MW01253323

Ulla Schmid
Moore's Paradox

Quellen und Studien zur Philosophie

Herausgegeben von
Jens Halfwassen, Dominik Perler und Michael Quante

Band 124

Ulla Schmid

Moore's Paradox

—

A Critique of Representationalism

DE GRUYTER

ISBN 978-3-11-037103-1
e-ISBN (PDF) 978-3-11-036649-5
e-ISBN (EPUB) 978-3-11-039241-8
ISSN 0344-8142

Library of Congress Cataloging-in-Publication Data
A CIP catalog record for this book has been applied for at the Library of Congress.

Bibliographic Information published by the Deutsche Nationalbibliothek
The Deutsche Nationalbibliothek lists this publication in the Deutsche Nationalbibliografie;
detailed bibliographic data are available in the internet at http://dnb.dnb.de.

© 2014 Walter de Gruyter GmbH, Berlin/Boston
Printing and binding: Hubert & Co. GmbH & Co. KG, Göttingen
♾ Printed on acid-free paper
Printed in Germany

www.degruyter.com

To my parents

The results of philosophy are the discovery of some piece of plain nonsense and bumps that the understanding has got by running up against the limits of language. They—these bumps—let us see the value of the discovery.

Philosophical Investigations §119

Acknowledgements

This book is essentially my PhD thesis which was accepted by the University of Basel in December 2012. While I was working on the thesis and revising it for publication, I received personal and academic support from many people. I wish to express my thanks to those whose contributions were vital for the thesis' completion.

First and foremost, I am indebted to my advisers, Emil Angehrn and Axel Seemann, for their patience, their understanding and their continuous encouragement. On many occasions, they helped me out of what seemed to me insurmountable difficulties (and often turned out to be molehills later), more often than I could have imagined it possible and necessary at the beginning of this enterprise. Emil Angehrn was a real *Doktorvater* to me, who never gave up on my project even though it took an entirely different course from the project I had originally intended to pursue. Axel Seemann took the place of Peter Goldie, who was designated to be my second adviser, after Peter's death in October 2011. Without Axel's commitment, I would not have been able to write my thesis in less than a year. His critical, but always constructive and most pointed feedback was most helpful. For the publication, I tried to implement the suggestions both my advisers made in their respective reports on my thesis. I am especially grateful for their support which went far above and beyond their duties and time as academic advisers.

Apart from my advisers, I also learned a lot from Joachim Schulte, in his seminars as well as 'off-stage'. To him, I owe the basis of my reading and understanding Wittgenstein. Despite his chronically tight schedule, Joachim provided helpful comments particularly on my second chapter (on Wittgenstein) and was an indispensable and almost unlimited source of advice, reference and anecdotes.

I am grateful to Dan Hutto and John Searle for inviting me to the University of Hertfordshire and the University of California at Berkeley, respectively. I spent exciting months in London in spring 2010 and had a good time in Berkeley in spring 2011. Many thoughts and ideas that found their way into my thesis originate from these times. Remarkably, and also unbelievably, I cannot remember it being raining in London, whereas it rained practically throughout my entire three months' stay in Berkeley. In spring 2013, Hans Sluga gave me the opportunity to return to Berkeley as his teaching assistant for the course *Later Wittgenstein*. This engagement contributed to sharpening my thinking about and with Wittgenstein and initiated a series of sedimentary changes in my form of life.

Thanks to being affiliated to the University of Basel, I enjoyed generous funding by the Swiss National Science Foundation, the University of Basel and the *Freiwillige Akademische Gesellschaft* Basel. Some of my funding was invested in hiking tours in the Alps that allowed me to see things from a different angle. The publication of my thesis was financially supported by the *Basler Studienstiftung* and the *Max-Geldner-Fonds* at the Humanities Division of the University of Basel. I am grateful to the deGruyter team, especially to Gertrud Grünkorn for her invitation to submit the manuscript and for her patience with my behaving as a typical author (despite good intentions) and to Maria Dassing for helping me cope with several TeXnical difficulties. The comments of several anonymous referees emphasised similar points Axel Seemann had noted earlier, and I hope to have sufficiently taken them into consideration.

At Basel, I had many lively and in-depth discussions with my colleagues and students. I wish to thank them for patiently sharing the twists and turns my project took, and for their participation in my seminars at the University of Basel none of which could have done without presupposing understanding of at least the first half of *Philosophical Investigations*. Three occasions seem to me worth mentioning here. Shortly before submitting my thesis, I had some very illuminating conversations on Moran's account with Jonas Held, who read and substantially commented the respective passages. The discussions in my seminar on Moore's Paradox in summer 2013 revealed even more and more radical facets of the paradox than I had recognised earlier. While I was preparing the book manuscript, I had the chance to read the PhD thesis of my colleague Benno Wirz. His treatment of the origins and the significance of philosophical thinking about light and darkness strengthened some of my fundamental views on philosophy as they become manifest in this book.

Jonathan Beale and Britt Harrison did a fantastic job at reading the proofs, some of which was done literally in the last minute, and significantly improved my English. I am especially grateful because the time was extremely inconvenient for both of them. My sister Maria Parker joined forces with them in eradicating my continuous violations of the English language. It goes without saying that all remaining Germanisms, cumbersome expressions, long sentences and all mistakes that managed to escape their eyes fully go to my account.

Two conversations in summer 2011 influenced the course my thesis took more than anything else and provided the key ideas for my argument. In our last conversation, Peter Goldie asked me, 'What is a thought?' and advised me to 'Be more radical!' He made me think about thoughts, and I hope to have followed his advice. Only some days after this conversation, I went to Konstanz together with my colleague Christoph Pfisterer to attend a lecture by John Searle. On this unforgettable journey, Christoph made me recognise the significance of Moore's Paradox (and the insignificance of the distinction between 'aliefs' and beliefs). Voilà, there we were.

My philosophical thinking was shaped first and foremost by Georg Meggle. I learned from Georg to handle authorities with care (in philosophy and elsewhere), to mistrust metaphysical thinking and to refrain from holding a philosophical position for reasons of convenience or simplicity. Last, but not least, I wish to thank my friends and family for supporting me during the last years. Most of my library coffee breaks ended in extensive discussions about the sophistications of philosophical, legal and everyday language (and planning the upcoming weekend) with Martin Sigrist. My final thanks is to my friend Eva, my sister Maria and my parents Jutta and Harald for their unconditional reassurance of the foundations of my life and their good company whenever we manage to spend our time together.

Contents

Introduction

In everyday conversation, the statement 'It is raining, but I don't believe it is', strikes us as absurd. We do not understand what the speaker wants to say. We do not know what to reply or how to go on. The question is, why?

It is hard to pinpoint what exactly makes this kind of statement absurd. It is not nonsensical in the way in which the sentences in Lewis Carroll's poem 'Jabberwocky' are absurd; it is a grammatically well-composed sentence of the English language, insofar as it does not contain imaginary words and it does not break any grammatical rules. It is not absurd in the same way as the sentence 'The present King of France is bald'; it does not conflict with our common knowledge that there is no present King of France. The statement is not absurd for empirical reasons, as is the sentence 'Yesterday, I rode my horse to the Moon and back' is; given that we know from experience it is impossible to visit the Moon by horse. That it might be raining whilst I do not believe it is, are not mutually exclusive facts, neither of which is absurd. The absurdity is not a product of a conceptual mistake, either, as the sentence 'On Mondays, tautologies are false' is. Finally, it is not absurd for logical reasons—from the point of view of propositional logic, its structure is identical to the structure of 'It is raining, but I don't believe it will last long'—and saying something like this might be wishful thinking, but it is clearly far from being absurd.

So there are no good reasons why, according to commonsense, it is absurd to state 'It is raining, but I don't believe it is'. There are several reasons one might consider this paradoxical. First, although statements like this are absurd, they can nevertheless be true. Second, making an analogous statement about what someone else believes say, 'It is raining, but Peter doesn't believe it is', is not absurd. Third, neither saying about oneself 'Yesterday it was raining, but I didn't believe it was', nor asking 'What, if it were raining, but I didn't believe it was?' would seem to be quite so absurd. This paradox, or catalogue of paradoxical facts about the statement 'It is raining, but I don't believe it is', is Moore's Paradox.

Moore's Paradox arises from the assumption that the statement in question is a meaningful sentence itself, that is, from the assumption that it is not nonsensical. It seems evident that this is the case: The statement 'It is raining, but I don't believe it is' is a conjunction of two meaningful sentences, 'It is raining' and 'I don't believe it is raining'. As G. E. Moore, who discovered the paradox, observes both of them have a definite meaning in English—the first one expresses the fact that it is raining; the second one expresses the fact that I don't believe it is raining. And how could a statement about the weather, conjoined with a statement about a person result in an absurdity?[1]

The conception of meaning underlying this assumption is that meaning is constituted by reference, that is, that the function of language is to represent and convey information about a language-independent world. Linguistic expressions, i.e. words or sentences, are supposed to stand for, or refer to, or denote objects and states of affairs. They do so in virtue of explicating the way in which objects and states of affairs are apprehended. This is their sense. In other words, the meaning of linguistic expressions is to refer to objects and states of affairs by means of articulating sense. The meaning of a word or a sentence is thus considered to be independent of the context in which it is used on any particular occasion as well as independent of the linguistic and extra-linguistic practices of those who use it.

I will argue in the following that this conception of language is radically mistaken. Language is here conceived as a means of conveying information to one another, be it about the weather, be it about one's state of mind, be it about anything you like. Yet, reducing the function of language to describing and re-porting what is the case in the world cannot and does not account for its use in everyday life. It does not accommodate the kinds of phenomena whose generation is conditioned on certain contextual features. Such a phenomenon arises from the statement 'It is raining, but I don't believe it is'. Its absurdity depends on the person who makes it, the tense and the kind of utterance in which it occurs. Because these factors are irrelevant to an account of meaning in terms of reference, such an account cannot but conclude that the absurdity generates a number of paradoxes. In my argument, I will exploit the distinctive absurdity involved in Moore's Paradox and argue that, contrary to the opposing view, the meaning of language resides in the use it finds in our everyday practice.

According to the view of meaning which I will scrutinise and reject in the following, every meaningful linguistic expression is meaningful in virtue of designating a corresponding object, the object it refers to. In this way, words stand for objects, which can be of any kind, physical objects, properties, processes, or relations, to name but a few. In the same way, sentences describe states of affairs, which are characterised as a certain constellation of the objects, which the words that are combined in the sentence refer to. This constellation is reflected in the syntax of the sentence. The meaning of words, accordingly, is provided by the object for which the word stands and the meaning of a sentence is provided by the state of affairs

---

1 *Cf.* George Edward Moore (1993), "Moore's Paradox", in *Selected Writings*, ed. by Thomas Baldwin, London/New York: Routledge, pp. 207–212.

which the sentence describes. The relation between a sign and its object is always an indirect one, it is mediated by the way in which the object is apprehended by the person who uses the sign. The meaning of a linguistic expression is constituted in that is articulates how a person apprehends an object. In this way, a linguistic expression indirectly designates the object.

This *referentialist* conception of language is so appealing that it has been taken for granted in most philosophical thinking ever since the Pre-Socratic times such that it seems natural to answer the question 'What is the meaning of a word?' with 'The object it refers to'. Its benefits are obvious: Separating the meaning of language from the practice of language apparently answers various questions concerning the meaning of natural languages. Firstly, it provides a criterion with which to distinguish meaningful from meaningless expressions. Whether a linguistic expression is meaningful or meaningless depends on whether it does or does not articulate a subject's apprehending an object. Secondly, it gives an account of meaning-identity, or meaning-uniformity, i.e. that different instances of the same expression, synonymous expressions, and intertranslatable expressions from different languages have the same meaning—they denote the same object. Thirdly, the view provides a simple method for assessing whether an expression is used correctly or incorrectly on a particular occasion, and whether a particular sentence is true or false. An expression is used correctly if it is used to refer to the object the word corresponds to, a sentence is true if it accurately describes the corresponding state of affairs. Last, not least, this view promises to clarify certain issues concerning linguistic practice: Languages are learned by learning which word stands for which object, and by learning how these words are combined to meaningful sentences. Being a competent speaker of a language is tantamount to being acquainted with its meaning and grammar in this way. And understanding another person's utterances in a language just amounts to grasping the sense of his words, i.e. the objects he or she seeks to describe.

This picture of language operates at two levels, the level of signs, that is, words and sentences, and the level of objects, which provides their meaning. Language and meaning are thus separate matters, which are connected by way of correlating items from one level with items from the other one. Words turn from meaningless sounds into meaningful signs in that they are attached to, or connected with objects. This view presupposes that our linguistic practices rely on a preliminary understanding of the object-level, i.e. on an understanding of what objects are, or what counts as an object, what kind of thing a particular object belongs to (e.g. physical objects, colours, experiences, properties, relations, abstract objects), and how individual objects interrelate. In other words, it presupposes that the ability to individuate, identify, re-identify and interrelate individual objects is prior to the mastery of our first language.

Accordingly, the primary purpose of psychological concepts is to refer to or describing a person's mental states and thereby identify them for the benefit of others. That is, they carry information about what a person feels, perceives, wishes or believes. The words used to express one's state of mind refer to corresponding mental phenomena, e.g. feelings, sensations, perceptions, wishes or beliefs. Sentences containing psychological concepts describe those certain psychological facts that are the case. For example, the sentence 'Peter believes it is raining', describes Peter as believing that it is raining.

So the suggestion is that the meaning of such words, psychological concepts, is constituted by reference to the phenomena to which they correspond. This contains a metaphysical assumption about the objects for which these psychological concepts supposedly stand, that is, about what our mental experiences are. Such a metaphysics of the mind is integrated into the more general metaphysical picture of the world, which is an integral part of the conception of language I outlined above. The world contains, or consists in, a variety of objects, states, phenomena, which we can discover and identify when we encounter them. The expressions of our languages are signs we use to represent them. Some of these states are states of ourselves; we become acquainted with them by undergoing them ourselves, or by inferring them from other people's behaviour. Such mental or psychological states are also particular individual phenomena which we can identify and associate with words. The relation we hold to psychological states, both our own and those of others', is of an epistemic kind, as is the relation we hold to the other things in the world.

Conceiving of the meaning of linguistic expressions in terms of reference, supports what one may call a *mentalist* conception of the mind, i.e. a conception of psychological phenomena as constituting their own uniform class of phenomena. For if psychological words have a distinctive meaning and do not come down to descriptions of behavioural sequences, their meaning must be to refer to phenomena of a distinct kind, the mental. As with any other kind of object, mental states are supposed to be self-standing phenomena, namely states of mind, that are individuable and re-identifiable by means of characteristic properties.

Thus, the conception of language, according to which linguistic expressions receive meaning by standing for corresponding objects, promotes the investigation into the meaning of psychological concepts to be a matter of clarifying the ontology of the phenomena to which they ostensibly refer. Representationalism provides such an ontology. It conceives of the mind as an aggregate of individual mental states, which are designated by psychological notions. The central claim of representationalism, which originates, in its modern form, from the writings of Descartes, Brentano, Husserl and Frege, is the idea that our elementary way of engaging with the world is to represent it. Representation is conceived as a function that serves to establish binary relations between a representing subject and a represented object. It is brought about by the subject representing the object in a particular way. This is to say that inasmuch as we interact with aspects of our environment, and inasmuch as our mind is concerned with the things around us, the connection between ourselves and the world is, first and foremost, one mediated by representation.

Representationalism does more than simply provide an ontology of the mind: It complements the conception of language at issue by yielding a theory about the fundamental way of engaging with objects that supposedly provides the foundations for mastering a language. It does so by deriving the capacity of linguistic expressions to refer to objects from the capacity of mental states to represent objects. On closer inspection, the function of language as conceived by the theory of meaning outlined above and the function of the mind as conceived by representationalism, run strictly analogously: As the individual units of a language (words, multiple-worded expressions, sentences) bear meaning in virtue of referring to corresponding objects or states of affairs, so do the individual units of the mind (mental states) have content in virtue of representing corresponding objects or states of affairs. This analogy is exploited by identifying the meaning of linguistic expressions as the content of mental states. The effect is that linguistic expressions are regarded as articulations of the results from a preceding mental process, i.e. the process of representing objects or states of affairs.

Thus, the following picture emerges: The primordial step in engaging with the world, is the generation of mental content that represents the world as we experience or apprehend it. Our states of mind can be then accompanied by expressive behaviour, gestures and facial expressions, which allow others to infer the state of mind we are in. Moreover, in order to express our states of mind, we have linguistic expressions at our disposal, words like 'to be sad', 'to see', 'to believe', or 'to wish'. By means of these words we represent ourselves or others as being in corresponding states of mind. Whether a particular linguistic expression is meaningful or not, depends on whether it does or does not articulate mental content. Whether a particular linguistic expression does or does not express a person's state of mind, depends on whether the person is or is not having the experience in question.

On this picture, the meaning of psychological concepts depends on representation in two ways. Without there being representational content, the relation between linguistic expressions and their corresponding objects could not be established in the first place. And without there being mental states that can be represented themselves, psychological expressions would have no object to refer to, and consequently would be meaningless. This position thus establishes a twofold priority of mental representation over linguistic expression: On the one hand, mental representation supposedly provides the relation between language and meaning, and, on the other hand, mental representation provides the objects of psychological concepts, i.e. mental phenomena.

Overview

In the following, I argue that this conception of the mind and its concomitant conception of language are radically mistaken. They presuppose that there is one gap running between language and meaning, and a second analogous gap running between mind and language. The conceptions seek to close these gaps by correlating items from each side with items from the other side, the nature of their relatedness ('representation') being left unclear. Linguistic expressions supposedly bear meaning insofar as they express representational content, and psychological concepts express mental states insofar as the former refer to the latter. The separations of language and meaning, and mind and language, respectively, established by these conceptions are irreversible. I argue that all efforts to reunite language and meaning, and expression and experience, once separated, are doomed to fail, and that all efforts to investigate either side of the gaps irrespective of its complement are useless for gaining insights in the meaning of linguistic expressions of our states of mind. As regards language, I argue that the meaning of linguistic expressions is not constituted by articulating the content of mental representation. And as regards the meaning of linguistic expressions of one's state of mind, I argue this does not consist in referring to corresponding psychological phenomena. In short, neither conception yields an adequate understanding of our everyday practices of expressing ourselves and understanding one another.

The proposal I make at the end of my investigation is to dispense with both conceptions and to approach linguistic phenomena from a radically different angle. Instead of converting questions of meaning and grammar into questions of metaphysics, I suggest that language be investigated as we encounter and use it, in everyday practice. Only if we stay on the rough ground of everyday language use and resist the temptations of metaphysical theorising about meaning and mind we will be able to philosophically appreciate language in its various functions, just as we do in commonsense. If we stop eschewing the complexity of our everyday linguistic practice for the sake of simplicity we will be able to see that neither meaning, nor the mental are enigmatic in essence. Understanding both is, in practice, easy for there is nothing hidden.

My investigation proceeds in three steps. In Chapter 1, I present a general outline of the representationalist theory of the mind, and confront it with the absurdity generated by statements like 'It is raining, but I don't believe it is'. According to the representationalist theory of mind and the conception of meaning in terms of reference, this absurdity gives rise to the aforementioned Moore's Paradox. Moore's Paradox appears to arise because assertions of the form 'It is raining, but I don't believe it is', are absurd although it seems that they ought not to be. I examine three different attempts to explain the absurdity within a representationalist framework and conclude that none of them can accommodate this phenomenon from ordinary language. My aim is to show that if one takes the assumptions about language, meaning and mind entrenched in representationalism for granted, one will inevitably misconceive both the absurdity underlying Moore's Paradox and its philosophical significance. I conclude Chapter 1 with the statement that the inability to cope with Moore's Paradox on a representationalist view of the mind, together with its referentialist conception of meaning, provides a reason to dispense with both views.

In Chapter 2, I develop an argumentation against both the representationalist theory of mind and the referentialist conception of meaning, which exploits Wittgenstein's remarks on Moore's Paradox and his considerations on rule-following and private language. My argument reveals that mental states, conceived of as particular individuable psychological phenomena, are neither necessary nor sufficient to ground the meaning of the associated linguistic expressions. Similarly, regarding assertions and other kinds of sentences as extensions of mental representation and conceiving of their structure in strict analogy with the corresponding mental states they allegedly articulate proves both intrinsically incoherent and an inappropriate means for gaining insights in the structure and function of language. That both misconceptions of language give rise to Moore's Paradox without being able to cope with the ghostly consequences thereby invoked provides sufficient reason to dispense with these very assumptions, or so I will argue. The conclusion of Chapter 2 is that the meaning of psychological concepts as well as of different kinds of sentences is constituted in our linguistic practices themselves, and not by anything external to them. Realising that the representationalist order of priorities (thought over language) is literally reversed yields the solution to Moore's Paradox. These results are substantiated in Chapter 3, where I first consider several objections, clarify some misunderstandings, and develop an alternative, practice-based conception of the meaning of linguistic expressions of belief and other states of mind. I close my investigation by articulating the lessons we ought to draw from Moore's Paradox.

1 Representationalism and Moore's Paradox

1.1 Introduction

In this chapter, I provide a general outline of representationalism, which serves to clarify the target of my investigation and is mainly terminological in character (Section 2.1). I focus on the foundational claims of representationalism, that is, those constituting its common theoretical framework, and mention controversies *within* this framework only in passing, without discussing them in detail or taking a stance in them. Since I will be concerned with the core of the representational theory in what follows, these differences do not affect the force of my argumentation.

At the core of representationalism lies the thesis that the function of the mind is to represent the world, that is, to disclose aspects of it to the subject. The subject forms particular representational states expressing either how the subject takes the world to be (cognitive states) or how he or she would like the world to become (conative states). One consequence of the representationalist assumptions worth highlighting here is that the relation between a person and his or her own states of mind, that is, between the bearer of a particular representational state and the representational state itself, is distinctive.

I introduce next Moore's Paradox as a challenge to the analogous representationalist assumptions about the meaning of language, in particular the claims that meaningful expressions serve as a means of representing reality, and that the meaning consists in designating a corresponding referent (Section 2.2). Moore's Paradox arises in connection with assertions such as 'It is raining, but I don't believe it'. These are absurd, but not contradictory. This is paradoxical: it is absurd to assert sentences of this kind, although they have a definite meaning and express an empirically possible state of affairs.

On a closer look, Moore-paradoxical sentences consist in a conjunction of two propositions, that p is the case and that I do not believe that p is the case. The first is a statement of facts, the second one a statement concerning the speaker's own state of mind. These statements are incommensurable with respect to formal-logical criteria. Since the relation between the speaker and his or her own state of mind is supposed to be distinctive, linguistic articulations of one's own state of mind appear to be asymmetric, compared with assertions about another person's mental condition. So the *prima facie* conjecture is that the second conjunct is responsible for the generation of Moore's Paradox. For this reason, the solution to Moore's Paradox issued from a representationalist point of view proceeds from the assumption that the second conjunct of a Moore-paradoxical assertion stands at odds with an additional, implicit statement about the speaker's state of mind.

I then examine three approaches to Moore's Paradox from within the representationalist framework, the approaches of John Searle, Sydney Shoemaker and Richard Moran (Section 3).[1] All of them endorse G. E. Moore's original approach. Moore's suggestion proceeds from the intuition that one normally believes what one asserts. More technically speaking, by asserting *that p is the case* the speaker implies *that he or she also believes that p is the case*. The person who asserts a Moore-paradoxical sentence, accordingly, implies (by the first conjunct) *that he or she believes that p is the case*, whereas he or she openly asserts *that he or she does not believe that p is the case*. Thus, the speaker of a Moore-paradoxical assertion is supposed to implicitly assert a contradiction, which is supposed to explain the absurdity of his or her assertion.

Summarising the approaches, I explain why this conclusion necessarily follows from taking for granted the representationalist view of the function of mind and language, and why this conclusion is a false solution to Moore's Paradox. I close this chapter by surveying the core claims of representationalism once again. This time, I focus specifically on its conception of language, which I will trace back to Frege's writings.

Notwithstanding wide agreement on the representationalist explanation of both Moore's Paradox and the absurdity of Moore-paradoxical sentences, Moore-paradoxical assertions are neither formal-logical, nor empirical contradictions. Thus, attempts to solve Moore's Paradox proceeding from the core claims of representationalism, necessarily fail. In the following chapter, I will argue that this is a good reason for abandoning the representationalist conception of mind and lan-

---

1 In the following, they will serve as paradigmatic representationalist accounts although they represent a small selection from only one of the two prevalent strands of the representationalist theory of mind, i.e. internalism. My selection results from three considerations. First, the distinction of internalism and externalism indicates a conflict *within* representationalism concerning the individuation of representational *content*. That is, both strands share the fundamental theoretical framework my investigation focuses on. For this reason, I only briefly review the distinction of internalism and externalism in this chapter and point to their common roots. In Chapter 3, I will clarify that, despite its apparent distinctness, externalism is affected by my argumentation in the very same way as internalism. Second, the views I discuss in more detail at this place more obviously endorse Frege's views on mind and language than externalist views do (see Section 4 of this Chapter). The argument from Moore's Paradox against representationalism I will present in the following chapter closely follows the argument Wittgenstein develops against Fregean views of mind and meaning. Elucidating the Fregean heritage in the basic claims constituting the framework of representationalism allows me to directly address and challenge its foundations. Third, Searle, Shoemaker and Moran stand *pars pro toto* for three ways of dealing with Moore's Paradox that are both available *within* the representationalist theory of mind and lead to a common 'solution'.

guage (Chapter 2). I will suggest an alternative understanding of meaning, which I will defend and clarify in the final chapter (Chapter 3).

1.2 The Theory of Representationalism

Representationalism is the doctrine that the mind engages with the world by representing it. Despite controversy concerning ontology and epistemology of the mind and concerning the function of representation in detail, the representationalist conception is the common denominator in mainstream philosophy of mind, past and present—from Aristotle to Searle, Descartes to Dretske, Kant to McDowell, Frege to the author of the *Tractatus*.[2] The central ideas captured by representationalism are the ideas of *perspectivity*, *veridicality*, and *mind-independence*. The *way* in which the world appears to me is different from how it appears to you or to Peter. Similarly, Peter, you and I can have different *attitudes* towards the same aspect of the world. I represent the world from my *perspective*, and how I represent the world partly constitutes my perspective on it. Further, the world need not be as it appears to me, to you, to Peter or anybody else, and not as we want it to be or become. We can be wrong in our beliefs, perceptions and assumptions, we can lie to one another, or unintentionally make false statements. Our desires can remain unsatisfied, our wishes wishful thinking, we can fail in carrying out our intentions. My representation of the world is *veridical*, if I represent it as it is, or if it becomes as I represent it. Still, the world, or reality is as it is, *prior* to and *independently* of whether, and how it is represented. It is the object of representation, and as such, objective.

1.2.1 Representation

The notions 'representation' and 'representing' are used in a relational sense as well as in a functional sense. On the one hand, they designate a two-place relation: a (representational) subject (an individual, or a person) relates to an object (a representational object, or *representatum*) by representing it. That is, the representationalist conception basically involves a primordial separation or distinction between subject and object, and yet a connection between them established in that

---

2 *Cf.* William Lycan (2008), "Representational Theories of Consciousness", *The Stanford Encyclopedia of Philosophy (Fall 2008 Edition)*, Edward N. Zalta (ed.), http://plato.stanford.edu/archives/fall2008/entries/consciousness-representational/, last access March 7th, 2012; William Lycan, Jesse Prinz (eds.), *Mind and Cognition. An Anthology*, Oxford: Blackwell 2008.

the subject represents the object. By means of representation, individual aspects of the world (representational objects) are singled out and (mentally) grasped by an individual (the representing subject).[3] The outcome of representing an object is that the subject entertains a representational state, or is in a state of representing. The *function* of token representational states is to represent objects as they are. As functional notions, 'representation' and 'representing' refer to the aim of token representational states, namely to disclose the representational object to the subject as it is actually constituted, that is, to deliver an accurate description of the object. If they do so, that is, if token representational states are veridical, the fulfil their function to the effect that the subject represents the object as it is. In this case, there is a representational *relation* holding between the token representational state in question and the respective representational object.[4]

The representationalist theory of mind presumes that the world represented by individuals is 'objective'. With respect to the ontology of representational objects, it is generally committed to 'realism' about the world 'external' to the subject. Although the views as to how realism ought to be further elaborated vary, realism minimally involves an ontological claim about representational objects and an epistemological claim about the way they are accessed in representing. The objects of mental representation are real in the sense that they are ontologically mind-independent. Thus, they are individuable independently of whether, in which way and from which perspective they are represented and their boundaries are identifiable by objective criteria.[5] Further, 'representation' denotes a uniform phenomenon, its function is identical for different individuals. The apprehension of representational objects thus is equally perspective-independent as the objects themselves. Under favourable circumstances, mental representation delivers knowledge about the respective representational objects *as they really are*. The nature of representational objects remains unchanged by being represented. Both claims result from the idea that representational states can be assessed with respect to their veridicality, that is, with respect to whether they represent their objects as they are.

---

3 There is some controversy whether, under which conditions and to which extent groups of individuals are suitable subjects of representation. This question and related questions concerning the ontology of groups have been discussed over the last thirty years under the heading of 'collective intentionality'.

4 *Cf.* Tyler Burge (2010), *Origins of Objectivity*, Oxford: UP, pp. 30–42. I will come back to this point when having a closer look at the notion of 'veridicality' in the context of representational content.

5 This is an ontological requirement on objects, not a requirement on the abilities of representational subjects. It does not imply that an individual representing an object need to be aware of the difference between its representational content and the corresponding object, or that it need to be able to individuate its object by means of citing criteria. *Cf.* Burge (2010), ch. 6.

The idea of veridicality implies that representational states and representational objects are comparable, which requires that the object represented by a particular representational state is identifiable beyond the respective state. The criteria by which any representational object is identifiable provide for the verifiability of representational states and, accordingly, must be objectively accessible.[6]

An individual subject's representational states interrelate according to certain principles, adding up to series, or sequences of interrelating representational states, that is, mental processes. The totality of an individual subject's representational states in this way constitutes an interlocking structure or system, which is regarded as tantamount to, or at least partly constitutive of, the subject's mind.

The relationship of the notions 'representation' and 'intentionality' is a matter of disagreement. Sometimes, they are used equivalently (for example, Crane (2003) and Searle (1983)), sometimes the notion 'intentionality' is deemed to include, but not be limited to that of representationality, that is, that intentional states contain non-representational elements (for example, Chalmers (2004)), or that there are some forms of intentionality, which do not include representational content at all.[7]

---

6 This framing of the relationship between world and representational content ought not to be taken to stark. One need not hold a special ontological view about the world. A naïve realism, as Searle suggests, would do. According to Searle, 'natural' or 'physical' facts, i.e. the constitution of the external world, just are independent of facts about the mental constitution of the representational subject. *Cf.* John Searle (1983), *Intentionality. An Essay in the Philosophy of Mind*, Cambridge: UP, pp. 158f. Alternatively, one might hold, for instance, that representational content is given non-conceptually on a subpersonal level, for example as a causally determined set of sense-data, and that a conceptual structure marks the transition from subpersonal to personal-level representation (as Russell and Quine do), which is compatible with idealism. Or one might hold that the environment causally determines the subpersonal content of (perceptual) representation, including the boundaries of the objects or events as they are represented. Still, in order to compare an object or state of affairs as it is represented with the environment, the object or state of affairs must be somehow identifiable, and hence individuable within the *environment*, regardless of the manner in which the representational content is generated.

7 The last claim is common in post-Heideggerian phenomenology, and appears frequently in contemporary philosophy of emotion. For a recent example of a phenomenological theory of emotions endorsing this claim, see Matthew Ratcliffe (2008), *Feelings of Being: Phenomenology, Psychiatry and the Sense of Reality*, Oxford: UP. For the others, *cf.* Tim Crane (2003), "The Intentional Structure of Consciousness", in Aleksandar Jokic, Quentin Smith (eds.), *Consciousness: New Philosophical Perspectives*, Oxford: UP, pp. 33–56; David Chalmers (2004), "The Representational Character of Experience", in Brian Leiter (ed.), *The Future for Philosophy*, Oxford: UP. Chalmers in particular advocates the view that the phenomenal character of experience is not entirely reducible to representational content. The phenomenal or 'subjective' quality of experience (its 'qualia') has been referred to in arguments against reductive theories of mind. The most influential contributions are Thomas Nagel (1974), "What is it like to be a Bat?", *The Philosophical Review*

I will use the notions 'mental states', 'intentional states' and 'representational states' interchangeably and sometimes use the notions 'experiences' and 'experiential states', without denying that at least some representationalist views hold that 'the mental' and 'intentionality' are *not* entirely analysable into representational states, and that 'experiences' and 'experiential states' involve non-representational elements, if they are not considered entirely non-representational.[8]

1.2.1.1 The Two-Component-Model of Representational States

The ideas of perspectivity, veridicality, and mind-independence respond to the commonplace intuitions that the world appears to different people in different ways, that one can take different attitudes towards the same state of affairs, and that the world *really is* not always as it *seems to be*. This observation can be formulated like this: In every instance of representation, the world is represented from a certain perspective as being in a certain way. These considerations are unified in a conception of representational states, which lies at the core of representationalism and is shared by all its versions, the *two-component model* of the mind. This model extends to all kinds of representational states including perceptual experience (as far as this is representational), and particularly applies to intentional and linguistic states.[9]

According to the representationalist view, representational states, or mental states, can be analysed into two components, a representational mode, and a representational content. The *content* of a representational state characterises the way in which the representational *object* is given to the representational subject. The *mode* of a representational state specifies the attitude the *subject* takes towards the representational object. The mode thus qualifies the representational subject's perspective and accounts for the difference between how the world is and how it seems to the subject.[10] The content accounts for the mind-independence of the

---

83/4, pp. 435–50, and Frank Jackson (1982), "Epiphenomenal Qualia", *The Philosophical Quarterly 32/127*, pp. 127–36.

8 John Searle, for instance, counts moods and non-intentional feelings as mental, but not as representational states, and moreover argues that the representational parts of the mind rely on a non-representational, but mental 'Background', comprising dispositions, capacities, skills, 'background beliefs' and so on. *Cf.* Searle (1983), chs. 1 and 6. I will discuss Searle's view on intentional representation later in this chapter.

9 *Cf.* Susanna Siegel (2011), "The Contents of Perception", in *The Stanford Encyclopedia of Philosophy* (Winter 2011 Edition), Edward N. Zalta (ed.), http://plato.stanford.edu/archives/win2011/entries/perception-contents/, last access August 17th, 2012.

10 The mode of a representational state ought not to be confused with the *mode of presentation* of a particular content. The former designates an attitude of the *subject's*, it qualifies the rep-

object it represents in having the function of representing its object as it is. So one can say that representational states decompose into two elements, an objective content-element, and a subjective attitudinal or modal element, which are united by the function of representation.[11]

Mode and content are of differing importance: Representing the world does not entail appraising it; yet, appraising the world entails representing it. That is, there are no representational states lacking content, since the content exercises the function of representing. For an attitude to be representational, it must have an object; and this object is specified by the content.

It is possible that a subject represents an object in a neutral way, without taking an attitude towards it. In this case, the subject entertains neutral representational contents, or neutral representational states, respectively (I will use these notions alternately). One may call this kind of representation 'representation as if', or hypothetical representation and contrast it with 'attitudinal representation'—the subject represents something as if it were the case, yet, without taking a stance to the veridicality of what he or she represents. If one imagines or hypothesises *that it is raining*, for instance, one entertains content-bearing states to which no truth-value is *assignable*. In this sense, the subject is indifferent towards the veridicality of what he or she represents.

By means of neutral representation, representational contents are most purely presented to the subject, as it were. That is, the subject takes notice of, or registers them, without forming an attitude as to whether the content is about something that exists in the way it is represented, or something desirable, or something to be brought about. Every representational state thus entails a neutral representational content.[12] So one may regard neutral representational content as the first outcome

---

resentational state as a whole, whereas the latter indicates the aspect under which an object is represented, it qualifies the representational *object*. Their significance differs in that the representational mode always contributes to the individuation of types and tokens of representational states, whereas the mode of presentation does so only under certain circumstances. I will come back to this point in the next section on content.

11 Not all kinds of representational content can be represented in all kinds of representational modes. Objectual content is accessible to perceptual modes, but only to some intentional and linguistic modes: I can see or smell or feel or hear a horse, I can desire or fear a horse, I can cry out 'Horse!', I can imagine a horse, but I cannot believe or intend or assume a horse without believing, intending or assuming that the horse is in a certain way or does certain things. Some modes allow simple objects in their contents, others require their content to be internally structured in a way, which is expressed by a sentence. These are called propositional attitudes. In each case, however, a whole representational state decomposes into mode and content.

12 A distinction similar to the one between neutral and attitudinal representational states is made by Chalmers (2004), who distinguishes between 'pure' and 'impure' representational properties.

of representing something, and taking up an attitude, e.g. a belief, towards that content as an additional step. Representational states consisting of mode and content would accordingly present more advanced stages of engaging with a particular object.[13]

Content and mode together type-identify representational *states*. I will, in the following, employ the following scheme: The totality of representational states is divided into different modes (belief, desire, fear, intention etc.), each of these modes comprises various *types* of representational content (apples, pears, that p is the case, that q is the case). The same content-type can figure in various representational modes, and the same representational mode can be related to different contents. A particular combination of a representational mode and a representational content constitutes a type of representational state (the belief that it is raining, the desire for an apple). The same *type* representational state can be instantiated at different times, and by different subjects. An individual representational state, or a *token* representational state, instantiates a particular type of representational state, in that it is held at a certain time and by a particular person (Peter's belief at time t_1 that it is raining). In brief, tokens of representational content are individuated by representational mode, time, and subject.

Representation itself can be subdivided into different *kinds*, with respect to the faculties a subject employs in representing the world. A distinction made frequently runs between perceptual, mental, and linguistic representation, as Burge (2010) suggests. Analogously, perceptual, mental, and linguistic states are differentiated as kinds of representational states. In this case, representational modes present subclasses of kinds of representation. For instance, perceptual representation divides into sense-modalities (vision, hearing, taste, etc.); mental representation includes beliefs, desires and intentions as well as emotions and sensations, and linguistic representation involves different kinds of sentences (assertions, questions, imperatives, and so forth) and forms of thinking in a natural language (inner speech, explicit reasoning).

According to Chalmers, having a pure representational property is tantamount to being in a state of representing the world as being in a certain way. Having an impure representational property amounts to being in the state of representing the world as being in a certain way in a particular *manner*, that is, in what I have called a representational mode. Crane (2003) similarly uses the word mode instead of manner to designate the attitudinal element of representational states. For Burge, neutral representational contents constitute the categories by which representational states are individuable, see Burge (2010); and Burge (1979), "Individualism and the Mental", reprinted in his (2007), Foundations of Mind, Oxford: UP, pp. 100–50.

13 This is a logical, not an ontogenetic or phylogenetic point. I want to leave it at this cautious consideration for the moment. I will come back to it frequently and it will be spelled out in the last section of this chapter.

The distinction has, or may have impact on the way in which the internal structure of the *content* of representational states is subsequently spelled out on particular representationalist views, and on its conception of how representational contents and objects are connected. Yet, it does not, at least, not necessarily affect the applicability of the two-component model as I described it, that is, the model according to which representational states are composed from a subjective mode- and an objective content-element, and instantiated by being had at a particular time. In the following, I will not be concerned with perception. Hence, I will only differentiate mental representation (mental or psychological states) from explicitly linguistic representation (utterances, or speech acts (including 'inner speech'), made in a natural language), and refer to their modes as *psychological modes*, and *kinds of sentences*, or *kinds of utterances*, respectively.

A token representational state is individuated by its mode, content, bearer and time of occurrence. Consequently, every representational state has *one and only one* bearer: No token representational state can exist without being had, and no token representational state can be had by more than one bearer.[14] As already mentioned, a token representational state can lack a mode. In this case, a representational subject represents an object or states of affairs without taking a stance on what he or she represents, for instance, without judging as to whether the content of his or her representational state is veridical. I will refer to these states as 'neutral' representational contents or states (in general), or as neutral thoughts or sentences (in the case of linguistic representational states, see below). Neutral representational states are thus individuated by representational content, bearer and time of occurrence only.

This has a consequence for the metaphysical status of tokens of representational states as well as for tokens of representational content: Their existence is

---

14 As I will elaborate in the last section of this chapter, this idea goes back to Frege's conception of states of consciousness. *Cf.* Gottlob Frege (1819), "Der Gedanke", *Beiträge zur Philosophie des Deutschen Idealismus 2*, pp. 58–77. I quote from Anthony and Marcelle Quinton's translation, published as Gottlob Frege (1956), "The Thought", *Mind (65/259)*, pp. 289–311.

A general difficulty resulting from this position concerns the possibility of collective or group intentionality. As mentioned above, it is a matter of ongoing debate whether groups and other collective entities can be treated as bearers of representational states or whether phenomena group intentionality must be reducible to the representational states of the individuals constituting a particular group. I have suggested elsewhere that the intersubjectivity characterising phenomena involving group intentionality is not only irreducible to individual intentionality, but that moreover individual intentionality must be regarded as rooted in social interaction. *Cf.* Schmid (2011) and Schmid (2013). If this is the case, investigating the phenomenon of group intentionality might allow to develop an independent argument against representationalism.

conditioned on there being a subject who has a certain representational content, or is in a state of representing the world in a certain way at a certain time. In this sense, particular representational states are *dependent* on their respective bearers, they belong, metaphysically speaking, to their bearers' properties.[15]

Although a person's token representational states cannot be 'shared' in the sense of being *transferred* to another representational subject, they are accessible to others by being represented themselves. For example, although I cannot *have* Peter's sadness that his mother died, I can *see* that Peter is sad, I can *feel sorry* that Peter is sad, I can *wish* that Peter's sadness were gone, or I can *tell* you that Peter is too sad to join us tonight. Of course, Peter can represent his own sadness in addition to bearing it. For instance, he can represent it by saying to himself 'This is the saddest feeling I ever had' or by reporting it to Harry. I will call this kind of representation 'meta-representation' for the reason that the represented objects are representational states. Representing someone as having a particular mental state is a kind of attribution, it amounts to ascribing a particular representational property to a bearer. Meta-representation requires possession of psychological concepts, i.e. concepts characterising representational states, but it need not be entirely cognitive in attitude (I can be scared by Peter's intention to visit war-shaken Syria next week).

Notably, having representational states is logically prior to representing representational states. Representing a particular representational state amounts to attributing the state in question to a bearer. The attribution, for example 'Peter is sad that his mother died', figures in the content of a meta-representational state, that is, it spells out the veridicality condition of the meta-representational state. Whether the meta-representational state is veridical, thus depends on whether the attribution corresponds to the analogous state of affairs, in the example the state that Peter is sad that his mother died. Being the measure of veridicality of meta-representational content-tokens, representational states are logically prior to and ontologically independent of being themselves represented. Once types of representational states, or representational content respectively, are instantiated by being had by a bearer, they are individual things, just as door-handles, trees, or red barns are. Thus, one can say that although token representational states exist in virtue of a subject's representing an object, they exist independently of and unalterably by being themselves represented by anybody.

---

15 *Cf.* Chalmers (2004), sect. 2; Joachim Schulte (2011), "Privacy", in Oskari Kuusela, Marie McGinn (eds.), *The Oxford Handbook of Wittgenstein*, Oxford: UP, pp. 429–50, here sect. 6. The page numbers I use (1–22) refer to the manuscript.

In summary, token representational states are most generally characterised in four respects: *structurally*, they comply with the two-component model (mode plus content); *ontologically*, they are independent of being represented, although *metaphysically*, they are bearer-dependent. *Epistemologically*, tokens of representational states fourthly are suitable objects of factual knowledge, since the existence of a particular representational state is an ontologically mind-independent state of affairs.[16]

Before I spell out the most central notion of representationalist theories, the notion of representational content, let me make a brief remark on the notation of representational states I will employ in the following. Recall that representation is a two-place relation between a subject, S, and an object, and that the subject represents the object at a certain time by means of a representational content, thereby having, or being in a representational state, or a mental state. A type representational state has a determinate mode (which might be neutral), M, and content, C, but a variable subject-place and a variable time index, t. A token representational state has a determinate mode, content, subject and time-index. I will symbolise types and tokens of representational states as follows:

$$\text{Mode}_{\text{time}}(\text{subject, content}), \quad \text{or} \quad M_t(S, C).$$

In the following, I will mainly be concerned with be so-called *propositional attitudes*. This notion designates the subclass of representational states, whose contents are articulated by means of simple or complex propositions. In the text, I will render propositional content as that-clauses and indicate them with italics, e.g. *that p is the case*. As regards notation, I will indicate propositional contents

---

16 The account of the mental thus explicated shows remarkable structural and metaphysical parallels with Descartes' conception of thinking as proceeding in individual 'ideas' each of which contains an "operation of the understanding" and a "thing represented by this operation", whereby the former is grasped as a subjective act, the latter as an objective thing. See René Descartes (1641), Meditations on First Philosophy, ed. and transl. by Michael Moriarty, Oxford: UP 2008; here: *Preface to the Reader*, p. 8 (pagination according to the French edition by Charles Adam and Paul Tannery, Paris: Vrin 1996). I owe this point to my colleague Benno Wirz who explores it in more detail in the course of his insightful investigation of the notions 'light' and 'dark' in philosophy, see his *Was Licht bedeutet und Dunkel verstehen lässt. Philosophie zwischen Affirmativität und Negativität*, PhD thesis submitted at the University of Basel, June 2014.—It is noteworthy, but possibly unsurprising that the aforementioned resemblance most often escapes the notice of proponents of represetationalism whereas denying one's ideas to be 'Cartesian' in spirit seems a prevalent move and almost an imperative in contemporary philosophy of mind. That it is no good strategy to escape arguments against the core claims of representationalism by alleging them to be directed against Cartesian straw-men, will be briefly taken up in the next chapter (Section 5).

with small letters, p, q, r. A propositional attitude accordingly reads $M_t(S, p)$, for instance, Peter's belief at time t_1 *that it is raining (r)* will be notated as $B_{t1}(P, r)$. Neutral representational contents will be symbolised with $-(S, p)$. Since I am not particularly concerned with the temporal dimension of representational states I will, for the most part, omit the time index.

1.2.1.2 Representational Content

The notion 'representational content' has two explanatory functions:[17] As I explained above, it serves as criterion to individuate types and tokens of representational states. Moreover, it specifies the *veridicality conditions* of representational states.[18] Siegel describes this function of representational content as follows:

> If an experience is inaccurate, then there is some mismatch between the experience and a situation. If there were no mismatch, the experience would be accurate. The conditions in which there is no mismatch are accuracy conditions. Analogous points hold for maps, stories and other mental states besides experiences that can be accurate or inaccurate.
> When we categorize token experiences as veridical (or veridical in certain respects), we are in the simplest case assessing them with respect to the situation in which they are had. If these classifications involve accuracy, then when we categorize an experience as veridical, we are saying that it is accurate with respect to this situation. (Siegel (2010), p. 31)

In other words, the type representational content instantiated in a token representational state describes reality in a certain way and thus spells out how the world must be, or what must happen in the world such that its instantiations are true, veridical, accurate, or adequate descriptions of their objects. As mentioned above, the idea of veridicality is central to representationalism, it is supposed to capture the insight that the world is not always as it seems to be, that representation is fallible. Representing an object was said earlier to be the function of representational states. The value of its instances, i.e. token representations, is expressed in terms of veridicality: A token representational state is true or false, accurate or inaccurate, adequate or inadequate, veridical or non-veridical, depending on whether its content does or does not match its object. The value of a token representational state thus is assessed by comparison with the objects they are supposed to

---

17 Burge mentions a third function, which is connected to his distinction between different kinds of representation, namely determining the internal structure of representational objects at different stages of abstraction. *Cf.* Burge (2010), pp. 37ff.

18 There are several notions employed to express this function of representational contents, Searle (1983) continuously calls them 'conditions of satisfaction', Siegel uses the term 'accuracy conditions'. *Cf.* Susanna Siegel (2010), *The Contents of Visual Experience*, Oxford: UP, and Siegel (2011). I will use these terms alternately.

represent. If a token representational state is veridical, its function is, in Searle's terms, *satisfied*.

A central characteristic all token of representational states, except from neutral ones, have in common thus is that they can be *evaluated* with respect to their veridicality, or accuracy, or as to whether they are satisfied, in virtue of having a content specifying the conditions under which this is the case. The criteria by which a particular representational state is evaluated vary across different modes of representational states. Burge explains this point as follows:

> Representational contents of beliefs and declarative sentences can be evaluated for truth or falsity—just as beliefs and assertions can be. Beliefs and assertions are true (or false) if and only if their representational contents are. Similarly, the representational contents of intentions and imperatives can be evaluated for whether their veridicality conditions are fulfilled. The veridicality condition (representational content) of an intention comes to be fulfilled, or is made veridical, if the intention is carried out in relevant action. The veridicality condition of an imperative comes to be fulfilled if the imperative is obeyed. The representational content of questions is to be understood analogously. The representational content of a perception can be evaluated for accuracy or inaccuracy—just as perceptions can be. Perceptions are accurate (their way of being veridical) if and only if their representational contents are.[19]

So, for instance, the belief that it is raining is true if and only if it is raining, the visual experience of a dagger is accurate if and only if there is a dagger in one's visual field, which is as it appears to be, and Peter's intention to go to London is fulfilled if and only Peter goes to London. The measure by which token representational contents and, *a fortiori*, token representational states are so assessable is the actual constitution of their respective objects.

There is some controversy with regard to the status of representational states that fail to be veridical, for instance, false beliefs, illusions, or hallucinations: Are non-veridical states to be counted as representational states? This question is raised in particular for perceptual representation: Are perceptual illusions perceptual states, and thus representational, or a different kind of mental state? For instance, is Macbeth's *hallucinating* a dagger pointing the way to Duncan's chamber an instance of *seeing*? The answer depends on how one conceives of the connection between perceptual contents and the objects of one's perception.

I have pointed out earlier that types as well as tokens of representational states need not have a mode, although they need to have a content. So the exception to

---

19 Burge (2010), pp. 38f. Burge's elaboration agrees with those of Searle (1983), ch. 1, and Siegel (2010), ch. 2.

the rule just formulated is the class of 'neutral' representational states, i.e. content-bearing states lacking a mode. This class of representational states bears veridicality conditions, but its tokens are not evaluable as to whether their respective veridicality conditions are met. A certain type of neutral representational states is thus coextensive with a certain type of representational content, e.g. the content-type *that it is raining*. Since representational states are essentially content-bearing states, neutral content presents the core component of any form of representation. Hence, it appears to be prior to composite states consisting of mode and content. The idea of neutral representational content is closely connected to the possibility of isolating an element from representational states that exclusively functions to represent a particular aspect of reality. I wish to account for the distinctiveness of neutral representational contents by distinguishing representation (the function of composite representational states) from reference (the specific function of representational contents).

In the following, I will use the term 'reference' to designate the function of representational content. I thereby diverge from the way Burge uses this notion. He distinguishes between reference and indication as two contrasting kinds of representation, thus differentiating among the elements of representational contents with respect to their function.[20] Since I will not be concerned with debates concerning the internal structure of representational content, I will consider 'representational content' the smallest unit, regardless of its internal structure and complexity. Accordingly, I will use the term 'reference' throughout in connection with (whole) representational contents. I will make an exception for the case of linguistic representation, that is, for the case in which representational content is expressed or articulated in a natural language. Linguistic expressions, words, multiple-worded phrases and terms, sentences, differ with respect to the way in which they exercise their referential function (if they have any). I will treat the reference of linguistic expressions separately below (section 'Language and Representation').

Analogously to the notion 'representation', 'reference' can designate both a function and a relation. The *function* of representational content is to refer to, or stand for, or designate a corresponding referential object, which can be a state of

---

20 Burge explains reference as the way in which singular terms represent, and indication as the way in which general terms represent. Reference need not include attribution, this is contributed by indication. Indicating terms serve to qualify and to help identifying, objects of referential notions (e.g. names or demonstratives). In Burge's example, the representational content expressed by the sentence 'The barn is red' contains a referring element ('the barn'), which is further specified by an indicating element ('redness'); *cf.* Burge (2010), pp. 31ff. The distinction itself needs a separate investigation. Since one could argue that the term 'barn' itself is an indication of the object singled out by 'that', it might turn out that the only referring terms are demonstratives.

affairs, a physical object, a relation, a mental state, or any other representational object. This function is fulfilled if the representational content represents the representational object as it is, that is, if the content is veridical. In this case, there is a reference *relation* holding between the representational content and the object in question, the content actually *has* a referent. If a particular representational content is non-veridical, it lacks a referent, that is, the object or state of affairs the corresponding content-type is supposed to refer to does not exist. However, at least in the case of linguistic and intentional representation, a non-veridical content-token maintains its referring function. For example, the content of a statement 'The present King of France is bald' uttered in 1793 lacks a referent (there was not a King of France any more at that time). Yet, it has the function to refer to the state of the world in which it is true that the present King of France is bald, and in this sense exerts the function of referring to something.[21]

The example leads to my final point concerning representational content. Although representational content need not be accompanied by a representational mode, at least some representational content comes in a *mode of presentation*. The mode of presentation indicates how the subject represents the representational object. It ought not be confused with the *representational* mode a representational state can have, which indicates an attitude the subject entertains towards the object he or she represents. The mode of a representational state contributes to individuating the state. In contrast, the mode of presentation qualifies the content without contributing to its individuation. It reflects the aspect under which the object is represented. Although mode of presentation and representational mode are related in that both express the subject's perspective on the object, they are not identical. To illustrate it with a common example, when Peter likes the Morning Star, the content of his representational state is the planet Venus, represented under a particular aspect, as the star that shines shortly before sunrise. The planet Venus is thus presented to Peter, or represented by Peter in a certain mode of presentation. The representational mode of Peter's representational state is an affective attitude, that of liking something. The mode of presentation affects representational content, inasmuch as it reflects the aspect under which an object is represented, it also occurs in neutral representation (for instance, when Peter represents the Morning Star in the premise of an inference, such as 'when the Morning Star shines, the sun will soon be rising'). The representational mode affects the whole representational state, it reflects the position a subject has towards the object. In a nutshell, the

---

21 Searle expresses this point in this way: The statement 'The present King of France is bald' is not about something in an *extensional* sense. Still, it is about an object in an *intensional* sense, that is, it is about a state of affairs, which is represented in the statement under a certain description. *Cf.* Searle (1983), p. 17.

mode of presentation designates the way in which the object appears to the subject, whereas the representational mode specifies the way in which the subject regards the object. The mode of presentation qualifies the representational object, whereas the representational mode qualifies the subject of representing.[22]

1.2.1.3 Three Claims Concerning Content

From this review of 'representational content', I now extract three claims, which are essentially involved in the representationalist framework. I will henceforth refer to them as the *Reference Claim*, the *Uniformity Claim*, and the *Priority Claim*. Together with the structural and ontological claims concerning representational states outlined earlier, the following claims constitute minimal conditions of representationalism. Every conception of the mind that is committed to the three of them will, by these standards, count as representationalist view.

(1) Reference.

The Reference Claim states that the function of content is to refer in the sense specified in the previous section. A particular content token fulfils this function— it takes the value 'veridical', or 'true'—if and only if there is a reference relation obtaining between the content in question and a corresponding object, that is, if the content matches a corresponding object. There are some specifications concerning the reference of linguistic expressions, which I will briefly outline in the next section. Note, once again, that I am not primarily concerned with perceptual content. I will leave aside the aforementioned question whether perceptual states exercise a referential *function* at all since affirming to this claim would entail that perceptual states continue to refer to their objects even if they are non-veridical, for instance, in case of hallucinations, illusions and so on. If reference was a function of perceptual states, the latter phenomena would have to count as non-veridical perceptual states, and this is denied by Searle and McDowell, for instance, whose respective conceptions of the mind otherwise qualify as representationalist.

---

22 *Cf.* Chalmers (2004). Although it might be confusing that the word 'mode' appears in both terms, it seems to me appropriate because both, the mode of presentation and the representational mode, together render the perspective the subject obtains to the object. As mentioned above, I will use the terms 'representational mode' and 'kind of representation', for linguistic representation 'kind of sentence' interchangeably, and sometimes refer to the mode of presentation of an object as the aspect under which the object is represented. My use of the term 'representational mode' conjoins Searle's notions 'psychological mode' (for intentional states) and 'illocutionary force' (for kinds of utterances).

(2) Uniformity of Content.
If two representational states have the same content, their veridicality conditions will be identical. If their veridicality conditions are identical, they will refer to the same object, since their veridicality conditions will be met by the very same state of affairs. Therefore, representational states having the same content will be veridical under exactly the same circumstances and so have a uniform value of reference, independently of time, mode and perspective of their occurrence.

Accordingly, *uniform* content-tokens represented in different modes of representational states, by different representational subjects, and at different times instantiate the same content-type. In this sense, uniform contents of particular representational states refer to the same kind of object or state of affairs. It is thus possible to extract an identical, or uniform, content-element from different tokens and different kinds of representational states. For example, my belief *that it will be raining* and Peter's hope *that it will be raining* are uniform in content, and so belong to the same *representational kind*. In this way, representationalism seeks to accommodate the perspective-independence of representational content. This is an enabling condition for analysing representational states into the two components mode and content, and of ascribing their actual representational function to the content-element.

(3) Priority.
The central intuition of the general representationalist view was said to be that the world need not be as it appears to be, it is ontologically mind-independent. The objects of representation are ontologically *prior* to being represented. More precisely, the representationalist assumptions imply that the objects of representational states are individuated prior to being represented, that is, the boundaries and criteria of individuation of representational objects are considered determinate. This follows from the conception of representational content as specifying the veridicality conditions of tokens of representational states and thereby referring to objects or states of affairs. A representational state has a referent if and only if the content succeeds in representing its object accurately. In evaluating token representational contents as to their veridicality, thus, one compares the content with the world. In order to state whether the content corresponds to an object or state of affairs the boundaries of the object or state of affairs must be identifiable as the object or state of affairs satisfying the veridicality conditions. Drawing on the world as the objective measure determining the veridicality of content would make no sense were it not possible to specify the object or state of affairs whose existence would make a particular representational content veridical independently of that content. The world must, in other words, be comparable with content. It

must be clear what an apple is in order to judge a particular representation of an apple veridical or non-veridical. Consequently, the boundaries of representational objects must be prior to and independent of what is represented by particular representational contents.

This has the following consequence for the metaphysics of representational states, given that representational states can themselves be represented in the content of meta-representational states: Representational states are ontologically prior to being represented. They present discrete phenomena independently of whether they are represented. That is, both representational modes and types of representational content have definite boundaries, independently of whether and how phenomena of these kinds are represented on a particular occasion. For example, Peter's belief that Harry intends to go to London tomorrow represents Harry's intention to go to London tomorrow, which itself represents the action of going to London at a particular time. According to the representationalist conception of content, the veridicality condition of Peter's belief is that Harry has the *intention* in question (independently of whether Harry's intention is carried out). Because Harry's intention is the truth-determinant of Peter's belief, intending must be a discrete psychological phenomenon whose boundaries and criteria of individuation do not depend on anybody's representation or judgment.

1.2.1.4 Language and Representation

The role language plays within representationalist views can be outlined as follows. Language is a device to convey information about the world, it is a kind of representing. Natural languages have the function to project thoughts about the world using a medium which is accessible and understandable by more than one person. A natural language accordingly presents a sign-system that enables communication, the exchange of information among the speakers of that language. Individual expressions from a natural language, linguistic expressions, serve to articulate representational content. Words, multiple-worded terms and phrases, sentences and parts of sentences are signs whose function consists in representing objects and states of affairs by means of articulating representational content.[23] Linguistic expressions are meaningful insofar as they fulfil this function, that is,

---

23 Disagreement concerns the kind of linguistic expressions from a natural language (in short: linguistic expressions) that are regarded as the smallest units of linguistic content, e.g. sentences, words, or more complex phrases, and whether different classes of words or sentences are conceived to exercise different representational functions. What matters here is mainly that the function of linguistic expressions consisting in or composed from the smallest possible meaning-bearing units is to refer to corresponding aspects of reality in the sense outlined in the last section. I will

insofar as they express representational content. So conceived, language is an indirect means of representing because it does so only in virtue of expressing content. The connection between language, content and world is characterised such that linguistic expressions stand for representational contents, which refer to corresponding objects and states of affairs. Representation by means of a natural language is characterised by three levels, the level of objects and states of affairs, the level of meaning or content (the way in which objects and states of affairs are represented) and the level of signs (the way in which meaning is articulated). An object or state of affairs can be represented in different ways, by means of different tokens of representational content, and a particular content can be expressed by different signs. Conversely, in an ideal language, every sign has only one meaning and thus refers to only one object or state of affairs, just as every content-type refers to only one kind of object.[24]

Accordingly, meaning is a function of linguistic expressions separate from, but still conditioned on reference. *Reference* is the function of linguistic expressions to *stand for an object or state of affairs*. Its value is assessed in terms of veridicality: a particular linguistic expression is veridical if and only if it corresponds to an actual object or state of affairs. *Meaning* is the function of linguistic expressions to refer to an object or a state of affairs *by means of articulating representational content*. This function is fulfilled if and only if a particular linguistic expression actually articulates a content, that is, if and only if it presents a description of a certain object or state of affairs, independently of whether this description is veridical. Yet, if a linguistic expression was not primarily to stand for an object, i.e. if its primary function was not reference, the expression would not refer to anything at first place. To put it differently, a linguistic expression is meaningful if it refers to an object or state of affairs in a functional sense, even if it does not actually has a referent.

---

not consider questions such as what structural features are necessary for a linguistic expression to be meaningful.

24 *Cf.* Gottlob Frege (1892b), "Über Sinn und Bedeutung", *Zeitschrift für Philosophie und philosophische Kritik 100*, pp. 25–50, particularly pp. 27–8. This paper has been translated by Max Black as Gottlob Frege (1948), "Sense and Reference", *The Philosophical Review 57/3*, pp. 209–30, and is contained as Frege (1980d), "On Sense and Meaning" in Peter Geach, Max Black (eds.), *Translations from the Philosophical Writings of Gottlob Frege*, Oxford: Blackwell 1980, pp. 56–78. The page numbers refer to the original pagination as indicated by the editors. I quote from this translation, using 'reference' instead of 'meaning' to translate Frege's *Bedeutung*, as Black suggests in his earlier translation, *cf.* Max Black (1948), "Introductory Note", *The Philosophical Review 57/3*, pp. 207f. Furthermore, I use the term 'meaning' approximately in the same way as Frege uses the word *Sinn* (usually translated sense) and the word 'reference' similarly to Frege's notion *Bedeutung*, thus differing from Black's translation. Thereby, I want to bring out the analogy of mental and linguistic representation which is drawn by representationalist views.

Consequently, the two functions of language can come apart in the following ways. Linguistic expressions thought or uttered on particular occasions can be meaningful without representing actual objects or state of affairs. In this case, their function of meaning is fulfilled, whereas their function of reference is not. Whereas, a linguistic expression cannot fulfil its function of reference without thereby fulfilling its function of meaning. On the contrary, meaningless expressions are characterised in that they do not represent any possible object, or in that they do not articulate representational content. Accordingly, the sentence 'the earth moves around the sun' is meaningful in that it refers to the state of affairs represented by the proposition *that the earth moves around the sun*, and it has a referent because the content it expresses is veridical. The sentence 'The present King of France is bold' is meaningful in the same sense, but uttered in 1793 it lacks a referent. The word 'gavagei' on the contrary is not meaningful because it does not express representational content.

Meaning and reference can come apart in another sense. As mentioned above, different signs can articulate the same content. For this reason, synonymous expressions and sentences from different natural languages are intertranslatable. The sentences 'Es regnet', 'It is raining' and 'Está lloviendo' have the same meaning in virtue of expressing the same content. Moreover, different contents can have the same reference, i.e. represent the same object or states of affairs, in virtue of rendering the object or state of affairs in different modes of presentation. Linguistic expressions articulating the respective contents do not have the same meaning, but the same reference. The expressions 'Morning Star' and 'Evening Star' refer to the same object, but do so under different descriptions, they do not have the same meaning.

Finally, one can utter words 'without meaning' (Searle), for instance, when practising their pronunciation. The respective words are not used as signs to designate corresponding objects and hence do not have a referential function. What decides whether a word is used 'with meaning' or 'without meaning' is whether it is connected with a referential object. What turns a word from a sound into a sign is a matter of controversy.[25]

In brief, the meaning of a linguistic expression consists in referring to an independently existing object or state of affairs. It does so by articulating representational content. Linguistic expressions translate representational content in a sign-system and in this capacity enable the exchange of information. In this way, the function of language is to convey information about the world.

---

25 *Cf.* Searle (1983), ch. 6. I will outline Searle's view on this matter later in this chapter. I will critically discuss the distinction of meaningless sounds and meaningful signs in Chapter 3.

The idea that the meaning of a linguistic expression is independent of the linguistic context in which it occurs imposes a requirement for the ability to use linguistic expressions as a means of representing as well as a means of conveying content to one another. The meaning of linguistic expressions is supposed to consist in referring to corresponding objects and states of affairs by means of articulating content. The competence of applying and understanding a particular linguistic expression thus presupposes familiarity with its reference, that is, the ability to individuate and/or recognise the object represented by the type of content it articulates. For instance, being able to use the word 'apple' requires familiarity with its reference (apples) to the effect that a competent user can discriminate apples (from one another, or, say, apples from pears) and recognise particular objects as apples. The word 'apple' is only a sign for the kind of object one is acquainted with. Minimally, familiarity with the reference of a linguistic expression requires the ability to discriminate its object from others, and/or to identify it as instantiating a general term. It is highly contentious what it means to be familiar with the reference of a linguistic expression, particularly with respect to the question which cognitive capacities are required. Broadly, one can distinguish between accounts that interpret 'familiarity with reference' in an intellectualist way, as knowledge of the general rule (a formal or general concept or a definition) connecting a particular sign with the corresponding object on the one hand, and anti-intellectualist accounts grasping the competence of applying and understanding a linguistic expression in virtue of acquaintance with the respective object that involves less demanding recognitional capacities.

A version of the intellectualist approach is prominently promoted by Gareth Evans in succession to Peter Strawson.[26] Generalising a proposal from Strawson concerning the individuation of particulars, Evans frames a requirement on understanding expressions designating concepts as well as such designating particulars:

> [A]nyone who has the grasp of the concept of being F must be able to understand what it is for an arbitrary proposition of the form [a is F] to be true (where a is an Idea [sc. a general concept, us.] which he possesses of an object). The Generality Constraint requires us to see the thought that a is F as lying at the intersection of two series of thoughts: the thoughts that a is F, that a is G, that a is H,..., on the one hand, and the thoughts that a is F, that b is F, that c is F,..., on the other. (1982, p. 209)

According to Evans, meaningfully entertaining a thought or making an utterance with the content *that a is F* presupposes the capacity to use both, *a* and *F* correctly

---

26 Gareth Evans (1982), *The Varieties of Reference*, Oxford: Clarendon Press, chs. 4.3 and 7, referring to Peter Strawson (1959), *Individuals. An Essay in Descriptive Metaphysics*, London: Methuen, p. 99

on indefinitely many other occasions, in other contexts, other tenses, or other subject-predicate combinations (1982, pp. 103ff. and 209f.). The idea behind the Generality Constraint is simple: The meaning of a term or a sentence consists in the content it expresses. Understanding a concept or a sentence accordingly just is gaining access to its content, that is eventually, what object or states of affairs it refers to. Concepts are general terms, whose instantiations on particular occasions refer to objects of the same kind. Hence, being able to understand the use of a general term on a particular occasion means to be able to connect the sign with the object it serves to designate—one must know, or be acquainted with what a word refers to in order to understand it. And, according to Evans and Strawson, this is possible only if the subject recognises on a particular occasion that a certain sign is an instantiation of a concept whose meaning is stable across different contexts. Mastery of the word apple accordingly requires knowing what apples are, i.e. knowing the general principle by which something counts as an apple and thus knowing the specific properties that distinguish apples from other kinds of objects.

The account of Strawson and Evans is criticised by Burge (2010, pp. 18f. and ch. 6) for being 'hyper-intellectualising' in that it suggests that discriminative and recognitional capacities do not only require the possession of general concepts, but also the individual's self-consciousness. Burge observes that

> Much ordinary cognition, particularly perceptual cognition, derives from instinctive extensions from paradigms or salient exemplars, rather than from general *conceptions* of differentiating principles that govern arbitrary instances of a kind. These extensions are subindividual and probably subconceptual. The principles governing such extensions need not be *conceived by the individuals* in whose psychologies the extensions are carried out. [...] Concept formation is often the product of such subindividual, subconceptual tendencies. Concepts mark abilities. The abilities can be explained by principles that apply to subconceptual processes and causal relations to the environment. The principles need not be known, represented, or even thinkable by the individual (even implicitly). (2010, p. 197)

The alternative Burge offers regards the acquaintance with discrete representational objects, or kinds of objects, which eventually underlies the competence of applying and understanding verbal expressions of content, as equally explainable by processes of reiterated encounters with particular objects of a kind. Familiarity with a sample, or a series of samples is sufficient in order to be able to recognise an object as belonging to a certain kind and to discriminate among particular objects. The principles uniting the instances of a kind of object and thereby enabling recognition and discrimination need not be thought intellectual in origin (they can rely on causal processes), nor be known to the individuals applying them. Picking out apples from other objects as well as recognising apples just requires having encountered apples before and the evolution of relevant mechanisms.

At any rate, the point of both accounts is that the capacity to discriminate and recognise objects as belonging to a certain kind, which is regarded a necessary precondition on the ability to use the corresponding linguistic expression, requires familiarity with the kind of objects in question. This is brought about either by acquaintance with samples, followed by a kind of (subpersonal) extrapolation, or in virtue of possessing the corresponding general concept that comprises definitory knowledge of the kind of objects in question and thus provides the criteria necessary for individuating and recognising its instantiations. The competence to apply and understand linguistic expressions thus derives from the ability to recognise and individuate the object, concept, or state of affairs it refers to.

Linguistic expressions do not only differ in meaning, but also with respect to their grammar, i.e. the role they play in a language. They do so in virtue of corresponding to different elements of the internal structure of content, which in turn refer to different kinds of things. For my purpose it suffices to broadly distinguish three groups of linguistic content, i.e. names and singular terms, concepts and sentences, which correspond to three groups of structural components of content, namely objects, (predicative) concepts, and propositions, respectively. Names and singular terms represent particular objects (including groups and abstract objects, such as the term 'theorem of Pythagoras'), concepts represent general objects (such as relations, properties, or predicates), and sentences represent states of affairs.[27] So, for example, the name 'Neil Armstrong' refers to the first man on the moon, the concept 'red' stands for the property of being red, and the sentence 'the King of France is bald' refers to the state of the world in which there is a King of France who is bald.

There are two further points of interest here concerning the question which part or parts of a sentence constitute its referring function. The representational function of concepts is variable. They can be used in a *referential* as well as in an *attributive* way. A concept refers to the corresponding general concept, if it is used as a general term. It refers to an object instantiating the corresponding general concept, if it is specified by other attributes. For example, in the sentence 'red is a warm colour' the word 'red' refers to redness in general (a general concept). In the sentence 'the red of my jumper is not quite the same as the red of my shirt', the word

---

27 Burge distinguishes between general and singular terms. The function of singular terms consists in referring to corresponding objects. General terms, in contrast, have an attributive function. They serve to qualify the referent of a token representational content and thereby contribute to its individuation. In his sample 'The barn is red', the term 'the barn' has the function of referring to an object, the term 'is red' indicates a property of the object referred to by the whole sentence. See Burge (2010), pp. 32ff.

'red' is used to refer to a particular object (the colour of my jumper) instantiating the general concept 'red'. Similarly, the uninflected verb 'to believe' refers generally to the phenomenon of believing or belief. The sentence 'Peter's belief is crazy' refers to a particular representational state, a belief, which is qualified by naming its subject (Peter) and ascribing a property to it (being crazy). The object the sentence is about is the belief.

In contrast, concepts exercise an attributive function if they serve to qualify a referring term, i.e. the element of the corresponding content, which picks out the object the whole representational state is about. In the sentence 'My jumper is red', the term 'is red' qualifies the object the sentence is about by ascribing a property to it, in the sentence 'My red jumper has a hole' the word 'red' serves to individuate the object among a class of similar objects (the red jumper, not the blue one). Similarly, the inflected forms of the verb 'to believe' serve to ascribe particular beliefs to the corresponding grammatical subjects, so for instance in the sentence 'Peter believes that is raining'. This sentence nicely brings out that one can analyse the meaning of linguistic expression on various levels. As a whole, the sentence expresses a proposition referring to the state of affairs *that Peter believes that it is raining*. In this sense, its meaning consists in conveying information about a certain psychological fact, it says that a particular person's mind is constituted thus-and-so. On a more fine-grained analysis, the sentence refers, with the name 'Peter', to a particular person, to whom it ascribes a particular representational state, a belief, which is further qualified by its content, a state of the weather.

The last example also brings out that propositions can change their function of referring to a state of affairs into an attributive function if they represent the content of a representational state which is referred to by the main sentence. This has the following consequence: When figuring in the subordinate clause following a psychological predicate, propositions do not themselves refer to particular states of affairs and therefore do not bear a referential value, i.e. they cannot themselves be assessed in terms of veridicality/non-veridicality or truth/falsity.[28] Yet, they maintain their function to represent veridicality *conditions*, but these are used to qualify the representational state represented by the main clause and thus serve to individuate and classify representational states. Propositions figuring in a subordinate clause continue to designate the veridicality conditions they express when constituting an autonomous sentence. In this sense, propositions have a uniform meaning independently of the role they take at a particular instance. For this reason, it is possible to extract content-identical elements from various repre-

---

28 Here, the Fregean roots of representationalism are obvious, *cf.* Frege (1892b) and Section 4 of this chapter.

sentational states, independently of the position they obtain within the internal structure of the content. For example, the contents articulated by the sentences 'Peter believes that it is raining', 'It was raining yesterday' and 'I wish that it is raining later' display a common element, the proposition *that it is raining*.

Thus, one can say that representationalist theories of mind involve a conception of language that defines meaning in terms of reference. Taking this conception of language together with the metaphysical claims concerning content outlined above has the following consequences for the meaning of psychological concepts, for instance belief, intention, desire, sadness and the corresponding verbs, 'to believe', 'to intend', 'to desire', 'to be sad': Psychological concepts are general terms. If psychological concepts are meaningful, they are so in virtue of referring to corresponding (types of) objects. These (types of) objects are discrete psychological phenomena, the states of believing, intending, desiring, or being sad. That is, psychological phenomena are ontologically prior to being represented by means of expressions from a natural language. The meaning of psychological concepts consists in articulating what I have called earlier meta-representational content, i.e. content specifying veridicality conditions that are met by corresponding psychological facts. In virtue of articulating content, psychological concepts have a uniform meaning across different contexts, and the truth-value of different psychological (instances of) concepts expressing the same content is identical independently of the subject and point of time of their use. Finally, the ability to understand psychological concepts on a particular occasion requires either the ability to understand them in all possible contexts in virtue of knowing their meaning (following the Generality Constraint) or acquaintance with a sample (following Burge). At any rate, it requires familiarity with the kind of things psychological concepts in general refer to.

1.2.1.5 Language and Content-Individuation

Whether or not language might have a function for the individuation of representational content, in addition to being a medium for articulating representational content, is a matter of controversy. Whereas internalist (or individualist) accounts hold that representing a certain content depends exclusively on the representational subject's intrinsic properties, externalist (or, as Burge prefers, anti-individualist) accounts claim that having (a certain kind of) representational states requires the subject's being related to his or her environment in certain ways. Which side one takes decides the question as to how representational content is individuated. Internalism about mental content holds that determining what representational states a subject has, i.e. which contents it represents, does not depend on how things are in the world 'external' to the subject. On this view, representational states, and representational content can be individuated by drawing on their subject's own psychological and/or physical properties (e.g. his or her cognitive and/or conceptual resources, sense impressions, the perceptual apparatus, or brain states). Consequently, language, that is, a publicly spoken, natural language, has no impact on the individuation of representational states; its primary function simply consists in articulating and thus conveying representational content. In contrast, externalism about mental content implies that, at least in some cases, the individuation of representational content, and thus of representational states, constitutively depends on the subject's relations to his or her environment, including his or her relations to the social and linguistic community he or she belongs to.[29]

According to externalism, there are two related ways the individuation of mental states may constitutively depend on language. Firstly, it is, to some extent, up to a linguistic community to establish the connection between words and their referents. Which words are used to articulate representational states about mind-independent objects (e.g. physical particulars or causal relations) is contingent on a certain community's practice. Differences across communities concerning the ways the reference of words is set up result in differences in meaning of homonymic expressions, and so in differences in the content of mental states involving the respective concepts. For example, in British English the word 'chips' refers to what is called, in American English, 'French fries'. In American English, the word 'chips' refers to what is called, in British English, 'crisps'. If a British person thinks or talks about 'chips' he or she represents a different thing than an American employing the word 'chips' and the corresponding concept. The respective concepts connected to the word 'chips' do not share their extension. Thus, the accuracy conditions of, for instance, the order to bring some 'chips' differ, once given by a British, once by an American person, respectively (familiarly so—the Englishman in New York will be disappointed to be served the referent for his concept 'crisps', and the American's wish will equally remain unsatisfied by the waiter's serving 'French fries' in Camden Town). Since the two kinds of representational content are different in extension and veridicality conditions, their individuation depends on those linguistic practices determining the referent of 'chips'.[30]

---

29 *Cf.* Max Deutsch, Joe Lau (2014), "Externalism about Mental Content", *The Stanford Encyclopedia of Philosophy (Spring 2014 Edition)*, Edward N. Zalta (ed.), http://plato.stanford.edu/archives/spr2014/entries/content-externalism/, last access June 7th, 2014.
30 I owe this everyday version of Putnam's Twin Earth example to Martin Sigrist. Putnam's point is slightly different, he makes it with respect to water, i.e. an object that naturally occurs in the protagonist's environment without being grounded in social conventions. If in some linguistic community the word 'water' is used for H_2O (a particular physically given stuff, that is) the thoughts

Secondly, in some cases the influence of linguistic or other social conventions is not restricted to establishing the reference of linguistic expressions, but includes determining the boundaries of the referent itself.[31] The individuation of a particular mental state constitutively depends on their subject's social environment or linguistic community in that the extensions of (some) concepts figuring *within* its content is determined by linguistic conventions, i.e. socially established norms or standards governing the usage of the relevant concepts. In other words, if the meaning of a concept depends on whether certain 'contingent matters' (Burge, 2003) about its range of applications are settled by a linguistic community the impact of linguistic conventions precisely consists in settling these matters. Given that meaning is conceived in terms of reference, this is to say that the boundaries of the referents corresponding to socially constituted concepts is fixed in the same way. Once the respective standards are established, the nature of such referents is independent of individual applications of the respective concepts in thought or speech and thus provides the content and a stable standard for evaluating the veridicality of corresponding representational states.[32] Although the standard might vary over time, across linguistic communities or discursive contexts (as in Putnam's examples), the meaning of the respective concepts is determinate in the particular instances of their application. Reversely, if the extension of a particular referent (for instance, an object, property, or process) is non-arbitrarily fixed (i.e. objectively, not socially) the meaning of the corresponding concepts is not, either; and so is not the individuation of content-bearing states representing any such referents. If the content of a mental state is based on non-arbitrary grounds

---

of its members employing the concept of water will be about H_2O. If in a different community the word 'water' refers to XYZ (a different physically given stuff) instead of H_2O its members will represent *XYZ* when thinking about 'water'. Thoughts employing the concept 'water' differ with respect to their their reference depending on whether they are had by members of the first or second community: Thoughts by members of the first community represent H_2O, thoughts by members of the second one XYZ. Their individuation depends on those linguistic practices determining the referent of 'water'.—The analogy holds nonetheless once there are things like chips or crisps, respectively. *Cf.* Hilary Putnam (1975a), "The Meaning of 'Meaning'", in Putnam (1975b), *Mind, Language, and Reality*, Cambridge: UP, pp. 215–71, here pp. 223–9.

31 Maybe the most famous example is the notion 'arthritis'. *Cf.* citeBurge1979; Tyler Burge (2006), "Postscript to Individualism and the Mental", ibid. pp. 151–81; (1986) "Individualism and Psychology", ibid. pp.221–53. The range of concepts he uses to exemplify and support his thesis in this article exceeds the range of concepts referring to 'social facts' in Searle's sense although the latter are the most obvious candidates to which his claims apply.

32 With Searle, one might say that these referents are ontologically subjective (qua constitutively depending on collective intentionality) and, at the same time, epistemically objective (qua being, once constituted, objective facts). *Cf.* John Searle (1995), *The Construction of Social Reality*, New York: The Free Press, pp. 8–12.

the mental state is individuable independent of whether and how the relevant concepts are used in a language.[33]

In this way, the claim that, in some cases, the individuation of mental states constitutively depends on language can be brought into accordance with the claim that representational states present language- and perspective-independent, 'objective' facts. Language—definitional standards, norms of usage, conventionally established ways of speaking—can influence the individuation of mental states as being of a certain *representational* kind—having a certain representational *content*—but only if specifying their content is otherwise underdetermined. However, language has no impact on individuating mental states as being of a particular *psychological* kind (what I earlier called their psychological *mode*). Whether or not a particular mental state is a belief, intention, wish, or thought, is not a matter of social conventions, but an ontologically (and also a phylogenetically and ontogenetically) prior fact.

To sum up, language serves, on a representationalist view, to convey information about objects and states of affairs. It does so by articulating representational content. In virtue of articulating representational content, meaningful linguistic expressions in general share the properties of representational content outlined above. The basic function of (meaningful) linguistic expressions consists in referring to corresponding objects, concepts or states of affairs and their veridicality depends on whether they succeed in doing so. The reference of particular linguistic expressions does not depend on the perspective from which they are uttered. That is, linguistic expressions used in different circumstances, by different persons or at different times with the same meaning signify the same veridicality conditions and therefore have the same referential value (being veridical or not). Moreover, the meaning of a term or sentence does not depend on the position it takes in a more complex expression, it continues its function of representing the corresponding object under a certain description without changing its veridicality conditions. So one can say that the meaning of a linguistic expression is uniform across different representational contexts. Since the meaning of linguistic expressions is the content it expresses, and since this function derives from the content's function to represent a mind-independent reality, the order of priorities is as follows: Objects

---

33 Such is the nature of the contents of the *most primitive and/or fundamental kinds of representational states* on which every other form of representation relies (such as perceptual beliefs and other perceptual states). The extension of the objects and states of affairs they refer to is not open to social discourse. Their contents are non-arbitrarily fixed, as product of the subject's perceptual apparatus, relevant subindividual processes and environmental conditions (*cf.* Burge (2010), p. 24).

and states of affairs are ontologically prior to being represented and representational content is prior to being articulated in a natural language with respect to its veridicality conditions and, as regards particular tokens, as well with respect to its individuation (which derives from the things it represents, however they are constituted).

1.2.1.6 Summary
In this section, I have given a general outline of the theoretical framework of the representationalist theory of mind. It is certainly not comprehensive, but I think the central notions have become sufficiently clear. The main idea of representationalism is that the primary function of the mind consists in representing mind-independent objects and states of affairs by means of framing veridicality conditions. I have outlined the general theoretical framework of representationalist views, explicating the function of representation, the central notion of 'representational content', from which I have extracted three claims as minimal conditions for a representationalist view to hold concerning content, and I have finished by giving an outline of the conception of meaning following from representationalism. Heal brings the basic ideas of representationalism into the following formulation, which I find very much to the point:

> [T]he world contains a variety of phenomena which people may come across and of which they may form some conception. Among these states are states of themselves, including beliefs. They come across them either by introspection [...] or in seeking to explain [...] the behaviour of themselves and those around them. The linguistic behaviour of the word "belief" is to be explained by unpacking the truth conditions of claims about beliefs; these in turn are explained by pointing to the conception people have of the phenomenon they have come across, a conception which will more or less accurately capture the nature of the pre-existing phenomenon. (Lurking behind this commonsensical-seeming account are further pictures e.g. of the world as already sliced by nature at the joints and awaiting only labelling from us, of empiricism as the right account of concept acquisition and of the correspondence theory of truth.)[34]

My investigation focusses on the claim that psychological or mental states are discrete phenomena that are ontologically prior to being represented. That is, psychological phenomena as well as the criteria that can be used for their individuation are conceived prior to and independent of the language used to communicate

---

34 Jane Heal (1994), "Moore's Paradox: A Wittgensteinian Approach", *Mind* 103/409, pp. 5–24, here pp. 17f. *Cf.*, for instance, the requirements Evans (1982) makes on the reference of concepts, and on the abilities involved in concept-possession, and Burge's view on the commonsense use of psychological expressions in Burge (1986), p. 224.

them in talking or writing. The grammar and meaning of psychological expressions are conceived as deriving from the ontological constitution of the phenomena they are supposed to designate. In the following, I will frequently refer to this view as 'referentialism concerning psychological concepts' and will argue that this view is false.[35]

In the next section, I raise a challenge for the representationalist conception of mind and language by introducing a phenomenon from ordinary language, which arises in some expressions involving first-person assertions of belief, i.e. involving the phrase 'I believe'. The phenomenon in question is Moore's Paradox. I will first outline the paradox, then explain the challenge arising from it for representationalism. I will continue by presenting four ways of approaching Moore's Paradox within the representationalist framework. Although these views radically diverge in detail, they nonetheless arrive at the same explanation of Moore's Paradox. This explanation, however, is false. I will argue that any approach to Moore's Paradox committed to the representationalist view of mind and its inherent referentialist view about meaning must arrive at this explanation and that this provides sufficient reason to dispense with the representationalist theory of mind. In the remainder of this chapter, I will connect the representationalist view of the mind with Frege's philosophy of mind and language and elaborate the analogies holding between them. In the following chapter, I will develop my argumentation against the representationalist conception of the mind exploiting Wittgenstein's considerations of Moore's Paradox as well as his arguments against the conceivability of a private language.

1.2.2 Moore's Paradox: A Challenge for Representationalism

Consider the following case: Someone resolutely says, in an assertive manner, 'It is raining, but I don't believe that it is raining.' This sounds puzzling, and you might ask 'What do you mean?', or 'Are you sure about what you are saying?' If he or she replies 'I am absolutely sure: It is raining, but I don't believe it is', you will possibly not take the speaker seriously, you might assume for instance that he or she is

---

35 The referentialist conception of language implies a mentalist conception of mental states, i.e. the view that mental states are discrete, language-independent, criterially identifiable psychological phenomena, but not necessarily a representationalist view of the mind. However, insofar as the representationalist theory of the mind transfers the two-component model from linguistic utterances to the structure of mental states and equally focusses on content as the constituting and individuating property of representational states, it presents a plausible, or at least, a convenient continuation of the referentialist conception of meaning endorsed by Frege and others.

making a joke, that he or she does not know how to use assertoric language, or that he or she is insane. It is, as G. E. Moore observes, "perfectly absurd or nonsensical to say such things as 'I don't believe it's raining, but as a matter of fact it is'."[36] Even worse, it is *"paradoxical* that it should be absurd to say them" (Moore (1993), p. 208). The question is, why? More specifically: Under what circumstances is it absurd to utter a sentence of this type? Why is it absurd? And why is this paradoxical?

It is not always absurd to utter, write, or think a sentence such as 'It is raining, but I don't believe it is raining'. It is *not* absurd to cite such a sentence as an example for an absurdity, as I just did. It is *not* absurd to say 'It is possible that it is raining and yet I don't believe it is raining', and equally to say it as a joke or a lie, that is, without meaning it seriously. It is only absurd to *sincerely assert* 'It is raining, but I don't believe it is'.

But why is this so? The sentences in question have the general structure '*p* is the case, but I don't believe that *p* is the case'. This structure, however, does not make these sentences absurd. Logically speaking, they present conjunctions of two independent propositions, the conjuncts being '*p* is the case' and 'I don't believe that *p* is the case'. The whole sentence can be paraphrased as $p \land \neg q$. It is clearly not absurd to sincerely assert either the sentence 'It is raining', or the sentence 'I don't believe it is raining'. So how can one explain that sincerely asserting their conjunction presents an absurdity? Approaches to answering this question from a representationalist viewpoint are the topic of the following discussion. Instead of trying to give an answer to this question straight away, I will characterise the phenomenon in more detail.

The name 'Moore's Paradox' does not refer to the absurdity of asserting a sentence of the type '*p* is the case, but I don't believe that *p* is the case' itself. It designates a *paradox*, or better a complex of paradoxes, generated by this absurdity.[37] The paradox consists in that the absurdity *ought not arise* at all, given the following observations: First of all, it is possible that what sentences like 'It is raining, but I don't believe it' express is *true*—it might well be the case *that it is raining and I do not believe it is.* It is, further, perfectly fine to assert that another person is in this situation, that is, to express the proposition from another person's point of view—there is nothing absurd in saying 'It is raining, but Peter doesn't believe it is'. Moreover, describing the same situation at a later time, 'It was raining, but I didn't

---

36 George Edward Moore (1993), "Moore's Paradox", in *Selected Writings*, ed. by Thomas Baldwin, London/New York: Routledge, pp. 207–212, here p. 207.

37 In the following, I will use the term 'Moore-paradoxical sentences' for sentences inducing Moore's Paradox, and I will use the singular term 'Moore's Paradox' throughout, although there are several reasons why it is deemed paradoxical that asserting a Moore-paradoxical sentence is absurd.

believe it', is as innocuous as describing it in the present tense form is absurd. Finally, a sentence of the type 'p is the case, but I don't believe that p is the case' does not generate any paradoxes if it presents the content of kinds of sentences other than assertion; if I, for instance, hypothesise, imagine, dream, or question the fact *that it is raining and yet I don't believe it is.*

Importantly, these observations confirm the above statement that Moore-paradoxical sentences are not, and cannot be traced, to either a formal-logical or an empirical contradiction, that is, they are neither contradictory according to the laws of traditional propositional logic, nor to the laws of physics, nor to the laws of psychology. They do not even contradict moral or social laws; uttering a Moore-paradoxical sentence does not necessarily amount to breaking a taboo. Moore-paradoxical sentences, such as 'it is raining, but I don't believe it' might sound like contradictions, but they are not. They are not formal-logical contradictions because the truth-values of the contents expressed by each conjunct, p and $\neg B(I, p)$, are independent of one another. And they are not empirical contradictions, either, for the state of affairs they express is not only conceivable, but even very likely to obtain.[38] If Moore-paradoxical sentences were tantamount to contradictions in either sense, they would always be false, regardless of the pragmatic context they stand in. But what they express can be a true description of a fact, and under certain circumstances, it also makes sense to say them. One just cannot sincerely assert them. For this reason, Moore prefers to characterise the assertoric use of sentences of this type as absurd rather than contradictory:

> "It is a paradox that it should be perfectly absurd to *utter assertively words* of which the *meaning* is something which may quite well be true—is not a contradiction." (Moore (1993), p. 209, original italics.)

As a consequence, it is an adequacy condition on any account of Moore's Paradox that its solution must not present the sentences giving rise to Moore's Paradox as a contradiction, or as implying a contradiction. *Any explanation of Moore's Paradox that renders Moore-paradoxical sentences contradictory, explicitly or implicitly, is false.* And any account of assertion and belief yielding such a solution is equally false. It is the aim of my argumentation to show that the representationalist view of the mind is such an account: The solutions to Moore's Paradox available within the representationalist framework *necessarily* render Moore-paradoxical sentences contradictory, or implying a contradiction. Therefore, representationalism is, as a theory of mind and language, at best inadequate, at worst false.

---

38 This point is emphasised and very cogently formulated by Richard Moran. *Cf.* Moran (1997), "Self-Knowledge: Discovery, Resolution and Undoing", *European Journal of Philosophy 5/2*, pp. 141–61, here pp. 143f.

The remarks just made indicate that Moore-paradoxical sentences violate two central claims of representationalism, the Reference Claim and the Uniformity Claim, although they appear to be perfectly in congruence with the laws of propositional logic. Before going into more detail here, it will be useful to make some further clarifications concerning the structure of Moore-paradoxical sentences. In its original form, the content of Moore-paradoxical assertions takes the form 'p is the case, but I don't believe that p is the case', or:

(1) $p \wedge \neg B(I, p)$.

Moore's Paradox is equally triggered by asserting a sentence of the two following types, (1') 'p is the case, but I believe that p is *not* the case', e.g. 'It is raining, but I believe it is not raining', and (1'') 'p is *not* the case, but I believe that p is the case', as in 'It is not raining, but I believe it is':

(1') $p \wedge B(I, \neg p)$,[39]   and

(1'') $\neg p \wedge B(I, p)$.[40]

(1') and (1'') are equivalent in that both present assertions of a belief whose content is contrary to what is asserted to be the case by the first conjunct, whereas (1) expresses one's disbelief of what one asserts to be the case. Heal and Williams argue independently that the versions significantly differ in their consequences, and that the difference should therefore be paid more attention to than it has been the case in the literature on Moore's Paradox.[41] Contrary to both, I think that paying too much attention to this point will obscure rather than illuminate the

---

39 *Cf.* John N. Williams (1979), "Moore's Paradox—One or Two?" *Analysis 39/3*, pp. 141–142.

40 *Cf.* Heal (1994), p. 6.

41 They explicitly mention Wittgenstein here, suggesting that his remarks on Moore's Paradox in *Philosophical Investigations* and elsewhere only take the first version into account. But contrary to this suggestion, Wittgenstein considers the respective alternative formulation of Moore's Paradox. At the most conspicuous place to search, in the remarks on Moore's Paradox published together with *Philosophical Investigations* (*PPF* Section x), Wittgenstein does not even mention the first version explicitly, but only considers sentences complying with the structure of the second. At other places, he uses both formulations alternately, e.g. in *Remarks on the Philosophy Psychology* I, §§ 485–487. *Cf.* "Philosophie der Psychologie – Ein Fragment. Philosophy of Psychology – A Fragment", in *Philosophische Untersuchungen. Philosophical Investigations*, transl. Peter M. S. Hacker, Joachim Schulte, 4th, substantially revised edition, Oxford: Blackwell 2009, pp. 182–243 (henceforth *PPF*) and *Remarks on the Philosophy of Psychology. Bemerkungen über die Philosophie der Psychologie* Vol. 1, ed. by G. E. M. Anscombe, Georg Henrik von Wright, Oxford: Blackwell 1980, henceforth *RPP* I. The remarks from *PPF* were first published and have usually been referred to as 'Part II' of *Philosophical Investigations*. The previous edition is *Philosophical Investigations. Philosophische Untersuchungen*, ed. by G. E. M. Anscombe, Georg Henrik von Wright,

actual difficulty with Moore's Paradox. After all, as both authors acknowledge, the three versions coincide in that sincerely asserting a sentence of either structure is absurd in the same way and for the same reasons. Resultingly, asserting a sentence of either structure equally induces Moore's Paradox. For this reason, I will not analyse the versions separately, but subsume them under the term 'Moore-paradoxical sentences'.

Earlier, I have shown that not every instance of uttering a Moore-paradoxical sentence is absurd. Let me now outline the few remarks I already made on both, the circumstances under which the paradox arises, and in what the paradox consists.

On the face of it, a sentence such as 'It is raining, but I don't believe that it is raining' seems odd. There is a strong tension in it, which makes it barely intelligible, almost contradictory. When asserted in everyday conversation, its sense is unclear and it almost prompts a reaction like 'What do you want to say?' At second glance however, it is difficult to specify why this is so. One might point out that, for example, "The sentence 'I believe it and it isn't true' *can after all be the truth*. Namely, when I really believe it and this belief turns out to be wrong."[42] A Moore-paradoxical sentence apparently describes a situation in which something is the case and, at the same time, someone does not believe that it is the case. Such a situation is not only conceivable, but indeed very likely to obtain for most parts of one's life, for example, when someone is ignorant of or agnostic about some matter of fact or other (as in (1)) or when someone wrongly believes something (as in (1′) and (1″)).

If one looks at each part of the compound sentence separately, it becomes even more puzzling that asserting a Moore-paradoxical sentence is absurd, and enigmatic how it can be asserted at all. A Moore-paradoxical sentence is a conjunction of two sentences, e.g. 'It is raining' and 'I don't believe that it is raining'. The first sentence states the weather to be such and such, the second one expresses the speaker's belief about the weather. Whether or not it is raining does (at least, as is widely accepted nowadays) not depend on whether anyone believes it is, and

---

transl. G. E. M. Anscombe, [2]Oxford: Blackwell 1958 (henceforth *PI*). Hacker and Schulte changed this for various reason in the revised edition of *Philosophical Investigations* (*cf.* the editors' preface). I use the citation suggested by Hacker and Schulte. Still, I use Anscombe's translation as the standard one and indicate where I use Hacker's and Schulte's instead. Furthermore, I deviate from Anscombe's translation in general wherever I find that a reasonable thing to do. I will not explicitly indicate minor changes (e.g. alternative words).
42 Ludwig Wittgenstein, *Remarks on the Philosophy of Psychology. Bemerkungen über die Philosophie der Psychologie* Vol. 2, ed. by G. E. M. Anscombe and Georg Henrik von Wright, Chicago: Chicago University Press 1980 (henceforth *RPP* II), here § 418.

so is the existence of someone's belief that it is raining independent of whether it is in fact raining or not. Within the framework of traditional propositional logic, nothing seems wrong with assertions of this type, either, however odd they may sound when uttered in everyday conversation. A Moore-paradoxical sentence consists in the conjunction $(p \land \neg B(I, p))$. That the proposition *that p is the case* appears in both conjuncts does not matter for the structure of the main sentence, because in the second one it appears only in the subordinate clause. It stands on a different level from the main clause, separated by the expression 'I believe', which removes its function as an autonomously referring sentence and turns it into an attributional function qualifying the second conjunct's predicate. Thus, Moore-paradoxical sentences can be just as well formalised as a conjunction of two independent propositions, $(p \land \neg q)$. The paraphrase only reassures that Moore-paradoxical sentences neither present formal-logical, nor empirical contradictions, but instead a conjunction of two propositions whose truth-values are independent of one another.

Yet, the assertion of a Moore-paradoxical sentence remains absurd, and this seems to result from the form of the asserted sentence, rather than from a certain contextual constellation of facts, in which the assertion is made. If someone asserts a sentence of the type '*p* is the case, but I don't believe that *p* is the case', one need not consider whether the proposition '*p* is the case' is true, or what beliefs the speaker actually holds. The paradoxicality of a Moore-paradoxical sentence is a conceptual, that is, a *grammatical* property of that sentence, not a matter of its content, or contingent facts concerning the speaker's psychology.

A major structural reason why Moore-paradoxical sentences are puzzling is the double appearance of the proposition *p is the case*, once in a positive, and once in a negative environment. For normally, the assertion *that p is the case* works similarly to the assertion of one's belief *that p is the case*. The assertions 'I believe it is raining' and 'It is raining' play a similar role in ordinary language, that is, one would use them to say similar things, and one would react to them in similar ways (*cf. RPP* I § 477). As Wittgenstein observes in a letter to Moore, if one asks someone whether there is a fire in the next room, and the answer is 'I believe there is', one cannot sensibly say "Don't be irrelevant; I asked you about the fire, not about your state of mind."[43] This suggests that the phrase 'I believe' in sentences such as 'I believe it is raining' is not always used to designate a feature of the speaker's psychology. Seen in this light, what Moore-paradoxical sentences reveal about the

---

43 Ludwig Wittgenstein, "Letter to G. E. Moore", October 1944, in *Cambridge Letters. Correspondence with Russell, Keynes, Moore, Ramsay and Sraffa*, ed. by Brian McGuinness, Georg Henrik von Wright, Oxford: Blackwell 1995, pp. 315–7. Henceforth *Briefe 257*.

expression 'I believe' when used in assertions, threatens to violate the Reference Claim. For, under certain conditions, it can be omitted without bringing about a change in the overall meaning of the sentence it belongs to. According to the Reference Claim, however, the meaning of psychological expressions consists in designating corresponding psychological facts, independently of the grammatical form in which they are used. If however the expression 'I believe' does not affect the meaning of an assertion 'I believe that p', it seems that it contributes nothing to the reference of the whole sentence. And this certainly cannot be a consequence, which a representationalist conception of language could straightforwardly accept.

A further observation is the occurrence of a radical change in the scenario as soon as one modifies a Moore-paradoxical sentence in either of the following ways. If instead of *asserting* a sentence like 'It is raining, but I don't believe it is' one says '*Suppose* it is raining and I don't believe it is', the absurdity disappears. This confirms the impression that one source of Moore's Paradox lies in a characteristic of the 'logic of assertion' as opposed to the 'logic' of other kinds of sentences. Whereas the assertion ($\vdash p$) is similar to the assertion ($\vdash B(I, p)$), the supposition ($-p$) is not similar to the hypothesis ($-B(I, p)$). Thus, the phrase 'I believe' can be omitted from assertions, but not from suppositions.[44] For this reason, *asserting* a Moore-paradoxical sentence is similar to asserting the contradiction ($\vdash p \wedge \neg p$), whereas merely supposing a situation expressed in a Moore-paradoxical sentence is not.

The second modification concerns the second conjunct, $\neg B(I, p)$. A change in the grammatical person or tense of its predicate 'believe' also removes the paradoxicality of a Moore-paradoxical sentence. Asserting 'Yesterday it was raining and I didn't believe it', is not paradoxical at all, one might want to explain why one did not take an umbrella and caught a cold. Likewise, the sentence 'It is raining, but Peter doesn't believe it is' is a perfectly uncontroversial description of an everyday situation. So another source of the paradoxicality of assertions of the type 'p is the case, but I don't believe that p is the case' is a characteristic of the grammar of the verb 'to believe'. More specifically, the paradoxicality originates from an asymmetry between the first-person singular present indicative and all other grammatical forms of the verb 'to believe'.

The disappearance of Moore's Paradox upon a change in the pragmatic context of a Moore-paradoxical sentence or in the grammatical form of the expression 'I believe' presents a challenge to the Uniformity Claim. The meaning of sentences, which represent the state of affairs *that p is the case and someone does not believe*

---

44 The notation is Frege's as introduced in his *Begriffsschrift* (1879), in Frege (1980e), pp. 1–20. I will come back to Frege in the last section of this chapter.

that p is the case, does not remain the same throughout all possible grammatical and pragmatic contexts. So it seems that the content articulated by the first-person present tense must deviate from the content expressed by all other forms. And this, too, is untenable on a representationalist view.

The challenge for representationalist theories of mind posed by Moore's Paradox is that the assertability of Moore-paradoxical sentences depends on the kind of sentence they are used in, on the point of view, from which they are uttered, and that its inassertability in the first-person present tense stands at odds with their possible truth. A solution to Moore's Paradox must answer two questions, what does the absurdity consist in?, and why does it arise? Given the representationalist framework, the solution must be consistent with the Reference Claim and the Uniformity Claim as integral parts of the representationalist framework. The strategy pursued in general roots in the following consideration: Moore-paradoxical sentences are similar to contradictions. However, they consist of two individually meaningful, but logically incommensurable sentences. Making them commensurable thus requires introducing a further proposition, which is tacitly conveyed by a Moore-paradoxical assertion and is in some way incompatible with either of the two explicitly stated propositions. The existence of this further proposition is to explain by the concept of assertion or by the concept of belief, because sentences of the Moore-paradoxical kind are absurd only if the word 'to believe' is used *assertively* in the *first-person present indicative*. So both, the logic of assertion and the expression 'I believe' deserve further attention.

1.3 Varieties of Representationalism

1.3.1 The Approach from Commonsense: Moore's Original Approach

Moore's writings include only an unfinished manuscript outlining his thoughts on the paradox.[45] In the first part of the document, Moore frames the paradox comprehensively. In the second one he sketches an explanation why it arises, which, though rudimentary, clearly shares strategy and outcome with the solutions proposed from representationalist positions.

---

45 According to Thomas Baldwin, Moore has discovered the paradox at some point in the 1930s. *Cf.* the editor's note to Moore (1993), p. 212. The manuscript contained in Baldwin's selection must have been written after Moore had presented the paradox in a lecture at the Cambridge Moral Sciences Club in October 1944, because he mentions several comments of Wittgenstein's concerning the paradox, and it was on this occasion that Wittgenstein came across the paradox for the first time.

Moore's characterisation of sentences such as 'It is raining, but I don't believe it is', or, in his original formulation "I don't believe it's raining, but as a matter of fact it is" (1993, p. 207), for the most part coincides with the description I have given when introducing the paradox as a challenge to representationalism. He states that statements of the structure 'p is the case, but I don't believe that p is the case' are absurd, when they are 'uttered assertively'.[46] Moore rules out the possibility that the absurdity originates from the pair of facts a Moore-paradoxical sentence describes, since it is logically and empirically conceivable that the conjoined propositions are true at the same time:

> The words 'I don't believe it's raining' when said by a particular person have a definite meaning in English: we can say that what they mean is something about his state of mind— what they mean can't be true unless his state of mind is one which can be properly described by saying he doesn't believe that; and so with 'as a matter of fact it is raining'. (Moore (1993), p. 209)

Therefore, the meaning of their conjunction "is something which might quite well be true, something which isn't a contradiction" (*ibid.*) and it is paradoxical that asserting a meaningful, possibly true sentence should be absurd.

Moore seeks the source of the absurdity in the pragmatics of assertion: With asserting something, one "implies" (*ibid.*, p. 210) that one believes that what one says is true. However, he does neither characterise the kind of implication, nor the reason why it holds any further than saying that the relation between asserting that p and believing that p usually holds. It is a matter of experience and presents a commonsense requirement on making an assertion (*ibid.*, pp. 210f.). The explanation Moore ends up with in the quoted manuscript can be brought into a nutshell as

---

46 Moore is reluctant to straightforwardly call such statements 'assertions' without giving any reason why (Moore, 1993, p. 207). It might be the following: As I elaborate in the following, representationalist views regard statements of the Moore-paradoxical kind as abridged, or implicit contradictions. Then, however, they present statements that one cannot rationally assert, given the referentialist conception of language I elaborated above. So it seems questionable whether Moore-paradoxical statements are assertable at all despite their being possibly true.—Nonetheless, I consider it innocuous to speak of Moore-paradoxical assertions and of asserting Moore-paradoxical sentences at this place, for several reasons. First, using the notions 'assertion' and 'to assert' in the context of Moore's Paradox has, by now, become an established manner of speaking. None of the other authors I discuss in the following shares Moore's hesitancy. Second, the observation that Moore-paradoxical statements are inassertible despite their being possibly true plays a role in both the representationalist interpretation of and solution to the paradox, and my criticism of them. Third, I do not agree with either the representationalist conception of assertion and its account of the meaning of the verb 'to believe'. I am thus not bound to use either term in a way compatible with the respective representationalist views.

follows: "In saying 'p' one *normally suggests* that one believes that p, or expresses a belief that p." (Williams (1979), p. 142, my italics.)

Moore explains the absurdity of asserting a sentence like 'It is raining, but I don't believe it is' by a pragmatic property of assertions. Asserting a proposition usually carries an implicit assertoric statement about the speaker's beliefs. Accordingly, asserting 'p is the case' is tantamount to asserting 'p is the case and I believe that p is the case', or:

(0) $\vdash p \rightarrow p \wedge B_{\text{impl}}(I, p)$ (Moore's Principle)

From applying this rule to Moore-paradoxical assertions it follows that the speaker of a Moore-paradoxical assertion implicitly contradicts him- or herself. A Moore-paradoxical assertion is a conjunction of the assertion 'p is the case' and the assertion 'I don't believe that p is the case':

(1) $\vdash p \wedge \neg B(I, p)$ (Moore-paradoxical assertion)

According to principle (0), the speaker implicitly asserts the sentence 'I believe that p is the case' by asserting the first conjunct, 'p is the case'. This however contradicts the second, explicitly stated assertion in a Moore-paradoxical sentence, 'I don't believe that p is the case' (the contradiction is underlined):

(2) $\vdash p \wedge \underline{\neg B(I, p)} \wedge \underline{B_{\text{impl}}(I, p)} \wedge B_{\text{impl}}(I, \neg B(I, p))$ $(0, 1)$.

That is, when I assert a Moore-paradoxical sentence,

> [T]here is a contradiction between what I implied and something that I said, though not between the two things I said. And I suggest that this is why it is absurd for me to say it, even though there's no contradiction between the two things I said. But now the question may be raised: What's meant by saying that I imply it? The only answer I can see to this is that is is something which follows from the following empirical fact: *viz.* that in the immense majority of cases in which a person says a thing assertively, he does *believe* the proposition which his words express. (Moore (1993), p. 210)

Soon after this passage, the manuscript breaks off. The general idea however has become clear: Moore-paradoxical sentences are absurd because they involve a contradiction between what is said, *that the speaker does not believe that p*, and what is thereby implied, *that the speaker believes that p*. In other respects, Moore's explanation remains unsatisfactory, and incomplete, particularly as regards the nature of the implication in question. Here, further considerations on the pragmatics of assertion would have been desirable to illuminate Moore's solution. Notwithstanding, his proposal to regard the absurdity in question as an implicit contradiction deriving from the pragmatics of assertion, expressed in 'Moore's Principle', is constitutive for representationalist approaches to Paradox in general.

1.3.2 The Approach from Speech Acts: Searle's Account of Intentionality

An early account of how it comes about that asserting that p implies that the speaker holds the belief that p is provided by John Searle's analysis of the structure of illocutionary acts.[47] Although Searle mentions Moore's Paradox only in a footnote (1969, p. 65 n. 1), the solution he offers deserves attention for various reasons. On the one hand, Searle locates the origin of Moore's Paradox in the 'logic of assertion', that is, in the conditions that make an utterance 'p is the case' a meaningful and sincere assertion of the proposition *that p is the case*. He thereby captures and elaborates Moore's original approach to the paradox: Because asserting that p is an expression of the speaker's belief that p, asserting a Moore-paradoxical sentence amounts to implicitly asserting that one does and does not believe that p is the case. On the other hand, Searle's treatment of Moore's Paradox relies on a conceptual interdependency of the notions belief, assertion, and truth that emerges from Searle's overall approach to speech acts in terms of intentionality. He thus provides a more steadfast analysis of the relation between asserting that p and believing that p than Moore, who handles it rather loosely. Moreover, the correspondence of assertion and belief is complemented by analogous relations pairing any one of the remaining kinds of speech acts with a respective kind of intentional states. This generalisation enables Searle to find equivalent phenomena to Moore's Paradox for the categories of speech acts other than assertion. As these points suggest, Searle's solution to Moore's Paradox stands in the context of his overall analysis of speech acts in terms of intentional states, which he elaborates in detail in his *Intentionality* (sc. Searle (1983)). It is therefore not only an option, but a need to contextualise it accordingly in order to properly understand Searle's conception of the relation between mind and language and its impact on Moore's Paradox. Eventually, Searle renders a profound theory of mind and language to the effect that his work can, up to a particular point, justifiably be regarded as a pioneering representationalist position *par excellence*, manifest in his understanding of language as well as of the relation between mind and world.

Language in its capacity as an institution as well as in its role as a medium of conveying meaning is, on Searle's view, derived from more primitive non-linguistic forms of representation. Philosophy of language is, for Searle, a branch of philosophy of mind. That Searle begins his philosophical investigations by analysing speech acts, serves 'pedagogic' (Searle) purposes only, because it is this kind of representation that he takes to be most familiar and least controversial. This strat-

---

47 John Searle (1969), *Speech Acts. An Essay in the Philosophy of Language*, Cambridge: UP.

egy does not make Searle a pragmatist, or a conventionalist about language;[48] and understanding him as such yields but a contorted and abridged picture of his elaborate philosophy. Quite to the contrary, the primacy of thought over language is and has ever been a core conviction of Searle's; it being evident that "[l]anguage is derived from Intentionality, not conversely" (Searle (1983), p. 5).

1.3.2.1 Assertion and Belief

Moore's own suggestion as to why assertions of the type '*p* is the case, but I don't believe that *p* is the case' are paradoxical is based on what I have called Moore's Principle (0). Moore's Principle reads that who asserts *that p is the case* also holds the belief *that p is the case*. On Moore's approach, the implicature the principle articulates has the status of an empirical generalization derived from an observation about everyday communication, that *typically* or *normally* a speaker who asserts *that p is the case* believes, or is expected to believe, *that p is the case*. A Moore-paradoxical assertion implies that the speaker holds contradicting or inconsistent beliefs. This conclusion is widely regarded to exhaust the absurdity of stating a Moore-paradoxical sentence in an assertoric mode.[49]

Searle, too, endorses Moore's Principle, that asserting *that p is the case* implies that the speaker also believes *that p is the case*. Searle's account as to why this principle holds however differs from the one Moore outlines. As already mentioned, Moore explains the implicature in question as an empirical generalization, based on an observation about everyday conversation. Here, the principle is tailor-made to answer Moore's Paradox, without fulfilling any further explanatory purposes, and appears as a product of somewhat off-hand heuristics. In contrast, Searle approaches the relation between belief and assertion systematically within his analysis of the illocutionary force of speech acts in general, where it exemplifies the relation between the different kinds of speech acts and the corresponding mental states.

Searle distinguishes five categories of speech acts, assertives, expressives, commissives (such as promises), directives (such as orders), and declaratives. Searle regards the five categories of speech acts exhaustive and mutually irreducible; and explains this matter of fact as deriving from the way in which the properties of

---

48 Moran (1997), for instance, criticises Searle's solution to Moore's Paradox for being conventionalist and finds it, for this reason, arbitrary and dissatisfying his desire for a metaphysically more steadfast solution.

49 *Cf.* for example Moore (1993), pp. 209f.; Williams (1979), p. 142; Mitchell Green, John N. Williams (2007), "Introduction", in Mitchell Green, John N. Williams (eds.), *Moore's Paradox. New Essays on Belief, Rationality, and the First Person*, Oxford: Clarendon Press, pp. 9f.

speech acts depend on intentionality. What makes a particular statement belong to one of these categories is its illocutionary force, the kind of thing one does by performing the speech act. Stating that something is the case belongs to the assertive class, apologising to the expressive one; promises and orders to do something are commissives and directives, respectively; and contracting marriages or declaring war are examples for the declarative class. Among the criteria determining into which of these categories a particular statement falls, there is one of particular importance in the present context, which is the *sincerity condition*. The sincerity condition requires the speaker of a particular speech act to have an intentional state of the corresponding kind[50] in order to succeed in performing a speech act. For this reason, the performance of a speech act necessarily is an expression of the psychological state specified in the speech act's sincerity condition, that is, the psychological state whose existence is a necessary condition for the speech act to be sincere.[51]

The sincerity condition of asserting that p is that the speaker believes that p, that is, an assertion is sincere only if the speaker believes what he or she asserts. Accordingly, a sincere assertion that p counts as an expression of a belief with the same content, more precisely, it entails that the speaker holds the belief *that p is the case*. On Searle's account, Moore's Principle directly results from the sincerity condition of assertion and presents an instance of the more general principle that a sincere speech act entails that the speaker has, at the moment of performing the speech act, a particular mental state. Applied to Moore's Paradox, Searle's account yields the following explanation: Sincerely asserting a sentence of the Moore-paradoxical type ($p \wedge \neg B(I, p)$) simultaneously expresses the speaker's belief that p is the case and that he or she doesn't believe that p is the case. By asserting the second conjunct ($\neg B(I, p)$) the speaker denies that the first conjunct's (p) sincerity condition, namely $B(I, p)$ is met. Hence, a sincere assertion of a Moore-

---

50 I will say more about the correspondence of intentional states and speech acts in the next section.

51 *Cf.* Searle (1969), pp. 64ff., (1983), pp. 9f. and ch. 6. Of course, Searle takes into account that the sincerity condition is not always met, e.g. when people lie or promise what they do not intend to do. His response is to modify the sincerity condition to the effect that it requires the speaker not to actually have a particular psychological state, but to acknowledge his or her responsibility for having it (*ibid.*, p. 62). The case of insincere speech acts has impact on Moore's Paradox only insofar as one can add another aspect to it, that, according to Searle, *insincerely* stating 'p is the case, but I don't believe it' lacks the absurdity a *sincere* assertion of a sentence with that structure would bear. I will not further discuss whether insincerely stating a Moore-paradoxical sentence in an assertive tone of voice is absurd, for it is questionable whether insincere statements present assertions at all. Instead, I will continue to use the term 'assertion' without adding 'sincere' at every instance.

paradoxical sentence implicitly denies that the very same utterance is a sincere assertion, and therefore is absurd. The result just is a remake of the solution Moore originally came up with:

$(0')$ $\vdash p \rightarrow \vdash p \wedge B_{impl}(I, p)$ (sincerity condition of assertions),

(1) $\vdash p \wedge \neg B(I, p)$ (Moore-paradoxical assertion),

(2) $\vdash p \wedge \underline{\neg B(I, p)} \wedge \underline{B_{impl}(I, p)} \wedge B_{impl}(I, \neg B(I, p))$ $(0, 1)$.

The difference is that the implicature involved in Moore's Principle has, on Searle's account, the status of a constitutive rule of assertions. Its generalised form holds with necessity for any sincere speech act, and is grounded in there being an internal relation between each category of speech acts and the corresponding kinds of mental states. This analysis enables Searle to generalise Moore's Paradox and to frame similar paradoxes for the other categories of speech acts.[52] Assertions *that p is the case* are sincere if the speaker believes *that p is the case*. Promises to carry out an action *A* are sincere if the speaker intends to do *A* because of his promising to do *A*. The sincerity condition of an order to perform an action *A* is the speaker's desire that the person to whom the order is directed does *A* because of the order. Expressions are sincere if the speaker holds the mental state he or she expresses, and declarations *that p is the case* are so if the speaker holds both, a desire and a belief *that p is the case*.

In the next section, I show how Searle conceives of the relation between intentional states and speech acts. I focus on the necessity of the implicature involved in Moore's Principle, and the necessity of the existence of five and only five categories of speech acts. This requires the explanation of two central technical terms in Searle's theory, the notion *direction of fit*, and the term *conditions of satisfaction*.

1.3.2.2 Belief and Assertion

As a preliminary formulation, Searle defines intentionality as "that property of many mental states by which they are directed at or about or of objects and states

---

[52] *Cf.* Searle (1969), p. 62; and (1983), p. 9. Exceptions are cases, in which the speaker distances him- or herself from the speech act just performed, for instance if an official in a railway station announces 'The train to Oxford will be on time, but personally, I don't believe it.' *Cf.* Searle (1983), p. 9n. 3, the example is Wittgenstein's in *RPP* I § 486. In this and similar situations, there are, so to speak, two persons speaking; the first conjunct of the utterance is asserted *ex officio*, on behalf of the railway company, whereas the second conjunct expresses the officer's personal belief. Such cases still sound odd, but they are not absurd in the way an actual Moore-paradoxical sentence would be.

of affairs in the world" (1983, p. 1). In the following, he clarifies the notion of intentionality in relation to a group of other notions associated with the mental—representation, consciousness, and intention—on the one hand, and in connection with linguistic notions—language and propositionality—on the other hand. The following picture emerges: Not all mental states are intentional states. There are particularly two dimensions of the mind that are not constituted by intentional states, the part that consists in the class of undirected, occurrent mental states, such as moods and some emotions, and the part of the mind constituting the 'Background' of any kind of mental activity that consists in a collection of (amongst other things) dispositions, skills, capacities, or fundamental beliefs about the world. Something similar holds for the relation between intentionality and consciousness: Not all conscious states are intentional—experiencing a state of anxiety or being in a state of panic without being afraid of something in particular, might be suitable examples. Conversely, not all of a person's intentional states are conscious, have ever been conscious, or will be conscious during the person's life. Full-fledged intentional states, such as the beliefs that the earth is round, that the ground is solid, or that cats don't grow on trees, the desire to live in a small village in a mountain area and so on, need never become consciously formulated or reflected on. Yet, such states can be efficacious in influencing their bearer's actions, his or her overall way of life and view of the world. According to Searle, such states, too, reside and work in the person's Background. Finally, intentionality encompasses more mental states than the class of states of intending, i.e. intentions, to φ. Although the notions 'intending' and 'intentionality' have the same etymology, 'intending' just means 'having an intention', whereas 'intentionality' covers the directedness of mental states in general without involving more than a terminological family resemblance to intentions. With this clarification, Searle distances himself from an agency-related conception of intentionality that grasps intentional states in terms of mental acts. Although states like hoping, believing, desiring or intending are devices by which intentional subjects relate to their objects, some aspect of the world or another, intentional states do not do so as outcomes of their subject's will, they do not involve intentions and so are not mental acts performed by their subjects. As Searle later clarifies, the class of intentions and the other classes of mental states differ with respect to their *direction of fit*, roughly the direction their intentionality takes, and their *conditions of satisfaction*, roughly the conditions specifying the circumstances under which an intentional state is 'successful'. I will come back to these notions in a moment.

Having thus distinguished intentional states from mental states, conscious states and states of intending, Searle spells out his account of intentionality by means of connecting it with his account of speech acts and language. According to Searle, the relation between intentionality and language, or speech acts respectively, is a relation of analogy in some respects, and of dependency in others. First of all, Searle characterises the function of intentional states as representation of mind-independent objects, "in the same sense of 'represent' that speech acts represent objects and states of affairs" (1983, p. 4). In brief: All intentional states are representational states, whereby 'representing' is not an activity carried out at will, and tokens of representational content are no 'pictures' in the subject's head. Paralleling intentional states and speech acts primarily concerns their overall structure: Such as speech acts consist of illocutionary force and propositional content, so are intentional states analysable into psychological mode and representational content. Notably, as mentioned in the last section, this analogy does not imply that the content of intentional states is necessarily linguistic, or even propositional. The latter applies only to propositional attitudes, such intentional states that have whole states of affairs as their objects, i.e. states whose content is expressed by a that-clause, e.g. the belief *that it is raining*.

Apart from this structural analogy, speech acts and intentional states exercise the function of representing reality in the same way. Searle characterises mode and content of representational states in terms of 'direction of fit' and 'conditions of satisfaction', respectively. Together, the two properties provide the criteria, by which speech acts and intentional states are classified, and constitute the aforementioned correspondence of each category of speech acts with an analogous class of intentional states. On the one hand, every speech act and every intentional state bears a particular *direction of fit* determining whether the representational content or the representational object of a representational state counts as the measure for the state to be satisfied. Assertive speech acts are intended to represent an independently existing world as it is. Their veridicality depends on whether their content matches its object, the world 'as it is' presents the yardstick of their truth. Assertive speech acts have the "word-to-world" direction of fit (Searle (1983), p. 7). It is, so to speak, the speech act's responsibility that its content complies with reality. In contrast, directive and commissive speech acts bear the world-to-word direction of fit: They represent how the world ought to be, and are supposed to bring about changes in the world, so as to bring it into line with their propositional contents. A directive or commissive speech act's success depends on whether or not it causes the relevant changes in the world; if it fails, it is the world's failure to comply, as it were, not the speech act's.[53] The fourth class of speech acts, expressives, has no direction of fit. The performance of an expressive speech act, an apology, for

---

53 The difference between commissives and directives consists in the subject specified in their respective propositional contents, i.e. who is supposed to carry out the action which would cause the world to comply with the speech act's content. In the case of commissives, such as promises, the speaker commits him- or herself to perform a particular action, and it is his or her responsibility

instance, itself suffices for the respective speech act to have succeeded in what it is supposed to do, namely to express the state of affairs it expresses, for instance the speaker's feeling sorry for having wronged someone else. Finally, declarative speech acts bear both directions of fit: They bring about a change in the world merely by representing it to be the case. The successful performance of declaratives has a special prerequisite, which distinguishes this category of speech acts from the four other classes. Declaratives presuppose the existence of an *institution* in virtue of which their speaker is endowed with the power to bring about the fact specified in a particular declarative's propositional content (Searle (1983), pp. 171f.). For example, the declaration *that the meeting is adjourned* makes it the case *that the meeting is adjourned* if the institution of adjourning the meeting in question exists, and if the speaker is institutionally endowed with the powers to adjourn the meeting. Prime Minister Chamberlain could only make Britain be at war with Germany by declaring war on Germany because it was a common institution among Britain and Germany that declaring war counted as the beginning of war and because Chamberlain was, *ex officio*, entitled to do so. Crucially, the scope of facts that can be brought about by declarations is restricted to institutional facts—it is, as Searle says, impossible for human beings to fry eggs just by declaring them to be fried.

Analogously, Searle classifies intentional states by their direction of fit. Beliefs are assessed in terms of truth or falsity, depending on whether their content matches the facts it is supposed to represent. Thus, they share in the direction of fit of the assertive class of speech acts, which Searle calls 'mind-to-world' in case of intentional states. Desires and intentions have a world-to-mind direction of fit, in that they are successful if they cause changes in the world such that they bring about the facts represented in their contents. With respect to their direction of fit, desires and intentions thus correspond with orders and directives. Finally, some intentional states, e.g. emotions such as remorse or pleasure *that p is the case*, are regarded neutral with respect to their direction of fit. Their content is not assessed in terms of veridicality.

On Searle's account, the notion 'direction of fit' fulfils a double function. Within each kind of representation, speech acts and intentional states respectively, it serves to categorise their members. In addition, it provides the link between speech acts and intentional states by establishing a correspondence of each class of speech acts with the class of mental states bearing the same direction of fit. As

---

to fulfil the proposition specified in the speech act. In the case of orders, the responsibility to bring about the state of affairs that complies with the speech act's content is imposed on another agent. *Cf.* Searle (1983), pp. 7f.

mentioned in the last section, Searle exploits this correspondence by specifying the sincerity condition of speech acts as a requirement for a speech act to be sincere, namely that the speaker holds a corresponding intentional state. The kind of correspondence in question is the agreement of speech act and intentional state in their direction of fit. For this reason, every speech act necessarily expresses an intentional state with the same direction of fit, the assertion *that p is the case* expresses the belief *that p is the case*, the promise to φ expresses the speaker's intention to φ, the order *that A be done* expresses the desire *that A be done*. Declarations, having a double direction of fit, express an intentional state with the world-to-mind direction of fit (the intention or desire to bring about *that p is the case*) and a second one with the mind-to-world direction of fit (the belief *that henceforth p is the case*). It is not necessary, though, that a speaker really has the intentional state expressed in a particular speech act; performing the speech act only commits him or her to having the corresponding intentional state. The sincerity condition is a normative requirement, which the speaker can fail to meet, deliberately (as in telling a lie) or unwittingly (as in promising something he or she cannot fulfil).

Central to Searle's account of intentionality is the term 'conditions of satisfaction', which is Searle's expression for 'veridicality conditions' (see Section 2.1.2 of this chapter). Intentional states having a direction of fit are content-bearing states. Their content specifies the conditions under which they are satisfied, or veridical. Beliefs are satisfied if they are true, and fail if they are false. A single belief *that p is the case* is satisfied if and only if it is true *that p is the case*. Similarly, intentions are satisfied if and only if the action they represent is carried out, and desires are satisfied if and only if they are fulfilled. Every mental state that has conditions of satisfaction is in the same sense of 'representing' a representational (or intentional) state. It is successful if and only if its representational content and the object the state is supposed to represent, match. In other words, on Searle's account, a mental state is an intentional state if its content represents its conditions of satisfaction. Thus, Searle's understanding of the term 'representation' is intended to be a functional, not an ontological one in that it serves to characterise what intentional states do, not what they are. The direction of fit and the conditions of satisfaction together individuate an intentional state in that the condition of satisfaction describes the state of affairs, which the state's representational content is supposed to match, under certain aspects and the direction of fit indicates whether the matching of content and world is supposed to already obtain, or whether it is supposed to yet be brought about. Except from bundling these properties of intentional states and speech acts and put them in a terminological nutshell, Searle does not concede any further meaning to the notions 'representation' and 'representing':

To say that a belief [or other intentional state] is a representation is simply to say that it has a propositional content and a psychological mode, that its propositional content determines a set of conditions of satisfaction under certain aspects, that its psychological mode determines a direction of fit of its propositional content, in a way that all of these notions—propositional content, direction of fit, etc.—are explained by the theory of speech acts. Indeed, as far as anything I have so far said is concerned, we could in principle dispense with the terms 'representation' and 'represent' altogether in favor of these other notions, since there is nothing ontological about my use of 'representation'. It is just shorthand for this constellation of logical notions borrowed from the theory of speech acts.[54]

Searle introduces the notion of representation as it applies to intentional states in analogy with the way speech acts represent reality, more precisely, of an independently existing world (for the objects represented need not really exist). The analogy consists in an interdependency of the notions 'representation' and 'conditions of satisfaction': Speech acts, insofar as they have a direction of fit, equally have conditions of satisfaction, which are identical with those of the corresponding intentional state specified in the sincerity condition. That is, a speech act will be

---

54 Searle (1983), p. 12. My insertion 'or other intentional state' needs a minor clarification: First, to repeat, Searle holds that not all representational content is propositional. So as regards non-propositional intentional states the word 'propositional' in the quotation ought to be read 'representational'. Second, strictly speaking, Searle holds that only propositional states with a direction of fit have conditions of satisfaction. However, it seems to me that the qualification as a representational state with a direction of fit (world-to-mind, mind-to-world or neutral) suffices for the state to have conditions of satisfaction for two reasons. On the one hand, it seems intuitively plausible that some intentional states, paradigmatically desires, can have both, a non-propositional content and conditions under which they are satisfied (the desire for a glass of water, for instance). One might say, of course, that in such cases the content of the desire is incompletely rendered and should rather read 'the desire that one has a glass of water'. But then it seems as if all representational content were, in fact, propositional; and that expressing it differently would always amount to an ellipsis of the content, as the exclamation 'Drink!' would be of 'I would like a drink, please bring me one, now'.
On the other hand, insofar as we are concerned with representational states, the notion of representational content is inevitable. The notion of content, however, implies there being a comparability between the representational content of a representational state and the object represented, which itself involves the possibility of assessing the relation between content and object in terms of accuracy, the possibility of being accurate involving more specific dimensions of assessing the contents of intentional states, be it truth/falsity, success/failure, satisfaction/dissatisfaction, or appropriateness/inappropriateness. For this reason, and especially taking into account the claim that representations always represent their objects in a certain way or under certain aspects (Searle (1983), p. 13), it seems inappropriate to restrict the scope of applying the notion 'conditions of satisfaction' to intentional states with *propositional* content only. For the interrelation of the notions 'content' and 'accuracy conditions', *cf.* Siegel (2010), Chapter 2, particularly pp. 30–42, and the introduction to this chapter.

satisfied if and only if the intentional state it expresses is satisfied. On Searle's view, this identity relation holds necessarily and for the reason that speech acts inherit their conditions of satisfaction from the intentional state they express. Making a speech act involves a "double level of Intentionality" (Searle (1983), p. 163), consisting in the intentional state specified in the sincerity condition and another intentional state, which Searle refers to as the 'meaning intention', i.e. the intention to represent a particular state of affairs by means of a linguistic utterance (and potentially to communicate this representation to another one). The assertion *that p is the case*, for instance, implies the belief *that p is the case* as its sincerity condition and entails the intention to assert *that p is the case*, i.e. to perform a speech act of a particular kind with a particular content by means of uttering the sentence '*p* is the case', as its meaning intention.[55] As a consequence of separating sincerity condition and meaning intention, it follows that a speech act's conditions of satisfaction differ from the speech act's conditions of success whereas this is not the case for intentional states. A speech act can be satisfied, but insincere, for instance, an assertion, which is true, but intended to be a lie. Conversely, a speech act can be successfully performed, but remain unsatisfied, for instance a promise, which is sincerely given, but never carried out.

Thus, speech acts are error-prone in two ways: They can be insincere if their sincerity condition is not met. They can fail to represent anything if either their condition of satisfaction is not met, or if the utterance is not a suitable means to express content, for example, if it does not comply with the syntactical or semantic rues of the language in which the speaker intends to express him- or herself. This results from the conception of language as a sign-system whose function is supposed to consist in referring to objects by means of expressing veridicality conditions, which is constitutive of the representationalist view in general (see Section 2.1.4), to which Searle in particular adheres. Intentional states by contrast can only fail to properly exercise their representational function. States, which have the mind-to-world direction of fit, fail by being non-veridical, states with the world-to-mind direction of fit, are unsatisfied if they fail to cause the world to change such as to fulfil the respective condition of satisfaction. Whereas, on Searle's account, speech acts constitute a complex kind of representation, which is analysable into several intentional states of an individual person, an individual's intentionality is not further analysable into more basic states of an organism.

Two points concerning the relation between meaning and meaningful language should not go without mention. Only the sincerity condition can be directly

---

55 For more detail on how to spell out the meaning intention of a given statement, *cf.* Searle (1983), ch. 6.

inferred from a particular statement, it is the corresponding intentional state with identical content. But the speech act itself neither supports unambiguous conclusions about the meaning intention, nor does it provide a clue as to whether the sincerity condition is fulfilled. By uttering a statement a speaker only signals that he or she is taking responsibility for having a particular intentional state, which would fulfil the sincerity condition. The speaker's 'real' meaning intentions might yet remain covert or camouflaged.

Moreover, that a particular utterance is meaningful, that is, that it bears conditions of satisfaction, thereby representing a state of affairs and expressing a corresponding intentional state, is not a property of the utterance itself. A speech act differs from a sequence of arbitrary sounds in that the former is uttered with meaning, the latter without.[56] What sounds like an assertion need not be one. For instance, if somebody utters the German sentence 'Es regnet' not with the intention to make a true statement, but to practice its pronunciation, or if someone utters random syllables that turn out to sound like a sentence in a language he or she does not speak. Searle regards the media in which content is expressed—sounds, ink-marks, gestures—as physical entities or complexes of physical entities. For this reason, they do not signify anything by themselves, they are, so to speak, dead. Yet, they can turn into signs that belong to a language, in which case they bear meaning.

So the question is, how does a sign manage to represent, or how is meaning attached to a sequence of sounds?[57] How does a *prima facie* 'brute' physical process (the generation of sounds) turn into an entity having normative impact (conditions of satisfaction, sincerity condition, conditions of success)? The brief answer is: The speaker's intentionality, more precisely, the speaker's meaning intention to this effect. The not so brief answer is: The speaker imposes the conditions of satisfaction of the intentional state he or she wants to express on the physical events constituting the utterance of the sequence of sounds. In virtue of

---

56 *Cf.* Searle (1983), p. 169, who refers to Wittgenstein remarks on the difference between uttering a sentence with meaning and uttering a sentence without meaning, and the relation of signs and content; *cf.*, for instance, *PI* §§ 501–18. Searle interprets Wittgenstein as objecting to understanding meaning as an introspective process. For Wittgenstein, however, Searle's claim that the presence or absence of a meaning intention or other intentional state could provide for the distinction of meaningful from meaningless sentences, is utterly misguided. It is part of an entire mythology of language, which reduces language to a means of conveying content about the world and accordingly deems language 'dead sounds' if it ostensibly fails to exercise this function. It is Wittgenstein's main purpose in his later years to identify, articulate and undermine this view. I will come back to this point in the following chapters.

57 A similar question is raised by Wittgenstein's interlocutor in *PI* §§ 431–5. I will discuss this point at more length in Chapter 3.

being caused by the meaning intention, the utterance henceforth constitutes the corresponding speech act with a particular illocutionary force and a particular representational content. This formulation indicates that making a meaningful speech act presupposes three things. Searle explicitly spells out only two of them in terms of the speaker's intentionality, first, the intentional state expressed in the speech act as its sincerity condition and second, the meaning intention that turns a particular utterance of sounds into a meaningful speech act. Implicitly, however, this formulation suggests that a speech act simultaneously is always also a tacit declaration of the very speech act the speaker wishes it to be: By means of intending the utterance in question to be a meaningful utterance, the utterance turns into the speech act it is supposed to be. For this reason, making meaningful utterances additionally presupposes there being an institution enabling the speaker to make utterances, which exists independently of the very act itself. This institution evidently is language itself. Spelling out Searle's account in this way, the meaning of a particular sentence does not only depend on what the speaker intends it to mean, but also on those constitutive rules by which a particular utterance, such as the expression 'It is raining' in an assertive tone of voice, counts as a speech act of a certain kind with a certain content, the assertion *that it is raining*, for instance. The range of possible speech acts thus is not only confined by the speaker's intentional states, but also by the rules constituting the logical, semantic and illocutionary properties of particular expressions in a certain linguistic context (for example, the English language in general, or a conversation at the baker's in particular). Seen in this light, speech acts appear as social facts, originally physical entities (here: sounds) that have adopted a conventional function (meaning) by a certain group's common acceptance of rules of the kind 'X counts as Y in context C', just as much as they are an individual speaker's representations of states of affairs.[58]

So presented, Searle locates two sources of meaning. On particular occasions, the meaning of sentences depends on the individual speaker's intentionality, on the veridicality conditions imposed on a sequence of sounds and on the direction of fit the utterance receives from expressing a particular kind of mental state. On the other hand, the meaning of particular sentences depends on their being embedded in our linguistic practices. Language is a social institution and as such generated in a social context, by 'collective intentionality'. One might now ask in which order of priority these two sources ought to be considered. Wittgenstein states in similar vein,

---

[58] Searle's account of social facts and their constitution from physical facts is spelled out in Searle (1995), and Searle (2010), *Making the Social World. The Structure of Human Civilization*, Oxford: UP.

[It] is quite possible that a sentence, e.g. 'It is raining', is at one time uttered as an assertion, at another time as a supposition (even if it is not prefixed by 'Suppose')—what renders it the one, what the other?—On the one hand, I want to answer: the game in which it is used. On the other hand: the intention with which it is uttered. How do these two tally with each other?[59]

Because Searle assumes a gap between the meaning of a sentence (its content) and the means of expressing it (the words uttered), Searle decides the question in favour of the speaker's intentionality and does not further pursue the question how language, considered as a practice, is constituted by intersubjective engagement. In recent years, he has even adjusted his earlier view of language as the system of social facts that provides the means for establishing all other practices and institutions. For he notes that, if language itself is an institution, a system of constitutive and regulatory rules, its origin cannot be explained by linguistically formulated constitutive rules on pain of circularity. Searle therefore shifts the emphasis from primarily conceiving language as a practice constituted in social interaction to conceiving it primarily as a means of representing reality that is "an extension and realization of the way the mind represents the world" (Searle (1983), p. 166). Consequently, the representational properties of speech acts, particularly their direction of fit and their conditions of satisfaction, "must derive from some fundamental features of the mind. The Intentionality of the mind not only creates the possibility of meaning, but it limits its forms" (*ibid.*). Thus, although he acknowledges the interplay of social practice and individual intentionality in grounding meaning, the driving force behind a speech act nonetheless remains the speaker's meaning intention. Only in this way it becomes conceivable, in Searle's opinion, how a series of 'physical events' can come to bear the logically interrelated normative elements analysed into sincerity condition, conditions of satisfaction and success, meaning, illocutionary force, representational content. In this manner, Searle eventually grounds the meaning of language in its function to represent and convey information about the world.[60] Its communicative and

---

59 *Manuscript (MS)* 136, 10.1.48, in Ludwig Wittgenstein (1998), *Wittgensteins Nachlass. The Bergen Electronic Edition*, Oxford: UP, available at http://pm.nlx.com/xtf/search?browse-collections=true, last access September 18th, 2012. The translation is Schulte's, in Joachim Schulte (1993), *Experience and Expression. Wittgenstein's Philosophy of Psychology*, Oxford: Clarendon Press, p. 152.
60 Searle actually *has* to make this move, on pain of turning the representationalist order of priority—thought over language—upside down, and thus condition mental states ontologically on language. In this point, his considerations match those of externalist (or anti-individualist) accounts that equally maintain the ontological independence of mental states despite conceding a certain role to language as regards the constitution and individuation of their content. The two kinds of influence language can have in these respects, establishing a representational connection

pragmatic functions and the entanglement of meaning within the contexts of concrete communicative situations, to which he had previously conceded a more prominent position in his earlier writings, now play a logically subordinate role.

Before coming back to Moore's Paradox, I will summarise Searle's account of the relation between intentionality and language. Intentional states and speech acts have the same primary function, which consists in veridically representing parts of reality under a certain aspect or causing reality to change in a way that generates their veridicality. Searle does not commit himself to a specific view of the structure of representational content and he considers demands for developing a more substantial ontology of representations than his conception in terms of conditions of satisfaction pointless. This strengthens his account and makes it a classic example of representationalism: Most evidently, Searle transfers the *two-component model* he had originally developed for speech acts to intentional states, analysing them into a psychological mode, characterised by a specific direction of fit, and a representational content, specifying the conditions under which an intentional state is veridical.

The content of an intentional state consists in a *representation* of a particular object or state of affairs that exists independently of its being represented. Intentional states are assessed by comparing their representational contents with their objects, primarily with respect to their truth/falsity, correctness/incorrectness or accuracy/inaccuracy. If the content accurately represents its object, they are successful or satisfied. So Searle holds a version of what I have called earlier the *Reference Claim*: The content of intentional states has the function of referring to corresponding aspects of an independently existing world. Sentences and other linguistic expressions are special referential devices, their meaning is constituted by referring to objects or states of affairs by means of expressing representational content. All tokens of a representational content-type have identical conditions of satisfaction, independently of the various modes in which it figures. Therefore, the *Uniformity Claim* is equally met.

Most evidently, Searle claims the priority of the mind over language: Function and purpose of speech acts, their illocutionary and representational properties

---

between words and pre-existing referents as well as determining the extension of otherwise underdetermined concepts, might be grasped (in Searlean terms) as laying down the constitutive rules for the further use of the respective words and concepts. Accordingly, they, too, depend on their being intentionality first, in this case, the collective intentionality of a linguistic community. Subsequent uses of so-established signs and concepts merely recall the rule constituting their meaning such that their reference, once established, remains unchanged by particular applications. See above, Section 2.1.5.

as well as their meaning, derive from intentionality. The capacity of representing reality of individual beings is the primary form of all other intentionality. The priority holds despite being seemingly at odds with the course of Searle's analysis (from speech acts to intentionality), since Searle models intentionality upon language for strategic purposes only, whereas he takes the logical priority to obtain in the reverse direction. Charging him with a conventionalist view of language and with ignorance of the psychological roots of assertion, as Shoemaker and Moran do, misses the point. Searle's considerations, on the contrary, issue in a strong prioritisation of thought over language. For this reason, his solution to Moore's Paradox results from an analysis of the mental conditions for making meaningful utterances, and not from an analysis of conventionalist or communicative issues surrounding language.

1.3.3 The Pragmatic Solution

In the previous sections, I have introduced two approaches to Moore's Paradox, Moore's original one and the one that follows from Searle's account of intentionality and speech acts. Because their respective solutions are based on considerations of the pragmatics of assertion, I will in the following resume them under the term 'pragmatic solution'. The pragmatic solution to Moore's Paradox runs as follows: Moore's Paradox consists in the contrast that Moore-paradoxical assertions are absurd, although their content, Moore-paradoxical sentences, can be true. Moore-paradoxical sentences can be true, because the state of affairs they describe is neither logically nor empirically impossible. For this reason, the absurdity roots in something external to the content of a Moore-paradoxical assertion. It derives from an illocutionary property of assertion. Assertions are characterised by implicating that the speaker also believes to be the case what he or she asserts to be the case. Asserting a Moore-paradoxical sentence, $\vdash p \land \neg B(I, p)$, implies that the speaker holds a content-identical belief, $B(I, (p \land \neg B(I, p)))$. Hence, asserting a Moore-paradoxical sentence is tantamount to asserting a contradiction between what one says *in* the content of one's assertion and what one says *with* the assertion (*cf.* Moore (1993), p. 210).

Given that language is a means to render representational content, the sentences 'I believe that p', and 'I don't believe that p' refer to corresponding facts about the speaker's state of mind, that the speaker does, or does not believe that p. They are true if and only if what they express is the case, namely that the speaker does (not) hold the belief that p. To put it differently, the sentence 'I believe that p is the case' is conceived, as per its grammar, as a self-ascription of the belief *that p is the case*. Asserting a Moore-paradoxical sentence amounts to representing the world as containing three states of affairs at the same time: *that p is the case*, *that the speaker believes that p* (by implication), and *that he or she does not believe that p*. That is, this approach regards Moore's Paradox as prompted by the speaker's conveying contradicting information about his or her current state of mind, or in that he or she implicitly states to believe a contradiction true. This fact is supposed to constitute the absurdity of asserting a Moore-paradoxical sentence, which is probably why Wittgenstein referred to this kind of explanation as drawing on "psychological reasons" (*Briefe* 257).

Moore, maybe not quite unintentionally,[61] but certainly not quite satisfactorily, does not qualify the relation between the assertion that *p* and the speaker's corresponding belief that *p* any further than saying it is an implication one usually draws from someone's asserting that *p*. The incompleteness of Moore's characterisation is accounted for on Searle's analysis of the conditions under which an utterance constitutes a speech act of a specific type (1969, ch. 3). There, he introduces the presence of a belief that *p* as a necessary condition for an utterance that *p* to be a sincere assertion (p. 65). Thus, he establishes the implicature in question as a conceptual relation between assertion and belief, in which the belief has logical priority over the assertion: Beliefs impose their conditions of satisfaction on assertions. Consequently, both are successful if their respective content is a true representation of the facts. This allows Searle to introduce the presence of the speaker's belief *that p is the case*, as the sincerity condition for an assertion *that p is the case*.

Notably, despite the difference regarding the nature of the relation holding between assertions that *p* and beliefs that *p*, Moore's and Searle's explanatory responses to Moore's Paradox share two central claims: On the one hand, their explanation presupposes that the speaker making a sincere assertion *that p is the case* implies that he or she holds a belief with identical content, the belief *that p is the case*. For this reason, both explanations agree in their consequence, that Moore-paradoxical sentences are, though not directly, still by implication, self-contradictory.

In that he concludes that an assertion that *p* therefore *counts as* an expression of belief that *p*, Searle suggests that the location of the source of Moore's Paradox is to be found in the illocutionary specificities of the speech situation. Introducing a 'conventional' element however is at odds with the representationalist's tendency to prioritise thought over language, and indeed as well as being at odds with the general approach Searle outlines: If the belief that *p* is logically prior to the assertion that *p*, and if a sincere assertion that *p* implies the belief that *p* in virtue

---

61 *Cf.* Green and Williams (2007), pp. 4–6.

of sharing its distinctive characteristic, being truth-directed, one would expect that the assertion '*p*, but I don't believe it' is absurd because the sentence '*p*, but I don't believe it' cannot be coherently *believed* at first place. Mental representation however is not an intentionally initiated process. That is, intentional states are simple and do not involve a further level of intentionality. In this respect, they contrast with speech acts, which Searle conceives as complex representational states.

This has the effect that the explanation why Moore-paradoxical assertions are absurd is not available for beliefs with Moore-paradoxical content on an approach focusing solely on the pragmatics of assertion. Does this mean that believing a sentence with Moore-paradoxical structure to be true, is absurd, but for different reasons than asserting the same content? Or does it mean that they are not absurd at all? Either way seems to have problematic consequences. If beliefs with Moore-paradoxical content turn out to be absurd for different reasons than assertions of the Moore-paradoxical type, or not absurd at all, it will be unintelligible why it is a conceptual, rather than a contextual feature of Moore-paradoxical sentences that they are absurd. More importantly, if Moore-paradoxical assertions are absurd for the reason the pragmatic solution suggests, whereas Moore-paradoxical beliefs are not, the claim to the uniformity of the contents of asserting *that p is the case* and believing *that p is the case*, respectively, risks breaking down. The content of the assertion 'It is raining' spelled out properly reads 'It is raining and I believe that it is raining', whereas the content of the belief 'It is raining' would need no further amendment. Thus, the veridicality conditions of an assertion *that p is the case* and a belief *that p is the case* would necessarily differ, and this seems to call into question Searle's claim that the conditions of satisfaction of a speech act are identical with the conditions of satisfaction of the corresponding sincerity condition.

On Searle's behalf, one may reply that the conditions of satisfaction of both, an assertion and its sincerity condition *are* identical; the assertion of a Moore-paradoxical sentence is absurd because the speaker announces that he or she makes an insincere assertion, not because the content expressed by the assertion is self-contradictory. That is, the second conjunct—I don't believe that *p*—and the sincerity condition—the speaker's belief that *p*—constitute a performative, not a formal-logical contradiction. But in this case, it seems to be at best arbitrary that Moore-paradoxical assertions are absurd, at worst, a corruption of everyday talk, as it were. It would remain an open question whether it is absurd to *believe* a proposition such as 'It is raining, but I don't believe it' and also to assert it in soliloquy. If the answer is no, there will be reason for doubting that assertions express beliefs with identical content. If an assertion of a Moore-paradoxical sentence is absurd, why not the belief it expresses? But if the answer is yes, which seems the correct answer on Searle's account—after all, he fundamentally holds that beliefs and assertions are two kinds of rendering representational content that differ only with respect to the device conveying the propositional content in question—the reason why believing a Moore-paradoxical sentence or saying it to oneself will remain obscure.

1.3.4 Interiors of the Mind—Must we Know our Minds for Having them?

This line of criticism is pursued by Sydney Shoemaker[62] and Richard Moran[63] against approaches to Moore's Paradox from the pragmatic or conventional properties of assertion. Both authors agree on the validity of Moore's Principle (0), i.e. that one believes what one asserts, and that an assertion that p therefore implies that the speaker holds the corresponding belief that p. They also agree that Moore's Principle holds because asserting that p is derivative from believing that p. They object, however, to restricting the investigation of Moore's Paradox to the case of overt assertions of Moore-paradoxical sentences because this supposedly leads to spelling out the absurdity of a sentence like 'It is raining but I don't believe it' in terms of eventually arbitrary practices regulating the illocutionary conditions of speech acts. They equally rule out the possibility that Moore's Paradox might arise from circumstances residing in the situational context in which a Moore-paradoxical sentence is asserted. Conditioning the generation of Moore's Paradox on the contingencies of social practices or situational circumstances however is deemed just as unsatisfactory as Moore's shoulder-shrugging appeal to an observation about everyday talk. For it seems that referring to conventions concerning everyday communication, even when backed by an account from speech act theory, is too weak to ground the conceptual rules violated by Moore-paradoxical sentences. The pragmatic solution is thus suspected of lapsing into a communitarian[64] or a stipulativist view[65] about the grammatical norms of language.

---

62 Sydney Shoemaker (1995), "Moore's Paradox and Self-Knowledge", in Sydney Shoemaker (1996), *The First-Person Perspective and Other Essays*, Cambridge: UP, pp. 74–93. Shoemaker particularly objects to approaching Moore's Paradox from Gricean meaning intentions, but his criticism equally applies to the solution presented by Searle and Moore.
63 Moran argues in particular against Searle and Crispin Wright. *Cf.* Moran (1997), which is turned into Chapter 3 of Moran (2001), *Authority and Estrangement. An Essay on Self-Knowledge*, Cambridge (MA): Harvard UP.
64 A prominent example is Saul Kripke, whose 'community view' follows from his treatment of Wittgenstein's considerations on rule-following. Familiarly, Kripke concludes from that nothing justifies the use of a linguistic expression on a particular occasion that there are no rules governing the use of language. Whether or not one uses an expression in the same sense as it was used before,

According to Shoemaker's and Moran's criticism, the pragmatic solution to Moore's Paradox takes too little notice of two further issues. The absurdity of Moore-paradoxical assertions equally affects beliefs with Moore-paradoxical content. As Moran observes, "Were someone to think to himself, as he looks out of the window, that it's raining outside and conjoin this with the thought that he doesn't believe that it's raining, his [complete] thought would risk incoherence in just the same way as it would if he were to assert the whole thought to someone else" (1997, p. 144). For this reason, there must be, secondly, something wrong about the state of affairs expressed in the content of a Moore-paradoxical assertion or belief. So believing something to be true must entail believing another proposition to be true such that, if a Moore-paradoxical sentence is believed, the content of this belief represents an internally incoherent state of affairs.

Even without further delving into the depths of speech act theory, it requires only a small step to recognise the common function of the assertion that p and the belief that p, both express the point that the respective subject considers p a true proposition. If there is any connection at all between the two, it consists in that asserting that p is the case inherits its illocutionary properties from believing *that p is the case* in virtue of being the linguistic articulation of the subject's belief *that p is the case*. If, as Moore's Principle suggests, asserting *that p is the case* expresses the speaker's belief *that p is the case*, the obvious conclusion is that it does so because the belief *that p is the case* similarly entails the subject's belief *that he or she believes that p is the case*. This consideration is expressed in Shoemaker's claim that beliefs are constitutively 'self-intimating', i.e. that it lies in the nature of the phenomenon of belief that a belief that p is the case $(B(S, p))$ generates the

---

is a fully empirical question. All one can do is hoping to use an expression meaningfully, and this works only as long as everyone agrees on using it in a particular way. *Cf.* Saul Kripke (1982), *Wittgenstein on Rules and Private Language*, Cambridge (MA): Harvard UP. Applied to Moore's Paradox, a communitarian view could either be concerned with Moore's Principle, or with the absurdity itself. It might read 'asserting that p implies the speaker believes that p because this is what we all think, or 'a Moore-paradoxical sentence is absurd because it has always been', or something similar.

65 This view would condition the absurdity of a Moore-paradoxical sentence on someone judging that it is. Asserting 'It is raining, but I don't believe it' is absurd if the speaker or hearer judges that the assertion is absurd, or if the assertion is or has been ruled out from meaningful language by a collective judgement within the speaker's community. With respect to the meaning of linguistic expressions, in particular to the truth-conditions of ascriptions of psychological states, this view is held by Crispin Wright. See Wright (1986), "On Making up One's Mind: Wittgenstein on Intention" in: Paul Weingartner, Gerhard Schürz, *Logic, Philosophy of Science and Epistemology. Proceedings of the 11th International Wittgenstein Symposium*, pp. 391–404, and Wright (2007), "Rule-following without Reason: Wittgenstein's Quietism and the Constitutive Question', *Ratio* 20/4, pp. 481–502. Kripke's and Wright's respective accounts will be examined in Chapter 3.

belief *that one believes that p is the case* $(B(S, B(S, p)))$. Moore's Principle, that asserting *that p is the case* implies that the speaker believes *that p is the case*, accordingly is supposed to derive from this property of belief.

Therefore, Shoemaker and Moran conclude that the origin of Moore's Paradox must reside in the metaphysics of the mind, particularly, the functional and epistemological features of belief, and that the absurdity of a Moore-paradoxical sentence must derive from the state of affairs which is expressed by the content of a Moore-paradoxical belief. This strategy is implemented in their respective work in different manners. Their accounts diverge, on the one hand, with respect to the conception of belief, and, on the other hand, with respect to the way in which they describe the situation ostensibly represented by a Moore-paradoxical belief.

1.3.5 The Approach from Metaphysics: Shoemaker's Higher-Order Belief Model

1.3.5.1 Functionalism about the Mind

Sydney Shoemaker is one of the earliest and most prominent advocates of functionalism, the view that the nature of mental states is determined by the causal roles they play within the economy of the mind and its interplay with bodily behaviour. Functionalism proceeds from an observational perspective on the mind and aims at rendering an explanatory model of the nature and function of mental states that is at least compatible with the scientific view of the world. Obviously, this approach presupposes that the mind actually is a phenomenon that can be successfully studied in this manner, that is, that the mind presents an object that seamlessly fits into the principles, methods and findings of natural science. Thus, it is assumed that the metaphysical and epistemic properties of the mind suit the investigative methods of an empirical science, psychology or cognitive science, for instance. According to Shoemaker, mental states are

> [C]haracterized and identified, not in explicitly mental terms, but in terms of their causal and other 'topic neutral' relations to one another and to physical inputs and outputs.[66]

Particular mental states accordingly are identifiable by indicating the location they occupy in relation to the rest of their bearer's psychophysical economy, in particular, by specifying their causal antecedents and the course of behaviour they dispose their bearer to further pursue. Peter's belief 'It will be raining soon' for instance appears, on functionalism, as the outcome of a conjunction of other

---

66 Sydney Shoemaker (1975), "Functionalism and Qualia", *Philosophical Studies: An International Journal for Philosophy in the Analytic Tradition 27/5*, pp. 291–315, here p. 307.

content-bearing states, perceptual input (the way the sky looks), or other beliefs (that rain was forecasted, that the weather-forecast is generally reliable). Together with the desire to stay dry, it 'poises' (Shoemaker) Peter to carry his umbrella when leaving the house, or to get the laundry inside, or to refrain from watering the plants, depending on what other mental states Peter currently entertains, or what courses of action Peter is currently engaged in. More generally, the functionalist conceives of the notion belief as denoting a uniform psychological phenomenon characterised by its causal role in an individual's economy of mental states. A belief *that p is the case* is the state that disposes the believer, given related desires and other beliefs, to act or behave in ways compatible with '*p* is the case' being a true description of facts.

The functionalist view of mental states seeks to complement, and react to, explanatory accounts of behaviour that are based entirely on externally perceivable signs.[67] This is achieved by upgrading psychological notions to full-blooded explanatory terms that have a substantial role to play in explaining and predicting certain processes and events happening in the world, the behaviour of human beings, whilst fitting them into a naturalist framework. Unsurprisingly thus, Shoemaker claims that mental states are "in principle eliminable", for the reason that

> [They] can be treated as synonymous with definite descriptions, each such description being formulable, in principle, without the use of the mental vocabulary. (1975, p. 307)[68]

Shoemaker endorses a representationalist version of functionalism, which agrees with the assumptions I have outlined above. Mental states are regarded as observable phenomena that are identifiable in virtue of bearing certain properties and hence exist independently of whether they are articulated in language or reflected upon. Articulations of mental states by means of psychological expressions primarily present descriptions of the respective states. They are based on evidence from behaviour, or inference from general laws describing the function of the mental, or, in the case of self-ascriptions of mental states, they express the content of the speaker's functionally generated higher-order beliefs (see below). The meaning of psychological concepts is constituted by designating corresponding phenomena, even if it might well be that they present synonymous abbreviations of more

---

67 *Cf.* Heal (1994), p. 13. Burge points to functionalism's being nonetheless a theoretical extension of behaviourism, see especially Burge (1979), pp. 135–7.

68 Notably, this statement does not claim the eliminability of mental *states*, but that of mental *terms*. It says only that whatever the ontological and functional properties of the mental consist in, psychological expressions denote empirically identifiable entities that can be described in non-mental terms.

complex definite descriptions. If mental states are identifiable in virtue of being embedded in causal relations, and if these relations are describable by means of general laws, the notions employed in these descriptions are general terms having a perspective-independent meaning. That is, psychological terms, such as 'to believe' or 'to desire', are supposed to have a uniform meaning, independently of their grammatical form applied in a particular case, and their meaning is exhausted by definite descriptions. Finally and most evidently, functionalism fully endorses the view that mental states exist prior to being mentally or verbally represented in so far as it treats mental states as discoverable and scientifically describable phenomena. The word 'belief' has a uniform meaning in all its instances, whether it designates a first-, second- or higher-order belief, is uttered from a first-, second- or third-person point of view, stands in a past, present, assertoric, hypothetical context and so forth. And, of course, the phenomenon of belief is prior to any linguistic expression of it. Accordingly, its structural and functional properties dictate the logical properties of the corresponding sign.

1.3.5.2 Self-Intimation and Higher-Order Beliefs

At first glance, functionalism seems to have little to say to Moore's Paradox. First of all, it is a paradox of assertion and so concerns a field that lies at best at the periphery of the focus of functionalism (which seeks to explain the mind). A sentence of the Moore-paradoxical type $p \wedge \neg B(I, p)$ involves but one explicit mention of a mental state. Yet, Moore's Paradox affects the functionalist understanding of belief as well: Although the conjunction of a statement about the mind and another one about the world looks harmless, its assertion is absurd in the by now familiar sense. This raises a certain dilemma for functionalism: On the one hand, Moore's Paradox suggests that the word 'to believe' manifests an asymmetry between its first and third-person present indicatives. On the other hand, functionalism is committed to the claim that psychological terms have a uniform meaning and so has no means at hand to accommodate this asymmetry which is a peculiarity of the concept of belief. Shoemaker's way of acknowledging this asymmetry whilst maintaining the core assumptions of functionalism consists in construing the metaphysics of the mind such that it renders a sound explanation of the origins of Moore's Paradox. His first move consists in transferring the *explanandum* from assertions of Moore-paradoxical sentences to beliefs with Moore-paradoxical content. This shift is undertaken in order to enable the investigation of the paradox without interferences from the circumstantial and illocutionary aspects inherent in the logic of assertions. In a second step, he analyses the functional properties of belief, arguing for the *Higher-Order Belief* (HOB) Model as a theory of mind that crucially involves the building of first-personal knowledge into the mind's architecture. The solution of Moore's Paradox Shoemaker eventually yields draws on the notion of self-knowledge and exhibits a significant overlap with the solution emerging from the pragmatic approach.

It is part and parcel of Shoemaker's account of the mind;

> [T]hat it is in any way constitutive or definitive of mental states, or of minds, or of the concepts of these, that these states intimate their existence to their possessors in a special and direct way.[69]

It belongs to the constitutive properties of mental states that their occurrence is immediately known to their subject. In other words, every mental state generates a corresponding belief that one has the mental state in question. Since this kind of belief is constituted by beliefs about one's mental states, it is labelled a class of higher-order beliefs. The Higher-Order Belief Model integrates Moore's intuition that, after all, one must know what one says and thinks, in a functionalist framework. This intuition echoes the Cartesian idea, that if there is anything knowable at all, it is the contents of one's own thoughts. As already mentioned, the Cartesian view of self-knowledge is framed in the following claims, that (1) knowledge of one's own mental states is infallible, that (2) it is a constitutive feature of mental states that they are known by their subject, and that (3) this kind of knowledge is available to introspection. Whereas Shoemaker considers the infallibility claim indefensible, he maintains the other two, that self-knowledge is a constitutive feature of being a minded creature, and that this knowledge is available to introspection. Casting the Cartesian idea into the formulation that beliefs are 'self-intimating', means that by having a mental state, e.g. believing something to be the case, the subject is acquainted with the mode and content of his or her mental state, e.g. the belief *that it is raining*.

The self-intimation thesis involves two component claims:

> First, if a belief is available, then its subject has the belief that she has that belief, and that second-order belief is available as well. Second, if a belief is available, then, if its content is presented as a candidate for assent, the subject will assent to it.[70]

---

69 Sydney Shoemaker (1988), "On Knowing one's own Mind", in Shoemaker (1996), pp. 25–49, here p. 25.
70 Shoemaker (1995), pp. 80f., *cf.* Shoemaker (1988) and Sydney Shoemaker (2009), "Self-Intimation and Second-Order Belief", *Erkenntnis 71*, pp. 35–51. At first sight, Shoemaker's claim appears to diverge from the intuition in that it does not explicitly designate the so generated higher-order belief as *knowledge*. But in virtue of construing the relation between first-order and higher-order

The self-intimation thesis thus involves a claim regarding the effect of having a belief that p on the subject's mental constitution, and a claim concerning the effect the presence of a belief that p has on the subject's further behaviour. The first claim presents the Higher-Order Belief Principle as an ontological claim about the constitution of the mind: The belief *that p is the case* brings about the second-order belief *that I believe that p is the case*, or:

(3) $B(I, p) \rightarrow B(I, p) \wedge B(I, B(I, p))$ (Higher-Order Belief (HOB) Principle). [71]

The second claim proposes a particular interpretation as to how at least one aspect of the causal role of available beliefs ought to be conceived, namely in terms of 'poising' the subject to assent to the proposition forming the content of his or her available belief. Assenting to the belief contents might take the form of either, affirming it in communication or thought, or taking a course of action that is conditioned on the proposition's truth. [72]

Reading the first part of the self-intimation thesis in the light of the second issues the following consideration. Believing that p is tantamount to being disposed to assent to the proposition that p in words or deeds. Believing *that I believe that p* analogously amounts to being disposed to assent to the proposition *that I believe that p*. Now, the belief that p entails the belief *that I believe that p*. Therefore,

---

belief as a conceptual one, the existence of a first-order belief that p provides sufficient grounds to justify the corresponding higher-order belief's counting as knowledge.

71 Strictly speaking, Shoemaker restricts the scope of the HOB Principle to available first-order beliefs only. On Shoemaker's view, available beliefs contrast with standing beliefs, which corresponds to a distinction between occurrent, i.e. beliefs that are conditioned on the subject's current circumstances and induce situation-specific courses of behaviour, and dispositional beliefs, i.e. long-term beliefs working in the background of the subject's mind. Standing beliefs can, given apposite situational affordances, turn into available beliefs and, of course, bear impact on what available beliefs a subject forms in a certain situation. In Peter's case, his belief that it will be raining soon is an occurrent belief, his belief that the weather forecast is generally reliable is a standing belief. Peter's standing belief, together with other informative states, conditions his available belief in that it is causally efficacious in Peter's forming the relevant available belief upon learning that rain has been forecasted. If the forecast seems very unlikely, or if, in a discussion, the topic turns towards meteorology, Peter's belief that the weather forecast is generally reliable might turn into an available belief and enter his situational reasoning. However, Shoemaker holds that standing and available beliefs are structurally identical, that is, they present informational or representational states with the same functional properties. For this reason, the distinction does not matter for my argument, although Shoemaker attaches some significance to it in the course of rejecting the objection that, without qualification, the self-intimation claim was too strong.

72 Note that this formulation, as the quoted one suggests, brings out that Shoemaker shares the representationalist conception of belief as a mental state of a certain kind, that is, with certain functional properties that contains a representation of what is the case.

believing that p does not only poise the subject to assent to the proposition *that p is the case*, but also to the proposition *that I believe that p is the case*. Shoemaker formulates this point as an interdependency between the two propositions' *assent conditions*, i.e. the conditions under which it is appropriate to hold either of them true (1995, p. 77f.). More specifically, the assent conditions of the proposition *that p is the case* entail the assent conditions of the proposition *that I believe that p is the case*—if I assent to the former, I thereby assent to the latter. Thus, Shoemaker acknowledges the kinship between affirming the proposition *that p is the case*, and affirming the proposition *that one believes that p is the case*, or the proposition:

$$\vdash p \text{ is similar to } \vdash B(I, p) .$$

This conclusion reveals a substantial kinship of the Higher-Order Belief Model and the pragmatic approach, which is not only of accidental nature. Shoemaker's claim to the similarity just formulated runs strictly parallel to Moore's Principle that assertions *that p is the case* count as assertions *that I believe that p* in virtue of implying that the speaker holds the belief *that p is the case*. The argument, for sure, is different. Shoemaker considers the case of sincere assertion only in passing, since he takes it to derive from the case of mental assent, by which he understands an "episodic instantiation of belief" (1995, p. 78), the act of judging a (neutral) thought-content true. And whereas Searle, and as far as one can say, Moore as well, proceeds from the illocutionary conditions of assertion as a communicative act, Shoemaker is cautious not to stray from his investigation of the constitutive features of the mind.

The argumentation Shoemaker pursues in establishing the self-intimation thesis involves two prongs. On the one hand, he argues from the impossibility of 'self-blind' reasoning, i.e. engaging in theoretical or practical deliberation without entertaining beliefs about the mental states involved. This prong, which I will only touch superficially, is primarily intended to yield the first part of the self-intimation thesis. On the other hand, the solution to Moore's Paradox is supposed to support the self-intimation thesis in its complete formulation.

Arguing for the claims Shoemaker adopts from Cartesianism, that it is a constitutive feature of mental states that their subject has corresponding second-order beliefs and that the second-order beliefs in question manifest specifically first-person knowledge, he imagines the case of a person who has only first-order beliefs but lacks that knowledge. The idea that rational processes, that is, theoretical and practical reasoning, could function properly in this case, is, in the following, shown to lead *ad absurdum*, from which Shoemaker concludes that the Higher-Order Belief Principle is correct. The brief version of the argument runs like this: Being a rational creature involves that one's first-order beliefs and desires fulfil two causal roles. First, they jointly produce rational actions (i.e. actions that can be rationalised by citing the beliefs and desires involved), and second, they cooperate such that they maximise the consistency of the creature's overall system of mental states. Successfully performing the first role is manageable on the basis of first-order states only. Accomplishing the second task, however, requires modifying one's beliefs and desires, if they stand in mutual conflict or if one acquires new evidence. Modifying one's first-order states in order to preserve or establish maximal consistency among them is a purposeful activity that presupposes the ability to form beliefs and desires concerned with the aim to keep one's first-order states in good order (*cf.* Shoemaker (1988), pp. 32f.). Hence, for being rational, an individual

> [M]ust be sensitive to the fact that there is the inconsistency, and must know what changes in his body of beliefs would remove it—and this requires knowledge [...] of what beliefs he has. (1988, p. 31)

That is, the functionalist account of mental states in terms of their causal efficacy, to jointly produce rational behaviour, could not render an adequate conception of the primary function of the mind (i.e. rational deliberation) unless it included the Higher-Order Belief Principle. The argument from rational deliberation on its own yet does not conclusively yield the claim that the second-order beliefs involved in adjusting one's first-order system constitute categorically distinct first-person knowledge. Still, Shoemaker's appeal to rationality at least suggests that this knowledge is knowledge that must be generated from 'within' the relevant set of first-order states, in that it is conceptually linked to entertaining mental states and does not require self-observation or other additional investigative efforts. If, on the contrary, this knowledge was not constitutively bound to having mental states in the first place, there would be no conflict between the presence of an inconsistency within one's first-order belief system and the desire for maximal overall consistency among one's overall set of mental states unless this inconsistency were accidentally discovered by the subject.

The second prong of Shoemaker's considerations, the argument from Moore's Paradox, is supposed to fully establish the self-intimation thesis, and thereby to accomplish the claim that first-person knowledge is a constitutive matter about being a minded creature at all.

1.3.5.3 Moore's Paradox goes HOB
Shoemaker's solution to Moore's Paradox is based on the thesis that beliefs are self-intimating. He further argues that the possibility of solving Moore's Paradox by means of the self-intimation thesis supports the thesis itself. I think that the value of his strategy does not only consist in the suggested solution itself, but also

in that Shoemaker acknowledges the challenge of Moore's Paradox taking it as an adequacy condition for any conception of belief, and any account of the meaning of expressions of belief, that it deliver a satisfying answer to the challenges of Moore's Paradox.

I have already indicated that Shoemaker is sceptical about explanations of Moore's Paradox that substantially draw on linguistic expressions of belief in communicative situations and approach a solution by analysing the logic of assertion with respect to its illocutionary features or the accompanying speaker's intentions. Shoemaker does not credit accounts related to speech act theory with the potential to explain why:

> [T]here is something paradoxical or logically peculiar about [the] idea of someone's *believing* the propositional content of a Moore-paradoxical sentence. [...] If we can come up with an explanation of this, then an explanation of why one cannot (coherently) *assert* a Moore-paradoxical sentence will come along for free, via the principle that what can be (coherently) believed constrains what can be (coherently) asserted. (1995, pp. 75f.)

In Shoemaker's view, pragmatic accounts have two main weaknesses: On the one hand, they divert attention from the contents of a Moore-paradoxical sentence to the circumstances granting the success of an assertion. Whether an assertion that p is successful is conditioned among others on whether it is sincere or insincere, that is, on the speaker's intentions regarding the effect of his or her utterance.[73] This allegedly obstructs the view as to what Shoemaker takes to really matter in explaining Moore's Paradox, i.e. the functional properties of belief. On the other hand, pragmatic accounts are suspected to wrongly reverse the order of priority in that they refrain from investigating the case of beliefs with Moore-paradoxical contents prior to the assertoric case. In a similar spirit, Shoemaker distances himself from accounts drawing on the circumstances of a Moore-paradoxical belief, particularly, from restricting the analysis to the case of conscious beliefs of this type (1995, p. 77).

Shoemaker's explanatory strategy presupposes that the metaphysics of belief, framed in functionalist terms, dictates the meaning of the word 'belief' and the range of its logically possible moves. The function of a sign—the word 'belief'—for its part, reflects the function of the entity thereby designated, that is the mental state of believing. If expressions of belief produce 'logical oddities', as it is the case in Moore-paradoxical sentences, they mirror confusions of some sort obtaining within the subject's belief-system. For this reason, Shoemaker is highly interested

---

73 This objection to pragmatist accounts does not necessarily hit Searle's solution of Moore's Paradox because he presupposes that the relevant assertion is sincere, *cf.* Searle (1969), p. 65.

in developing a solution to Moore's Paradox abstracted from circumstantial conditions of the instantiations of Moore-paradoxical sentences in thought and speech. Notably, isolating the *explanandum* from its *in situ* environment to scrutinise it *in vitro* has a not insignificant side-effect: It constricts the investigative focus to the absurdity of Moore-paradoxical beliefs and leaves aside the relational aspects of Moore's Paradox that come into play in verbal utterances of Moore-paradoxical sentences. Moore's Paradox does not only consist in the contrast between the possible truth and unassertability of Moore-paradoxical sentences, but also in the contrast between their absurdity in the first-person present indicative and the possibility to sensibly express the same proposition in other grammatical persons, tenses and modes. Insofar as Shoemaker regards beliefs containing Moore-paradoxical sentences the original source of the paradox, he focusses on the first contrast and seems unaware of the other one or, if he is, he attaches only minor importance to it. That is, Shoemaker considers Moore's Paradox on the level of content, leaving aside the grammatical impact it has on the level of signs, i.e. language. Although he thereby implements his conviction that grammar derives from ontology (plus conventional modifications), this move precludes the possibility that an adequate solution to Moore's Paradox might indeed emerge from an investigation of grammar (including its conventional aspects), as opposed to coming from a metaphysical inquiry, whereas it does—or so I will argue in the next chapter.

What emerges is the extent to which Shoemaker is most concerned with establishing a solution to Moore's Paradox which is more robust, in the sense of logically more stringent, rather than appealing to circumstantial and conventional factors could achieve. Thus, in order to answer the questions why one cannot believe a Moore-paradoxical sentence, and why one cannot believe that one has a belief with a Moore-paradoxical content, he proposes an argument that proceeds solely from the notion of belief without further qualification. Notably, this requires him to investigate both, the meaning of the word 'to believe' and the metaphysics of belief. The former is inevitable because, in its original form, Moore's Paradox is framed as a paradox from verbal expressions of belief or disbelief. Shoemaker intends to derive the absurdity of Moore-paradoxical assertions from judgements about the truth of Moore-paradoxical sentences in general and so can be expected to give an account of the relationship between asserting and believing *that p is the case*. The latter describes Shoemaker's main target, tracing the unbelievability of Moore-paradoxical sentences to the constitutive conditions of belief.

Shoemaker argues that the functional properties of the phenomenon of belief are responsible for a Moore-paradoxical sentence to be absurd when judged true. According to the self-intimation thesis, holding a belief *that p is the case* causes the subject to equally hold the belief *that I believes that p is the case*. The Higher-Order Belief Model accounts for the incoherence of a belief with Moore-paradoxical content analogously to the pragmatic approach based on Moore's Principle (0) for the case of assertion, namely *via* the principle that having a belief that p implies having the belief *that one believes that p* (1995, p. 80):

(3) $B(I, p) \rightarrow B(I, p) \wedge B(I, B(I, p))$ (Higher-Order Belief (HOB) Principle).

Applying the HOB Principle to a Moore-paradoxical sentence accordingly explains the incoherence of such a (first-order) belief by a resulting pair of second-order beliefs with contradicting contents (the belief *that one believes that p* and the belief *that one does not believe that p* (underlined)):

(4) $B(I, (p \wedge \neg B(I, p)))$ (Moore-paradoxical belief),

(5) $B(I, (p \wedge \neg B(I, p))) \wedge B(I, B(I, (p \wedge \neg B(I, p))))$ (3, 4),

(6) $B(I, p) \wedge \underline{B(I, \neg B(I, p))} \wedge \underline{B(I, B(I, p))} \wedge B(I, B(I, \neg B(I, p)))$

(distribution principle). [74]

Remarkably, the account Shoemaker gives for the interdependency of the assent conditions of the belief that p with those of the belief *that I believe that p* parallels the pragmatic conception of the interrelation between asserting that p and believing that p. The formalisation nicely brings out that this explanation indeed runs analogously to the explanation of its correlate, the absurdity of asserting a Moore-paradoxical sentence, as resulting from a contradiction (underlined) between the contents of two first-order beliefs:[75]

(0) $\vdash p \rightarrow p \wedge B_{impl}(I, p)$ (Moore's Principle),

(1) $\vdash p \wedge \neg B(I, p)$ (Moore-paradoxical assertion),

(2) $\vdash p \wedge \underline{\neg B(I, p)} \wedge B_{impl}(I, p) \wedge B_{impl}(I, \neg B(I, p))$ (0, 1).

---

74 *Cf.* Christoph C. Pfisterer (2011), "Ist Glauben ein psychisches Phänomen?" (MSS), draft paper presented at Vienna, March 2011, p. 5.

75 Note that both the pragmatic and the HOB-based explanation consider having two beliefs whose contents contradict each other the cause of Moore-paradoxical sentences' being absurd. Kriegel (2004) objects to Shoemaker's solution to Moore's Paradox that doing so relies on the additional assumption that the contents of a person's individual representational states form or ought to form a coherent system to the effect that they stand in direct logical relations to one another. That is, the two explanations proceeding from Moore's Principle must grant that having two distinct beliefs with contradicting contents is tantamount to a single self-contradictory belief, or that $B(I, p) \wedge B(I, \neg p) \leftrightarrow B(I, p \wedge \neg p)$ holds on every level of believing. If a person's representational states were not transparent to one another in this way Moore's Paradox would be unsolvable, Kriegel argues, for there is, in general, nothing paradoxical about having distinct beliefs with contradicting contents. *Cf.* Uriah Kriegel (2004), "Moore's Paradox and the Structure of Conscious Belief", *Erkenntnis* 61/1, pp. 99–121, especially pp. 109–11. Kriegel's point is not quite

Moore's Paradox, conceived as originating from the incoherence of asserting or believing something that nonetheless can be the case, is in both cases explained in psychological terms. Whereas the pragmatic model locates the origin in the logic of assertion, Shoemaker draws on an ostensible architectural feature of the mind, namely the tendency to produce meta-representations of what one takes to be a true representation of reality. Representing a state of affairs in an affirmative context— the judgement 'p is the case, but I don't believe that p is the case', manifest in a belief or assertion that this proposition is true—is supposed to be accompanied by an at least implicitly held belief that one takes the content of one's affirmation to be a true representation of the respective state of affairs. The accompanying belief is located at one level higher than the original, explicit representational state is; the assertion that p is accompanied by the belief *that p is the case*, the belief that p by the belief *that one believes that p*. So the claim that beliefs constitutively generate self-knowledge and the solution to Moore's Paradox seem to nicely complement each other.

1.3.5.4 Difficulties within the HOB Model

Shoemaker's account of belief, self-intimation and Moore's Paradox raises three worries. First, conceiving of belief as a functionally determined psychological phenomenon does not render an adequate conception of the notion of believing and its grammatical properties. Particularly, it does not account for the impossibility of sensibly ascribing a false belief to oneself. Second, the self-intimation thesis invites an infinite regress of higher-order beliefs because it constructs higher-order beliefs

---

wrong. As will become clear in this section, his requirement is provided for by Shoemaker's and Moran's appeal to the person's rationality and his or her resulting commitments to the coherence of his or her belief system. For Searle, regarding distinct beliefs with contradicting contents and self-contradictory beliefs as equivalent (at least, as regards their paradoxicality) is not a question; as far as I can see, he remains tacit on this point.

I doubt the force of Kriegel's argument, but will remain agnostic about that matter. Shoemaker considers first- and second-order beliefs phenomena of the same kind, beliefs namely, which are equally integrated in the constitution of a person's mind. If (available) beliefs are dispositions to assent to propositions articulating their contents the subject of a Moore-paradoxical belief is apt to affirm that p is the case, that he or she does not believe that p is the case (the content of his or her first-order belief), that he or she believes that p is the case, and that he or she believes that he or she does not believe that p is the case (the content of his or her second-order belief). The subject is thus prone to assent to a formal-logical contradiction mirroring the fact that he or she holds beliefs with contradicting contents, which might be sufficient to meet Kriegel's requirement.—Whether or not appealing to a person's rationality and the allegedly entailed commitment to coherence among his or her belief-contents provides the solution of Moore's Paradox is a different question, which I will discuss later in this section.

as functionally identical with first-order beliefs. This moreover raises a problem concerning Shoemaker's account of the first-personal epistemic privilege, manifest in a distinctive kind of self-knowledge. Finally, the HOB account renders Moore's Paradox as based on a tacit formal-logical contradiction within one's belief contents, which is, as I have argued above, false. These points are related: According to Shoemaker's solution, judging a Moore-paradoxical sentence is tantamount to affirmatively ascribing a false belief to oneself. And his explanation of Moore's Paradox and the self-intimation thesis are mutually supporting, they stand and fall together.

The conception of belief entrenched in Shoemaker's Higher-Order Belief Model includes the representational claims about content and combines them with a functional conception of psychological modes. Belief is conceived as an observable phenomenon, something that is at work *within* the mind of its bearer, independently of how things are *outside*. Beliefs about one's own beliefs are meta-representational states and thus identical in character to beliefs about whatever else in the world.

Concentrating on the interrelations between beliefs of first- and higher-orders, the functionalist account Shoemaker establishes is at risk of losing sight of one crucial element of the notion of belief, that believing that p entails believing that p is true. The way Shoemaker conceives of belief comes down to handling beliefs as photographs, as it were, which may turn out to be true or false pictures. This becomes obvious from his solution of Moore's Paradox (6) that locates the grounds of Moore's Paradox in believing to hold beliefs with contradicting contents ($\neg B(I, p) \wedge B_{\text{impl}}(I, p)$). Thus, judging a Moore-paradoxical sentence true is reduced to judging that one believes a contradiction, that is ascribing a false belief to oneself.

But according to Shoemaker's conception of belief in functional terms, that believing that p is being disposed to behave in ways appropriate to p being the case, it is not obvious why this should be absurd at all. Introducing self-intimation as an additional function of belief does not yield the absurdity, either, because self-intimation delivers *factual* knowledge about one's own mental states. However, that knowing that one holds two contradicting beliefs is incoherent is not entailed by the functionalist conception of belief. To arrive at this conclusion, which he takes to be the key for explaining Moore's Paradox, Shoemaker appeals to two additional assumptions, firstly that one is concerned with the belief contents of rational beings only and secondly that this primarily means the presence of an overall desire for maximal consistency among one's belief system.

Shoemaker endorses Moore's Principle in his claim that the assertions 'p' and 'I believe that p' equally express the speaker's belief *that p is the case*. He explains the implication involved in the principle by means of the Higher-Order Belief Model. On this model, both assertions have the same assent conditions because first-order beliefs automatically generate corresponding second-order beliefs. Second-order beliefs differ from first order beliefs only regarding their content (being about one's own beliefs), not regarding the functional properties they have *qua* being beliefs. That higher-order beliefs are supposed to be functionally identical with lower-order beliefs, however, makes the HOB Model susceptible to infinite regress. For the higher-order belief reiterates the conditions imposed on the first-order representation. Given the principle that believing that p implies believing that one believes that p, it seems unavoidable that it implies that one also holds a belief about the second-order belief, to the effect that one believes that one believes that one believes that p, and a corresponding fourth-order belief etc. Holding a single belief, that is, seems to generate an infinite number of higher-order beliefs:

$$(3') \ B(I, p) \rightarrow B(I, p) \wedge B(I, B(I, p))$$
$$\rightarrow B(I, p) \wedge B(I, B(I, p)) \wedge B(I, B(I, B(I, p))) \quad \textit{etc. ad inf.} \ [76]$$

In order to avoid this effect Shoemaker introduces a belief stopper at the second-order level, the level of knowing one's own beliefs. Forming second-order beliefs, i.e. beliefs with the content *that I believe that p is the case*, he argues, requires mastery of the concept of belief and the concept of oneself, whereas holding first-order beliefs *that p is the case* does not. According to Shoemaker, this difference amounts to a categorical difference between the conceptual capacities needed for having first- and second-order beliefs, respectively. Beliefs on even higher levels in contrast do not require the mastery of concepts beyond those already required for having second-order beliefs do. Thus, Shoemaker concludes,

> If having the second-order belief that one has an available first-order belief is just having that available belief together with the concepts of belief and of oneself and an appropriate degree of rationality, it would seem that having that second-order belief should also count as having the third-order belief that one has it, that this in turn should count as having the fourth-order belief that one has that one, and so on ad infinitum. (Shoemaker (2009), p. 43)

---

[76] Despite the analogy between the HOB Principle (3) and Moore's Principle (0), the pragmatic approach need not lead to infinite regress of the sort

$$(0') \ \vdash p \rightarrow p \wedge B(I, p) \rightarrow p \wedge B(I, p) \wedge B(I, p \wedge B(I, p)) \quad \textit{etc. ad inf.}$$

Without additionally endorsing (3), the pragmatic account does not face the regress problem because it is concerned with assertion and not with belief.

That is, Shoemaker claims that although the higher-order belief principle (3) holds for any belief or assertion, and although 'belief' is a functionally uniform phenomenon on all levels, the meta-belief implied by the principle is not liable to produce further meta-beliefs of even higher orders. It is questionable though that Shoemaker can continue attaching quite such importance to the qualitative difference between having first-order and higher-order beliefs. And this contrasts with the core thesis of his model, that beliefs are essentially self-intimating. If they are, having a first-order belief will generate a corresponding second-order belief. So if the mastery of the concept of belief is necessary for having second-order beliefs, and if, at least, insofar as rational subjects are concerned, there is no first-order belief without bringing about a corresponding second-order belief, it seems necessary for having beliefs at any rate. That this would indeed make the functionalist view more plausible is supported by the following, very simple consideration. Believing that p presupposes the ability to distinguish what one believes from what is real, that is being aware that one's beliefs can be false. This ability, however, involves mastering the concept of belief, even for first-order beliefs. Shoemaker could easily integrate this consideration into his own account (for it indeed follows from the self-intimation thesis) if he was not to opt for allowing the possibility of holding first-order beliefs without having mastered the concept of belief.

Thus, holding principle (3) together with the claim that having second-order beliefs presupposes mastery of the concepts of belief and of oneself, yields the conclusion that mastery of the respective concepts is a necessary condition for having beliefs at all. Or, to put it the other way round, believing that p is either a sufficient condition for the corresponding second-order belief in that it already involves the necessary capacities for generating second-order beliefs, or it isn't. In the latter case, the self-intimation claim is not fully exhausted by the Higher-Order Belief Principle, which exclusively spells out the functional properties of belief.

According to Shoemaker, believing is a uniform phenomenon across all occasions. Consequently, he conceives of first-order and second-order belief alike, as theoretical or factual belief that a particular proposition—*that p* or *that I believe that p*—is true. That is, knowledge of one's own state of mind does not categorically differ from knowledge of another person's state of mind. Self- and other-knowledge supposedly rely on different modes of access (introspection *vs.* observation) and to hold to different degrees of completeness. Yet, explaining the distinctiveness of first-personal knowledge in virtue of having privileged access to one's own states of mind *via* the HOB Principle does not answer the question as to why it is only one's own mental states that automatically generate corresponding second-order beliefs.[77] With respect to this explanatory gap, the Higher-Order Belief Model

---

[77] This point is made in Moran (2001), ch. 1.4.

stands, *pars pro toto*, for accounts of self-knowledge advocating the view that self-knowledge, regardless of its possible idiosyncrasies, presents a kind of perceptual or, more generally, factual knowledge, that is, knowledge that certain facts regarding one's own psychological constitution are true.[78] I have argued elsewhere that the theoretical conception of self-knowledge makes it hard to see just in what respect self-knowledge ought to be distinctively first-personal if this knowledge basically does not differ from knowledge of other facts generated by observation and inference. Conceptions of self-knowledge as factual knowledge cannot plausibly accommodate the specific first-personality of this kind of knowledge other than by stipulation (Schmid, 2011).

Shoemaker in principle agrees with Moore's approach to Moore's Paradox by means of drawing on Moore's Principle, that asserting that *p* implies that the speaker also believes that *p*. Although he proposes a different account of grounds (self-intimation of beliefs) and nature (functional property of beliefs) of the implication involved, he arrives at the same result: asserting a Moore-paradoxical sentence amounts to ascribing a false belief to oneself. Even if this was correct (which it is not), it would not explain the absurdity responsible for Moore's Paradox without drawing on further principles, external to Shoemaker's concept of belief. For according to the functionalist conception of belief as a definite psychological phenomenon, and of self-knowledge as factual/empirical knowledge, there is nothing wrong with describing oneself as holding a false belief. That there *is* something wrong with self-ascribing a false belief only follows given that the respective subject is a rational subject (otherwise the connection of Moore's Paradox and the self-intimation claim would not hold) and as such has mastered the concept of belief.

Yet, the result is false. Asserting a Moore-paradoxical sentence amounts to asserting a possible truth, not to asserting a contradiction. Further, this result is

---

78 *Cf.* Christopher Peacocke (1996), "Our Entitlement to Self-Knowledge", *Proceedings of the Aristotelian Society New Series 96*, pp. 117–58; Peacocke (2003), "Action: Awareness, Ownership, and Knowledge", in: Johannes Roessler, Naomi Eilan (eds.), *Agency and Self-Awareness: Issues in Philosophy and Psychology*, Oxford: UP, pp. 84–111; Peacocke (2009), "Mental Actions and Self-Awareness (II): Epistemology", in Lucy O'Brien, Matthew Soteriou (eds.), *Mental Actions*, Oxford: UP, pp. 192–215; Tyler Burge (1996), "Our Entitlement To Self-Knowledge", *Proceedings of the Aristotelian Society New Series 96*, pp. 91–116; Akeel Bilgrami (1998), "Self-Knowledge and Resentment", in Crispin Wright, Barry C. Smith, Cynthia Mcdonald (eds.), *Knowing Our Own Minds*, Oxford: Clarendon Press, pp. 207–42; and most empirical accounts of self-knowledge and self-awareness. See, for example, Elisabeth Pacherie (2007), "The sense of control and the sense of agency", *Psyche 13/1*, pp. 1–30. Comprehensive collections of articles concerning questions related to the notion of self-knowledge are Quassim Cassam (ed.), *Self-Knowledge*, Oxford: UP 1994 (a collection of 'classics'); Wright, Smith, Mcdonald (1998); and Roessler, Eilan (2003).

questionable in the light of what it is to have mastered the concept of belief, which is a necessary presupposition for rendering Moore-paradoxical sentences contradictory at first place. The concept of belief, well understood, does not provide for the possibility of representing oneself as holding a false belief at present (whereas it allows the self-ascription of past false beliefs and considering the possibility that one might have a false belief at present). In this light, Shoemaker's claim that a person assenting to a Moore-paradoxical sentence affirmatively represents him- or herself as entertaining a false belief, which is considered absurd, seems incoherent for conceptual reasons.[79]

Interpreting, as Shoemaker does, affirmative Moore-paradoxical sentences as representing discrepancies within the subject's mental architecture moreover eventually detracts from the point that Moore's Paradox is a multiple relational paradox and is not comprehensively explained by a rational deficiency on part of the subject. That the Higher-Order Belief Model locates the origin of Moore's Paradox in contradicting contents at the level of second-order beliefs is symptomatic for the more specific problems of functionalism about the mind. The result that an assertion of a Moore-paradoxical sentence amounts to ascribing contradicting (second-order) beliefs to oneself is wrong, because beliefs with Moore-paradoxical content can be true.[80]

In conclusion, Shoemaker's Higher-Order Belief Model invites objections to the functionalist conception of belief and the resulting conception of self-knowledge as well as to his own proposal as to how Moore's Paradox should be explained. First, the Higher-Order Belief Model omits two core elements of the notion of belief, that beliefs aim at truth and that having beliefs requires mastery of the

---

79 I will come back to this point after my discussion of Moran's approach to Moore's Paradox in the next section.

80 There are a number of modified versions of functionalism that seek to account for one or several those problems in the light of Moore's Paradox, e.g. by introducing specific first-person elements into the concept of belief (as Heal (1994) does), by amending the relation between first- and second-order belief with an additional epistemic relation that in turn is made responsible for the asymmetry of the grammatical first person, or by introducing new technical details into the Higher-Order Belief Model. See the contributions in Green and Williams (2007), Kriegel (2004), and for a critical discussion of the literature on Moore's Paradox, Christoph C. Pfisterer (2008), "Moore's Paradox, Behaupten, Urteilen", in *Conceptus 91*, pp. 41–62, The page numbers I use (1–14) refer to the manuscript. Such efforts will however not succeed because the difficulties manifest on Shoemaker's account concern some of the basic assumptions of functionalism, *viz.* the understanding of 'belief' as a scientific notion, the conception of its grammar as derivative from the metaphysics of belief, the construction of the metaphysics of belief in functional terms, to name a few.

concept of belief. Second, Shoemaker's conception of the epistemic asymmetry of first-personal statements concerning one's own state of mind is too thin. Although he claims self-knowledge to be a constitutive feature of having mental states, this knowledge is supposed to be a kind of observational knowledge. It is questionable, however, whether appealing to the constitutiveness of this relation alone suffices to acknowledge that a person's relation to his or her own beliefs is a first-personal, not a third-personal one. Finally, Shoemaker's approach to Moore's Paradox, tracing its origin to an alleged self-representation as holding a false belief, yields a false solution of Moore's Paradox and moreover indicates an inherent incoherence resulting from his misconception of the notion of belief.

1.3.6 The Approach from Epistemology: Moran's Transparency Condition

Moran agrees with the general approach to solving Moore's Paradox I have presented so far. He considers Moore's Paradox resulting from Moore's Principle concerning assertions, that asserting *that p is the case* implies that the speaker also believes *that p is the case*. Moran joins Shoemaker in criticising the pragmatic approach to Moore's Paradox. Considering Moore's Paradox as a paradox arising from the pragmatics of assertion, in his opinion, falls short of explaining the absurdity of Moore-paradoxical beliefs and thus overlooks the point that the absurdity of Moore-paradoxical assertions must be inherent in some aspect of its content, rather than its illocutionary force. For this reason, Moran, too, seeks to derive Moore's Principle from an analogous principle about beliefs, agreeing with Shoemaker that having knowledge of one's own beliefs—true beliefs about one's own beliefs—is a constitutive feature of having beliefs. So he treats an adequate conception of self-knowledge and the solution to Moore's Paradox as interrelated questions.

Accordingly, Moran gives a still different account for the reason why the implicature expressed in Moore's Principle is valid. Despite agreement on the general approach to Moore's Paradox as well as on the solution eventually rendered, Moran's conception of belief and self-knowledge significantly deviates from Shoemaker's. The most important difference consists in Moran's spelling out of the notions 'belief' and 'self-knowledge' in normative instead of functional terms. In contrast with Shoemaker and also with Searle, Moran develops an account of belief-formation, self-knowledge and statements concerned with one's own beliefs that considers the subject of belief as a mental agent. Shoemaker identifies Moran's alternative approach to the phenomena of belief and self-knowledge as coming from an epistemological rather than, like Shoemaker, from a 'metaphysical' standpoint.[81] Shoemaker's observation is right insofar as Moran proceeds from the question, how do I come to know what my beliefs are?, rather than, what is a belief? His main concern is the interrelation between the way one comes to hold particular beliefs and the way in which one subsequently represents one's own beliefs. Yet, Moran's account of self-knowledge is intrinsically connected with his account of the ontology of belief. This, too, crucially differs from Shoemaker's in that Moran conceives the distinctiveness of self-knowledge as resulting from a specific first-personal perspective on one's own beliefs. This perspective is presented as subjective in a literal sense, it is the perspective an agent takes on his or her deeds. Consequently, Moran considers self-knowledge as practical knowledge in Anscombe's terms,[82] which is reflected in a certain peculiarity of making assertions about one's own belief, which in turn provides the solution to Moore's Paradox. For this reason, Moran attaches more attention to the meaning of first-person present tense assertions of belief than has been done in the accounts I discussed above.

In comparison with Searle's and Shoemaker's respective accounts of belief, Moran's account harbours two idiosyncratic strands. On the one hand, he conceives of mental states, in particular beliefs and intentions, as resulting from their subject's mental agency, that is, from deliberation of reasons.[83] On the other hand, Moran separates two categorically distinct standpoints which one can, in principle, adopt towards one's own mental constitution. The conception of mental states as an outcome of mental agency is connected with a conception of oneself as their subject, the *transcendental* or *deliberative* stance. It is complemented by a conception of mental states as discrete phenomena, which is connected with a conception of oneself as an empirical being, the *empirical* or *theoretical* stance. This move goes hand in hand with reassessing the implication inherent in Moore's Principle in normative terms, as articulation of *practical*, as opposed to factual self-knowledge.

In the following, I will present Moran's account in three steps, beginning with Moran's considerations on the meaning of the expression 'I believe'. Moran takes

---

81 *Cf.* Sydney Shoemaker (2003), "Moran", in *European Journal of Philosophy 11/3*, pp. 391–401.
82 *Cf.* Richard Moran (2004), "Anscombe on Practical Knowledge", *Philosophy 55* (Supplementary Volume), pp. 43–68; and G. E. M. Anscombe (2000), *Intention*, 2nd edition, Cambridge (MA): Harvard UP.
83 At least, beliefs and intentions must be *describable* as conclusions of a practical syllogism. This requirement can be met without an explicit reasoning process taking place. Beliefs, as intentions, are regarded commitments—not to an action but to the truth of their propositional content. Similarly to Shoemaker, one might say, Moran conceives of believing as being prone to assent to a proposition, though not in virtue of having a disposition-like state, but of a normative commitment. I will come back to this point later.

it for granted that the semantic and grammatical properties of this expression derive from analogous properties of the phenomenon of believing. His account of the ontology of believing and its intrinsic connection with self-knowledge will be the topic of the following section. Thereafter, I will explain Moran's answer to the questions what the absurdity of Moore-paradoxical assertions consists in, and why it arises. In the final section, I will show that the way in which Moran takes his account to yield the solution to Moore's Paradox does not structurally diverge from the solutions I have presented so far. I will argue that this provides a reason not only to reject his solution to Moore's Paradox, but also to resist his account of the mind.

1.3.6.1 The Transparency of 'I believe'
According to Moran,

> [A] first-person present-tense question about one's beliefs is answered by reference to (or consideration of) the same reasons that would justify an answer to the corresponding question about the world. (Moran (2001), p. 62)

Moran calls this feature the "transparency of one's own thinking" (1997, p. 146), that is, that coming to know what one believes about a certain subject-matter does not proceed by considering how things are with oneself, but considering how things are with the subject-matter one is interested in. The idea Moran grasps with the notion 'transparency' is formulated as part of Evans' conception of the epistemic grounds for ascribing mental states to oneself (1982, pp. 224 ff.).[84] Inspired by a remark of Wittgenstein's,[85] Evans describes the process of deliberation by which one simultaneously forms a belief about a certain issue and comes to know what one believes regarding the very same issue as follows:

---

84 The notion itself originates from Roy Edgley (1969), *Reasons in Theory and Practice*, London: Hutchinson. *Cf.* Moran (2001), pp. 60f.

85 Wittgenstein is reported to have said, in an Oxford discussion, "If a man says to me, looking at the sky, 'I think it will rain, therefore I exist,' I do not understand him." Christopher Coope, Peter Geach, Timothy Potts, Roger White (eds.), *A Wittgenstein Workbook*, Berkeley/L.A.: University of California Press 1972, p. 21. Note, that this remark is published without any contextualisation, though it appears under the heading "'I' (Consciousness; *Äusserungen*")". Whether Wittgenstein actually makes the point Evans takes him to make, remains an open question. Be it as it may, it is mistaken to interpret Wittgenstein as making substantial claims concerning the metaphysics of belief, at this place or elsewhere. On a Wittgensteinian picture, 'transparency' characterises the *grammar* of the expression 'I believe', and not, as on Moran's account, the *metaphysics* of belief. I will discuss this point later in this section and in Chapter 2.

[I]n making a self-ascription of belief, one's eyes are, so to speak, or occasionally literally, directed outward—upon the world. If someone asks me 'Do you think there is going to be a third world war?' I get myself in a position to answer the question whether I believe that *p* by putting into operation whatever procedure I have for answering the question whether *p*. [...] If a subject applies this procedure, then necessarily he will gain knowledge of one of his own mental states: even the most determined sceptic cannot find here a gap in which to insert his knife. (Evans (1982), p. 225)

The notion of transparency captures the similarity of statements concerned with one's own beliefs, with statements concerned with the content of one's beliefs. The similarity of statements that *p* and statements *that I believe that p* consists in what Shoemaker has called 'sameness of assent conditions' (see previous section), that the circumstances justifying affirming one of the statements equally justify affirming the other. What Shoemaker explains by drawing on the Higher-Order Belief Principle and a conception of belief as disposition, is, on Moran's account, captured by the notion of transparency, accompanied by an agentive understanding of belief: If the epistemic grounds of judging the proposition *that p is the case* and judging the proposition *that one believes that p is the case* coincide, then judging *that p is the case* enables the subject to equally judge *that he or she believes that p is the case*. Conversely, the transparency of thinking means that judgements that one has a certain belief and judgements to the truth of the respective belief-content are, from the first-person point of view, based on the same grounds. Consequently, the judgement *that one believes that p is the case* is, from the first-person point of view, interchangeable with the judgement *that p is the case*.

Yet, this makes it look as if the content articulated by the sentence '*p* is the case' were identical with the content of the sentence 'I believe that *p* is the case' and that, consequently, the expression 'I believe' were not a referring term. Its function would accordingly not consist in representing one's own state of mind, but in characterising the way in which the content of one's belief is represented. This, however, would separate the first-person present tense from the other grammatical inflections of the verb 'to believe' in that the respective functions of the inflected verb 'to believe' and the phrase articulating the content of the ascribed belief would be exactly the opposite as it is in its other forms: Whereas in the sentence 'Peter believes that it is raining' the proposition that it is raining serves to qualify the belief ascribed to Peter, the expression 'I believe' in Peter's sentence 'I believe that it is raining' would serve to qualify the content of Peter's representational state. The peculiar outcome would be that, from a first-person point of view, one could represent anybody's beliefs except one's own, and it would even seem that, from a first-person point of view, one could not even refer to oneself. Moreover, this kind of reasoning, which Moran regards as constitutive for what he designates the

'Presentational View',[86] would straightforwardly issue in the result that Moore-paradoxical assertions are nothing but formal-logical contradictions, expressed in a slightly cumbersome manner:

(7) $\vdash p \equiv \vdash B(I, p)$,

(1) $\vdash p \wedge \neg B(I, p)$ (Moore-paradoxical assertion) ,

(8) $\vdash p \wedge \neg p$ (7, 1) .

And, as Moran rightly remarks, Moore-paradoxical assertions are not contradictions, but describe two independent states of affairs which, as a matter of fact, are very likely to be simultaneously the case. Moran further argues that if the expression 'I believe' were to designate a mode of presentation and not a mode of representation, it would be prevented from being a meaningful psychological expression. This would severely violate the Generality Constraint, together with the related claims about reference and uniformity of content. On the one hand, someone's capacity to apply the concept expressed by the verb 'to believe' to oneself would not enable him or her to equally apply the concept to other persons, and *vice versa*. This, however, is the condition of the mastery of concepts formulated by the Generality Constraint (see Section 2.1.4 of this chapter). On the other hand, the sentences 'I believe that p is the case' and 'Peter believes that p is the case' would not express the same proposition and hence not refer to the same state of affairs because, as explained above, the expression 'I believe' would lack any referential function. Taking the first-person present indicative as asymmetric in this extreme manner would however mean that there is a verb, or better a class of verbs (the psychological ones) which lack a grammatical form (*cf.* PPF § 98). And this ultimately contravenes the principle that the possibility of representing particular states of affairs is not bound to the perspective from which they are represented. For the Presentational View yields the conclusion that one could not represent one's own state of mind as the very same empirical fact others can think or talk about (*cf.* Moran (1997), p. 145).

So the question is, how can asserting that one believes that p count as an assertion that p is the case *and* have the function of referring to a particular person?[87] It seems fairly obvious that in asserting 'I believe it is raining outside' I, U. S., refer to the same psychological fact as someone else does with the statement 'U. S. believes that it is raining outside'. However, Moran's considerations themselves suggest that the first-personal assertion differs from the statement 'U. S. believes that it is

---

86 *Cf.* Moran (1997), pp. 144f.; and Moran (2001), ch. 4.1.

87 *Cf.* Richard Moran (2003), "Responses to O'Brien and Shoemaker", *European Journal of Philosophy* 11/3, pp. 402–19, particularly pp. 404f.

raining outside', even if I was to utter the latter, in two respects. On the one hand, the former is based on different epistemic grounds, the weather, and not the designated person's psychological life. On the other hand, the expression 'I believe' is, for this very reason, *transparent* and allows to utter and understand the statement equally as a statement about the weather.

In order to reconcile what one may call the *logico-semantic continuity* of the expression 'I believe', that is, its conformity with the logical and semantic rules governing the application of the verb to believe in all other grammatical forms, with its *epistemic asymmetry*,[88] Moran declares the expression 'I believe' to have two functions, the usual referential one and an additional expressive one. Conse-

---

88 Both terms are Bar-On's, *cf.* Dorit Bar-On (2004), *Speaking my Mind. Expression and Self-Knowledge*, Oxford: UP, pp. 6–11; and Bar-On (2009), "First-Person Authority: Dualism, Constitutivism, and Neo-Expressivism", *Erkenntnis 71*, pp. 53–71. The contrast of epistemic asymmetry and logico-semantic continuity reflects the general problem of the meaning of *avowals*, that is, first-person present tense assertions of belief and other mental states. Avowals apparently conform with statements using other grammatical forms of the same predicates, for instance, statements about another person's state of mind, in that they can enter processes of reasoning, serve as premises in logical inferences, and in that their predicates comply with the Generality Constraint. The asymmetric properties of avowals—exemplified above with assertions of the structure 'I believe that *p* is the case'—includes their resistance towards error through misidentifying the subject of the self-ascription and the self-ascribed state, the subject's authority over their veridicality, and the fact that they are not made upon reflection on one's own state of mind. It is a matter of ongoing debate whether the continuity and asymmetry of avowals can be reconciled at all or whether either can be reduced to the other or a more basic function of the mind (typically, it is the asymmetry, which is considered reducible). Moreover, disagreement concerns questions such as which of the enumerated characteristics essentially belong to avowals, if any can be given at all, and which mental states are avowable in the strict sense at all. At any rate, conceiving the asymmetry of avowals as an epistemic one invites considering avowals as expressions of distinctive self-knowledge, as Moran, too, suggests (see below). This brings us back to the question, in which sense and on which grounds is it justifiable to consider knowing one's own mind epistemologically distinctive at all? I have treated this question elsewhere (Schmid, 2011) and will no longer pursue it here. The particular problem of immunity to error through misidentification has been framed in succession to Wittgenstein's considerations on the meaning of the first-person pronoun in the *Blue Book* (*BB*). *Cf.* Ludwig Wittgenstein (1958), *The Blue and Brown Books*, Oxford: Blackwell, pp. 66f. It was initially discussed by Shoemaker, to whom we owe the term 'immunity to error through misidentification' (Sydney Shoemaker (1968), "Self-Reference and Self-Awareness", *The Journal of Philosophy 65/19*, pp. 555–67) and taken up, among others, by Evans (1982), ch. 7; John Campbell (1999), "Immunity to Error through Misidentification and the Meaning of a Referring Term", *Philosophical Topics 26/1-2*, pp. 89–104; Peter Michael Stephen Hacker (1990d), *Wittgenstein: Meaning and Mind. An Analytical Commentary on the Philsophial Investigation, Part II: Exegesis*, Oxford: Blackwell, ch. 4; and Crispin Wright (1998b), "Self-Knowledge: The Wittgensteinian Legacy", in Wright (1998a), pp. 13–45. I will discuss the meaning of avowals together with the notion itself in Chapter 3, Section 2.2.

quently, the content of the judgement 'I believe that p is the case' simultaneously *refers* to a particular psychological state and *expresses* that the person has arrived at it by considering whether p is the case. If this has been the case, the judgement simultaneously *reports* and *avows* the person's state of mind. For this reason, it expresses the proposition *that the person believes that p is the case* and the proposition *that p is the case*. Avowing one's belief—asserting 'p is the case' or 'I believe that p is the case'—hence amounts to making a self-ascription of belief that complies with what Moran calls the *transparency condition*, i.e. that it is based on considering evidence for and against p, not on one's own state of mind.[89] The reverse holds, too: The assertion that the proposition 'p is the case' is true, or more simply, the assertion *that p is the case* expresses the person's judgement *that he or she believes that p is the case* insofar as it expresses his or her judgement as to the truth of p. In contrast to what the Presentational View suggests, Moran interprets the similarity of the assertions *that p is the case* and *that I believe that p the case* not as a relation of identity, but of mutual implication:

(9a) $\vdash p \rightarrow \vdash p \wedge B(I, p)$ et

(9b) $\vdash B(I, p) \rightarrow \vdash B(I, p) \wedge p$ (Transparency Claim) .[90]

Moran suggests that avowals be taken as constituting a subclass of ordinary ascriptions of psychological predicates that additionally comply with the transparency condition. Both types of avowals, *that p is the case* and *that I believe that p is the case*, accordingly have a double function: They convey information about the external world (*that p is the case*) *and simultaneously* about the state of mind of the person issuing them, *that he or she believes that p is the case*.

However, understanding the expression 'I believe' both as a transparent and referring term immediately raises a puzzle: In virtue of the referential function of 'I believe', an avowal of belief, i.e. an assertion of the kind 'I believe that p', is primarily a claim about a psychological fact, that a particular person's state

---

89 *Cf.* Moran (2001), ch. 3.3. Moran here explicitly draws on Anscombe's distinction between predicting and expressing one's intention that one will φ at a later time. *Cf.* Anscombe (2000), pp. 55 and 92. Moran applies this distinction to the case of belief: Avowing one's belief expresses both, a description of a psychological state of the person's, and his or her awareness of the commitments involved in the concept of belief.

90 It follows that asserting (or believing, respectively) *that p is the case* is logically equivalent to asserting (or believing) *that I believe that p the case* if the conditions of transparency are met (Moran's view of Moore's 'normal circumstances'). Other than the 'Presentational View' suggests, they are not identical. As will become clear later, Moran deems the equivalence in question a normative requirement to the effect that there are cases in which it breaks down. See Section 3.6.3 of this chapter.

of mind is constituted such that it contains the belief that p. Yet, in virtue of the transparency of 'I believe', it is based on reasons that speak for and against the truth of p (the belief-content), not about considerations on the person and his or her beliefs and, for this reason, implicitly expresses an assertion *that p is the case*. The puzzle resulting from transparency consists in it being possible to "answer a question about the beliefs of a particular person [...] not by considering the evidence about that person, but by considering the evidence about some wholly distinct matter of fact. [...] Without a reply to this challenge, I don't have any right to answer the question that asks what my belief is [with regard to the question whether it will rain] by reflection on the reasons in favor of an answer concerning the state of the weather" (Moran (2003), p. 405).

That is, Moran interprets Moore's Principle—that, under certain circumstances, asserting that p implies asserting that one believes that p—as an outcome of the way, in which one arrives at the judgements *that p is the case*, and *that one believes that p is the case*, respectively. He amends it in the reverse direction, asserting that one believes that p implies that one also asserts that p. Both implications hold if the respective judgements are made on identical epistemic grounds, and they hold in virtue of the transparency of forming beliefs by rational deliberation. In other words, Moran, like Shoemaker, conceives of Moore's Principle as a peculiarity of belief, not of assertion. Its validity in the case of assertions is piggybacking on an analogous principle concerning the connection of believing that p, and believing *that one believes that p*, which must, according to Moran, equally be conceived as complying with the transparency condition.

1.3.6.2 The Transparency of Belief

Moran's suggestion becomes more intelligible upon reconsidering his conception of belief. The notion of belief undergoes substantial revision on Moran's account in that he emphasises the first-personal dimension of believing. This amounts to a radical break with Shoemaker's understanding of beliefs as functional states that are 'at work' within a person's mind, disposing him or her to think and act in ways consistent with his or her belief contents. It further spells out the intentionality of belief in stronger terms than Searle's conception of belief as an intentional *state* with conditions of satisfaction and direction of fit. On Moran's account, beliefs are not simply mental states, not even directed mental states, which a subject entertains and whose veridicality is a matter of fact. A belief *that p is the case* is regarded as a subject's *commitment* to the truth of a proposition. From the first-personal perspective, it is *not* just a matter of fact whether one's beliefs are veridical. The relation one has to one's own beliefs is more appropriately characterised by the subject's responsibility for ensuring that what one believes corresponds with the facts, and relatedly, for maintaining consistency among one's belief contents. For this reason, a person must not treat the questions whether p is the case and whether he or she believes that p is the case separately.

Moran conceives of the belief *that p is the case* as the believer's commitment to the truth of the proposition p, which is (logically) preceded by considering whether p is the case and making a judgement as to its truth. The subject takes up a position towards one aspect of the world, expressed in the propositional content of the belief. The content of one's beliefs present the conclusion of a process of reasoning that aims at answering the question whether, or not, p is the case. Accordingly, the belief *that p is the case* just is the person's assent to the proposition *that p is the case*, which can be represented as the conclusion of a practical syllogism. The first-personal standpoint towards the mental is thus characterised as a relation of authorship. Being the author of one's own mind is supposed to condition the double function of avowals, reference to and expression of one's state of mind. The transparency of avowals is so derived from the analogous property of beliefs, that is from their immediate answerability to the person's deliberation.

Moran's understanding of the mind does not simply deliver a modified functionalist view from a different perspective, as Shoemaker (2003) seems to believe. In contrast, it focuses on a dimension of subjectivity that is essentially excluded from the functionalist viewpoint. In virtue of being answerable to the subject's deliberation about the states of affairs represented in their content, the mental states constituting the first-person perspective comply with the *transparency condition*, that a subject knows that he or she has these states by considering their content only. The transparency condition both grants and requires that taking a position towards a particular issue delivers both the grounds for believing the issue in question and the grounds for ascribing that belief to oneself. It follows from the transparency condition that, from a first-personal point of view, making a judgement *that p is the case* about the external world, expresses an implicit judgement *that I believe that p is the case*, ascribing a mental state to oneself. That is, both statements—that p and *that I believe that p*—equally represent one's state of mind. Moran concludes that

> [A] judgment of one's own belief that is arrived at in a way that respects the Transparency Condition can nonetheless be seen as retaining its reference to a particular person and her belief (2003, p. 410)

because

> [I]n both the question [what do I believe?] and the answer [I believe that p], the ostensible reference to oneself is genuine [...] Hence, when successful, answering such a question can

count as arriving at knowledge about oneself, knowledge about the belief of a particular person, since that is what the question is about. (*ibid.*, p. 414)

In this way, Moran maintains that avowals articulate self-knowledge in a robust sense of knowledge, as factual knowledge that one endorses a particular state of mind and simultaneously fulfil the transparency condition. When someone has made up his mind about a certain issue in accordance with the transparency condition, and articulates his conclusion in an affirmative statement *that p is the case*, "[w]hat he has gained, and what his statement expresses, is straightforward knowledge about a particular person, knowledge that can be told and thus transferred to another person" (Moran (2001), pp. 105f.).

The aim of Moran's argument from transparency is to reveal self-knowledge as a constitutive feature of having beliefs and intentions, of being a rational agent, without relying on some kind of mental mechanism, whose proper functioning is beyond the agent's control. In Moran's words, the term transparency designates the quality of relating to the mind from a first-person point of view to the effect that, from a first-person point of view, the mind is nothing but the subject's own perspective from which the very subject relates to the world by means of mental activity. It is the subject who constitutes him- or herself in that he or she takes a stance towards the world, and constantly evaluates, revises and re-creates his or her own perspective. Only if mental states comply with the transparency condition, they are, in contrast to non-intentional states, 'up to the agent', in the sense that they are "answerable to [the agent's] sense of reasons and justification" (Moran (2003), p. 406). Conforming to the transparency condition is a necessary condition for a subject's authority to answer a question about his or her state of mind by pointing to facts beyond it, and thereby, for his or her self-conception as a rational agent.

The notion of transparency demarcates the categorical difference between a person's relation to his or her own beliefs, and the relation to other people's beliefs. Another person's beliefs stand on a par with whatever other representational objects there might be. They are accessed by representing them as an outcome of observing the other and inferring his or her beliefs from his or her behaviour. If one is concerned with deliberating whether p is true, another person's beliefs count among the evidence one takes into consideration in developing one's position towards p. In contrast, one's own beliefs just are what delineates one's position towards p. Inasmuch as one holds a belief concerning p, one has made up one's mind and the question whether p is true is decided, raising it additionally thus is redundant. With regard to another one's beliefs, it is possible to have a range of different attitudes, for instance, one may or may not trust or agree with them or take them into account in making up one's mind about what is the case. In one's own case, "there is no distance between them and how the facts present themselves to me, and hence no going from one to the other" (Moran (1997), p. 147).

In other words, Moran's account has the effect that one's belief that p and one's self-knowledge thereof, considered from a first-person point of view, have to be considered as based on the very same reasons, although from a third-person perspective, one is concerned with *two* separate states of that person, the person's belief *that p is the case* and the person's self-belief *that I believe that p*. Conversely, it is this feature that categorically distinguishes the first-personal, or subjective, from the third-personal, or empirical, perspective on the mind. So the epistemic authority a subject bears in virtue of transparency gives rise to a *prima facie* implausible conception. The main difficulty runs parallel to the puzzle of transparency regarding the meaning of avowals. The states of affairs *that p is the case* and *that I believe that p is the case* must be distinguishable even from the first-personal point of view, and hence, both must be independently representable—after all, this was Moran's objection to the Presentational View. If these were, from the first-personal perspective, *not* different matters of fact, a person could not regard his or her own beliefs as fallible in virtue of being about an belief-independent world.

Moran treats the transparency of a person's judgement *that he or she believes that p is the case* to the judgement *that p is the case* not as a functional property, but as a normative requirement on believing *that p is the case*. According to Moran, the belief that p is the case is tantamount to the commitment to the truth of p. Hence, by judging *that one believes that p is the case* one is required to recognise that one is committed to the truth of p, i.e. that one is required to assent to the question whether p is the case. This presupposes that one has arrived at the judgement *that one believes that p is the case* in a transparent fashion, by considering matters regarding p, not towards one's state of mind. The judgement concerning one's own belief is transparent only if the belief thereby expressed is answerable to reasons that speak for and against the truth of p. Only in this case the subject has the *authority*, and also the responsibility, to treat the questions whether p is the case and whether he or she believes that p the case, and the respective answers, alike. That is, if and only if a judgement *that one believes that p is the case* obeys the transparency condition, the subject has authoritative first-personal knowledge of his or her belief as well as the authority concerning the entitlement to treat questions concerning a certain state of affairs and questions concerning one's corresponding belief as the same. In general, the extent to which a person enjoys authoritative self-knowledge is determined by the extent to which his or her mental states are answerable to the person's deliberation on their respective content.

Yet, one can fail to meet with this requirement. On Moran's account, a judgement *that I believe that p* is the case represents the state of affairs *that a particular subject believes that p is the case*, which is independent of the state of affairs constituting the content of the respective belief. Hence, it is possible to consider one without considering the other, in particular, to consider the question whether one believes that p in the same way as one would consider the question whether another person believes that p, for instance, by way of observing one's behaviour, connecting it with relevant past actions and drawing inferences from that. If one ends one's self-investigation by concluding *that I believe that* p, this judgement is not made by considering the question whether p is the case. The self-ascription of the belief *that p is the case* is made independently of reasons one might have to judge that p is true and hence not answerable to the person's potential deliberation concerning p. Of course, such a self-ascription can be true, it is a judgement that a certain contingent fact obtains. If it is, it presents an expression of factual knowledge about one's state of mind. But it does not express the person's authoritative self-knowledge, the kind of knowledge he or she would enjoy only if her judgement was made in accordance with the transparency condition.

1.3.6.3 Moore's Paradox as a Failure of Transparency

Treating transparency and authoritative self-knowledge as normative requirements, Moran concedes the possibility of lacking one or the other, for instance in cases of self-deception and weakness of the will, but also, if one fails to draw the right conclusions from one's evidence and later does not adjust the resulting (false) beliefs. Granting the possibility of failure with respect to transparency is crucial to accommodate the phenomenon of self-deception, which he describes as the situation in which a person has false beliefs about his or her own state of mind, such that he or she is, intentionally or unintentionally, unaware of what he or she really believes, feels, desires, or intends. In this case, one cannot arrive at judgements concerning one's own state of mind by way of considering evidence concerning their representational content.

One fails to meet the requirements imposed by the transparency condition if, for instance, one can explain one's behaviour best as expressing the belief that p, whereas one's conscious considerations of the question whether p always end up with the conclusion that p is false. Likewise, it is manifest in situations in which one's self-image clashes with the impressions others have of oneself, in which one does not recognise one's real motivation for acting in certain ways, in which one acts against what one takes to be one's intentions, or in which one does not implement what one intends to do. For once, there seems to be a gap between the subject and his or her intention or belief. That there is a gap where there ought not to be, apparently indicates that the person is not the subject of his or her respective intentions or beliefs in the strongly authoritative sense described in the last section, that, as it were, the first-personal route to come to know them is blocked.

Moran explains the appearance of this gap by distinguishing two ways in which one can position oneself to one's own mind. From the transcendental, or deliberative stance, one conceives oneself as the author of one's own mind. One does not distinguish between questions about one's psychological states and questions concerned with what they are about. This stance is the truly first-person stance, manifesting the conception of oneself 'as transcendency'. It contrasts with the empirical, or observational stance, from which one regards oneself with the eyes of another, as it were, as a psychological being among many others (a 'facticity', in the Sartrean language that Moran employs here).[91] The empirical stance lacks the particular normative dimension present on the transcendental stance, in particular, it lacks the commitments and rational responsibilities connected with authoritative self-knowledge. Considering questions about one's own psychology from the empirical stance does not proceed by deliberating over those reasons that speak for and against facts external to one's mind, but by reflecting on one's own state of mind as if it belonged to another person. One's own mind here figures as the object of one's investigation. In this way, the empirical stance amounts to a self-alienated position, a standpoint from which one is utterly unclear about what one really thinks, wants and feels.

To illustrate situations like these, Moran gives examples such as the akratic gambler (who takes it to be his firm intention to stop gambling, but frequently finds himself at the gaming tables)[92] and the self-deceived analysand who does not (want to) recognise her deep conviction that her brother has, in early childhood, betrayed her. The crucial point here is that both the gambler and the self-deceived analysand are, from the transcendental stance, unaware of what they really believe and intend, respectively. That is, Moran deems it possible that, under certain circumstances, one lacks knowledge of the beliefs and intentions one would form if one was to consider the matter they are concerned with. One fails to comply with the transparency condition *even though* the states in question belong to the paradigmatic class of states delivered by pure rational deliberation, and must have been brought about in this manner.

Once the empirical standpoint is taken, however, it is quite difficult to return to one's original, transparent self-conception. For whatever conclusions one might arrive at when considering the question what one is up to, from an observational point of view, seeing these conclusions and endorsing them are two quite different

---

91 *Cf.* Moran (2001), ch. 3.2; and Jean-Paul Sartre (1970), *Das Sein und das Nichts. Versuch einer phänomenologischen Ontologie*, German transl. Julius Streller, Hamburg: Rowohlt pp. 91–121.
92 Moran borrows this example from Sartre together with the emphatic distinction of a first-personal self-conception as one of transcendency and a third-personal self-conception as one of facticity. *Cf.* Moran (2001), chs. 3.2 and 3.4, drawing on Sartre (1970), pp. 75f.

matters. It is of course possible, and in cases most useful too, to arrive at a new interpretation of some of one's own behaviour, as well as it might be, in cases, necessary to attempt to 'influence one's mind from the outside', as it were. An *akratic* gambler, knowing that he will never stop gambling just because he has formed the (hypothetical) intention not to return to the casino, might, for instance, tell his friend to occupy him all evening. Odysseus let himself be bound to the mast in order to save himself from temptation. However, one could not succeed in changing one's mind if these measures were not, in the end, initiated from the transcendental stance and if their outcome was not endorsed by the subject, that is, if one was not ready to accept their outcome as one's own work.[93]

That it is not sufficient to deliberate about one's mind in order to find out what one really thinks, reflects "the priority of what I've been calling the transcendental over the empirical point of view" (Moran (1997), p. 158). The priority is twofold. On the one hand, it is only by way of deliberately making up one's mind that one's mental life comes into existence at first place. Only subsequently, can one consider it empirically. Having already committed oneself to the world being thus and so is the *conditio sine qua non* for having an object for self-reflection from the theoretical stance. But "were one not a rational agent, there would be no psychological life to have empirical views about at first place" (Moran (1997), p. 151). On the other hand, coming to know one's mind by means of theoretical self-investigation is initiated and carried out from the deliberative point of view. And whether the conclusions of one's attempts to get clarity about one's mind by coming up with an observationally generated explanation are sound, still depends on whether one can endorse them through one's transcendental stance, whether, that is, one can reproduce them by considering the issue they are about on one's own.

Distinguishing the deliberative from the empirical stance lays the basis for Moran's explanation of Moore's Paradox. Together with the Transparency Claim, the distinction is supposed to provide for situations of self-deception, in which first- and third-personal standpoint can come apart. In such situations one can truly assert a Moore-paradoxical sentence. In that case, however, one's assertion will be absurd because it would, when taken seriously, undermine the person's status as an author of his or her mental states, which to maintain is a central point of Moran's view. Moran illustrates this with an example from a psychoanalytic setting (1997, p. 152). It pictures a situation, in which a person holds the belief that *p* (that her

---

93 For a more detailed discussion of the various ways of making up one's mind and changing it based on Moran's distinction of two stances to oneself, see Pamela Hieronymi (2009), "Two Kinds of Mental Agency", in O'Brien, Soteriou (2009), pp. 138–62; and Moran (2001), ch. 4.3

brother betrayed her), and (theoretically) acknowledges that she does, without arriving at p in deliberation. Before the analysand has accepted that she believes that her brother betrayed her, she acts in accordance with the belief that p whilst insisting, in reflection or discussion of the issue, on the truth of *non-p*, or whilst in denial that her actual doings are better describable as based on her belief that p, rather than on her avowed belief that *non-p*. Confronted with the proposition that she might believe that her brother betrayed her, the role of this belief is primarily restricted to an exclusively explanatory one, she might consider it as a suggestion (of her psychoanalyst's, say) to reconsider her behaviour in this light. However, as long as she does not integrate it into her first-personal stance, she is caught in the unsettling situation that she has, from the deliberative point of view, every reason to avow her belief that *non-p*, whereas, from her empirical point of view to herself, everything speaks in favour of her believing the truth of the contrary, that p. Moran lets his analysand come to believe as an effect of her psychoanalytical treatment that she indeed believes that she was betrayed by her brother. But unless this belief does become manifest in her experience of certain situations, she has not actually endorsed her self-belief. Theorising about oneself is not the same as actually endorsing what one has theoretically concluded—and endorsing one's beliefs about a certain issue makes theorising about what one believes about the matter obsolete.

Moran describes the analysand's situation as a situation of inner conflict consisting in a person's holding two beliefs about herself with contradicting content. The conflict is apparently due to the analysand's having arrived at her respective self-beliefs by means of different methods to find out what she really believes about p. From the *transcendental* standpoint, she has considered the question whether her brother did betray her (p), and arrives at the conclusion that he didn't (*non-p*). Because this procedure meets the transparency condition she has thereby prepared the grounds for forming the belief *that she believes that non-p*. From her *empirical* point of view, she might have thought about her doings and feelings, events like arguments with her brother or her parents, her mistrusting relationships with other people. All things considered, she has concluded that it is true that she believes that her brother betrayed her, *that she believes that p*. This is to say, she believes two contradicting propositions to be true about her own state of mind, that she does and does not believe that her brother betrayed her.

The analysand's deliberative stance is so constituted that it endorses the belief *that her brother didn't betray her, that non-p is the case*, and the belief *that she nevertheless believes that he betrayed her, that she believes that p is the case*. If she were now to articulate her attitudes towards her brother, she might say 'I believe he betrayed me, but of course, he actually didn't' (or something to this effect) and thereby *she intends to make a true statement*. The structure of her sentence is then of the Moore-paradoxical kind:

(10) $\vdash \neg p \wedge B(I, p)$ (Moore-paradoxical sentence)[94]

The assertion sign here indicates that the following Moore-paradoxical sentence articulates the analysand's answer to the question what her beliefs are about p, from the deliberative point of view. That is, when making a Moore-paradoxical assertion she has committed herself to its truth. It might well be that the sentence is true from her empirical perspective of herself—that p is not the case, and that she believes that p is the case—and yet, Moore's Paradox arises from its assertion.

Moran describes Moore's Paradox as a clash between the possibility of conceiving of the situation articulated in a Moore-paradoxical sentence from the empirical standpoint one takes to oneself and one's self-conception as a rational agent (1997, p. 151). Because a Moore-paradoxical sentence presents, in cases of self-deception or other kinds of inner conflict, a commitment of the author, such a clash is unavoidable from his or her point of view as a rational subject (i.e. the transcendental stance). One cannot 'opt out' of one's self-conception as a rational agent and switch to a detached theoretical mode of self-contemplation, because the deliberation that proceeds from the observational stance is, too, initiated from the transcendental standpoint. As said above, this feature constitutes the general priority of the transcendental over the empirical stance.

How does the priority of the transcendental stance relate to the case of stating or believing a Moore-paradoxical sentence to be true? Analysing the sentence in Moran's terms, it presents a conjunction of an avowal of belief and a report about a belief. The conjunction itself is avowed. Its author thereby commits him- or herself to its truth, and knows that this is the case. The author is thereby, knowingly, committed to the truth of the avowal as well as to the truth of the report, but not necessarily to the truth of the content of the reported belief. That is, the author holds the following conjunction true and thereby contradicts him- or herself (underlined):

(10) $\vdash q \wedge B(I, \neg q)$ (Moore-paradoxical sentence) ,
(9a) $\vdash p \rightarrow \vdash p \wedge B(I, p)$ (Transparency Claim) ,
(11) $\vdash q \wedge \underline{B(I, q)} \wedge B(I, \neg q) \wedge B(I, B(I, \neg q))$ (10, 9a) .

Since the Transparency Claim (9) applies only if the transparency condition is met, i.e. only to statements made within the transcendental stance, the transition from (10) to (11) is only valid if the statement of a Moore-paradoxical sentence (10)

---

94 (10) does not translate into (1), but is identical with ($1''$).

presents an avowal. Here, the author self-ascribes two beliefs with contradicting contents. Given the double function of avowals on Moran's account, one has to distinguish between two readings of a Moore-paradoxical sentence, which are simultaneously present in its assertion or belief.

From Moran's elaborations as to how the meaning of expressions, reports and avowals of psychological 'facts' is constituted, and how these types of statements interrelate, it is clear that Moran is convinced that the semantic core of avowals and reports does not differ. Both types of statements are taken to first and foremost describe a state of affairs, and therefore to be truth-apt depending on whether they truly or falsely represent what is the case. Crucially, the meaning of the psychological predicate involved is uniform, that is, reports and avowals refer to the *very same* facts. With stating a Moore-paradoxical sentence, one does not describe one kind of belief with the first conjunct, and another one with the second, although the subject has come to know them by different epistemic methods.[95]

From a descriptive standpoint, there is nothing absurd about asserting a Moore-paradoxical sentence. Because from a descriptive standpoint the questions whether *p* or *not-p* and whether I believe that *p* or I don't believe that *p* are independent, reporting a Moore-paradoxical sentence will be tantamount to asserting two independent states of affairs. From the deliberative standpoint, however, the speaker of a Moore-paradoxical assertion judges that he or she is at once committed to the truth of *p* and the truth of *non-p*. *Avowing* a Moore-paradoxical sentence equals asserting a contradiction and thereby ascribing a false belief to oneself. The author of a Moore-paradoxical avowal thus confesses his or her own irrationality within his or her self-conception as a rational subject. So he or she compromises the condition that, if any, enables him or her to hold that very sentence true. Avowing a Moore-paradoxical sentence is absurd in that involves an unwitting declaration of bankruptcy of the author's self-conception as a rational being, and thus a denial of the precondition for him or her to be a mental agent in the first place.

From the author's empirical point of view, in contrast, the conjuncts involved in (10) designate two independent facts, a fact about the weather, say, or the author's brother, and a fact about the author's state of mind. Nothing speaks, from the theoretical point of view, against their co-occurrence. Sentence (10) alone does not represent any inner conflict on the part of its author, because it does not bear a normative dimension that would be the case if the utterance is made from the transcendental stance. So it seems to be fine to report a situation in which both,

---

95 Moran rejects this possibility in discussing a suggestion from Georges Rey. *Cf.* Moran (1997), pp. 152f.; Moran (2001), pp. 85ff.; and Georges Rey (1989), "Towards a Computational Account of *Akrasia* and Self-Deception", in Amelie Oksenberg Rorty, Brian McLaughlin (eds.), *Perspectives on Self-Deception*, Berkeley: University of California Press, pp. 264–96.

'*p*' and 'I don't believe that *p*', are true by means of a Moore-paradoxical sentence, as long as one does so from a detached, an observer's point of view of oneself. All there is to wonder, in this case, is how it comes about that a person is alienated from his or her *true* self to an extent that he or she does not notice the absurdity that comes with asserting a Moore-paradoxical sentence.

In summary, Moran presents Moore's Paradox as a paradox of irrationality, consisting in a clash between the results of finding out what one believes in two different manners. *Avowing* a Moore-paradoxical sentence is rendered a commitment to one's own rational deficiency delivered by a rational subject. *Reporting* a Moore-paradoxical sentence enacts this conflict in that the author is apparently unaware of the compromising implications for his or her rationality manifest in that statement. Yet, the statement itself describes a perfectly conceivable situation.

I have stated at the outside of the chapter that Moore's Paradox has several aspects: Assertions of sentences with the structure '*p* is the case, but I don't believe that *p* is the case' sound absurd *although* they can be true statements of facts. One reason why it arises is that asserting *that p is the case* is similar to asserting, in the fist person present indicative, *that one believes that p is the case*. On Moran's view, the similarity in question derives from Moore's Principle, which he grounds in the way beliefs are constituted and endorsed from a subject's deliberative perspective on particular aspects of the world. That is, insofar as one actively takes a stance towards a certain issue, one arrives, by deliberating whether *p*, at both, the conclusion *that p is the case*, and the conclusion *that one believes that p is the case*. From the transcendental stance, replying 'I believe that *p* is the case' to the question 'What do you believe about *p*?' is equivalent to the reply '*p* is the case'. The transparency condition has the effect that asserting or believing a sentence of the Moore-paradoxical type from the authoritative first-person point of view amounts to asserting or believing that one is committed to the truth of a formal-logical contradiction, '*p* is the case, but *p* is not the case'. And thus confessing that one's beliefs are in rational disorder, this seems to severely violate one's conception of oneself as a rational agent. In contrast, judging a Moore-paradoxical sentence from the empirical point, according to Moran, seems to be perfectly fine. Reporting a Moore-paradoxical sentence, that is, using the sentence to describe what is the case, does not involve the normative dimension present in avowing the same sentence.

To put Moran's account of Moore's Paradox in a nutshell, assenting to a Moore-paradoxical sentence is not absurd at all, if this is done from an empirical standpoint. If, in contrast, a Moore-paradoxical sentence is judged true from a transcendental standpoint it is tantamount to judging a contradiction true and therefore ascribing a false belief to oneself. Unsurprisingly, given that Moran retains the validity of Moore's Principle, his account, too, interprets Moore's Paradox as originating from an indirect assertion of a contradiction. The absurdity of Moore-paradoxical assertions reflects the inconsistency of the states of affairs they represent from the standpoint from which they are made. Yet, asserting a Moore-paradoxical sentence is not tantamount to asserting a contradiction. It is, therefore, not, at least not only, a matter of the content which a Moore-paradoxical assertion expresses, but, first and foremost a matter of asserting it. Because Moran takes Moore's Paradox to be not a problem of the grammar of a particular kind of sentences, but a problem of the ontology of a certain mental phenomenon, he is, as Shoemaker is, blind to the aspects of Moore's Paradox concerning the logic of assertion.

1.3.6.4 The Opacity of Transparency: Objections

Moran's account of the meaning of the assertoric use of 'I believe' concludes, *via* a metaphysical inquiry into the nature and epistemology of belief, that Moore's Paradox is the assertion of a contradiction, which is, as I have repeatedly said, symptomatic of an underlying problem with his account of believing as well as of his explanation of the meaning of the verb 'to believe'. Before discussing Moran's own approach to Moore's Paradox, I will briefly comment on Moran's interpretation of some passages from Wittgenstein's considerations of Moore's Paradox. I will then specifically scrutinise Moran's solution to Moore's Paradox, in tandem, where appropriate, with Shoemaker's account.

Throughout his account of belief, self-knowledge and Moore's Paradox, Moran refers to Wittgenstein's remarks on Moore's Paradox and the meaning of first-person present tense expressions of one's state of mind. However, Moran's enterprise to bring together Wittgenstein and the "last great Cartesian [i.e. Sartre, us.]" (Moran (1997), p. 141) in order to deliver a robust understanding of first-personal knowledge not only seems hazardous, it actually is. Most of Wittgenstein's arguments in his later writings on the philosophy of psychology[96] involve an argumentative strand against what one may call a Cartesian view of the mind. This is hardly reconcilable with the Cartesian thesis of self-knowledge as Moran advocates it in accordance with Shoemaker's characterisation thereof (Shoemaker (1988), pp. 25ff.). In my next

---

96 These are published in *Philosophical Investigations*; *Remarks on the Philosophy of Psychology* (both Volumes); *Last Writings on the Philosophy of Psychology. Preliminary Studies for Part II of Philosophical Investigations. Letzte Schriften über die Philosophie der Psychologie. Vorstudien zum zweiten Teil der Philosophischen Untersuchungen* (*LWPP*), 2 Volumes, Georg Henrik von Wright, Heikki Nyman (eds.), Oxford: Blackwell 1982; and *Zettel* (*Z*), ed. by G. E. M. Anscombe, Georg Henrik von Wright, Oxford: Blackwell 1967. They are prepared in the lectures published as the *Blue Book* and the *Brown Book* (*BrB*).

chapter, I will develop an argument against the views I presented in the foregoing, including Moran's, which is partly based on the same material Moran refers to, yet offers an alternative interpretation. Because my aim will be argumentative, not exegetic, I will not go into detail on differences in Moran's and my respective interpretations. Instead, I will highlight now what I take to be misguided about Moran's reading.

Prima facie, appealing to the notion of self-knowledge for the purpose of locating the origins of Moore's Paradox may seem to accommodate several points that appear frequently in Wittgenstein's considerations on Moore's Paradox.[97] In particular, Moran seems to be able to explain that one cannot meaningfully claim, assert or affirm 'I believe wrongly'.[98] Secondly, he gives a comprehensive accounts of the reasons why the statements 'p' and 'I believe that p' equally count as expressions of the speaker's belief that p (*RPP I* §§ 462–500, especially 469–77 and *PPF* § 102); and that lastly one's attitude towards one's own verbal expressions of belief is "wholly different" from that of others (*RPP I* §§ 704–19 and *PPF* § 103). According to Moran, it would be meaningless to assert 'I wrongly believe that p', the short form of Moore's Paradox, because this statement would undermine the speaker's self-conception as a rational agent. Transparency moreover seems to offer a useful specification of Wittgenstein's claim that the absurdity of the assertion 'p, but I don't believe it' is rooted in the attitude towards one's own expressions of belief. Wittgenstein's characterisation suggests that although one does not 'see and hear' (*PPF* § 99) one's own words expressing what one believes, one is familiar their content.

Moran spells out Wittgenstein's suggestion as identifying a conceptual link obtaining between one's beliefs and corresponding self-beliefs. It follows that one does not learn or infer the contents of one's own beliefs from articulating them in language, because one already immediately knows one's beliefs (or the contents of one's beliefs) in virtue of having them. Whereas my utterance 'I believe that it will be raining' informs others about my state of mind and thus counts as evidence,

---

97 These remarks are, partly overlapping, published in *Remarks on the Philosophy of Psychology* I and *PPF*, x.

98 Moran here refers to the following remark: "If there were a verb meaning 'to believe falsely', it would not have a meaningful first-person present indicative." (*PPF* 92, translation Hacker/Schulte, original: "Gäbe es ein Verbum mit der Bedeutung 'fälschlich glauben', so hätte das keine sinnvolle erste Person im Indikativ des Präsens." (from *MS* 137, 91b) Note that Wittgenstein's remark does, in contrast to Moran's interpretation, *not* aim at explicating the conditions involved in having a self-conception as a mental subject, but at explicating the grammar of psychological predicates as part of his considerations of Moore's Paradox. The difference is crucial: Wittgenstein intends this remark to apply to the conditions of using the concept of belief, whereas Moran interprets it as a remark concerning the conditions of subjectivity.

for others, that I also entertain related mental states (e.g. the intention to take an umbrella with me), I am in no need of learning what I have in mind because I am already acquainted with it by judging it to be true. 'Self-ascribing' a state of mind by means of an avowal is not a matter of guesswork, they are apparently presented by the person with a degree of certainty as knowledge would be. So the reasons in favour of interpreting avowals as articulations of self-knowledge appear overwhelming. If avowals do not present knowledge of one's beliefs, why not and what else?

One should not, however, read Wittgenstein as claiming that an assertion 'I believe that p' or simply 'p' entails a self-ascription of belief. It presents an expression of belief, not an articulation of knowledge of the contents of one's own beliefs. In this respect, it resembles other behavioural expressions: 'I believe it will rain soon' is similarly expressed by the utterance as by bringing the laundry into the house or taking an umbrella or raincoat or not watering the lawn. According to Wittgenstein, an assertion such as 'I believe that p' is as much an articulation of knowledge about a particular person, as moaning or groaning is—not at all. On the contrary, the reasons just cited in favour of considering avowals articulations of knowledge speak, on a closer look, exactly against doing so. For normally, the word 'knowledge' is used precisely when what is known is, in principle, accessible, comprehensible and verifiable by others such that it can be subject to doubt, discussion, mutual persuasion, and changing one's mind; and the content of avowals normally lacks all of these characteristics.[99] The objects of knowledge are in principle objective or public—whereas 'self-knowledge' along the lines of Moran is intrinsically subjective or private.[100] Against Moran's interpretation, Wittgenstein regards expressing one's state of mind by means of psychological concepts, in this respect, on a par with expressing one's state of mind by means of gestures or facial expressions.[101]

---

99 *Cf. PI* §§ 246–7, 404–14; *PPF* §§ 307–15. There are statements sharing the basic features of avowals (i.e. groundlessness, certainty, authority) whose subject-matter does not concern one's own psychological constitution. Sentences like 'I have two hands, 'Cats don't grow on trees', 'No one has ever been on Mars', and other truisms are equally beyond doubt. Like avowals they lack the distinct features of knowledge, and one should, following Wittgenstein, not treat them as such. *Cf.* Ludwig Wittgenstein, *On Certainty* (*OC*), ed. by G. E. M. Anscombe, Georg Henrik von Wright, New York: Harper & Collins 1969, especially the opening §§ 1–65. In Chapter 3, I will propose to understand statements concerning one's current state of mind similarly as expressions or manifestations of one's own perspective.

100 This objection analogously affects the notion 'practical knowledge' used for 'knowledge of one's intentions' in succession to Anscombe.

101 *Cf. BB*, p. 67, *PI* § 244, *RPP* I § 472, *PPF*, ix. I will clarify this point in Chapter 3.

Finally, if having beliefs itself implies that their subject has the corresponding self-knowledge it is evident that articulations of what one believes will simultaneously be implicit expressions of one's knowledge that one believes the respective fact. Notably, this conclusion is not conditioned on whether an expression of belief occurs in thought or speech, that is, it holds independently of the presence of a another person who might draw the inference to the higher-order belief. Thus, considering self-knowledge as an intrinsic feature of having beliefs avoids leaving the grammar of expressions of one's belief-contents to the contingency of social conventions. Surmising that it is a socially constituted rule governing the logic and semantics of expressions of belief, such as an appeal to a Searlean constitutive rule that might run 'an utterance that p counts as expression of belief that p in an assertoric context', becomes redundant. More importantly, if the link between beliefs and corresponding higher-order beliefs is considered a conceptual link, it follows that expressions of belief, both, the phrase 'I believe that p' and the simple 'p', *always* convey that the subject believes that he or she believes that p. Establishing a conceptual link between a particular belief and the relevant higher-order belief entails that whatever happens on the level of first-order beliefs induces corresponding changes on the level of second-order beliefs.

Having a closer look at Moran's explanation of Moore's Paradox, it emerges that neither the structure of a Moore-paradoxical sentence, nor the statement of it in the first-person present indicative *per se* raises Moore's Paradox. Moran maintains the claims that the meaning of sentences is to refer to states of affairs by means of articulating propositional content, and that their truth solely depends on whether the sentences succeed in accurately describing the fact they are supposed to describe. Now, the state of affairs expressed in a Moore-paradoxical assertion certainly is empirically and logically conceivable, and the statement that this fact obtains here and now can be a true report of what is the case. A problem arises only if a Moore-paradoxical sentence is avowed, that is, asserted or believed under the conditions of the transcendental stance. In this case, a Moore-paradoxical sentence amounts to describing oneself as holding contradictory propositions true. Moran characterises this as a situation of inner conflict. So Moore's Paradox seems primarily not to consist in the contrast between the absurdity of Moore-paradoxical assertions and their possible truth, but in that the assertion is intended to make a true statement from a standpoint from which the fact it expresses ought not to be true, namely that one holds a false belief. According to Moran, the incoherence of a Moore-paradoxical assertion derives from the state of affairs it represents in connection with the constitution of the perspective from which it is represented.

It is questionable, though, whether Moran's proposal is coherent by his own standards. In his own words, a person cannot 'opt out' of the transcendental stance, it remains dominant even if the person is maximally alienated from some part of his or her mind. Why, then, should it be possible to describe one's own mental constitution by means of a Moore-paradoxical sentence from the empirical stance *without* thereby bringing in the paradox?

This question hints at a problem entrenched in the assumptions of Moran's account of the meaning the verb 'to believe'. Moran grants the possibility of making a statement of a sentence with Moore-paradoxical structure in the first-person present indicative without inducing the paradox, as long as this statement is made from the empirical stance.[102] The possibility derives from Moran's conception of the meaning of assertions containing the expression 'I believe'. This is supposed to be primarily and always descriptive. It can be used in the reportive sense only, if the speaker is alienated from the belief he or she thereby refers to. This is to say that Moran considers it possible to assent to the proposition *that one believes that p without* thereby committing oneself to the truth of the respective belief-content that *p*.

However, in assenting to a proposition, to be clear, in judging, asserting or believing a proposition, one judges, asserts or believes that the proposition is true—this belongs to the respective concepts of judgement, assertion and belief Moran employs. But this cannot meaningfully be done with the proposition *that I believe that p* unless one thereby also makes a judgement, assertion or belief to the truth of *p*. Assenting to a proposition just is assenting to its truth, that is, it is impossible to assent to a proposition without assenting to its truth. Assenting to the proposition *that one believes that p* presupposes having mastered the concept of 'to believe' as the state of mind in which its bearer takes something to be true. If one assents to the proposition *that one assents to p*, one assents to its truth, and that means nothing else than that one assents to the truth of the proposition *that one assents to the truth of p*. This is to say that in judging, asserting or believing *that one believes that p* one *always* judges, asserts or believes that *p* is true, regardless

---

102 His solution to Moore's Paradox relies on this possibility. The second conjunct must be interpreted as uttered from the empirical standpoint. The analysand arrives at her belief that her brother has betrayed her by way of self-observation and she reports the proposition that she has this belief from the empirical standpoint. Interpreting the second conjunct as an avowal of belief is not a way open to Moran. Because the Transparency Claim (9) would, in this case, apply to both conjuncts, thus assenting to a Moore-paradoxical sentence would be equivalent to straightforwardly assenting to a formal contradiction, $q \wedge \neg q$. But a Moore-paradoxical sentence is *not* a contradiction, and acknowledging that it isn't constitutes the reason for Moran to introduce the distinction of two self-reflective stances at first place. Moran apparently conceives cases of utmost self-deception as possible precondition to make a Moore-paradoxical assertion from an empirical standpoint. One can also imagine a Moore-paradoxical assertion from an empirical standpoint as a confession of one's own imperfect rationality.

of the way one has arrived at the conclusion *that one believes that p*, whereas a supposition that one believes that *p* does not entail a supposition concerning the truth of *p*. If this was not the case the Transparency Claim would not be justified at first place.

That it is nevertheless *conceivable* that a certain proposition is true while one does not believe it is, does not imply that it is possible to *assert*—or judge, or believe—this to be the case. Talking about the conceivability of a particular situation belongs to a hypothetical context, not to an assertoric one. That is, it is not possible to *meaningfully* judge a sentence of the type '*p* is the case, but I don't believe that *p* is the case' at all (although one might pretend that one does, or imagine this to be the case), not even in order to give a true description of what one believes to be the case, as one supposedly would do from the empirical stance. In other words, it is wrong to regard statements made from the empirical stance as genuine reports, i.e. statements that are, though not advanced with the same impetus as avowals are, nevertheless intended to deliver true descriptions of what is the case. The empirical stance, as Moran constructs it, is a hypothetical standpoint, a standpoint from which one may theorise about oneself, or make assumptions about what might be the case if this and that were true about oneself. It is not a standpoint, though, from which one can make truth-apt statements *about* one's own beliefs as others can do. Although there is a limited sense in which one can give reports of one's beliefs even in the present tense (e.g. in 'I often believe on Wednesdays that it was, in fact, Thursday'), the expression 'I believe' as it is at issue here cannot be sensibly used as an assertion about, a report or a description of one's state of mind, for this would require, among others, that it were possible to assert Moore-paradoxical sentences without thereby being absurd, and to assert sentences like 'I falsely believe that *p*'. Saying 'I believe it is raining', or 'I believe my brother has betrayed me' amounts to manifesting one's belief, speaking out of it, as it were, not about it. It thus seems highly questionable whether a theoretical stance in the detached, third-personal way Moran constructs it may be regarded a practical conceivability at all, or whether it is not rather a theoretical construction only. Moran's 'solution' to Moore's Paradox points to a difference in asserting and supposing *that I believe that p* and so restates one of the reasons for Moore's Paradox to arise whilst leaving it as unintelligible as before. The absurdity of Moore-paradoxical assertions seems indeed to derive from a feature about the context in which they are expressed, not from the supposed fact they report to be the case.

This consideration not only shows that it is impossible that a Moore-paradoxical sentence be intended as a *report* of what is the case by Moran's own standards, but it also calls Moran's explanation into question why the paradox arises if a Moore-paradoxical sentence is avowed. As mentioned earlier, this explanation requires that the second conjunct of a Moore-paradoxical sentence (10), $B(I, p)$, presents a report about one's belief that p, supposedly without making a statement about p as well. But in this case, the author of this self-report does not intend the report to be true, because otherwise, he or she would be using the expression 'I believe that p is the case' in its full sense, including that he or she is committed to the truth of p. If, alternatively, the expression was used from a theoretical point of view about oneself the sentence might run '$\neg p$ is the case, and it might seem to others that I (here and now) believe that p is the case'. But this is hypothetising and not absurd at all, and thus reinvites the paradox. Or, as it appears to be the case in Moran's example, one might say '$\neg p$ is the case, and I seem to believe that p is the case'. And this is either irony or nonsense. So conceiving of Moore's Paradox as an outcome of avowing an inner conflict constituted by the (avowed) conjunction of an avowal of the belief that $\neg p$ and a report of the belief that p, as Moran does, conflicts with his claim that the transcendental stance is not only prior to the empirical stance, but even unavoidably present if one draws conclusions from the empirical stance.

Given that it is an essential feature of the concept of belief that believing that p is believing that p is true, the assertive use of the expression 'I believe' always differs from its hypothetical use in that the former is virtually interchangeable with the simple assertion *that p is the case* while its meaning is preserved. In contrast, the latter is *not* interchangeable with the supposition *that p is the case* without thereby changing the meaning of its content. In other words, it is part and parcel of the concept of belief that the following two propositions are true:

$\vdash B(I, p)$ is similar to $\vdash p$,   and

$-B(I, p)$ is not similar to $- p$.[103]

Remarkably, Moran's and Evans' notion of transparency is tailor-made to capture the similarity of asserting that p and asserting that one believes that p. However, the claim that the similarity is always in place is inconsistent with the Generality Constraint and raises the worry that it necessarily results in a version of the Presentational View, according to which the expression 'I believe' is non-referential.[104]

In order to avoid these consequences, Moran maintains that although the deliberative stance is ontologically prior to the theoretical stance, assertions made

---

103 *Cf.* Schulte (1996), p. 196.

104 I will argue in the next chapter that the claim is true. It provides reasons to give up the Generality Constraint as well as the claim that the expression 'I believe' indeed has the function it apparently has, namely to refer to the person it uses and attributing to him or her a particular mental state. This seems to leave the expression 'I believe' bereft of meaning in assertions, but it does not, as I will explain in Chapter 3.

from the former nevertheless constitute a semantic subclass of the latter and that it is therefore possible to make an assertoric report that one believes that *p* without thereby making an assertion concerning the truth of *p*. Yet, his subsequent explanation of Moore's Paradox has shown that it is questionable whether Moran can reconcile the ontological priority of the deliberative standpoint with the semantic priority of the descriptive semantics of the expression 'I believe'. Furthermore, given that the semantics of a concept like 'to believe' are supposed to derive from the ontology of the phenomenon thus designated, doubt is shed on Moran's claim that the assertoric use of the expression 'I believe' always and primarily constitutes a description of a state of affairs from a perspective-neutral standpoint. As I have elaborated above, this claim is a precondition for his solution to Moore's Paradox. Yet, Moran's proposal that Moore-paradoxical assertions are to be regarded as (potentially true) self-reports of inner conflict contradicting one's self-conception as a rational thinker is false, although he rightly distinguishes theorising about from making up one's mind and although his account of the similarity of asserting *that one believes that p* and asserting *that p is the case* in terms of first-personal asymmetry makes sense.

1.3.7 The Rational Solution

Moran attaches immense significance to the normativity of mental activity, such that he straightforwardly denies that self-knowledge, though a constitutive feature of having mental states, is acquired by introspection—a claim that is central to Shoemaker's version of functionalism. Thereby, he obscures that in fact, his and Shoemaker's accounts of self-knowledge and their conceptions of the mind are not categorically distinct.[105] For both agree on what Shoemaker has presented as a straightforward Cartesian claim;

> [T]hat it is implicit in the nature of certain mental states that any subject of such states that has the capacity to conceive of itself as having them will be aware of having them when it does, or at least will become aware of this under certain conditions. (1988, p. 31)

Self-knowledge, the knowledge of the kind and content of one's current mental states, comes with being a rational thinker—this is the Cartesian core of both, Moran's and Shoemaker's accounts. The kind of self-awareness in question, which is also common ground for both, is further qualified as non-perceptual

---

105 On the similarity of their respective accounts of self-knowledge and first-personal authority, and their connection with Evans' claims about transparency, see also David H. Finkelstein (2008), *Expression and the Inner*, Cambridge (MA): Harvard UP, ch. 6.

self-knowledge. The paradigmatic states a subject has access to in this way are his or her own propositional attitudes, specifically those that play a role in rational deliberation. Self-ascriptions of mental states, such as 'I believe that p is the case', articulate self-knowledge and, for this reason, enjoy specific epistemic security. Both authors maintain that self-knowledge is factual knowledge, that is to say that its content truly represents the subject's state of mind. On Shoemaker's account, this follows from the Higher-Order Belief Principle, which includes that the automatically generated second-order beliefs are of the same kind as first-order beliefs, namely beliefs that a state p is the case. On Moran's account, this follows from maintaining that the meaning of psychological predicates is uniform across all grammatical forms, that therefore avowals, reports, and third-person statements of a particular person's state of mind refer to the same fact, and that the states of mind expressed by avowals are not different in kind from those expressed by other types of sentences.

Moran's and Shoemaker's conceptions diverge, as clarified above, most obviously with respect to the constitution and function of the mind—functional units embedded in causal relations *vs.* commissive states resulting from and initiating mental activity governed by rational norms—and with respect to the epistemology of the specific kind of self-knowledge—non-perceptual introspection *vs.* practical knowledge.

Notwithstanding these differences, which are certainly significant—Moran's conception of mental states in terms of rational commitments presents a radical turn in understanding the mind from functionalism to a more adequate, agential conception, one which pays tribute to the role of the subject in the first place—their divergence does not affect the representationalist core of both views. On Moran's account, the subject's first-person, transcendental stance persists in addition to the empirical perspective on the mind, which is not exclusively the subject's. Interestingly enough, Moran does not make any effort to reject functionalism, which is, I think, indicative of his general benevolent attitude towards Shoemaker's views. For the explanations, inferences and descriptions of a person's mental constitution, which an observer's point of view yields, be it the subject's own one or another one's, remain the same in kind and purpose. They present descriptive reports of psychological facts, and in this light, it seems that Moran's account can integrate Shoemaker's Higher-Order Belief model or an equivalent representationalist conception of the mind as a descriptive model for mental ongoings, whilst amending it with an account of the origin and the driving force of mental activity, the subject's rational thinking. Especially so, since Shoemaker equally appeals to rational principles as normatively binding guidelines for a person's thinking. What remains obscure on Shoemaker's account, is the origin of the demands of rationality for consistency and coherence among the beliefs that constitute one's mental system and the subject's striving for compliance with them that present the force motivating the subject to adjust his or her belief system from time to time. The role of rationality becomes more lucid on Moran's account in that he conceives of rational deliberation as the grounds of belief-formation and treats it as a requirement on authoritative or transparent self-knowledge.

It is thus unsurprising that Moran and Shoemaker explain Moore's Paradox in almost complete unanimity by way of pointing to a deficiency in a subject's rationality, which a Moore-paradoxical sentence ostensibly articulates. The statement of a Moore-paradoxical sentence, 'p is the case, but I don't believe that p is the case' (or its cousins), when considering its structure alone, ostensibly does not exhibit any abnormalities whatsoever. Moore's Paradox is supposed not to be rooted in the properties of the sentence at all, neither in its pragmatics, nor in its semantics. Rather, its origin is sought and found in a clash between the metaphysics of the mind, the conditions of possibility of rational thinking and what a Moore-paradoxical sentence reveals about the subject's current state of mind without explicitly being mentioned. In particular, the statement of a Moore-paradoxical sentence is taken to describe the subject as believing a formal contradiction, or holding beliefs with contradictory contents. Asserting a Moore-paradoxical sentence thus amounts to self-ascribing a false belief. From the subject's perspective, however, the state of inconsistency he or she self-ascribes is untenable given his or her self-conception as a rational thinker, and his or her striving—however grounded—to abide the requirements of rationality. In the end, Moore's Paradox is rendered, on both accounts, as a problem of irrationality.

The argument from self-knowledge goes like this: A sentence of the type $p \wedge \neg B(I, p)$ refers to the state of affairs that something, p, is the case and a particular person does not believe that it is the case. Since this state of affairs presents a conjunction of two propositions whose truths are independent of each other, it is neither logically nor factually impossible. The sentence itself is semantically and structurally inconspicuous. But assenting to it, that is, holding it true, unexpectedly provokes Moore's Paradox. Since Moore's Paradox is triggered independently of whether the sentence in question forms the content of a belief or an assertion, and thought is prior to speech, the paradox cannot be due to the pragmatic conditions of assertion, either. Hence, it must be sought in some implicit description it delivers about its author's mental constitution, most likely a contradiction or inconsistency among his or her beliefs. Given the maintenance of the Cartesian claim to self-knowledge, a rational defect in this sense is happily found among the person's self-beliefs. Hence, what Moore's Paradox is all about, is a kind of inner conflict deriving from the clash between the person's *de facto* limited rational capacities, and his or her self-conception as a rational thinker.

Is this a plausible explanation of Moore's Paradox? I do not think so, for several reasons. First of all, as is the case with the pragmatic approach, the argument from self-knowledge reduces Moore's Paradox to the statement of a *formal* contradiction among the contents of either, second-order (Shoemaker) or first-order (Moran) beliefs. However, a Moore-paradoxical sentence neither contains, nor implies a formal contradiction. If it did, sincerely asserting, or truly believing it would not merely be absurd, but *conceptually* impossible. Since both, belief and assertion, aim at truth, it is ruled out for *logical* reasons to assert or believe what one knows to be a falsity, in this case, a formal contradiction. This point affects all representational accounts and I will come back to it in my general discussion of the representationalist solutions to Moore's Paradox in the next section.

There are further, more specific reasons to reject the attempt to solve Moore's Paradox by drawing on the constitution of the mind. Approaching Moore's Paradox from self-knowledge begs the question. Shoemaker and Moran acknowledge that Moore's Paradox has to do with the absurdity of assenting to a Moore-paradoxical sentence that somehow contrasts with the potential truth of the fact thereby assented. But they draw the wrong conclusions. The argument from self-knowledge seeks to explain why assenting to a sentence of the type '*p* is the case, but I don't believe that *p* is the case' is absurd by means of explaining what is absurd about the fact it allegedly implies, the subject's (confession of his or her own) irrationality. Therefore, Moran and Shoemaker are concerned with the questions, what does assenting to a Moore-paradoxical sentence actually state to be the case? and what aspect of this matter of fact gives rise to the absurdity in question? The first move accordingly consists in conceiving a Moore-paradoxical sentence as an elliptical statement of facts, that is, one that does not explicitly mention all relevant aspects of the matter of fact it describes. In particular, the author of a Moore-paradoxical statement '*p* is the case, and I don't believe that *p* is the case' does and need not mention *that I believe that p is the case* since this is, from the first-person point of view, sufficiently accommodated for by assenting to the simple proposition *that p is the case*.

So the problem with assenting to a Moore-paradoxical sentence is ostensibly sourced in the assumption that its subject-matter is described from a particular perspective, the perspective of a rational, self-knowing subject: If an assertion of a Moore-paradoxical sentence in the first-person present tense were not to express the subject's rational deficiency, it would not be absurd. Moore's Paradox is accordingly taken to derive from the 'absurdity' of the fact a Moore-paradoxical belief or assertion allegedly expresses if it is true (and its author believes that the sentence is true). As an articulation of the subject's self-beliefs, the sentence is absurd *because* it can be true. Moore's Paradox however consists in that a sentence such as 'It is raining, but I don't believe it' is absurd *although* it can be true. That is, the contrast between the absurdity of a Moore-paradoxical statement and its potential truth (absurd although possibly true), turns into a causal relation (absurd because possibly true). Insofar as Shoemaker and Moran engage with Moore's Paradox within their respective accounts of self-knowledge, they misconceive it. What they seek to explain is actually distinct from Moore's Paradox. For Shoemaker, it is the impossibility of 'self-blindness' for rational beings, for Moran it is the case of self-deception or inner conflict. For this reason, Moore's Paradox is given a contorted interpretation, and is dissolved rather than resolved.

That the rational solution misses the point is partly due to an unnecessary and indeed wrong constraint introduced at the outset of Moran's and Shoemaker's respective investigations. As I have mentioned above, both reject pragmatic approaches to Moore's Paradox because they bring to bear the illocutionary conditions of assertions and are supposed to consequently fail to account for the absurdity of beliefs with Moore-paradoxical content. On the prejudice that mental representation is prior to linguistic representation, and thus belief to assertion, Moran and Shoemaker reverse the explanatory order proceeding from the question why a Moore-paradoxical belief is absurd. For this reason, they fully concentrate on the mental conditions of belief, conceived as a certain mental phenomenon, and elaborate on the ontology of belief and the structural and epistemological conditions of self-knowledge, conceived as holding beliefs about one's own beliefs. Accordingly, they end with an explanation of Moore's Paradox, which comes down to pointing to a clash between a person's *de facto* irrationality and his or her *de dicto* rationality.

However, the additional assumptions about the ontology of belief, the rational constraints on the constitution of a rational thinker's mind, the structure and consequences of inner conflict and so on and so forth add up to an enormous metaphysical weight piggybacking on the solution to Moore's Paradox. This sharply contrasts with the *prima facie* simplicity of Moore's Paradox. ''Tis obvious to the common man', Hume would say, that a sentence such as 'It is raining, but I don't believe it' is absurd, and one would not expect the absurdity of particularly this sentence to reside in an inconsistency among mental states that are at least one level away from the level of explicit articulation, even less in an inner conflict of existential dimensions. On the other hand, if a sentence with a Moore-paradoxical structure that can be justly called to bear existential significance is stated affirmatively, such as 'My mother died, but I don't believe it', one would not determine the existentiality of this statement in a breakdown of its author's self-conception as an autonomous, rational thinker, but rather in his or her emotional state and particular sensibility; and it would be more than inappropriate to answer such a statement with simply pointing to the ostensible self-contradiction of the subject's.

The most obvious strategy for solving Moore's Paradox consists in having a closer look at the conditions of assertion and the grammatical rules of the verb 'to believe', which together seem to produce the similarity of an affirmative Moore-paradoxical statement with a statement of a formal contradiction and simultaneously prevent it from lapsing into a straightforward formal contradiction. But Shoemaker and Moran have deprived themselves of the possibility of taking this route in their shared prejudice that it would not be likely to yield an explanation free from conventional interferences, and their shared striving for a metaphysically more steadfast solution. This initial move eventually is motivated by two assumptions, which I have earlier called the Priority Claim and the Reference Claim. Because thought is prioritised over language the conditions of asserting that p are taken to derive from their mental relatives, judging that p and believing that p, and thus the focus is fixed on the conditions of *mental* assent only. And because psychological concepts are supposed to refer to psychological phenomena and to inherit their logical features from the qualities of their referents, the investigation cannot but proceed as a metaphysical and epistemological enterprise. Ironically, the resulting account of Moore's Paradox does not make a difference to the account presented as the supposedly insufficient and imprecise pragmatic account—a Moore-paradoxical sentence must either reduce to a formal contradiction or it isn't absurd at all.

1.3.8 The Representationalist 'Solution' to Moore's Paradox

The explanations of Moore's Paradox I presented in this chapter agree in their analyses of the paradox as well as in their solutions with Moore's original considerations. According to Moore, the paradox is that asserting sentences of the structure 'p is the case, and I don't believe that p is the case' is absurd when at the same time there are three considerations that suggest that there ought not to be an absurdity. First, Moore-paradoxical assertions are absurd although they can be true, and although they have a clearly defined meaning. Second, sentences of the Moore-paradoxical kind are not absurd if they present the content not of assertions, but of other kinds of sentences. Finally, assertions with the content expressed by a Moore-paradoxical sentence are not absurd if the verb 'to believe' takes a grammatical form other than the first-person present indicative.

Of these three aspects of Moore's Paradox, two factors are systematically overlooked on representationalist accounts of Moore's Paradox, the logic of assertion, and the meaning of the expression 'I believe'. This is not surprising, for these two matters are fixed as part of the theoretical framework of representationalism: Assertions allegedly comply with the two-component model in virtue of constituting a class of representational states articulated in a natural language, thus being analysable into illocutionary force (assent) *plus* representational content (a proposition). The meaning of the verb 'to believe' is said to consist in designating a corresponding psychological phenomenon, the phenomenon of believing. Therefore, the grammatical properties of the expression 'I believe'—including the peculiarities Moran alone finds noteworthy—are supposed to derive from corresponding peculiarities of the ontology of belief. As a representational state, belief similarly complies with the two-component model, sharing its structure with assertion, i.e. assent (here: a psychological mode) *plus* representational content (a proposition).

The function of assertion and the meaning of the expression 'I believe' are fixed within the general framework of representationalism. Hence, the paradox seems only interpretable as the discrepancy between the absurdity of asserting a sentence with the structure $p \wedge \neg B(I, p)$ and the possible truth of the proposition thereby asserted. The puzzlement is augmented by the fact that neither of the two sentences conjoined in a Moore-paradoxical sentence is meaningless, and that the states of affairs they refer to are mutually independent. Moore observes that the sentences 'It is raining' and 'I don't believe it is raining' have a definite meaning and each of them can be true regardless of whether the other one is. Conjunction is not a logical operation that would change the reference of the sentences it unites. Following the representationalist considerations, thus, the question is: Why is asserting a meaningful, possibly true conjunction of two independent states of affairs nevertheless absurd?

According to the conception of language intrinsic to representationalism, the meaning of a sentence derives from the content it expresses, that is, from the state of affairs it represents. Thus, the absurdity of Moore-paradoxical assertions is taken to derive from the content a Moore-paradoxical sentences expresses when it is asserted. Because the sentences conjoined in a Moore-paradoxical assertion have a definite meaning and are incommensurable in formal-logical respects, representationalist approaches consider their conjunction as elliptical statements of the content actually expressed. Moore-paradoxical assertions are thus conceived as involving an implicit third conjunct that provides for their absurdity by being inconsistent with either of those explicitly stated.

The accounts I have presented agree in explaining the existence of the third conjunct *via* Moore's Principle, that one normally believes what one asserts. Accordingly, the content of the assertion that p is the case not only represents the state of affairs that p is the case, but simultaneously expresses that the speaker believes that p is the case. Spelling out what the content of a Moore-paradoxical assertion refers to comprehensively delivers, according to the principle, the proposition that p is the case and, by implication, that the speaker believes that p is the case and that the speaker does not believe that p is the case and, again by implication, that the speaker believes that he or she does not believe that p is the case. The representationalist answers to the question, why Moore-paradoxical assertions are absurd, claim *una voce* that they are because they express a contradiction between what the speaker explicitly states and what he or she implies to be the case, although his or her explicit statement can be true.

Despite consensus on the general strategy to approach Moore's Paradox *via* Moore's Principle, the presented accounts disagree in their conception of the implication involved. Moore and Searle locate its origin in the pragmatics of assertion. Due to the brevity and sketchiness of Moore's notes on the paradox, all there is to learn from them is that the principle holds as a commonsense requirement on making an assertion. Under ordinary circumstances, a person asserting that p is expected to also believe that p. On Searle's more elaborate account of the pragmatics of assertion, Moore's Principle holds because the sincerity condition of asserting that p is that one simultaneously believes that p. If an assertion is sincere it implies that the speaker believes what he or she asserts to be the case.

Shoemaker and Moran criticise the pragmatic approach to Moore's Paradox for its supposed inability to explain the incoherence of believing a Moore-paradoxical sentence, from which they conjecture the absurdity of Moore-paradoxical assertions derives. Therefore, both consider a modified version of Moore's Principle to hold for belief, that believing that p implies that one also believes *that one believes that p*. In other words, both take it to be an ontological feature of believing that one knows one's beliefs by having them. According to Shoemaker, it is a constitutive property of belief that having a belief that p generates a corresponding higher-order belief *that I believe that p*. The implication is here conceived as representing a functional property of belief. In contrast, Moran argues that Moore's Principle holds because the epistemic grounds for judging that p are, from the first-personal point of view of the person making the judgement, identical to the epistemic grounds for judging *that I believe that p*. That reflecting on one's own beliefs is transparent to reflecting on their contents, in other words, that a belief that p and the corresponding authoritative knowledge *that one believes that p* are preceded by the same reasoning, is introduced as a requirement on being a rational thinker.

Notwithstanding, all of them arrive at the same explanation of Moore's Paradox: Moore's Paradox arises because assertions (or judgements, if you wish) of the type 'p is the case, but I don't believe that p is the case' are absurd for the reason that, by implication, they assert a formal-logical contradiction. And this is false. Moore-paradoxical assertions are not contradictions, neither explicit, nor implicit ones. For if they were, they could never truly represent a certain state of affairs. But they can, and this insight is amongst the initial motivations for the solution of Moore's Paradox from a representationalist viewpoint.

Taking a closer look at the solutions to Moore's Paradox, all of them would appear to allow the possibility of asserting a Moore-paradoxical sentence without thereby uttering a contradiction. One could make a Moore-paradoxical assertion against the commonsense requirements on assertion (Moore), that is, without simultaneously holding a content-identical belief, or one could insincerely assert a Moore-paradoxical sentence (Searle). A Moore-paradoxical belief might fail to generate the corresponding second-order belief because of a functional error (Shoemaker). And finally, it is possible to describe one's state of mind by means of a Moore-paradoxical assertion if one fails to comply with the transparency condition (Moran). In these cases, Moore-paradoxical sentences do not express contradictions. Following the respective authors' own lines of thought, the paradox does not arise in these cases unless one takes contextual features into account, e.g. the possible reactions of a hearer. However, in these cases Moore-paradoxical sentences cannot be considered absurd, either, and this runs in the face of their commonsense appearance.

Yet, the point is that those cases in which Moore-paradoxical assertions are absurd and hence generate Moore's Paradox are explained as implicitly involving formal-logical contradictions. According to the representationalist approach, Moore-paradoxical statements are absurd if they express a formal-logical contradiction. This 'explanation' of Moore's Paradox, however, is indefensible partly because it is incompatible with the representationalist assumptions themselves. First of all, it loses sight of the puzzle from which the representationalist investigation departed, that Moore-paradoxical assertions are absurd although they can *simultaneously* be true—and according to the representationalist solution, this cannot possibly be the case. Reducing Moore-paradoxical sentences to formal-logical contradiction is moreover only held possible in first-person present tense assertions, which violates the assumption that the veridicality of a sentence, or mental content is independent of its context, in particular of its subject's perspective.

More importantly, though, the representationalist explanation of Moore's Paradox has some rather dubious consequences with regard to the logical properties of Moore-paradoxical sentences. Granted, for the sake of argument, that Moore-paradoxical assertions and beliefs were absurd for the reason that they present covert contradictions. Asserting or believing a sentence of the Moore-paradoxical kind, 'p is the case and I don't believe that p is the case', amount to asserting or believing 'I believe that p is the case and that p is not the case' and thus to self-ascribing a false belief (I falsely believe that p is and is not the case). The opposite of asserting or believing a Moore-paradoxical sentence would be tantamount to asserting or believing a tautology, or to self-ascribing a false belief, i.e. either self-ascribing a true belief or not self-ascribing a false belief—in which case neither a tautology nor anything else is self-ascribed. As to the former case, self-ascribing a true belief is 'I believe that p is the case and p is the case', or $B(I, p) \wedge p$. Should we regard an assertion of this an assertion of a tautology?[106] Neither of the two principles introduced so far, i.e. Moore's Principle and the Transparency Condition, suggest so, for their respective results read $p \wedge B(I, p) \wedge B(I, p) \wedge B(I, B(I, p))$ and $p \wedge p$. Even if one reiterates the transformations, e.g. by adding further higher-order beliefs or amending them with the formula 'and p is true', the best one can get at is assertively repeating a proposition time and again. This might make a truth in Brave New World (where 62400 repetitions are sufficient),[107] but not in propositional logic.

The assertion of a negated Moore-paradoxical sentence for its part is neither tantamount to asserting a tautology, nor to self-ascribing a true belief:

$$\vdash \neg(p \wedge \neg B(I, p)) \quad \leftrightarrow \quad \vdash p \vee \neg B(I, p) \quad \leftrightarrow \quad \vdash B(I, p) \quad \rightarrow \quad p \,.$$

The idea behind the representationalist solution was to integrate Moore's Paradox into its own theoretical framework whilst leaving its foundational assumptions in place, particularly, to secure that the inferential and referential properties of Moore-paradoxical sentences do not differ from those of 'ordinary' sentences. The operations open to the representationalist handling of Moore's Paradox were thus limited to transforming Moore-paradoxical sentences in accord with the laws of propositional logic. Explaining the particular absurdity of Moore-paradoxical state-ments by reducing them to formal-logical contradictions is so attractive because it seems to accommodate the intuition that asserting a Moore-paradoxical sentence is similar to asserting a contradiction as well as to validate the laws of proposi-tional logic. Yet, on a closer look neither impression sustains. On the one hand, the negation of a Moore-paradoxical assertion does not share the formal-logical properties of a tautology—which it ought to if it were reducible to a formal-logical contradiction. On the other hand, what would be the intuitive opposite of a trans-formed Moore-paradoxical sentence, that is, ascribing a true belief to oneself or asserting 'I believe that p, and this is true', does not amount to either, the negation of a Moore-paradoxical sentence or a tautology. There seems to be a gap in logic, a failure to accommodate the specific absurdity of Moore-paradoxical assertions with respect to both their formal-logical behaviour as well as their way of being understood in everyday language. In the light of these considerations, Moore's Paradox appears as a paradox concerning propositional logic once its scope is extended from the hypothetical context of logical inquiry to statements made in the practice of language. This is to say that Moore's Paradox first and foremost

---

106 Wittgenstein asks this question in *RPP* I § 489 and takes it up in § 715.
107 *Cf.* Aldous Huxley (1994), *Brave New World*, London: Flamingo Classics, p. 60.

casts doubt on the assumptions that assertions were analysable as judgement *plus* proposition, as the two-component model suggests, and that their logical and semantic properties were a matter of their content only and eventually derivative from the state of affairs they allegedly represent. Quite to the contrary, the characteristic absurdity of Moore's Paradox suggests that the meaning, and thus also the inferential potential and veridicality conditions, of statements is less independent of their linguistic context than representationalism allows.

The representationalist solution, finally, begs the question as regards the concept of belief. The claim was that the absurdity of asserting a Moore-paradoxical sentence consists in the speaker's self-ascribing a false belief. Yet, the representationalist theory does not provide a good answer to the question as to why it is absurd to assert a sentence of the form 'I falsely believe that p'. I have earlier pointed out that doing so is ruled out for conceptual reasons in that believing "aims at truth", to borrow from Williams, i.e. that believing that p means nothing but believing that p is true just as asserting that p means nothing but asserting that p is true.[108] For this reason, the assertion 'I falsely believe that p' is absurd (*cf.* Williams (1970), p. 137; *PPF* § 92; and Pfisterer (2008), pp. 6f.). However, representationalist accounts cannot explain the origin of this constitutive feature of the concept of belief. Whereas it seems possible to explain the truth-directedness of assertions in virtue of their speaker's intentions to make a true statement there is no analogous explanation in the case of believing. Moran's appeal to rationality as the origin of a person's commitment to the truth of his or her beliefs results in explaining the absurdity of believing 'I falsely believe that p' by drawing on the person's irrationality, that is, his or her failure to recognise this absurdity and to subsequently abandon the false belief. Yet, considering Moore-paradoxical statements declarations of the person's irrationality does not straightforwardly explain their absurdity. For there is nothing intrinsically wrong about a statement such as 'I am irrational'. Contrarily, if such a statement is true, asserting or believing it would be a matter of honesty rather than absurdity.

The difficulty apparently consists in that there is no non-circular way of explaining the truth-directedness of believing *within* the mental realm, i.e. in virtue of other mental states (such as second-order beliefs) or capacities (such as rationality).[109] More precisely, referring to the normative or architectural features of belief does not account for the properties of the words 'to believe' and 'belief',

---

108 Bernard Williams (1970), "Deciding to Believe", in Bernard Williams (1973), *Problems of the Self*, Cambridge: UP, pp. 136–51, here p. 136.
109 Dummett raises this as an objection against Frege, *cf.* Michael A. E. Dummett (1992), *Frege: Philosophy of Language*, London: Duckworth, ch. 10. I will come back to it in my conclusion to Chapter 2.

in particular, for their restricted applicability in the first-person singular. The point in a nutshell is that the grammatical features of the words 'to believe' and 'belief' are supposed to derive from the metaphysics of belief, but that the metaphysics of belief do not sufficiently account for the grammar of the words 'to believe' and 'belief' (I discuss this point in more detail in the following chapters). In this case, however, assuming that the truth-directedness of belief would ground the truth-directedness of assertion is unjustified. But that ought to be the case if assertions were articulations of beliefs and as such inherited their properties from their mental equivalents, judgement and belief. That is, the order of priority representationalist views take for granted, i.e. thought over language, is equally called into question.

The representationalist approach to Moore's Paradox suffers from two claims that, first, the referential function of the expression of 'I believe' must be preserved at all costs on pain of rendering the expression meaningless. Second, that the claim that assertions and other statements as well as belief and other propositional states were analysable into two distinct elements, i.e. representational mode/illocutionary force and representational content, is equally not negotiable on pain of abandoning the principle that representational content were perspective-independent. The prior decision to conceive of meaning in terms of reference pre-determines the logic of assertion as well as the concept of belief and thus allows for exactly one way of interpreting Moore's Paradox, i.e. as a discrepancy between the apparent inassertability of Moore-paradoxical sentences and their possible truth. For this reason, all representationalist views discussed regard Moore-paradoxical assertions as meaningful sentences whose absurdity reflects a corresponding paradoxicality of the state of affairs they describe. Yet, I argued in response to Moran's solution that the similarity of asserting 'I believe that p' and 'p is the case' understood, on Moran's account, in terms of transparency and interchangeability, is always in place. Notwithstanding, holding this does, *pace* Moran, not necessarily commit one to a Presentational View concerning the meaning of the assertoric use of 'I believe'. It does so only on the assumption that similarities and differences in *meaning* among different sentences must rely on corresponding and foregoing similarities and differences in *reference*. Abandoning this claim has the effect that asserting a Moore-paradoxical sentence will always be similar to asserting a straightforward formal-logical contradiction, without entailing one. Moore-paradoxical assertions never present meaningful reports although they never reduce to formal-logical contradictions, either. Rather than taking Moore-paradoxical judgements—whether overt or tacit—at face value, as a meaningful sentence indicating the speaker's failure of rationality, their apparent similarity to formal-logical contradictions renders them, at least for the most part, meaningless.

In the next chapter, I will argue in detail that the representationalist conception of language is wrong in exactly this respect, *viz.* that it defines the meaning of linguistic expressions in terms of reference. In the remainder of this chapter, I will explicate the conception of language that the representationalist account of meaning takes for granted in its core claims, that is Frege's philosophy of language.

1.4 Shared Assumptions: Frege's Legacy

In the previous sections, I have surveyed three representationalist solutions to Moore's Paradox, which were shown to basically present variations of Moore's original proposal. To put the consideration lying at the core of represenationalist approaches to Moore's Paradox in a nutshell: Moore's Paradox arises because normally one believes what one asserts (Moore's Principle). Applied to Moore-paradoxical assertions and beliefs, this assumption renders them implicit or tacit contradictions and this is taken to explain their absurdity. In this section, I want to reconsider the two ideas that, forming the basis of the representationalist framework in general, are operative in all the suggested solutions to Moore's Paradox discussed so far, which are the two-component model of thought and the conception of belief as psychological phenomenon. Both originate in a well entrenched philosophical view about the logical structure and function of assertions and about what beliefs are (namely discrete psychological phenomena), which, probably not coincidentally, displays striking parallels with Frege's philosophy of language, his conception of thought and his account of assertion.[110]

In the following, I will give a brief and very schematic outline of Frege's views on these matters and demonstrate how they are at work in the core assumptions of representationalist accounts. In doing so, I have two aims. First, I want to give a clear picture of the general foundations of the representationalist framework against the background of its varieties I presented in this chapter, and I find the fundamental representationalist assumptions most conspicuously spelled out in

---

110 This is not to claim that all representationalist accounts explicitly refer to Frege. Here is not a place for a historical inquiry. Rather, the views Frege spells out present what one may call philosophical commonsense views about the logic of assertions and the concept of belief, which themselves can be traced to Aristotle and Descartes, and frequently appear in this or that guise in philosophical thinking. In my opinion, connecting representationalism with Frege, though, can be justified better than only by pointing to existing parallels, for the influence of Frege's writings on twentieth century analytic philosophy can be hardly underestimated. This influence, one may conjecture, has meanwhile been so thoroughly entrenched in the foundations of philosophy that it is usually taken for granted without further reflection.

Frege's writings. Second, I want to prepare the grounds for the next chapter. There, I will argue that the representationalist conception of the structure and function of language and its related conception of mental states are responsible for the fact that representationalist approaches to Moore's Paradox necessarily fail to deliver an adequate solution to Moore's Paradox since they suggest a misguided approach to analyzing what the paradox consists in. I will further argue that this is a sufficient reason for abandoning the representationalist picture on thought and language altogether. Since my argument is based on Wittgenstein's writings and Wittgenstein often employs a similar terminology to Frege, it will be easier to comprehend the force of the argumentation in the following chapter once the Fregean roots of representationalism have been excavated.

Drawing on Frege provides a terminologically and structurally coherent model of the logic of assertion, the conception of belief and their interdependency as they are intrinsic to representationalism. In framing this model, I will stay as closely to Frege's own writings as possible. However, the resulting picture is inevitably, given the limitations of space, more idealised and schematic in character than a thorough interpretation of Frege's writings would demand, but of course, the focus of my investigation lies elsewhere. Hence, I will refer to the model as the Fregean one (when using Fregean terminology) or the representationalist one (when using a more representationalist language), although I am well aware that interpretations of Frege diverge and that the grounds for ascribing a pre-representationalist theory of the mind and language to Frege have only recently been brought into question.[111]

1.4.1 Sense and Reference

The basic insight of Frege's philosophy of language is the distinction between the sense and the reference of a linguistic expression, which together account for its meaningfulness. Thereby, he acknowledges that the function of referring to or designating a corresponding object does not fully account for the meaning of a linguistic expression. The distinction, which Frege draws in *Über Sinn und*

---

111 *Cf.* François Recanati (1995), "The Communication of First-Person Thoughts", in John Biro, Peter Kotatko (eds.), *Frege, Sense and Reference: One hundred Years Later*, Dordrecht: Kluwer, pp. 95–102; and Christoph C. Pfisterer (2009), "Gedanken beleuchten. Frege und Davidson zum Problem der Prädikation", *Deutsche Zeitschrift für Philosophie 57/4*, pp. 583–95. For the standard interpretation, see Michael A. E. Dummett (1981), *The Interpretation of Frege's Philosophy*, Cambridge (MA): Harvard UP; and Dummett (1992). For an earlier critical response to Dummett's interpretation, see Peter Michael Stephen Hacker, Gordon P. Baker, *Frege. Logical Excavations*, Oxford: Blackwell 1984.

Bedeutung (*On Sense and Reference*),[112] answers to two puzzles arising on his view that linguistic terms—words, complex phrases, sentences—are signs or names whose function consists in referring to corresponding objects. The first puzzle affects statements of identity, the second one concerns the substitutability of subordinate clauses, or parts of them, particularly with respect to indirect speech and reports about propositional attitudes.

Frege notes that there is a crucial difference between identity statements of the kind '$a = a$' and of the kind '$a = b$' with regard to their respective 'cognitive value' (*Erkenntniswert*). Whereas identity statements of the first kind hold *a priori*, identity statements of the second kind present substantial achievements of human knowledge, that is, statements whose truth is not always *a priori* obvious. For example, the statement 'Hesperus is Hesperus' is obviously true, whereas the statement 'Hesperus is Phosphorus' is not. Both statements are true, and thus are not distinguishable with respect to their reference. Yet, the statement 'Hesperus is Phosphorus' transports a statement about the world, it contains the discovery that the names 'Hesperus' and 'Phosphorus' both designate one and the same thing, the planet Venus. This consideration reveals that identity statements of the form '$a = b$' have a different cognitive significance from identity statements of the form '$a = a$'. This difference cannot be accounted for if the meaning of a sign is equated with its reference. Therefore, the meaning of a sign—a word, a phrase, or a sentence—cannot be determined by considering its reference only.

The same conclusion follows from a puzzle concerning subordinate clauses. Expressions that, in virtue of having the same referent, are intersubstitutable under ordinary circumstances lose their substitutability if they appear in the subordinate clause of an ascription of a propositional attitude. For example, the names 'Hesperus' and 'Phosphorus' are mutually substitutable under ordinary circumstances because the identity statement 'Hesperus = Phosphorus' is true. The argument 'Hesperus shines at night; Hesperus is Phosphorus; therefore, Phosphorus shines at night' is valid. This is not the case if the first premise presents an ascription of a propositional attitude, in which either name appears in the content of the subordinate clause. The argument 'Peter believes that Hesperus shines at night; Hesperus is Phosphorus; therefore, Peter believes that Phosphorus shines at night' is not valid. For it is possible that the premises are true and the conclusion false, for instance, if Peter does not believe that Hesperus is Phosphorus, or if Peter correctly identifies Phosphorus with the morning star, and so quite naturally believes that Phosphorus shines in the morning, but not in the evening. This, too, would not be explainable if the meaning of an expression was fully determined by its reference.

---

112 Frege (1892b); Frege (1948); and Frege (1980d).

For if this was the case, expressions having the same reference would be mutually substitutable regardless of the context in which they stand. Since the reference of 'Hesperus' and 'Phosphorus' is identical, substituting one for the other would neither change the reference of the term or the sentence to which it belongs, nor would it change the logical properties of a sentence, to whose reference it contributes.

Frege solves both puzzles by distinguishing the reference of an expression from its sense, that is, the object an expression denotes from the 'mode of presentation', i.e. the way in which it is conceived by means of a given expression. The referent of a term is the object it designates. The sense of a term captures its cognitive value, that is, the way in which the object is presented to cognition, or some aspect of the designated object which is available to cognition. The term itself expresses a sense. Frege describes the interrelation of these three notions as follows:

> The regular connection between a sign, its sense, and its referent is of such a kind that to the sign there corresponds a definite sense and to that in turn a definite referent, while to a given referent (an object) there does not belong only a single sign. The same sense has different expressions in different languages or even in the same language. To be sure, exceptions to this regular behaviour occur. To every expression [...] there should certainly correspond a definite sense; but natural languages often do not satisfy this condition, and one must be content if the same word has the same sense in the same context. (1892, pp. 27f.)[113]

The distinction between the sense and reference of a term or expression accommodates the following characteristics of natural languages: The same object can be conceived in different ways, and thus referred to under different descriptions. For example, the planet Venus can be conceived as the 'morning star' and the 'evening star'. The expressions 'morning star' and 'evening star' have the same reference, but different senses. The same sense can be expressed in different languages, and the respective expressions are thereby mutually translatable. For example, the sentences 'Napoleon ist tot', 'Napoléon est mort' and 'Napoleón està muerte' express the same sense and thus the same meaning, which makes them mutually translatable. The same goes for synonymous expressions in a single language. Further, some expressions have a sense and so can be used meaningfully without referring to anything, for example the name 'Pegasus' or the sentence 'The King of France is bald'. Finally, the distinction contains a solution to the first puzzle. The identity statements '$a = a$' and '$a = b$' have the same referent, but not the same sense. Hence, their respective cognitive value and their respective meaning is different.

---

113 The last qualification serves to account for homonymous words, such as 'bank', which in some contexts denotes a financial institution, in others refers to a riverbank, and in still others presents the name of a train station.

As to the second puzzle, Frege further suggests that the reference and the sense of a term coincide when the term appears in the subordinate clause of a propositional attitude description. A term so situated loses its ordinary function to refer to either an object or a truth-value and instead refers to the sense or the thought it expresses. Accordingly, in subordinate clauses, only signs denoting the same sense are interchangeable, whereas signs expressing different senses cannot be mutually substituted even if they ordinarily refer to the same object. The meaning of the sentences 'Peter believes that Hesperus shines at night' and 'Peter believes that Phosphorus shines at night' is not identical because the expressions 'Hesperus' and 'Phosphorus' here refer to different objects (the evening star and the morning star, respectively). Similarly, the meaning of the sentences 'Peter believes that the battle of Waterloo was lost by Napoleon' and 'Peter believes that Bonaparte was defeated in the *Belle Alliance*' are not identical, although the thoughts expressed in the respective subordinate clause refer to the same event and have thus have the same truth-value.

Frege's solution to the second puzzle thus draws on the distinction between sense and reference and, in addition, reassesses the referential function of subordinate clauses. It follows that the sentences contained in the subordinate clause of ascriptions of propositional attitudes lose their status as self-standing descriptions, that is, as linguistic terms referring to 'their own' objects.[114] Instead, they specify concepts which are ascribed to grammatical subjects and thus serve to qualify the respective referent of the main sentence.[115] The sentence 'Peter believes that the earth is round' refers to Peter, who is characterised as believing what is specified in the that-clause, that the earth is round. Neither the earth nor its actual shape contribute to the reference of the whole sentence, and so do not matter for its truth-value, either. Rather, they qualify the predicate ('believes'), specifying the content of Peter's belief.

---

114 Frege considers every sentence to be a name for its truth-value, 'The True' or 'The False', respectively. The truth-value of a sentence constitutes the object it refers to, i.e. its reference. The reference of a sentence becomes manifest in the sense of a sentence, and, where applicable, under a certain mode of presentation. This conception parallels the case of individual objects, which are designated by names, and can also be presented under different modes. For instance, the second planet of our solar system is designated by the name 'Venus', which is the reference of the words 'Hesperus' and 'Phosphorus'. The case for sentences runs parallel: The Pythagorean theorem presents a mathematical truth, it is hence a name for The True, and it is the sense of its respective geometrical and arithmetic notations.
115 This point is almost unaltered contained in the representationalist conception of language that I explained above (section 'Language and Representation'). *Cf.* Burge's elaborations on reference and attribution in Burge (2010), pp. 30–42.

The conclusion concerning the content of mental states rendered in indirect speech anticipates Frege's conception of the metaphysical status of mental states, which I will further explain in the next section. Notably, it also recalls what was said earlier in this chapter about the metaphysical status of mental states conceived upon the assumptions of representationalism. According to representationalism, types of representational states are instantiated in that they are had by a bearer at a certain time. The individuation of any particular representational state thus requires denoting its bearer and the time at which it occurs. Without reference to its bearer a mental state does not exist, and hence cannot be identified as a discrete state at first place. In that their instantiation depends on there being an individual to whom a particular state belongs, representational states are metaphysically bearer-dependent states, or properties. Further, since language is supposed to be a means of representing objects it would be surprising if the metaphysical properties of an object did not carry over into the grammatical properties of the linguistic expressions by means of which they are articulated in a natural language. One would expect that expressions denoting representational states would be constituted by some kind of predicates or concepts. The phrase 'belief that the earth is round' does not refer to a single mental phenomenon unless it is associated with a particular person, say, as 'Peter's belief that the earth is round'. Thus, grammatically speaking, the grammatical status of referring terms of psychological predicates mirrors the metaphysical dependency of token mental states on their respective bearers, although the expressions rendering the representational content, taken in isolation, may consist of or contain referring terms.

The capacity of originally autonomous terms to lose their ordinary function of reference when appearing in the content-clause of a sentence ascribing a representational state to a particular person and to take on the function of a predicative expression is theoretically grounded in Frege's distinction of sense and reference outlined in this section. I will now explain the metaphysics of thought and assertion as they are presented in Frege's philosophy of meaning.

1.4.2 Fregean Thoughts and the Two-Component Model

In his paper *Der Gedanke* (*The Thought*),[116] Frege is actually concerned with the question of what the word 'true' signifies, and to what kinds of things it is appropriately applied. As a by-product of answering this question, he develops a conception of what thought is, providing a view of how mind, world and the mean-

---

116 Frege (1819, 1956).

ing of sentences hang together, which strongly resembles the representationalist view.

In this article, Frege distinguishes between the material world as it objectively exists (the 'outer world') and the world as it is apprehended by individuals (the 'inner world'). This distinction roughly corresponds to the representationalist distinction between the world as it is and the world as it is represented. Frege's next step is to state that the word 'true' designates things that are both immaterial and objective. For this reason, Frege rules out material objects as well as subjective experiences, e.g. sense impressions, feelings and sensations, as possible members of the class of things that can be true, as well as any relations obtaining among them (Frege (1956), pp. 292f.). Rather, the word 'true' applies to things existing in a 'third realm' alongside the world of material objects and the world of subjective (*sc.* qualitative) experience, namely thoughts. Frege characterises a thought as

> [S]omething for which the question of truth arises. So I ascribe what is false to a thought just as much as what is true. So I can say: the thought is the sense of a sentence without wishing to say as well that the sense of every sentence is a thought. The thought, in itself immaterial, clothes itself in the material garment of a sentence and thereby becomes comprehensible to us. We say a sentence expresses a thought. (1956, p. 292)

From this passage already, the outline of Frege's conception of thought, language and their relation becomes visible: (1) A sentence expresses a sense; (2) the sense of a sentence is something different from the sentence; (3) the sense of a sentence is immaterial; (4) an immaterial sense becomes comprehensible in the guise of a material sentence; (5) the sense of some (kinds of) sentences is a thought, namely (6) the sense of a sentence that can be judged to express something true or false is a thought, for (7) what is true or false, is a thought. Close to the end of the article, Frege adds a definition of facts (8): "A fact is a thought that is true." (p. 307)

In the following, Frege specifies this outline, elaborates the way in which thoughts are apprehended by an individual's consciousness and further qualifies the differences between thoughts and experiences. First of all, he enlists different kinds of sentences, imperative, interrogative and indicative sentences and sentences expressing desires or requests (p. 293).[117] All of them have or express a sense, but only the sense of interrogative and indicative sentences, i.e. questions and assertions, sentences "in which we communicate or state something" (p. 293),

---

117 The analogy to Searle's analysis of speech acts is evident. Searle endorses Frege's conception of different kinds of sentences with respect to both taxonomy and structure of speech acts. *Cf.* Searle (1969) and above, Section 3.2.

is a thought.[118] Importantly thus, Frege holds that one and the same thought can be contained by different kinds of sentences, namely 'sentence-questions' and assertions, for instance, the question 'Is it raining?' and the assertion 'It is raining' both contain the thought *that it is raining* and each of them contains "something else"; the indicative sentence additionally contains an assertion, the question contains a request. What Frege arrives here just is the two-component model as I have presented it at the outset of this chapter:

> [T]wo things must be distinguished in an indicative sentence: the content, which it has in common with the corresponding sentence-question, and the assertion. The former is the thought, or at least contains the thought. So it is possible to express the thought without laying it down as true. (p. 294)

In other words, although a thought itself is true or false, and thus decides whether an assertion is an expression of something true or false, the thought can be presented to a subject without thereby being judged to be true or false. That is, one can entertain the thought *that it is raining* without thereby having (yet) committed oneself to its truth. Frege's view that assertions were decomposable into a general content-bearing element and a subjective element, the act of affirming or denying a particular content, appears as early as in his *Begriffsschrift*. It is reflected in the notation Frege introduces here and refines in his paper *Function and Concept*,[119] which I have already been using throughout this chapter:

---

118 Frege introduces some further qualifications regarding the relation of particular sentences and thoughts. Only those indicative sentences can be said to express thoughts, which are meant seriously, i.e. are actually uttered with the intention of saying something true. In the case of lying, pretending, telling stories or acting, indicative sentences fail to meet this condition. These sentences do not contain assertions and therefore do not express a thought, although they have a sense. Moreover, if indicative sentences contain expressions, which taken by themselves present exclamations or other indicators of their speaker's mood or feelings, e.g. 'thank God', 'alas', 'well', and the like, what these expressions express does not belong to the thought. *Cf.* Frege (1956), pp. 294f. Thirdly, the same thought can be expressed by different sentences, for instance, synonymous sentences or a sentence translated into different languages—the sentences 'It is raining', 'Es regnet', and 'Està lloviendo' all express the thought that it is raining at a certain place to a certain time. Finally, sentences containing indexicals or demonstratives or that otherwise relate to the speaker's situation must be treated as abbreviations. In order to arrive at the thought thereby expressed, the additional information that is contained in the speaker's uttering the sentence under his or her particular situational circumstances, must be amended. For example, Peter's sentence 'This is my book' contains the thought 'The book located at location l at time t is owned at time t by Peter', whereby the proper name also has to be given a definite description. *Cf.* Frege (1956), pp. 297f.
119 It is contained as Gottlob Frege (1891), "Funktion und Begriff", lecture at the *Jenaische Gesellschaft für Medizin und Naturwissenschaft* (January 9th, 1891), in Frege (1962), *Funktion, Be-*

A judgment is always to be expressed by means of the sign ⊢. This stands to the left of the sign or complex of signs in which the content of the judgment is given. If we *omit* the little vertical stroke at the left end of the horizontal stroke, then the judgment is to be tranformed into a mere *complex of [thoughts]*; the author is not expressing his recognition or non-recognition of the truth of this. [...] In this case we *qualify* the expression with the words '*the circumstance that*' or '*the proposition that.*' (1879, pp. 1f., original italics.)

This separation of the *act* from the *subject-matter* of judgment [and equally of assertion, us.] seems to be indispensable; for otherwise we could not express a mere supposition—the putting of a case without a simultaneous judgment as to its arising or not. We thus need a special sign [in addition to the horizontal] to be able to assert something. To this end I make use of a vertical stroke at the left end of the horizontal [...] Thus here we are not just writing down a truth-value, [...] but at the same time saying that it is the True. (1891, pp. 21f., my italics.)

The assertion sign '⊢' consists of a horizontal line, '–', (the 'content-stroke' or simply the 'horizontal')[120] and a vertical stroke (the 'judgment-stroke'), '|'. The horizontal line indicates that a neutral proposition follows, i.e. one that has not or not yet been judged true or false. Adding the vertical stroke symbolises that the following thought has been judged true, and turns a neutral sentence, a sentence towards which its author has an indifferent attitude, into a particular assertion.

Given Frege's notion of sense, one can expand this consideration such that it applies to all kinds of (grammatically complete) sentences: The same sense can be expressed in a neutral sentence, i.e. a supposition, as well as contained by different kinds of sentences, such as wishes, desires, imperatives, assertions, requests, and so on. This amendment makes the idea Frege formulates here coincide with the representationalist conception of mental states and utterances as decomposable into content and psychological mode or illocutionary force. Analogously, one may introduce further symbols into Frege's notation designating the modes different from judgement, for instance, '?' for requests, '!' for imperatives and the like. The question 'Is it raining?' could thus be rendered '? – p', the imperative 'Make it rain!' '! – p' and so on.[121] The crucial point to note here is that, according to Frege, different kinds of sentences can contain one and the same sense, and that the sense of a sentence remains untouched by the kind of sentence, in which it appears, as well as by the wording chosen to express it on a particular occasion. Accordingly, the sense of a sentence exists independently of whether and under which circumstances it is expressed in language. In the same respect, the truth or

---

griff, Bedeutung: Fünf logische Studien, ed. by Günther Patzig, Göttingen: Vandenhoek & Ruprecht, pp. 16–37; translated as Frege (1980b), "Function and Concept", in Geach, Black (1980), pp. 21–41.

120 Frege introduced the sign as 'content-stroke' in Frege (1879), § 2. He changed its name in Frege (1980b).

121 *Cf.* Schulte (1993), pp. 140f.

falsity of a particular thought, e.g. *that it is raining in London on the morning of July 14th 2012*, is independent of whether it is thought or articulated by an individual person.

These characteristics of thoughts simultaneously distinguish them from subjective experiences or, as Frege calls them, 'ideas', among which he counts sense-impressions, creations of one's imagination, sensations, feelings, and moods (1956, p. 299). Ideas are, in terms of their existence, essentially dependent on their bearer. First, ideas are had: "An experience is impossible without an experient. The inner world presupposes the person whose inner world it is." (*Ibid.*) Second, ideas are individuated by their bearer: My headache is distinguished from Peter's headache in that my headache belongs to my consciousness, whereas Peter's headache belongs to Peter's consciousness. This property rules out that one could access or even compare one another's experiences—nobody can feel my pain, have the visual impression of grey the sky causes on my retina etc.[122]

Thoughts, on the contrary, exist independently of a particular person's consciousness and, for this reason, can be had by different individuals, and communicated (in assertoric sentences) to one another. The thought *that it is raining in London on the morning of July 14th 2012* can occur to various people, at various times and places, without it needing to be altered. If this was not the case, Frege argues, one and the same thought (in Frege's example, that expressed by the Pythagorean theorem) might be true for me and false for Peter. In this case, however, truth would be a notion whose applicability were restricted to the content of my own consciousness (p. 301). Since this seems an unbearable consequence to Frege, he concludes that thoughts "are neither things of the outer world nor ideas" (p. 302), but constitute a 'third realm' of reality, which is both immaterial and beyond the consciousness of individual persons.

1.4.3 From Thought to Thinking

A thought enters the 'inner world', i.e. the consciousness of an individual person insofar as this person apprehends the thought. A general thought is particularised in a person's thinking. Frege here distinguishes three stages:

---

[122] Frege carefully distinguishes between the objects of sense-impressions and the sense-impressions themselves: Whereas the objects of sense-impression exist in the outer world, independently of being perceived, sense-impressions exist only within a single person's consciousness. The grey sky exists independently of whether I see it and can be perceived by another person just as well, but my visual impression of the grey sky ceases to exist if I close my eyes, and it cannot be shared by anybody else. *Cf.* Frege (1956), pp. 299–302.

(1) [T]he apprehension of a thought—thinking,
(2) the recognition of the truth of a thought—judgment,
(3) the manifestation of this judgment—assertion. (1956, p. 294)

Stage (1) presents what Frege has called earlier the "putting of a case" (Frege (1980b), p. 21). Here, a thought is grasped by an individual's consciousness as a supposition and thereby transformed into a "complex of ideas" (Frege (1879), p. 2) belonging to the content of the person's consciousness. Subsequently, the person can take up an attitude towards the thought (stage (2)), he or she may ask whether it is true or assent to it. In the first case, the thought constitutes the content of a question, in the second case, it presents the content of a judgement (*cf.* Frege (1956), pp. 293f.). At stage (3), the person's judgement or request is expressed by an assertion or question-sentence. So it seems that a thought need not be articulated in a sentence of a natural language until this stage, thereby being made communicable.

Suppositions, that is, neutrally entertained contents, bear a distinct role on this model. They amount to the "putting of a case without a simultaneous judgment as to its arising or not" (Frege (1980b), pp. 21f., as quoted above). As such, they present the primary way in which thoughts are apprehended by individual persons. Only in a second step, does a supposition become the object of the person's judgement as to its truth or falsity, and it takes a third step to express the judgement in language, as an assertion. In a supposition, a thought is introduced into a particular person's consciousness. Here, the realm of thought, which exists external to an individual's consciousness, and the inner world of an individual person, whose existence depends on that person, are connected. Once the thought has been grasped in thinking, it persists within an individual person's consciousness. Here, it can become the content of a judgement or a question and/or 'interact' with the other 'inhabitants' of this person's consciousness, e.g. thoughts, ideas, sensations and so forth. That is, the characteristics of thinking a thought are the same as those of ideas—it takes a person to think a thought, and thinking a thought, though not the thought itself, has a bearer, and only one bearer:

> The apprehension of a thought presupposes someone who apprehends it, who thinks. He is the bearer of the thinking, but not of the thought. Although the thought does not belong to the contents of the thinker's consciousness yet something in his consciousness must be aimed at the thought. But this should not be confused with the thought itself. (Frege (1956), p. 306)

The function of suppositions consists in particularising general thoughts and thus making them suitable objects for an individual person's reflection, which proceeds by entertaining the supposition in different kinds of sentences (e.g. requests, imperatives, or judgements). To illustrate the role of suppositions, Wittgenstein deploys the following picture:

> Imagine a picture representing a boxer in a particular fighting stance. Well, this picture can be used to tell someone how he should stand, should hold himself; or how he should not hold himself; or how a particular man did stand in such-and-such a place; and so on. One might (using the language of chemistry) call this picture a sentence-radical. Frege probably conceived of the "supposition" along these lines. (*Philosophical Investigations*, p. 11 note)

In the light of these two quotations, Frege's version of the two-component model can be further specified. Earlier, Frege describes questions and assertions as being composed from a thought, which presents their content, and 'something else', the question or judgement. Now, the question or judgement belong to the things the person who has apprehended a thought does with his or her instantiation of the thought, they are, in this respect, *subjective*, i.e. elements of this person's consciousness, and hence intrinsically dependent on this person's consciousness and inaccessible by others. The content of a question or judgement, in contrast, is objective, it is just the particular guise a general thought is given by the person's apprehending it. Thus, a supposition is not only the first, but also the most general form in which a thought can persist within a person's consciousness. A supposition *that p is the case* quintessentially expresses a thought, or, more generally speaking, a sense, insofar as it just contains an instantiation of the thought, without adding a further, subjective element. As such, one and the same supposition can be extracted from different kinds of sentences, by 'purifying' them, as it were, from all their subjective elements, including their modes. Therefore, what is actually communicable as well as actually communicated in different kinds of sentences is the supposition, which bears the complete sense of a sentence.

Wittgenstein's comparison of suppositions with chemical radicals pinpoints the double role suppositions bear on Frege's account. A chemical radical is, as the *Oxford English Dictionary* defines, "an atom or group of atoms regarded as a (or the) primary constituent of a compound or class of compounds, remaining unaltered during chemical reactions in which other constituents are added or removed."[123] The same properties apply to a supposition: A supposition is the primary constituent of sentences, and it remains unaltered by subjective elements entering the sentence throughout the person's reflection. Wittgenstein however uses the comparison of suppositions with chemical radicals to criticise Frege's

---

[123] *Cf.* "radical, adj. and n.", John Simpson, Edmund Weiner (eds.), *OED Online*, Oxford UP: March 2014, http://www.oed.com/view/Entry/157251?rskey=dOZCOF&result=1&isAdvanced=false#eid, last access March 18th, 2014.

conception of assertion. As I will explain in detail in the next chapter, conceiving assertions and other kinds of sentences as containing a uniform content-element, a supposition or a sentence-radical, is misguided and does not render an adequate account of their use in language.

1.4.4 Frege in Representationalism

The parallels between Frege's account of how mind, world and language are connected, with how the representationalist view conceives of this issue are, I think, now obvious. They can be summarised as follows: According to Frege, a thought, whose object is any state of affairs in the world, becomes the object of a person's reflection in virtue of its neutral representation in a supposition. In a next stage, such a particularised thought is judged to be true or false. Eventually, this judgement is articulated in an assertion. On the representationalist view, a type representation of a state of affairs is instantiated when a subject represents the state of affairs. The subject subsequently takes up an attitude towards his or her token representation, it has a mental state, for instance, a belief that the state of affairs he or she represents is true. The mental state finally can be articulated in a corresponding kind of sentence, e.g. in an assertion that the respective state of affairs obtains. Crucially, on both Frege's account and the representationalist view, language comes in only at the last stage, when it comes to articulating the judgement or the content of mental states. A part of the subject's consciousness, thoughts and representational contents need not yet be expressible in a natural language.

From this further presentation of Frege's account it becomes clear that all the elements I specified at the outset of the chapter as the fundamental constituents of representationalism are present in Frege's account as well. This is most apparent with regard to the two-component model—the idea that particular mental states and different kinds of sentences are composed from an objective content and a subjective act, a psychological mode or illocutionary force is part and parcel of both Frege's account and the representationalist view of the mind. Further, the relation of content-types, token mental states and sentences on representationalism is conceived in analogy to the relations obtaining between thoughts, judgements and spoken sentences, on Frege's account. Thoughts and content-types are independent of and unalterable by their apprehension by individual minds. The same holds for the reference of thoughts (their truth-values) and content-types (their referential objects), respectively. The state of affairs that it is raining at a particular location on a particular time, or that a particular person has a certain experience at a particular time obtain irrespectively of whether they ever come to a person's mind. Likewise, the truth of mathematical propositions is independent of their being discovered; the laws of physics are valid and unchangeable whether or not they are recognised by a particular community.

Moreover, being independent of being thought by an individual, thoughts and type representations exist prior to being grasped by individuals, and mental acts or states are prior to being articulated in sentences of a natural language (Priority Claim). Different kinds of sentences, which differ only in their 'subjective' parts (the choice of words, their mode and/or possible further expressions of a person's feelings, moods etc.), can still be identical in content. Reversely, the same sense, thought, or type representation can constitute the content of different mental states or utterances, such as one can believe, hope, predict, request, or doubt *that it is raining in London on July 14*[th] *2012* (Uniformity Claim).

Also, a claim corresponding to the Reference Claim results from Frege's conception of how the contents of particular acts of the mind and particular sentences are related to objective thoughts. Sentences manifest mental states, mental states contain thoughts, thoughts exist independently of and prior to being instantiated in thought or speech. Hence, sentences denote something (according to Frege, the truth-value of a sense or a thought), which exists independently of being expressed in a sentence and ensures that the sentence is meaningful.

Eventually, Frege's account relies on a distinction between an outer, objective, and an inner, subjective realm, which basically corresponds to the representationalist distinction between the world as it is, and the world as it is experienced by individual persons. The outer realm comprises the material world as well as the realm of thought, which both exist independently of being perceived, or apprehended or otherwise interacted with. This is the publicly shared world, accessible to everyone endowed with the prerequisite cognitive and sensory faculties, and in virtue of this it is communicable to one another. The subjective, inner realm in contrast consists in the interior of a particular person's consciousness and includes his or her thinking, and his or her ideas, sensations, feelings and so on. This realm is essentially dependent on having an individual bearer. According to Frege, experiences would not exist, were it not for there being somebody to experience them, and thinking would not take place, were it not for there being somebody doing the thinking. Yet, what belongs to a person's consciousness, his or her thoughts, experiences, sensations and so forth, occurs independently of anybody's reflection on it. That Peter is in pain is just as much a name of 'The True' or 'The False' as the cat being on the mat. Therefore, what occurs within the inner realm can become the object of its bearer's or another person's reflection, and yet is, in its quality of belonging to the bearer's subjective experiences, *stricto sensu* accessible only by him- or herself. That is, although my judgement *that Peter is in pain*, and Peter's judgement *that I am in pain* contain the same thought, *that Peter is in pain*, I am in principle excluded from participating in Peter's pain.

It is thus but a small step for Frege to conclude that "everyone is presented to himself in a particular and primitive way, in which he is presented to no-one else" (1956, p. 298) and that it is this primitive way, in which entertaining thoughts about oneself is grounded. And yet, since these thoughts are concerned with states of affairs different from their bearer's reflecting on them, they are in principle comprehensible to others. Consequently, if Peter articulates the fact that he is in pain in language by means of the sentence 'I am in pain', "he must use the 'I' in a sense which can be grasped by others, perhaps in the sense of 'he who is speaking to you at this moment'" (*ibid.*). In an avowal, thus, the word 'I' is used to *designate* a particular person in a double way, a subjective and an objective one, and the same holds, to be sure, for the respective first-person expression of his or her inner state.[124] This is just another way of saying that whatever else avowals do, they represent their subject as having a particular mental state from an objective, or descriptive, point of view—which is the formulation I employed earlier when characterising the representationalist conception of first-person present indicative expressions of mental states.

It is this complex of ideas on the interrelations of mind, world and language that tempts into conceiving of the 'primitive way' in which an individual is acquainted with the contents of his or her own consciousness in epistemological terms, as a distinctive epistemic privilege or authority, or a special access everyone has to the occurrences taking place in his or her 'inner world'. Although nobody can be as certain of the occurrence of a particular mental state as the person having it, the occurrence of the mental state yet is an objective fact and as such presents a suitable object of thought. Consequently, psychological predicates are supposed to designate corresponding psychological phenomena, which likewise constitute and grant the meaning of psychological predicates, and whose presence decides the correctness and accuracy of articulations of psychological facts in their particular instantiations. Accordingly, the function of their grammatical first person is to ascribe a particular psychological state to oneself, that is, to describe oneself as having a particular psychological state. The meaning of avowals, on this conception, derives from this general picture: They have a descriptive meaning in the first place, they are thus 'semantically continuous' with all other inflective forms. In Fregean terms, one can extract the same thought from Peter's avowal 'I am in pain' and my assertion 'Peter is in pain', which is expressed by the supposition that Peter is in pain. The asymmetric properties of avowals are additives, deriving from the special way in which their author is related to their content.

---

124 The claim that first-person present indicative expressions of mental states were doubly referring in this sense will be examined in the next chapter.

It is this very same complex of ideas which motivates the representationalist approach to solving Moore's Paradox by 'psychologising' it, that is, by introducing a further assertion of belief. As I argued in this chapter, this approach inevitably results in rendering Moore-paradoxical sentences, when uttered assertively, logical contradictions, which they are not, and thus must be considered false. As I will argue in the next chapter, it is because this complex of ideas provides the conceptual foundations for representationalism that it is impossible to account for Moore's Paradox on a representationalist view. Thereby, I will discern the two-component model of mental states and speech acts and the claim that psychological expressions always denote corresponding psychological phenomena to be the main reasons why representationalism cannot but arrive at the wrong solution. I will develop an argument from Moore's Paradox to the conclusion that the fact that Moore's Paradox cannot be integrated in this complex of ideas provides sufficient reason to give up these very assumptions and thus to discard the representationalist theory of the mind.

1.5 Summary

In this chapter, I presented a general outline of the representationalist view as to how the mind is structured (in a psychological mode together with a representational content), how it apprehends the world (by representing it), what constitutes the meaning of psychological expressions (reference to a corresponding psychological phenomenon), and how mind and language interrelate (Section 1.1). I distinguished two core presuppositions and three consequent claims, which together span the framework of representationalism.

Fundamental to representationalism are the two-component model and the assumption that the meaning of words and sentences consists in designating an independently existing referent, a state of affairs or an object. These core conceptions reveal a commitment to three claims, which I labelled the Reference Claim, the Uniformity Claim and the Priority Claim, respectively.

The two-component model presents mental states and verbal utterances as decomposable into a mode- and a content-element. The content-element specifies the accuracy conditions of the mental state it belongs to, i.e. those external conditions under which a particular mental state contains an accurate representation of its corresponding object, or under which a particular sentence presents an accurate depiction of the state of affairs it refers to. Modelling sentences on the two-component model already entails the claim that it is the primary function of language to describe reality. Every meaningful sentence, irrespectively of what is done with it, conveys information about a certain aspect of reality.

The Reference Claim is primarily a claim about the content of mental states. It results from the view that the objects an individual represents in the content of his or her mind exist prior to, independently of, and invariant to being apprehended at all, and that an individual engages with reality as it represents it. The notion 'representation' thus denotes the function of the mind that aims at establishing a two-place relation, holding between its subject and a representational object. The object, which is taken to consist in a state of affairs, an event, an object, or other entity, is apprehended in virtue of the subject representing it. Any such representation can subsequently become the content of various attitudes of the subjects, and any instance of representation can fail in terms of veridicality. At any rate, it *stands for*, and in this sense, refers to the object itself beyond the boundaries of the mind.

On representationalism, language presents a special kind of way of representing the world. Hence, all that was said about the structure and function of (non-linguistic) mental states equally applies to utterances and linguistic thoughts. Words and sentences denote corresponding entities, concepts or states of affairs, which simultaneously warrant the meaningfulness of a particular expression, and establish whether a particular expression is correctly used, i.e. whether it accurately represents its referent. The main function of language is thus to describe the world as it is, and this function is maintained throughout different kinds of sentences.

The Uniformity Claim serves to secure that the same object or state of affairs can be represented in different modes, and expressed in different kinds of sentences, without thereby undergoing any alterations. And according to the Reference Claim, different mental states, and different kinds of sentences have the same content if and only if they refer to the same object or state of affairs. According to representationalism, it is thus possible to extract one and the same content from different mental states or kinds of mental states, and analogously, from different sentences or kinds of sentences.

The Priority Claim clarifies the relation between mind and language, prioritising mental representation over linguistic representation. It does so in two ways: First, mental representation is the *genus proximus* of linguistic representation, linguistic representation thus presents a subspecies of the activity of representing an object or states of affairs in general and inherits all the structural and functional properties of mental representation. Second, psychological states themselves are suitable objects of mental as well as linguistic representation. As all other representational objects, psychological states thus exist independently of being themselves represented in mind or language. Hence, psychological states exist prior to being articulated in thought or speech, and sentences deploying psychological expressions thereby represent corresponding psychological states.

In the following (Section 1.2), I presented Moore's Paradox as a challenge to the representationalist view. Moore's Paradox arises upon asserting sentences of the type 'p is the case, but I don't believe that p is the case'. The challenge to the representationalist view consists in the point that assertions of this type are absurd, they are in some way paradoxical, although what they express can actually be true. Thus Moore's Paradox neither constitutes a logical, nor an empirical contradiction. As a further complication, the two conjoined sentences of which it is comprised are incommensurable under formal-logical aspects—the first conjunct is concerned with an external state of affairs, the second one with the speaker's attitude towards this state of affairs—since they concern two entirely distinct matters of fact. The possibility that the first conjunct could, in some way or other, generate the paradox, was swiftly ruled out for several reasons. Instead, the second conjunct, in particular the phrase 'I believe', was found to be responsible from prompting the paradox, together with a distinctive property of assertion. So the *prima facie* conjecture was that the absurdity originates from the 'logic of assertion' and the grammar of the verb 'to believe'.

Subsequently, I presented three versions of the representationalist view and their respective approaches to explaining Moore's Paradox alongside the solution, which was originally suggested by Moore himself, Searle's pragmatist approach and the two approaches from rationality and self-knowledge proposed by Shoemaker and Moran (sections 2.1–2.6). Neither view *exploits* the prima facie impression, i.e. that the absurdity of Moore-paradoxical sentences results from the use of assertions and of the expression 'I believe' in everyday language. Instead, all focus exclusively on the contrast of the absurdity of Moore-paradoxical sentences with their possible truth. In perfect unanimity thus, the discussed proposals were shown to proceed from the commonplace assumption that "[i]n saying 'p' one normally suggests that one believes that p, or expresses a belief that p." (Williams (1979), p. 142) An assertion that p is the case thus implies the speaker's belief that p is the case. That an assertion could be so amended was explained by the grammatical asymmetry of avowals. Accordingly, a Moore-paradoxical assertion 'p is the case, but I don't believe that p is the case' implies the speaker's belief that p is the case, and hence implicitly entails the assertion 'I believe that p is the case'. Hence, one arrives at the conclusion that Moore-paradoxical assertions present contradictions between one of the explicitly stated conjuncts and an implicit, additional statement.

Yet, Moore-paradoxical sentences are not contradictions, neither logical nor empirical ones—which is recognised by the representationalist views I discussed themselves. However, as I have argued, there is no other solution available within the representationalist paradigm, particularly in the light of the two-component model and the assumption that psychological expressions always designate corresponding psychological phenomena.

In the last section, I traced the complex of assumptions constituting the core of the represenationalist view back to Frege's conception of thought and assertion. I have thereby paved the way for the next chapter, in which I will develop an argument from Moore's Paradox that, whilst rejecting each of the core representationalist assumptions, will yield the conclusion that we ought to relinquish the representationalist view of mind and language.

2 Moore's Paradox Revisited

2.1 Moore's Paradox Reconsidered

In the last chapter, I presented Moore's Paradox as a challenge to the representationalist theory of the mind and its concomitant views concerning the meaning of language, its constitution and function. I argued that none of the representationalist approaches to Moore's Paradox yields an adequate solution of the paradox, and I argued that this is necessarily so, given the framework of representationalism. Consequently, my conclusion was that one should drop those presuppositions that prevent representationalist views from accommodating Moore's Paradox. As suitable candidates to give up, I have suggested the representationalist conception of assertion along the lines of the two-component model, and of the meaning of the expression 'I believe', which was said to supposedly consist in designating a corresponding mental phenomenon. Yet, since these are part and parcel of the representationalist framework, my suggestion is that we should dispense with representationalism altogether.

In this chapter, I elaborate an argument from Moore's Paradox, which will in particular be directed against the representationalist conception of language, and amend it with an argument to show that the representationalist conception of how the meaning of psychological expressions is constituted (namely by reference to corresponding phenomena) is false. I will continue by sketching an alternative view of the meaning of psychological concepts (Chapter 3). I will treat Moore's Paradox alongside other borderline cases of everyday language and close the inquiry with some thoughts on the lessons to be learned from Moore's Paradox with respect to the logic of assertion, the concept of belief, and the philosophical treatment of concepts from everyday language. I first reconsider Moore's Paradox for the purpose of clarifying once more what is at issue.

Moore's Paradox is induced by sincerely asserting a sentence of the form 'p is the case, but I don't believe that p is the case'. It is, under ordinary circumstances, absurd or nonsensical to say 'It is raining, but I don't believe it is raining', in the sense that one would not know how to respond to such a statement. Most likely, one would react by saying 'What do you mean?', which would be perfectly appropriate. Yet it is hard to pinpoint exactly why such sentences are absurd, and what this absurdity consists in. For one thing, there are cases in which it makes sense even to assert a sentence of this form. If a close friend calls you up and states, in a stern voice, 'My mother just died, but I don't believe it', it would be inappropriate to answer 'Don't be absurd, but tell me what you really want to say'. For another thing, sentences like that are conjunctions of two grammatically and semantically inconspicuous sentences, neither of which is absurd in itself. The sentences 'p is the case' and 'I don't believe that p is the case' are, taken for themselves, perfectly intelligible statements that a certain fact obtains. Finally, Moore-paradoxical sentences are not contradictions either, for the two propositions conjoined in a Moore-paradoxical sentence are not mutually exclusive, neither under formal-logical aspects, nor from an empirical point of view.

Although Moore-paradoxical sentences are not contradictions, it is noteworthy that they involve the same proposition twice, *that p is the case*, once in a positive, once in a negative sentence: one conjunct is affirmed (It is raining), the other one negated (I do *not* believe that it is raining), separated only by the expression 'I believe'. This suggests that there is something about the expression 'I believe' that makes Moore-paradoxical sentences appear *similar to* contradictions[1] and, at the same time, prevents them from constituting a *kind of* contradiction.[2] Hence, the absurdity of assertions taking the form 'p is the case, and I don't believe that p is the case', seems to be not merely a coincidental or empirical issue, as Moore proposes, but rather a conceptual issue, inherent in their structure.

The paradox consists in that asserting these sentences *is* absurd, but *ought not to be*, given three considerations. Moore specifies them as follows. First, Moore-paradoxical assertions are absurd, although they can be true. Second, sincerely asserting a sentence of the type 'p is the case, but I don't believe that p is the case' is absurd, although saying or thinking a sentence of this type in another pragmatic context is not (e.g. in a supposition). Third, asserting sentences of this structure is absurd, although asserting the same content from another person's point of view, or in another tense of the verb 'to believe' is not. The absurdity in question thus gives rise to Moore's Paradox because it is a unique feature of a class of sentences expressing a particular kind of fact, *that p is the case and that someone does not believe that p is the case*, in a particular pragmatic context, an assertion, and from a particular perspective, that is, in a particular inflective form of the verb 'to believe', the first-person present tense. Moore's Paradox arises only under these circumstances.

---

1 The relevant sense of 'similar' will be clarified in the next section.

2 I take it to be relatively obvious that the absurdity of Moore-paradoxical sentences is not merely a matter of asserting that one does not believe something to be the case. The utterance 'It is raining, but *I don't believe* that Chelsea won the cup' might be puzzling (due to an abrupt change in subject), but it is not absurd in the sense the utterance of a Moore-paradoxical sentence would be. And the assertion 'It is raining, but I don't believe that we need to change our hiking plans', is perfectly sensible. That Moore-paradoxical sentences are absurd, has two sources, that two sentences involving the same proposition are conjoined in an assertion, and their being separated by the (negated) expression 'I believe'.

The representationalist explanations of Moore's Paradox I presented in the previous chapter agree in their analyses of the paradox as well as in their solution with Moore's original considerations. Throughout, the paradox is interpreted as the discrepancy between the absurdity of asserting a sentence with the structure $p \wedge \neg B(I, p)$ and the possible truth of what is thereby asserted. The question worrying the representationalist is, how does it come that a true description of the facts, or, in case of Moore-paradoxical belief, an accurate representation of what is the case, is nevertheless absurd?

In the light of there being three reasons Moore gives for the generation of the paradox, there are two factors that play a role in the generation of Moore's Paradox which are neglected by the representationalist approaches to Moore's Paradox: the logic of assertion and the meaning of the expression 'I believe'. This is actually not surprising, for these two matters are set within the theoretical framework of representationalism and belong to its core. Assertions are supposed to comply with the two-component model; the meaning of the word 'to believe' is taken to consist in designating a corresponding psychological phenomenon. For these reasons, both are not negotiable, even the less for the purpose of providing a solution to a small paradox like Moore's. Where it is seen that they are indeed challenged by Moore's Paradox, efforts are taken to explain how Moore's Paradox can be solved in accord with them, by making use of the third option only. That Moore's Paradox in this way is reduced to a contradiction and so brought to disappearance is accepted as a more or less undesirable side-effect—after all, one might say, it's just an implicit contradiction, that doesn't really count. That it does count, that this ought to be taken seriously, and that this, as a last consequence, undermines these very assumptions of representationalism, is what I will argue in this chapter. I will do so by employing two arguments of Wittgenstein's; the argument contained in his remarks on Moore's Paradox published in *Philosophy of Psychology – A Fragment* (Section x), and several strands from his argument against the conceivability of a private language.

2.2 Wittgenstein on Moore's Paradox

Wittgenstein's most prominent remarks on Moore's Paradox are published in *Philosophy of Psychology – A Fragment* (Section x, §§ 86–110) where they appear as an assemblage of thematically related remarks taken from various manuscripts and rearranged in a more or less random order.[3] As it is often the case with Wittgen-

---

3 Joachim Schulte has, at various places, comprehensively described the editorial process of Wittgenstein's writings. Difficulties in understanding and interpreting Wittgenstein's published

stein's published remarks, their coherence is not plainly obvious. This makes it tempting to pick out single remarks in order to illustrate and support one's own argument irrespective of their original context. Consequently, this manner of adopting Wittgenstein's philosophy (which is rather a manner of adapting it) regularly generates misinterpretations, makes Wittgenstein look unnecessarily enigmatic and eventually obscures rather than illuminates his views. Moran provides a good example here in that he calls Wittgenstein in line with Sartre ("the last great Cartesian" (Moran (1997), p. 141)) witness for his account of self-knowledge and the asymmetry of avowals. Ironically, Wittgenstein's remarks on Moore's Paradox include an argument to the contrary of Moran's view. Section x of *PPF* is not only composed quite carefully, but also Wittgenstein there unfolds a complex argumentation from Moore's Paradox against the core ideas of representationalism. The argumentation is divided in five separate but interlocking arguments, addressing in turn (1) the two-component model in general (§§ 87–9), (2) its functionalist version (§§ 90–2), (3) the Reference Claim with respect to psychological concepts (§§ 93–100), (4) the Uniformity Claim (§§ 101–5), and (5) the prioritisation of thought over language (§§ 106–9). It further outlines an alternative conception of the meaning of the word 'belief' (§ 102), which I will take up in the closing chapter.

2.2.1 Contextualisation

Let me first try a rough contextualisation of Wittgenstein's considerations on the concept of belief in *PPF*, Section x. The grammar of the words 'belief' and 'to believe' belongs to the domain of language concerned with expressing, articulating and understanding one another's psychological condition by means of psychological concepts. Understanding this region of language, as it were, in both its scientific

---

remarks often originate from the way in which the respective editors proceeded in selecting and translating passages from Wittgenstein's manuscripts. During the editorial process the manuscripts underwent several rounds of selection, some of which were performed by Wittgenstein himself. The published remarks often present abridgements of Wittgenstein's original trains of thoughts, whose most important or most concise steps and conclusions have been selected for publication, often to the effect that it is not obvious that Wittgenstein actually pursues arguments and does not arrive 'out of the blue' at his insights. *Cf.* Schulte (1993); Joachim Schulte (1996), "Es regnet, aber ich glaube es nicht", in Eike von Savigny, Oliver Scholz (eds.), Wittgenstein über die Seele, Frankfurt: Suhrkamp, pp. 194–212; and his introduction in Ludwig Wittgenstein, *Philosophische Untersuchungen. Kritisch-genetische Edition (PU)*, ed. by Joachim Schulte, Frankfurt: Suhrkamp 2001. The sources of the remarks on Moore's Paradox in *Philosophical Investigations* are *MSS* 130, 132, 133, 137 and 169. Some of the remarks have also been published in Wittgenstein's *Remarks on the Philosophy of Psychology* and *Zettel*, often in a more encompassing context.

and its everyday variants, counts among Wittgenstein's major concerns during the last years of his life. He attaches particular importance to the question how the meaning of psychological concepts is constituted, in which sense they can be said to relate to the psychological phenomena they express, and what psychological phenomena are conceived to be in different contexts of discourse.

Wittgenstein's concern is not so much to criticise and develop particular psychological theories,[4] but rather to articulate the modalities of the use of psychological language both in scientific and everyday contexts. Contrary to psychological theories and contrary to representationalist theories, Wittgenstein's inquiry is a grammatical inquiry, not an investigation into the metaphysics, the function and the ontology of the mind. Unsurprisingly his approach therefore yields different results; e.g. with respect to the meaning of psychological concepts, or with respect to his appreciation of ordinary ways of talking about experience.

There is often an observable clash between the easiness of using psychological concepts in everyday circumstances and the confusion that arises when using such concepts in scientific discourse. This confusion concerns their grammatical behaviour as well as the ontology of psychological phenomena they supposedly designate. Wittgenstein is interested in two things in particular. First, he is concerned with rendering a 'map' of psychological concepts, i.e. with laying out their use, their mutual relationships, and the places they occupy in language. The purpose of this somewhat cumbersome seeming method is to arrive at a better understanding of their meaning than it would be available by explaining them in a concise, but abridged and one-dimensional way. Second, he is concerned with bringing to light views that, being deeply entrenched in our commonsense way of thinking and speaking about the mental, unreflectedly carry over into our scientific investigations of the mind, where they hold us, so to speak, captive such that most often its results cannot but present psychological phenomena in a distorted way. Wittgenstein discerns several tendencies and temptations in our ways to reflect on the nature of the mind lying at the bottom of the confusion, to which he comes back over and over again in his later writings. I shall mention three prominent

---

4 Exceptions are Wolfgang Köhler's developments in Gestalt psychology and William James' *Principles of Psychology*. The latter were, as the legend wills, for a certain period of time the only academic books Wittgenstein tolerated on his bookshelf. Wittgenstein indeed appreciated James' ideas, although he considered his explanation of the connection between emotions and expressions of emotion mistaken. *Cf. RPP* I §§ 451–6; *RPP* II §§ 321–35; William James (1890), *The Principles of Psychology*, 2 Volumes, New York: Dover; Wolfgang Köhler (1933), *Psychologische Probleme*, Berlin: Julius Springer (the revised German edition of his (1929) *Gestalt psychology*). For Wittgenstein's quotations from and allusions to these and other authors, see the impressive register from Hans Biesenbach (2011), *Anspielungen und Zitate im Werk Ludwig Wittgensteins*, Bergen: Wittgenstein Archives.

ones to characterise the broader context in which the remarks on Moore's Paradox stand inasmuch as they are concerned with the concept of belief. These are, firstly, the striving for finding laws of utmost generality and uniformity governing the function of language and of the mind; secondly, the entrenched aptness to model the mental as an inner realm of its own, for instance, as a subjective, private realm, removed in one distinctive way or another from the epistemic reach of others—in structural analogy, but ontological opposition to the 'outer' realm of physical objects—which, thirdly, usually goes hand in hand with referentialism with regard to psychological concepts.

In this context, Wittgenstein's remarks on the concept of belief inspired by Moore's Paradox have, as I will argue in this chapter, severe implications for a variety of core metaphysical assumptions regarding the nature, function and epistemology of beliefs and other psychological phenomena that are entrenched in contemporary philosophy of mind and related sciences, e.g. psychology and cognitive science, just to mention the two most prominent. In particular, I will argue that the argument from Moore's Paradox provides the basis for decisively and finally rejecting the core assumptions of representationalism.

Insofar as they concern the concept of belief, the three mentioned metaphysical themes become thematic in the remarks constituting *PPF*, Section x. Wittgenstein notes here and at related places[5] that the verb 'to believe' exhibits a characteristic asymmetry in the semantic and logical properties of its first-person singular present indicative, when used in assertions, in comparison to its other grammatical forms. In virtue of its grammatical asymmetry compared with other verbs, the verb 'to believe' presents a counter-example to the view that the meaning of concepts consists in a uniform core which is present in every instantiation of the concept, independently of its particular pragmatic and grammatical context. This suggests that the meaning of the words 'to believe' and 'belief' is not backed by a referent. That is, there is no such thing as a uniform, definable phenomenon of belief the presence of which could be criterially identified (whether by subjective or objective criteria) whenever someone 'holds' a belief. It thus seems that we should understand it by no means as a "matter of course, but as a most remarkable thing that the verbs 'believe', 'wish', 'will' display all the grammatical forms possessed by 'cut', 'chew', 'run'" (*PPF* § 93), particularly that they continue in the first-person singular present indicative. Notwithstanding, they *do* so as a matter of fact, and it would intuitively seem most awkward, an offspring from a behaviourist nightmare ('you believe it's raining, but what do I believe?'), if they didn't. But accepting that this is so does not automatically support the conclusion that it is for the reason that

---

5 *RPP* I, *RPP* II and *MSS* 130, 132, 133, 137, 169.

there was some sort of a common referent providing coherence among, in terms of semantic continuity between, the grammatical forms of the verb 'to believe'. The grammatical characteristics of psychological concepts do not themselves allow for metaphysical conclusions regarding the nature of the mental. Turning the grammatical inquiry into a metaphysical enterprise yet contributes to constituting the framework of the representationalist view. This issues in the claim that psychological concepts had an unchangeable uniform meaning independently of their inflection, and the concomitant claim that a sentence 'I believe that p' referred to a designated inner state, the belief that p. This is a step in the wrong direction and does not at any rate render any illuminating explanatory results concerning the meaning and the use of psychological expressions, or the metaphysics of mind. This is what I will argue in the following.

2.2.2 Moore's (Un-) Discovery

Wittgenstein's engagement with Moore's Paradox began with a talk given by G. E. Moore at the *Cambridge Moral Sciences Club* in October 1944. On that occasion Moore presented the paradox for the first time. Wittgenstein, who was present at Moore's lecture, reacted enthusiastically in a letter to Moore, which he wrote the following day:

> Dear Moore,
> I should like to tell you how glad I am that you read us a paper yesterday. It seems to me that the most important point was the "absurdity" of the assertion "There is a fire in this room and I don't believe there is." To call this, as I think you did, "an absurdity for *psychological* reasons" seems to me to be wrong, or *highly* misleading. (If I ask someone "Is there a fire in the next room?" and he answers "I believe there is" I can't say: "Don't be irrelevant. I asked you about the fire, not about your state of mind!") But what I wanted to say was this. Pointing out that "absurdity" which is in fact something *similar* to a contradiction, though it isn't one, is so important that *I hope you'll publish your paper*. By the way, don't be shocked at my saying it's something "similar" to a contradiction. This means roughly: it plays a similar role in logic. You have said something about the *logic* of assertion. Viz: It makes sense to say "Let's suppose: p is the case and I don't believe that p is the case", whereas it makes *no* sense to assert "⊢ p is the case and I don't believe that p is the case". This *assertion* has to be ruled out and *is* ruled out by 'common sense', just as a contradiction is. And this just shows that logic isn't as simple as logicians think it is. In particular: that contradiction isn't the *unique* thing people think it is. It isn't the *only* logically inadmissible form and it is, under certain circumstances, admissible. And to show this seems to me the chief merit of your paper. In a word it seems to me that you've made a *discovery*, & that you should publish it.
> I hope to see you privately some day.
> Yours sincerely
> L. Wittgenstein[6]

We can extract the following observations from the letter: (1) Moore's Paradox concerns an absurdity, which arises if—and only if—sentences that take the form 'It is raining, but I don't believe it' are asserted. (2) The absurdity does not occur for "psychological reasons", that is, it does not result from a fact concerning the speaker's mind. Wittgenstein can therefore be expected to disagree with representationalist explanations of Moore's Paradox because, as I have explained in the previous chapter, these have to appeal to an implicitly conveyed fact about the speaker's mind. (3) Assertions of the type $p \land \neg B(I, p)$ are "similar" to assertions of contradictions of the form $(p \land \neg p)$ in that they, too, make no sense. (4) Such assertions therefore have to be and actually are excluded from use in everyday language.[7] (5) The absurdity of Moore-paradoxical sentences shows that logic is more complex than logicians think it is. (6) In particular, it illuminates something about the "logic" of assertions. (7) It is conceivable that asserting a Moore-paradoxical sentence makes sense under certain circumstances.

Remarkably, Wittgenstein does not mention the word 'truth' once in the context of Moore's Paradox. The representationalist question of 'Why can a true description be absurd?' and its corresponding answer, because it truly represents an absurd state of affairs, seem to have no role in Wittgenstein's approach to Moore's Paradox. The notion 'truth' is, for Wittgenstein, inextricably interlaced with the logic of assertion. Contrary to all the views discussed, Wittgenstein consequently focusses on the contrast between assertions and other kinds of sentences, particularly suppositions in the Fregean sense, that display a Moore-paradoxical structure, and relatedly on the meaning of the expression 'I believe'. This peculiarity persists throughout Wittgenstein's considerations of Moore's Paradox and contributes to the radicalness of Wittgenstein's argument.

---

6 *Briefe* 257, original emphases.

7 Wittgenstein makes use of the word 'nonsense' in a descriptive, not a normative sense. In the *Tractatus* (*TLP*), the word 'nonsense' designates expressions that lack a sense in Frege's use of the word, e.g. in *TLP* 3.03ff. In Wittgenstein's later writings, the notion 'nonsense' comprises utterances or sentences that do not provide a clue how to continue thinking or talking from them or how to respond to them—every response could be right and wrong at the same time. Nonsensical expressions in this latter sense do not play a role in language, either in general, or within a particular speaking situation. In that they are of no use although they are composed in accord with grammatical rules, they are 'ruled out by commonsense'. Formal-logical contradictions constitute one class of nonsensical expressions, Moore-paradoxical sentences another one. This is one of several similarities between sentences of both classes. See Ludwig Wittgenstein, *Tractatus logico-philosophicus. Logisch-philosophische Abhandlung*, ed. by Joachim Schulte, Frankfurt: Suhrkamp 2003; and *cf.* Hans-Johann Glock (1996), *A Wittgenstein Dictionary*, Oxford: Blackwell, pp. 258–64.

Approaching Moore's Paradox as a grammatical problem allows a critical examination of the two issues in grammar that have always already been pre-established in adopting a representationalist framework: the 'logic of assertion', which was explained in terms of the two-component model, and the meaning of the word 'belief', which was explained as denoting a corresponding mental state. Seen in this light, Moore's Paradox raises serious doubts for the representationalist assumptions concerning the function of assertions as well as on the constitution of the meaning of psychological concepts. Moreover, approaching Moore's Paradox from a grammatical point of view relieves the investigation of the pressure to yield a coherent metaphysical picture of the mind as an *explanans* for the peculiarities of grammar. Thus breaking with the striving for generality makes it possible to regard Moore's Paradox not as a wayward phenomenon that had to be integrated by all means in an otherwise neatly functioning and easily operatable theory, but as a phenomenon that sheds light on several aspects of the use of psychological concepts and calls the very point of drawing up theories of language into question that satisfy one's desire for generality and simplicity on pain of being inadequate to understand language in practice.

As early as in the letter, Wittgenstein emphasises that the absurdity of asserting a sentence of the form '*p* is the case, but I don't believe that *p* is the case' makes the assertion *similar to* a contradiction, although it is not a formal contradiction ($p \land \neg p$). What Wittgenstein means by 'similarity' becomes clear from a series of remarks that are concerned with Moore's Paradox in the context of first-person expressions of one's state of mind and published in the first volume of *Remarks on the Philosophy of Psychology*, §§ 460–504. In § 472, Wittgenstein notes that the first-person present indicative of psychological concepts can, under certain circumstances, be omitted from utterances, without thereby changing what the utterance expresses:

> I want to say first of all that with the assertion 'It's going to rain' one expresses belief in [what one asserts] just as one expresses the wish to have wine with the words 'Wine over here!' One might also put it like this: 'I believe *p*' means roughly the same as '*p*' and it ought not to mislead us that the verb 'believe' and the pronoun 'I' are present in the first sentence. We merely see clearly from this that the grammar of 'I believe', is very different from that of 'I write'.
>
> But when I say this, I don't mean that there may not be also big similarities here; and I am not saying what *kind* of differences there are. ((Real and imaginary unit.))
>
> For [bear in mind] that what is in question here are similarities and differences of concepts, not of phenomena. (*RPP* I § 472)

That is, one can express one's beliefs, wishes and so forth by means of different kinds of utterances, and insofar as several utterances serve to express one's state of mind, such as the utterances 'I wish you would bring me some wine' and 'Wine over here!' express the speaker's wish to have wine, they are *similar* to one another. What Wittgenstein means with expressions such as 'similarity' and 'roughly the same' in this context is clarified a couple of remarks later:

> What does it mean to say that 'I believe p' says roughly the same as 'p'? We react in roughly the same way when anyone says the first and when he says the second. (§ 477)

Asserting a Moore-paradoxical sentence such as 'It is raining, but I don't believe that it is raining' accordingly is similar to a contradiction because the sentences 'I don't believe that it is raining' and 'It isn't raining' are similar. Thus, Wittgenstein writes to Moore, they ought to be handled similarly in logic as they are in everyday situations. In 'commonsense' talk, Moore-paradoxical assertions are generally 'banned' or 'ruled out' from usage due to their unintelligibility, though they are 'admitted' as intelligible sentences in special circumstances.[8]

Note that Wittgenstein does not attach much normative weight to expressions such as 'banned from' and 'admitted', related expressions are merely 'withdrawn from circulation' (*PI* § 500) because they do not have a role to play in everyday communication. Wittgenstein hereby indicates that the use of certain sentences makes no sense in everyday language, although the sentences are unobjectionable from a *stricto sensu* logical or grammatical point of view. That they make no sense should not be mistaken for a normative claim (just as little as Wittgenstein's earlier use of the word 'nonsense'); he thereby only means, in the spirit of *RPP* I § 477, that one wouldn't know how to respond to a sentence such as 'Milk me sugar!' (*PI* § 498), even if all its elements, when taken in isolation or in other combinations, make sense (in this case the words 'milk', 'me', and 'sugar'). From Wittgenstein's point of view, this is pretty much all there is to the absurdity of Moore-paradoxical assertions. They are

> [C]ontradiction[s] only to the same extent as 'I'm incapable of pronouncing any word with four syllables'; or 'I can't speak a word of English'. If this latter is a kind of contradiction; still the assumption 'Suppose I couldn't speak a word of English' is not. (*RPP* I § 503)[9]

---

8 Examples of situations can be found at various places in *RPP* I and II, Searle mentions one in (1983), p. 9n. I will come back to this point later in this chapter.
9 The German original is more elusive in the first case: "ich kann kein viersilbiges Wort aussprechen", and the second, of course, originally reads: "Ich kann keinen einzigen deutschen Satz sagen" (*ibid.*) An important note regarding this quotation concerns the words 'assumption' [*Annahme*] and 'suppose...' [*angenommen, ...*]. Wittgenstein uses them for Frege's 'supposition' [*Annahme*], the mere "putting of a case without a simultaneous judgment as to its arising or not." (Frege (1980b), p. 21; *cf.* previous chapter.) To repeat, in representationalist terms, the words

I will now disentangle Wittgenstein's argument from Moore's Paradox in *Philosophy of Psychology – A Fragment*, x, simultaneously using it as substantial criticism of the fundamental claims of representationalism.

2.3 The Argument from Moore's Paradox

2.3.1 Assertion and Belief

At first sight, it might seem not fully comprehensible why Wittgenstein begins to discuss Moore's Paradox and its relevance to the logic of assertions by asking the following questions:

> How did we ever come to use such an expression as "I believe..."? Did we at some time become aware of a phenomenon (of belief)? Did we observe ourselves and other people and so discover belief? (*PPF* § 86)

One might of course simply ascribe this to a change in Wittgenstein's priorities. Yet, scrutinising the meaning of the expression 'I believe' is not an accidental move in the context of Moore's Paradox. After all, it is mainly responsible for Moore-paradoxical assertions to be undeniably absurd without being contradictory. Since the assertions '*p* is the case' and 'I believe that *p* is the case' are similar in meaning, the assertions '*p* is the case, but I don't believe that *p* is the case' and '*p* is the case, but *p* is not the case' are similar, too. That they are similar but not identical in meaning is shown in that, in contrast to asserting a Moore-paradoxical sentence, supposing a Moore-paradoxical sentence was true makes sense, but supposing a contradiction was true doesn't.

If representationalism was true, the phrase 'I believe' would describe the speaker's or thinker's own state of mind, and it would do so whenever it is used. A Moore-paradoxical sentence then consists in a conjunction of two ordinary sentences, a statement of facts and an avowal of the speaker's state of mind. Hence, a Moore-paradoxical sentence would, as I explained in the last chapter, in every instance

---

'supposition' and 'assumption' designate 'neutral' representational contents, i.e. those elements of representational states that constitute the representational state's accuracy conditions, without thereby contributing to its truth value. As announced in the last chapter, I will continue to use the words 'supposition' and 'assumption' in Wittgenstein's manner, in order to indicate that we are concerned with sentences whose only function is to represent (Fregean) thoughts, which are, as it were, pure meaning-bearers, or, again in Wittgenstein's terms "sentence-radicals" (*cf. PI*, p. 11n.; Schulte (1993), pp. 140f.

represent two independent states of affairs, one about the world and one about the speaker's mind. Because neither conjunct is nonsensical in itself, the representationalist is required to take Moore-paradoxical assertions as abridged descriptions of facts, which implicitly entail an additional description of facts that stands at odds with either of the other two. So representationalism can hardly avoid psychologising Moore's Paradox. This, as I have argued, inevitably leads to the conclusion that the person making a Moore-paradoxical assertion thereby asserts a contradiction.

This result is however problematic for two reasons. First, Moore-paradoxical sentences are neither logical nor empirical contradictions. So the representationalist conclusion that it is an implicit logical contradiction, is false because it would prevent Moore's Paradox from arising in the first place. Let us assume for the sake of argument that the proponent of representationalism managed, as he or she apparently believes he or she can do, to give a good argument why the implicit contradiction read into Moore-paradoxical assertions suffices to make the assertion appear contradictory and simultaneously is too implicit to be a real one. This suggestion would have the potential for an acceptable radio Yerevan joke. However, it would endanger the representationalist's commitment to the uniformity of content if one and the same sentence was absurd when asserted, but not when supposed, questioned, hypothesised and so forth. But you can't have the cake and eat it, you must opt for one of the following: *Either* asserting a Moore-paradoxical sentence amounts to asserting a contradiction. *Or* asserting a Moore-paradoxical sentence does *not* imply an additional contradictory assertion. Because of the internal relation between the Reference and the Uniformity Claim, it is not feasible on a representationalist conception to discard one of them whilst keeping the other.

The following problem arises however for each option: In the former case, the contradiction persists, as demanded by the Uniformity Claim, across all kinds of sentences containing a Moore-paradoxical sentence, including suppositions. In the latter case, the representationalist has no means at hand to integrate the absurdity of Moore-paradoxical sentences, because the two conjunct propositions are incommensurable under formal-logical aspects, that is, their truth-values are independent of one another, in that the states of affairs they refer to are neither logically nor causally or otherwise related. Consequently, my suggestion developed in this and the following chapter is simply to give up both claims, which is tantamount to dispensing with representationalism altogether. I now outline the arguments from Moore's Paradox against the central representationalist claims in more detail along the lines of *Philosophy of Psychology – A Fragment*, x.

2.3.2 The Two-Component Model

2.3.2.1 From Thought to Assertion

Representationalism hinges on the two-component model of thought and speech, according to which all representational states and utterances are decomposable into a mode and a content-element. This model basically originates from and corresponds to the Fregean conception of thought and assertion, in the guise of which it presents the target of Wittgenstein's first argument in *PPF* §§ 87–9.[10] To repeat, on Frege's view, assertions decompose into a neutral content, a thought, which turns into a particular assertion with a specific truth-value by a mental act, a judgement. Thoughts are conceived as abstract sentence-radicals $(-p)$ yielding, in a condensed manner, the general meaning of their particular instances. Thereby, they set the veridicality conditions of particular sentences, whereas they lack a truth-value, unless they are instantiated as the content of particular assertions. Analogously, representational content-types represent object-types and bear veridicality conditions, but become assessable in terms of veridicality only if they figure as the content of particular representational states. The general content-type or sentence-radical is logically prior to its instantiations, even in cases where it is accessible to an empirical person only by abstracting from particular token representations or token judgements, respectively. The two-component view implies that it is possible to isolate the content-element from every particular representational state and that utterances or representational states that are identical in content are identical in meaning (see previous chapter).

What if Moore's Paradox is seen from Wittgenstein's angle, as a paradox concerning the logic of assertion rather than a paradox concerning a particular constellation of facts about a particular person's mind? Then, Wittgenstein suggests,

> Moore's paradox can be put like this: the expression "I believe that this is the case" is used like the assertion "This is the case"; and yet the *hypothesis* [*Annahme*] that I believe that this is the case is not used like the hypothesis that this is the case. (*PPF* § 87)

On the two-component model of thought, one would expect a particular content to remain the same, regardless of the sentence, or type of sentence it appears in. But this is not the case when one compares the assertion 'p is the case, but I don't believe that p is the case' with the content-identical supposition. Whereas asserting a Moore-paradoxical sentence is absurd, supposing, questioning or hypothesising

---

10 *Cf. Briefe* 257; *RPP* I, §§ 471ff.; *PI* p. 11n.; Schulte (1996), p. 195f.; and (1995), p. 140.

it is not:

$$\vdash (p \wedge \neg B(I, p)) \text{ is similar to } \vdash (p \wedge \neg p), \quad \text{whereas}$$
$$-(p \wedge \neg B(I, p)) \text{ is } not \text{ similar to } -(p \wedge \neg p).$$

Asserting a Moore-paradoxical sentence sounds similar to asserting a contradiction because in most ordinary communicative situations the assertions 'p is the case' and 'I believe that p is the case' are used interchangeably, whereas in a different grammatical context the two sentences cannot be mutually substituted (e.g. in another tense or in an assumption). This means trouble for the two-component model, because all instances of the sentence 'I believe that p is the case' should have the same meaning, that their subject believes that p is the case. But this is called into question by Moore-paradoxical sentences. What is more, now it seems that the assertions *that p is the case* and *that I believe that p is the case* are more closely related in meaning than the assertion *that I believe that p is the case* and the supposition *that I believe that p is the case* are. This, too, shouldn't be the case on the two-component model, for the meaning of a sentence was decisively conditioned on the content it articulates, not on the kind of psychological or pragmatic mode in which it is embedded.

From a representationalist viewpoint, Moore's Paradox has the effect that the wrong sentences are commensurable under formal-logical aspects: the assertions 'p' and '$B(I, p)$', which apparently describe different facts, even different types of facts, seem comparable in meaning to the effect that the conjuncts of Moore-para-doxical sentences, p and $\neg B(I, p)$, appear incompatible. In contrast, the meaning of asserting and assuming the very same fact, $B(I, p)$, radically differs. Unless the representationalist denies that Moore-paradoxical assertions are paradoxical, he or she is required to transform a Moore-paradoxical assertion into a sentence that contains two commensurable elements whose conjunction constitutes an inconsistency for logical reasons (for Moore's Paradox is a conceptual issue) and thus explains the incompatibility of the two conjuncts. Since there is a structural similarity between the two conjuncts of a Moore-paradoxical sentence in that the same proposition, *that p is the case*, appears once in a positive, and once in a negative context, separated only by the expression 'I believe', there seem to be two possible strategies, eliminating the expression 'I believe' or duplicating it in a way that produces the requested inconsistency.[11]

---

[11] Heal, for instance, formulates: "[T]he solution must identify a contradiction, or something contradiction-like, in the Moorean claims." (1994, p. 6) Their oddness is accepted to consist in some conceptual tension, not in empirical improbability.

2.3.2.2 The Photographic Model: Against Functionalism

In order to make the two conjuncts of a Moore-paradoxical sentence comparable, one might argue that a description of one's beliefs ($B(I, p)$) indirectly involves a description of the contents of one's beliefs (p); such as a description of a photograph can function as a description of what it portrays:

> 'Basically, in using the words 'I believe…', I describe my own state of mind—but here this description is indirectly an assertion of the fact believed.'—As, in certain circumstances, I describe a photograph in order to describe what it is a photograph of. (*PPF* § 90)

On this assumption, the expression 'I believe' could be bracketed in a Moore-paradoxical sentence, which one might render like this:

$$\vdash p \wedge \neg B(I, p) \quad \rightarrow \quad \vdash p \wedge \neg [B(I,]p) \,.$$

This suggestion evidently reduces the absurdity raising Moore's Paradox to asserting a formal contradiction (which it isn't) and does so regardless of the kind of utterance in which it appears, i.e. not only in case of assertions. But Moore's Paradox arises only if a Moore-paradoxical sentence is asserted, not if it is questioned, assumed etc. This argument aside, the comparison of beliefs and photographs suggests that one could handle a belief just like a photograph, in particular, that one could 'impartially' state whether what one believes to be true is actually true, such as one can state whether a photograph is an accurate or a good picture of its object, and such as one can state that one's own sense-impressions are delusive or veridical: "But then I must be able to go on to say that the photograph is a good one. So also: 'I believe it's raining and my belief is reliable, so I rely on it.'—In that case, my belief would be a kind of sense impression." (*PPF* § 90) In this way, conceiving of belief in terms of its veridicality conditions only, such as Searle does, or in terms of its functional properties, as a functionalist-cum-representationalist model would do, assimilates beliefs to sense impressions, that is, to such mental states, which one could, in one's own case, assess 'from the outside' such that one could sensibly judge that one has false beliefs. This is likely to neglect the important conceptual feature of belief that "beliefs aim at truth",[12] a reason why,

---

12 Williams (1970), p. 136; *cf.* also *PPF* § 92. Williams formula encapsulates three characteristics of beliefs. First, they are assessable as to their truth or falsity. Second, believing that p means nothing but believing that p is true. Upon recognising that one holds a false belief one will thus abandon the belief. Third, and most importantly here, one cannot *intend* to falsely believe something. Note that Shoemaker (1995) is aware of that problem and tries to solve it by means of his Higher-Order Belief model, although this means to introduce the additional, non-functionalist assumption of a desire for maximal rational consistency within one's own belief system. I mention this point

as Wittgenstein puts it, "[O]ne can mistrust one's own senses, but not one's own belief" (*PPF* § 91).

The comparison of beliefs with photographs moreover demonstrates what has been suspected before, that it is not possible to extend a Moore-paradoxical sentence by introducing, as a third conjunct (underlined), the content of the belief stated in the second conjunct, like this:

$$\vdash p \wedge \neg B(I, p) \quad \rightarrow \quad \vdash p \wedge \neg B(I, p) \wedge \underline{\neg p}.$$

For this conjunct would, though commensurable with the first one, persist independently of the belief stated in the second conjunct. But the second and the third conjunct, the speaker's belief and the content of the speaker's beliefs, are not independent of one another, but, as Moran has pointed out, internally related facts *from the speaker's point of view.*[13]

This is to say that it is conceptually ruled out that one takes one's own current beliefs as empirical facts, such as one can treat other people's beliefs or one's own sense impressions. This matter of fact brings us back to the asymmetry of the first-person present indicative of the verb 'to believe' that was already touched on in the discussion of Moran's view. The asymmetry was supposed to consist in a special error-resistance of self-ascriptions of (some) mental states deriving from the epistemic certainty of knowing one's own mind, and as such found responsible

---

mainly because it is the reason why Searle cannot account for Moore-paradoxical beliefs. On his account of intentionality, beliefs are defined as representational states with the mind-to-world direction of fit and the conditions of satisfaction that what is believed, is true. From this definition, it does not follow that believing that the conditions of satisfaction of one's own current beliefs are unfulfilled is absurd, as it would have to be the case to run Moore's Paradox for Moore-paradoxical beliefs. On the possibility of believing Moore-paradoxical sentences, *cf.* the conclusion of this chapter.

13 Notwithstanding his own argument, Moran maintains the possibility of treating one's own beliefs alongside the beliefs of other people, from a fully detached but still first-personal point of view (characterised as self-alienation), which he introduces as an *explanans* for Moore's Paradox using an example from a psychoanalytic setting. In the previous chapter, I have already called into question that Moran's explanation of the example is plausible, among others for the reason that precisely the phenomenon of self-alienation from one's beliefs, as Moran conceives of it, is conceptually ruled out by the concept of belief. The more plausible description of the case, as Moran presents it, is that the person is confused about what to believe with regard to her brother, she does not hold two contradictory beliefs about what she believes with regard to her brother. This suggests that self-deception does not mean to have false beliefs about the state of one's own mind, but to deceive oneself on matters in the world, e.g. by being ignorant towards specific aspects of an issue (in Moran's case, for example, the brother's actual behaving towards the analysand). See Severin Schroeder (2006), "Moore's Paradox and First-Person Authority", *Grazer Philosophische Studien* 71, pp. 161–74 (especially pp. 169f.); and the previous chapter, Section 3.6.3.

for the generation of Moore's Paradox. It was used to explain why asserting *that p is the case*, and asserting *that I believe that p is the case* are similar, whereas supposing *that p is the case* and supposing *that I believe that p is the case*, are not. If the two assertions are interchangeable, they are so in both directions:

(9a) $\vdash p \;\rightarrow\; \vdash p \wedge B(I, p)$ *et*

(9b) $\vdash B(I, p) \;\rightarrow\; \vdash B(I, p) \wedge p$, [14]

and, for a Moore-paradoxical assertion:

(12a) $\vdash p \wedge \neg B(I, p) \;\rightarrow\; \vdash p \wedge \neg B(I, p) \wedge \neg p$,

(12b) $\vdash p \wedge \neg B(I, p) \;\rightarrow\; \vdash p \wedge B(I, p) \wedge \neg B(I, p)$.

It is obvious that, if the representationalist's flirt with the asymmetry of 'I believe' *necessarily* yields (a version) of this proposition as the solution to Moore's Paradox, this attempt to integrate Moore's Paradox into representationalism, too, will be doomed to fail.[15] Wittgenstein's following argument (*PPF* §§ 94–8) is tailor-made to show just that.

2.3.2.3 The Elimination of the Meaning of 'I believe'

If the absurdity of asserting '*p* is the case, but I don't believe that *p* is the case' is not due to an additional statement about the world, it must entail an implicit statement about the speaker's mind, which stands at odds with the second conjunct, 'I don't believe that *p* is the case'. This is the next step Wittgenstein suggests one might take and this is the move all of the discussed views make: Making an assertion implies that the speaker believes what he or she asserts. Hence, an assertion *that p is the case* always carries an implicit assertion about the speaker's state of mind, *that he or she believes that p is the case*. For this reason, it is possible to infer from an assertion to the speaker's state of mind. This matter of fact comes to bear, for instance, in examinations—questions such as, 'When did Nietzsche write the *Genealogy of Morals*?' or 'what is $\sqrt{26569}$?' do not aim at coming to know a historical or mathematical fact, but at testing what the student knows, i.e., at coming to know something about the student's mind. In situations like this, the answer will be primarily understood as conveying information about the speaker, rather than the subject-matter in question.[16]

---

14 Obviously and not coincidentally, this just is Moran's Transparency Claim, *cf.* the previous chapter, Section 3.6.1.

15 The same holds, *mutatis mutandis*, for Moore-paradoxical beliefs, as was explained in the last chapter.

16 *Cf. PPF* § 94; Schulte (1996), p. 200.

If this is a conceptual feature of assertion, it will always be possible to amend an assertoric sentence with the expression 'I believe that…'. Asserting 'p is the case' additionally entails asserting 'I believe: p is the case'. Reversely, if the meaning of the expression 'I believe' consisted in indicating the speaker's mental assent to the following proposition, it would be fully replaceable by other means of expressing the same thing, for example, an assertive tone of voice. This consideration nicely yields the result that asserting *that p is the case* is similar to asserting *that I believe that p is the case*, whereas supposing *that p is the case* and supposing *that I believe that p is the case* are not similar in the same way. It thus brings out the asymmetry of avowals of belief, which are characterisable, among others, as 'immediate expressions' of belief. What one does here is to isolate the expression 'I believe' from an assertion and turn its meaning into an adverbial one, making an assertion sound more empathetic, or colourful, or honest (*cf. PPF* §§ 95–7).

Accordingly, it seems that the expression 'I believe' could be omitted from assertions, because these are made in an assertive tone of voice anyway (to put Moran's Transparency Condition in a nutshell). The assertion 'p is the case, but I don't believe that p is the case' would, in this case, be equivalent to the assertion 'p is the case, and p is not the case'. This would, however, carry things too far, because Moore's Paradox would not arise at all. Asserting a Moore-paradoxical sentence would be nothing but a cumbersome way of asserting an ordinary logical contradiction (*cf. PPF* §§ 96–8). Wittgenstein here explores the claim that the expression 'I believe' was asymmetric in the sense described. He concludes that in this case, the expression 'I believe' would lack a sense, and in this way would cease to be a continuation of the other grammatical forms of 'to believe'.[17] Ironically, emphasising the asymmetry of the expression 'I believe' renders it a redundant ornament of a simple assertion; and rather than solving Moore's Paradox, the strategy at hand results in dissolving the absurdity into a contradiction:

(13) $\vdash B(I, p) \;\rightarrow\; \vdash p$

(14) $\vdash p \wedge \neg B(I, p) \;\rightarrow\; \vdash p \wedge \neg p$.

Moreover, if the expression 'I believe' were only an indicator of one's own state of mind serving to allow others to draw inferences towards one's own state of mind another claim by representationalism would be undermined; namely the claim

---

17 This line of argument is paralleled at a later stage of the private language argument, where Wittgenstein objects to a referential picture of meaning with regard to sensation-words: "That is to say: if we construe the grammar of the expression of sensation on the model of 'object and name', the object drops out of consideration as irrelevant." (*PI* § 293, transl. Hacker/Schulte) The same follows if one applies this model to the meaning of the phrase 'I believe' once it is hypostatised in the manner described.

that psychological concepts have a uniform meaning regardless of the grammatical form in which they are used. It would be impossible, that is, to represent one's own beliefs, and reflect on or communicate them, even though beliefs are, by the Priority Claim, facts that exist independently of being represented in language.[18]

One could however try to save the original idea, the idea which lead to claiming that asserting that p implies believing that p. This idea was to produce, in a Moore-paradoxical assertion, a third conjunct by implication, which is commensurable with either of the two explicit ones. Taken together with the relevant one of them, one would render a Moore-paradoxical assertion logically incoherent. Since the attempt to generate an additional statement standing at odds with the world-related conjunct (p) bears the dubious consequences just mentioned, the third conjunct must be an implicit statement about the speaker's state of mind. So one starts as in the case just discussed: Asserting *that p is the case* is tantamount to asserting *that p is the case and I believe that p is the case*. In contrast to the previous continuation, one maintains that the expression 'I believe' not only indicates, but represents that the speaker believes the proposition. The expression 'I believe' in the content of a Moore-paradoxical sentence would accordingly be opaque, not transparent, that is, its meaning would only consist in referring to the speaker's belief *that p is the case*. This line of thought is familiar by now: Asserting that p implies believing that p has already been Moore's proposal to explain his own paradox. It eventually leads to the conclusion that asserting a Moore-paradoxical sentence amounts to asserting 'p is the case, and I don't believe that p is the case, and I believe: p is the case, and I don't believe that p is the case'. This is just the result encountered in the last chapter:[19]

$$\vdash p \;\rightarrow\; \vdash p \wedge B(I, p) \quad \text{(Moore's Principle)}$$
$$\vdash p \wedge \neg B(I, p) \;\rightarrow\; \vdash p \wedge \neg B(I, p) \wedge B(I, p) \wedge B(I, \neg B(I, p)) \,.$$

What the representationalist has achieved by 'psychologising' Moore's Paradox in this manner, i.e. amending it with an assertion about the speaker's state of mind, is to have introduced an additional conjunct into a Moore-paradoxical assertion, consisting in an implicit assertion about the speaker's state of mind, which contradicts the original explicit assertion about the speaker's mind. This is certainly a

---

18 This extreme view of the asymmetry of avowals roughly amounts to what Moran has called, and rejected as, the 'Presentational View'. *Cf.* Moran (1997), pp. 144f., (2001), ch. 4.1; the previous chapter, Section 3.6.1; and Chapter 3, Section 2.3.

19 *Cf.* propositions (0)–(2), first appearing in the context of the solution offered by Moore, Section 3.1.

respectable conclusion, as it fully satisfies the representationalist adequacy conditions imposed on a solution to Moore's Paradox (as Heal (1994) suggests) and, at least superficially viewed, fits into the overall representationalist framework. Nonetheless, what is here presented as an explanation of why Moore-paradoxical assertions are absurd once again renders them as logical contradictions, and thereby explains away the original absurdity. Moore's Paradox cannot be accommodated within the representationalist conception of avowals as error-resistant self-ascriptions of independent facts, whether the expression 'I believe' is, so to speak, withdrawn from circulation in virtue of its asymmetry, or taken to represent the speaker's belief as an independently existing fact, as every other expression would do.

2.3.2.4 Against Referentialism I: The 'Phenomenon' of Moore-Paradoxical Beliefs

According to the Reference Claim, types of representational content inherit their properties from the phenomena they depict. The asymmetry of the first-person present indicative of 'to believe' accordingly is supposed to derive from the phenomenon it refers to, the speaker's current psychological state of believing. So it cannot be just a matter of grammar that asserting a Moore-paradoxical sentence raises Moore's Paradox. On the contrary, that it occurs must lie in the nature of belief, more precisely, in the attitude one has towards one's own beliefs. Since assertions are in general supposed to be articulations of content-identical beliefs, the next step is to focus on the phenomenon of Moore-paradoxical beliefs, in the hope to find something about the construction of Moore-paradoxical beliefs that explains the Moorean absurdity. As in the case of asserting a Moore-paradoxical sentence, the content of a Moore-paradoxical belief must somehow be amended to an internally commensurable, but inconsistent conjunction. If one keeps the assumption in place that the phrase 'I believe that p' represents the state of affairs *that the speaker holds the belief that p*, that is, that the expression 'I believe' designates that the following proposition is believed by the subject, there are again two ways to go.

On the first alternative, the phrase 'I believe', when appearing in the contents of a (meta-)belief, is supposed to be sufficiently provided for by the (meta-)belief itself. For instance, the content of Peter's (meta-)belief 'I believe it is raining' is just the same as the content of Peter's (simple) belief 'It is raining'. The expression 'I believe', which figures in the content of the meta-belief, is provided by Peter's believing the simple proposition 'It is raining' on the additional assumption that Peter, *qua* being a believer, knows that he believes 'It is raining' by entertaining that belief only without explicitly representing himself as believing 'It is raining'. In other words, the fact that the subject believes the proposition introduced by the expression 'I believe' is already entailed by the fact that it figures in the content of a (meta-)belief; and this is familiar to the subject. The subject of a (meta-)belief, which is about his or her own beliefs, need not additionally indicate that a particular proposition within his or her (meta-)belief is believed by him- or herself, because, as a matter of fact, the proposition in question is, by figuring in the content of a (meta-)belief, already believed by the subject. The belief *that I believe that p* could then be paraphrased as 'I believe: *p*'. This move makes the expression 'I believe' transparent, it need not even be replaced by a tone of voice or gesture, as it might be in the analogous case of asserting *that I believe that p*. For the subject of a belief *that I believe that p* need not communicate to anyone else in which mode the represented fact that *p* stands. Following this suggestion, entertaining a belief sufficiently indicates that its content is believed, such that possible occurrences of the phrase 'I believe' are redundant. The expression 'I believe' can therefore be dropped from a belief with Moore-paradoxical content as well, such that the subject believes a formal contradiction:

$$B(I, p \wedge \neg B(I, p)) \quad \rightarrow \quad B(I, p \wedge \neg p) \, .$$

In this way, analysing Moore-paradoxical beliefs in terms of transparency, as Moran advocates it, has the consequence that there are no Moore-paradoxical beliefs.

If, alternatively, the expression 'I believe' represents the state of affairs *that the subject believes that p* in a way that is opaque to the subject of a (meta-)belief with this content, the fact that the simple belief figures in the content of a (meta-)belief duplicates the expression 'I believe'. The (meta-)belief would be rendered as follows: 'I believe: I believe that *p*', which just amounts to 'I believe *that I believe that p*' or $B(I, B(I, p))$. A belief with Moore-paradoxical content accordingly would be accompanied by a meta-belief of the sort: 'I believe: *p* and I don't believe that *p*'. Then, the subject's belief content is tantamount to:[20]

$$B(I, p \wedge \neg B(I, p)) \quad \rightarrow \quad [B(I, p \wedge \neg B(I, p))] \wedge [B(I, B(I, p \wedge \neg B(I, p)))] \, , \text{ or}$$

$$(13) \quad [B(I, p) \wedge \underline{B(I, \neg B(I, p))}] \wedge [\underline{B(I, B(I, p))} \wedge B(I, B(I, \neg B(I, p)))] \, , \quad \text{or}$$

$$(14) \quad B(I, [p \wedge \underline{\neg B(I, p)}] \wedge [\underline{B(I, p)} \wedge B(I, \neg B(I, p)))]) \, .[21]$$

Therefore, according to the representationalist framework, believing or asserting a Moore-paradoxical sentence on either conception of the expression 'I believe'

---

20 The square brackets have no logical force. The first pair contains the simple belief, the second one comprises the meta-belief, the contradiction being underlined. The outcome is identical with the formalisation of Moore's Paradox on the Higher-Order Belief Model, see previous chapter, Section 3.5.3, proposition No. 6.

21 It is, unfortunately, not that easy. Whether or not you agree on the validity of deducing proposition (14) from (13) depends on your view as to how an individual subject's belief contents relate

comes down to believing or asserting a formal contradiction, $q \land \neg q$. And this conclusion does not render Moore-paradoxical beliefs and assertions absurd, nor has it to do with articulating inner conflicts, but with logic: Someone who believes or asserts a Moore-paradoxical sentence refers to a logically and empirically possible state of affairs. He or she does not state or believe a formal contradiction.

But can't we say that the expression 'I believe' is both transparent from the first-person point of view and opaque from a third-person point of view, as Moran (1997), (2001) and Heal (1994) suggest? Well, of course we can; and this suggestion takes up the representationalist's earlier radio Yerevan-joke on the contradictoriness of Moore-paradoxical assertions (it would be a good one, if it wasn't a sad fact that it is such a widely accepted view in philosophy of mind). For the suggestion, once spelled out, would read approximately, 'Moore-paradoxical beliefs and assertions are absurd, because, from *my* point of view, they are nothing but beliefs and assertions of formal contradictions, whereas, from your point of view, they aren't, of course'. This would radically break with the Uniformity Claim, because the first-person present indicative instantiation of the proposition $p \land \neg B(S, p)$ would not be identical in meaning with all other instantiations of the very same proposition, that is, it would not refer to the same state of affairs. The absurdity would arise only for the speaker, not for the hearer of a Moore-paradoxical assertion. This would have the effect that their respective reference were constituted by different states of affairs—my belief *that p is the case and I don't believe that p is the case*, represented from my point of view, would be a different state of affairs from my belief *that p is the case and U. S. doesn't believe that p is the case*, represented from your point of view. However, this contradicts the claim presupposed by the representationalist solution to Moore's Paradox, that beliefs were 'objective' facts existing indepen-

---

to one another, and so eventually on your views on the ontology of belief. If you have a substantial account of belief, and think of beliefs as discrete entities or events, such as books or photographs are, you will not agree with the last step: From Peter's having a book on Descartes and a book on Hume it does not follow that Peter has a book on Descartes and Hume. If, in contrast, 'having beliefs' is considered an attributive affair, a process, a disposition, or an action, say, the step from (13) to (14) is valid: If Peter is a jolly fellow and Peter is a good fellow, it follows that Peter is a jolly, good fellow.

However, if you opt for the first alternative, as Shoemaker for instance does, an additional principle must be introduced in order to explain as to how exactly holding beliefs with contradicting contents accounts for the absurdity of Moore-paradoxical assertions (which motivates Kriegel's (2004) criticism of Shoemaker's solution, see Chapter 1, Section 3.5.4.). On Shoemaker's, and similarly on Moran's view, this is provided for by his appeal to the subject's rationality, *viz.* the requirement to strive for maximal consistency among the contents of one's belief system. *Cf.* the previous chapter, Sections 3.5.2, 3.5.4, 3.6.2, and 3.7

dently of and prior to being represented from whatever perspective. Suggesting that asserting or believing a Moore-paradoxical sentence was contradictory to a degree just sufficient to be absurd, but not to count as a 'real' contradiction, does not render the content of Moore-paradoxical assertions and beliefs absurdities, but the representationalist assumptions themselves. The philosophical significance of Moore's Paradox consists in that the possibilities to approach Moore's Paradox open on representationalism reveal representationalism to be an eventually self-undermining model of the mind. The absurdity characteristic of Moore's Paradox has no space among the fundamental representationalist assumptions regarding the concept of belief, and the logic of assertion.

2.3.2.5 Asymmetry contra Uniformity

Let me further clarify the last point. One of the adequacy conditions on a conception of the meaning of avowals is that any such conception should yield two properties, semantic continuity and epistemic asymmetry (see Chapter 1, Section 3.6.1). The first is to secure that psychological predicates, such as the verb 'to believe', continue into the first-person present indicative without thereby adding or losing some facet or other of the respective concept's general meaning. That psychological concepts do not vary in meaning across their inflections is indisputable on a representationalist view, since their meaning is assumed to consist in designating corresponding psychological phenomena, whose existence and properties are independent of whether they are themselves represented, and if so, equally of the perspective from which this happens.

Conceiving of the asymmetry of the first-person present indicative of psychological concepts as an epistemic asymmetry seeks to circumvent ascribing a different meaning to this inflective form. That is, the asymmetry generating the possibility of transparency, i.e. of abandoning the phrase 'I believe' from assertions and belief-contents, is shifted from the content into the modal properties of the respective representational state or utterance. It is not the case, on this picture, that the first-person present indicative of psychological concepts had a different meaning, i.e. a different reference in comparison with all their other grammatical forms, but that the reference in this case is distinctively subjective. On this view, one's way of relating to one's own mental states is characterised as exclusive to the subject and yet supposed to involve reference to an objective fact. This consideration seems to be supported by the course Wittgenstein's argument takes in *PPF*, x: One does not speculate about one's own beliefs (*PPF* § 99), or infer from one's own behaviour to one's own psychological states, as others would do (§ 100), and finally, one obtains a "wholly different" attitude towards one's own words than others do (§ 103).

Taking this consideration into account and applying it to Moore's Paradox, it results very much the solution Moran has proposed: If the attitude in question (of which he conceives as distinctively first-person knowledge) is in place, then the phrase 'I believe' is transparent and can be omitted from the sentence. If, in contrast, the attitude is absent because the person is 'alienated' (Moran) from him- or herself, then the expression 'I believe' is opaque and sustains. Let us go through this proposal once again.

I have shown that, if the attitude in question is present, Moore-paradoxical assertions and beliefs will come down, one way or another, to asserting or believing a contradiction and that this has the consequence that Moore's Paradox is eliminated:

$$\vdash p \wedge \neg B(I, p) \quad \rightarrow \quad \vdash p \wedge \neg B(I, p) \wedge \neg p\,,$$
$$\vdash p \wedge \neg B(I, p) \quad \rightarrow \quad \vdash p \wedge B(I, p) \wedge \neg B(I, p)\,.\,^{22}$$

If the relation holding between the expression 'I believe that p is the case' and the subject's corresponding belief *that p is the case* was always asymmetric, the first-person present indicative of the verb 'to believe' would always be replaceable by a non-representational expressive device (tone of voice, facial expression, gesture, and the like), and the same would hold for all other psychological concepts.[23] That is, if the first-person present indicative of psychological predicates always articulated one's epistemically subjective relation to one's own beliefs, it would lack a descriptive meaning. Therefore, it would lack the meaning it ought to have as the continuation of the respective predicate into the first-person present indicative. In this sense, psychological predicates would actually be bereft of this inflective form. Instead, there would be a class of expressions that would curiously *appear* to be the first-person present indicative form of ordinary psychological predicates, whereas in fact they would present non-representational, verbal substitutes for more 'primitive' performative indicators of their user's state of mind.

If the first-person present indicative had this and only this subjective meaning, the expression 'I believe' could not be used in contexts other than assertions, particularly not in suppositions. Thus, the Uniformity Claim would be violated—

---

22 The first transformation presents the conclusion from conceiving the attitude in question in terms of practical self-knowledge along the lines of the transparency model, the second one of conceiving it in terms of theoretical or introspective self-knowledge, along the lines of the Higher-Order Belief Model. *Cf.* the previous chapter, Section 3.5 (propositions (6), (9a, b), (11)).
23 One could, for instance, substitute the sentence 'I'm afraid of the financial crisis' with making a fearful face and crying 'financial crisis!', the sentence 'I intend to go to London tomorrow' with a decisive utterance such as 'I am going to London tomorrow', or, very simply, the sentences 'I'm in pain' with crying 'Ouch!' and 'I need help' with 'Help!' *Cf. RPP* I §§ 462–472; *PI* § 244.

for there would, first, be a class of inflected forms which, though phenotypically continuous with all other grammatical forms of one and the same predicate, would not have the meaning captured by the predicate's general referent. To put it the other way round, psychological concepts would not comply with the Uniformity Claim, because applying them to oneself in a present tense assertion would differ in meaning from all other forms insofar as it would not represent the speaker's state of mind, but indicate or express it.[24] To maintain that avowals are semantically continuous sentences, more precisely, to claim that psychological predicates were meaning-preserving concepts across all instances, seems to me more than questionable under these conditions.

If, in contrast, the asymmetric attitude towards one's own psychological states were either always absent or always irrelevant to the meaning of the first-person present indicative, this form would always have a descriptive use, which would be the immediate semantic continuation of the other inflections of psychological concepts. This would enable us to sensibly saying things like 'I seem to believe that *p*', or 'I believe I hope you will come' (*cf. PPF* §§ 99, 103–5; *RPP* II § 4=*Z* § 79), but it would equally reduce the meaning of the first-person present indicative of psychological concepts by its asymmetric, transparent aspect, leaving only the descriptive, opaque one. In consequence, the meaning of first-person present indicative of psychological concepts would always consist in referring to the state of affairs that the speaker has the state of mind denoted by the respective concept.

If the expression 'I believe that *p*' was always ineliminable in this manner even from the contents of sentences represented in an assertoric mode, it would be impossible to explain why Moore-paradoxical assertions sound absurd, or contradiction-like. For in this case, the meaning of sentences such as 'It is raining, but I don't believe that it is raining' would come down to describing two mutually independent states of affairs, the state of affairs *that it is raining* and the state of affairs *that I don't believe that it is raining*. They would be as absurd as the sentences 'It is raining, but I haven't broken my leg', or 'It is raining, but I don't

---

24 If the meaning of an assertion like 'I believe that *p* is the case' were to be spelled out, it would read approximately like this conjunction: '*p* is the case and the speaker believes that *p* is the case and the speaker knowingly believes that *p* is the case' (however one's conception of the term 'knowingly'). The state of affairs represented by this formulation contains the state of affairs *that the speaker believes that p is the case*. But this does not suffice to state the Uniformity Claim fulfilled. For the state of affairs the sentence at hand is taken to refer to is much more complex than that referred to by the other inflective forms of 'to believe', which only designate the state of affairs *that a particular person believes that p is the case*. It additionally claims the speaker to have the capacity of authoritatively knowing his or her own beliefs. One could with the same kind of argument support the claim that the words 'thunderstorm' and 'rain' are meaning-identical, because the concept of a thunderstorm refers to a state of affairs that involves the presence of rain.

believe that Chelsea has won the match'. Asserting a Moore-paradoxical sentence would accordingly come close to two utterances made by different speakers, as if Peter said 'It's raining', and I immediately replied 'But I don't believe it' (*cf. RPP* II § 420).[25] In other words, this account of the meaning of the expression 'I believe' would bring us back to the photography model of belief, which has been rejected earlier because of its inadequacy with respect to the internal relation of the concepts belief and truth. Moore's Paradox would disappear on this model, and the verb 'to believe' would lack a grammatical form, though this time the one that is used in ordinary assertions and can be omitted or replaced by a tone of voice, or similar expressions such as 'I say that p' or 'I think that p' (*cf. PPF* § 107).

The claim that the first-person present indicative of psychological concepts could have both meanings at once was rejected in the last section. The last option open to a referentialist conception of the meaning of 'I believe' is proposing that the phrase 'I believe' sometimes has a descriptive meaning, sometimes an expressive meaning: That, in other words, the distinctive first-person attitude is sometimes present, sometimes absent. This suggestion does not only sound slightly wishy-washy, it also raises several worries. First, it would not be possible to determine whether the expression 'I believe' would have one or the other meaning in a particular assertion from the assertion alone. The criterion for this is whether the speaker stands in a distinctive first-person relation to the respective belief, and this is a question leading beyond the utterance. This is to say, unless one knows whether the attitude is present it would not be possible to determine the truth-conditions of the asserted sentence, let alone its particular truth-value. The assertion 'I believe that p is the case' could, without further knowledge, be an assertion about the speaker's mind only (*that N. N. believes that p is the case*) if the attitude was absent. It equally could be an assertion about the world (*that p is the case*), if the attitude was present. It could also be taken to refer to two kinds of belief, the objectively knowable and the subjectively knowable kind.[26] The reference of the first-person present indicative of the verb 'to believe', and analogously of other

---

25 As Searle, Wittgenstein and, to some extent Moran, note, there are situations, in which asserting a Moore-paradoxical sentence makes sense. These situations all involve a dissociation of the subject of the first conjunct, *that p is the case*, from the subject of the second conjunct, *that I do not believe that p is the case*. However, these cases ought to be considered as confusing the hearer, an expression of a pathological state of mind only insofar as they express the speaker's confusion about the meaning of what is said. In this case, they are better conceived as nonsensical than as describing inner conflicts (see Section 3.8 of the last chapter). *Cf.* Searle (1983), p. 9n.; Moran (1997), pp. 152ff.; Wittgenstein *RPP* I §§ 708 and 816.

26 But see Moran's critique on Rey discussed in the last chapter, Section 3.6.3. *Cf.* Moran (1997), pp. 152ff.

psychological predicates, would be indeterminate such that one had to further refer to the context, in which the assertion stands, or the speaker's intentions, with which it is uttered. Taking shelter in citing further determinants of the meaning of particular sentences that lie beyond the contents of this sentence, however, is no way out on representationalism, as Moran and Shoemaker are careful to point out against the pragmatic solution. And it would be only to the worse if what one's belief-contents really are were indetermined in the same way, if they concern one's own state of mind.

Admittedly, one could argue that the indeterminacy of the meaning of the expression 'I believe' is due to the limitation of our vocabulary and is relevant only on the general level. Actually, which state of affairs of the expression 'I believe' in every token sentence 'I believe that p is the case' refers to is determinate, but as a matter of fact we use the same expression for both alternatives, e.g. we use the word 'bank' in one sense to denote a financial institution, in another to designate a riverbank. The representationalist could even suggest that we ought to introduce a new word into ordinary language that captures the asymmetric meaning of the expression 'I believe', whilst leaving the expression 'I believe' with its descriptive meaning only in order to provide a continuation of the verb 'to believe' into the first-person present indicative. Or, one could propose to use one's own name instead of the first-person pronoun when using the expression in a descriptive manner, such that 'I believe that p is the case' was to express that one believes the proposition *that p the case*, whereas, in order to describe one's state of mind, one would say 'N.N. believes that p the case'.[27]

---

[27] Wittgenstein discusses a similar suggestion in the *Blue Book* (*BB*), where he focuses on the meaning of the first-person pronoun 'I' and proposes, from the point of view of solipsism, to distinguish between a subjective (transparent, error-resistant) and an objective (quasi-third-personal, error-prone) use. As I mentioned earlier, the subjective use of the first-person pronoun is particularly distinctive in that it is immune to error through misidentification. Wittgenstein however does not exploit this distinction in order to investigate a putatively distinctive, possibly epistemic first-person attitude towards oneself, manifest in the asymmetries of avowals. Rather, he aims at showing that the distinction between objective and subjective in the sense described renders its own idea of subjectivity inconceivable. His argument in the *Blue Book* in this way is related to the argument I presented here. Wittgenstein concludes that the meaning of neither the first-person pronoun, nor psychological predicates is constituted by referring to a person or a psychological phenomenon, respectively. *Cf. BB*, particularly pp. 66ff. Regrettably, I cannot further engage with this argument at this place. There is a wide literature on first-person reference in addition to the topic of self-knowledge already mentioned. My interpretation of the respective passage (that Wittgenstein holds a 'no-reference view' (Wright (1998b))) short-cuts the interpretation Hacker suggests in his commentary to *Philosophical Investigations* §§ 398–411, and is in line with John Campbell (1999), "Immunity to Error through Misidentification and

Notwithstanding the additional difficulties imported by either of these attempts to get more precision into ordinary language, pointing to the determinacy of the expression 'I believe' once it is instantiated, though with good intentions, fails to show a way out of the trouble. Rather, it leads back to the start: If every token assertion containing the expression 'I believe' is either expressive or descriptive, it will either be transparent and thus redundant, or opaque. So the meaning of every assertion and every belief with a Moore-paradoxical content would either be tantamount to a formal contradiction (in the expressive cases), or it would lead to a conjunction of two independent propositions (in the descriptive cases). This idea would face the additional difficulty that one must introduce a criterion by which to discern which of the two uses one faces at a particular instance. Here, one might be tempted to appeal to the peculiar subjective kind of self-knowledge— and immediately find oneself with the question as to the criteria by which one would recognise this and thus distinguish one's own expressive from one's own descriptive use of 'I believe' (see the next section on private language). Either result, as I have discussed at length in the previous sections, makes Moore's Paradox disappear; neither does accommodate the absurdity characteristic of the assertive use of Moore-paradoxical sentences.

2.4 The Logic of Assertion

2.4.1 Avowals contra Descriptions

The last section exacerbated the confusion concerning the expression 'I believe' to substantial *aporia*. For it seems that assertions prefixed by 'I believe…' do not always present descriptions of one's state of mind, do not always articulate a transparent relation to one's own beliefs, never do both at once, and the last argument resulted in the claim that they do not have either function at all. Instead of further engaging in combinatorics about meaning, it is time to bundle the implications Moore's Paradox has with regard to the foundational claims of representationalism. These were, firstly, that sentences of the form 'I believe that p' always described

---

the Meaning of a Referring Term", *Philosophical Topics 26/1-2*, pp. 89–104. *Cf.* Peter M. S. Hacker (1990d), *Wittgenstein: Meaning and Mind. Part II: Exegesis §§ 243–427*, Oxford: Blackwell, pp. 267–90. Reactions to Wittgenstein's conclusion that the word 'I' does not refer to a person range from incomprehension *via* indignation to resistance, especially from scholars who otherwise sympathise with Wittgenstein's views, but strongly disagree with this conclusion. Both, Wright (1998b) and Evans (1982), for instance, conclude that Wittgenstein must have been 'simply' mistaken.

what happens in the speaker's mind, and, secondly, that the structure of speech acts as well as mental states complied with the two-component model. I engaged with the first assumption in the previous section and I focus on the second one in this section. Finally, in the last section of this chapter (Section 5), I will present an independent argument against the claim that the meaning of psychological concepts is constituted by reference. The main mistake included in the representationalist framework will turn out to be the idea that mental states constituted a special sort of discrete phenomena, the psychological kind, to which their bearer entertained an epistemic relation that, though distinctive, simultaneously grants the meaning(fulness) of corresponding words. In order to understand why, it will be useful to have a look at the way in which the expression 'I believe' and in which assertions are used.

The *aporia* spelled out in the last section is an inevitable consequence of adopting the representationalist claim that the words 'I believe' always refer to a fact about the speaker's state of mind. The crucial error of representationalism in trying to cope with Moore's Paradox consists in psychologising the paradox right from the start, taking it as a paradox "for psychological reasons" (*Briefe* 257), as Moore suggested and Wittgenstein immediately criticised. Once this step has been made, it will be just a matter of course that every meaningful utterance of the expression 'I believe', whatever else it does, carries a report or a description of one's own state of mind. Even Moran, who takes its asymmetry most seriously, takes it for granted that avowals constitute a subclass of reports on one's own state of mind. This picture clashes with the impression that avowals undeniably exhibit asymmetries. Recognising the latter triggers making all kinds of more or less grotesque twists in order to acknowledge their asymmetries, whilst integrating the former into the two-component model of assertion and its cousin, the principle of content-uniformity. This has the effect that representationalist views eventually seek shelter in assuming a distinctive epistemic attitude towards one's own mind that is exclusively reserved for the subject.

The basis for considering avowals asymmetric consists in several observations about the use of the expression 'I believe': One does not infer from one's own utterances or observations of one's own behaviour to one's own state of mind, and the assertions 'I believe that p' and 'p' are used in similar ways. That much is familiar and common ground, and is itself puzzling enough. The *aporia* concerning the meaning of 'I believe' comes in with the representationalist next step, assuming that avowals are at the same time expressions of one's own mind and statements about the speaker's mind. In a series of remarks published in *Remarks on the Philosophy of Psychology* I (§§ 493–504) that are closely related to the remarks on Moore's Paradox in *Philosophy of Psychology – A Fragment*, Wittgenstein critically engages with this claim. He writes:

The difficulty becomes insurmountable if you think the sentence 'I believe…' states something about the state of my mind. If it were so, then Moore's Paradox would have to be reproducible if, instead of saying something about the state of one's own mind, one were making some statement about the state of one's own brain. *But the point is that no assertion about the state of my brain (or whatever else) is equivalent to the assertion which I believe*—for example, 'He will come'. (*RPP* I § 501, my emphasis)

According to Wittgenstein, the main error with the representationalist picture lies in treating avowals—the assertion 'which I believe'—as (at least partly) equivalent with assertions about the speaker. For this amounts to overloading avowals with a statement of facts, which is, as it were, made from the outside, from an 'empirical' point of view. And as Wittgenstein points out, making a statement about one's state of mind 'from the outside' has as little in common with an expression of one's state of mind as a statement about one's brain states has:

> Now would a sentence ascribing to myself—or to my brain—such a condition that I reply 'Yes' to the question 'Will he come?' and also exhibit such-and-such other reactions—would such a sentence amount to the assertion 'He will come'?
> Here one might ask 'How do you imagine I have been informed about this state of mind?—By experience, say? Do I then want to predict from experience that I will now always answer such a question like *this*, etc.?' (*RPP* I § 503)

That is, in taking avowals as ascriptions of belief which are articulations of an epistemic achievement, we introduce a kind of internal observer, whose insights result in statements of facts about oneself, statements that count as factual knowledge about oneself. The reason for treating avowals as self-ascriptions is quite clear— one wants to ensure that they are statements about facts, one wants to allow them to present a suitable inferential basis for explaining and predicting the speaker's behaviour, and one wants to maintain that psychological predicates do not deviate from other verbs, but have the same meaning in all their inflective forms. But if one tries to maintain all this by taking avowals as both expressions and descriptions of one's state of mind, one would be treating avowals as if two persons were speaking at the same time, as if there was a subjective entity (a Freudian '*Instanz*') for playing the expressive part, and another, 'objective', entity reporting what is going on in the person's mind. So the person could say, playing the part of the Super-Ego: "'It is raining, and the ego believes so,' and might go on 'So I shall probably take an umbrella with me'" (*RPP* I § 708), and that 'hybrid' person indeed would be able to "pronounce 'I don't believe it is raining; and it is raining'." (*RPP* I § 495) It is possible to imagine a situation in which such utterances make sense, think of the railway officer announcing 'The train to Oxford will be on time, but, personally, I don't believe it', or the soldier, who adds to the military reports stating the facts as he has observed them that he does not believe his own reports (*RPP* I §§ 486–7).

The point Wittgenstein makes in these remarks is that the sense of such utterances would be unclear. How could they be used? How would one react to them? What sense could others make of them? One would "have to fill out the picture with behaviour indicating that two people were speaking through my mouth" (*PPF* § 105). That is, one could imagine situations in which an assertion of a Moore-paradoxical sentence would not be absurd, situations that involve a kind of dissociation from oneself, e.g. when one personally does not believe what one is obliged to say *ex officio* or as a particular group's speaker, or when one suffers from a dissociative disorder. Conceiving of avowals in this double way, however, as expressions-cum-descriptions of one's state of mind, would make the dissociative case the normal one—and one would actually have reason to wonder why these two voices usually chorus. One would treat the assertion 'I believe that *p* is the case' as a description from one's internal observer's point of view. But this is not the same as *expressing* one's state of mind, it is *speaking about* one's mind as if one was speaking about one's brain states, which one has learned from observation.

However, avowals are immediate expressions of one's state of mind, they do not rely on self-observation, one does not infer from them to one's state of mind, and they do not serve as evidence for how one's own future course of actions will turn out (*cf. PPF* §§ 107–8, *RPP* I § 705). Most representationalist views acknowledge this. But it will be only puzzling if the default case were, as the representationalist conception of avowals suggests, that avowals were both expressions and descriptions of one's state of mind. Here, the following question quite naturally imposes itself:

> Why is it that I cannot gather from my own assertion 'It is going to rain' that I believe this? Can't I draw any interesting inferences at all from the fact that I said this? If another one says it, I infer, for example, that he will take an umbrella with him. Why not in my own case? Of course, here it is tempting to say: In my own case, I do not *need* to draw this inference from my words because I can draw it from my state of mind, from my belief itself. (*RPP* I § 704, my translation)

The temptation Wittgenstein here alludes to is the temptation to grasp the asymmetry of avowals in epistemological terms. What is striking is that it seems inconceivable that one could meaningfully use the words 'I believe...' to assert one's beliefs without thereby making a statement about them from a point of view that could, in theory, be taken by another person, that one could use such assertions in a way different from thereby stating a fact about one's own psychology. Starting like this will, as I have argued in the last section, inevitably lead into the 'insurmountable difficulty' that Wittgenstein holds we are confronted with in Moore's Paradox. The lesson to be learned from this is, as Wittgenstein puts it, to recognise it as a *misconception* that the words 'I believe' meant "something internal *as well as* something external" (*RPP* II § 335, my emphasis), to give up the idea that avowals were descriptive in a double way, describing the contents of one's mind as well as one's state of mind itself. Rather than taking avowals as articulations of an asymmetric attitude one has to a special realm of facts, facts about one's states of mind—and what else could this attitude be, then, if it weren't an epistemological one, a matter of access?—one should take the asymmetry of the first-person present indicative of psychological predicates as a grammatical issue, consisting in a different attitude one has to one's own words, just as one has a different attitude towards one's own facial expressions, one's gestures or exclamations, all of which serve equally well as expressions of one's state of mind as avowals do. To put it in a nutshell, the difference in question is not an epistemological issue, but a matter of what one does with one's own utterances as compared with those of other people. Asking for an explanation as to why this is so, which will most likely lead into an investigation into the ontology of this special realm, the mind, itself is grounded in a misconception: a misconception of the logic of assertion along the lines of the Fregean two-component model, that is, of a view of assertion as assent to truth-evaluable propositions, which always aim at telling the truth about what is the case, and what isn't.

2.4.2 Assertions in Everyday Use

Having taken the argument to a point where representationalism is caught between *aporia* and absurdity, it might be useful to step back and reconsider the two-component model in general. The two-component-model was said to basically analyse mental states into a psychological mode plus a representational content, and speech acts into an illocutionary force plus a representational content. The psychological mode or illocutionary force, respectively, symbolise the attitude the subject takes towards the object. The content-element presents, for propositionally structured representational content, a 'sentence-radical', *that p is the case*, onto which a performative element, such as 'S believes…', 'S desires…' etc. is tacked. The two-component view is expressed in Frege's notation such that a horizontal stroke in front of a proposition, $(-p)$, indicates that the following is a neutral thought *that p is the case*. As explained in the last chapter, a neutral thought has truth conditions, but is not assigned a truth-value. Adopting representationalist terminology, it expresses that the subject entertains a representation of a certain state of affairs, but does not inform us whether the subject has formed a particular attitude towards it. This information is conveyed by prefixing an additional sign, in Frege's original model the 'judgment-stroke', |, signifying that the thought has been judged true. The notation can be amended by other symbols representing the respective other psychological modes, such as ? (for questions), ! (for desires) etc.[28] A full representational attitude accordingly is notated as $\vdash p, ? - p, ! - p$ and so forth.

The Fregean notation does not only suggest that representational states are decomposable into a mode and a content element, but also that the mode is an adjunct to the content, which is replaceable by another one whilst leaving the content element intact. The idea inherent in this suggestion, which is endorsed in representationalist accounts, is that one could isolate a representational element from any representational state as the determinant of the state's accuracy conditions, or, for linguistic representation, a 'sentence-radical' constituting the meaning of their propositional content. Although the accuracy conditions of a representational state are specified in its content, the representational content-element itself bears no truth-value. Representing or articulating a set of accuracy conditions alone does not yet involve stating whether they are fulfilled or ought to be fulfilled. This happens once a previously neutral representational element is presented in a particular psychological mode, or articulated in a certain pragmatic context.[29]

In this light, it seems as if complete representational states and speech acts are advanced stages of simple contents. Asserting that something is the case appears to be a more complex phenomenon than merely assuming, or positing, or thinking, or representing that something is the case, insofar as it involves an additional mental act, the act of assenting or denying that a certain state of affairs obtains whilst maintaining the properties of the thoughts they contain. The two-component model assumes a linear gradient in complexity, so to speak, leading from neutral thoughts or representations of states of affairs to beliefs, desires, assertions, orders and so forth. The supposed advance is that attitude-specific properties involving an attitude or a kind of commitment on part of the speaker's as to whether and how a particular proposition relates to the actual world are grafted upon a content whose accuracy conditions would otherwise not be actualised. Accordingly, neutral representations of objects or states of affairs are regarded prior to complete token representational attitudes (*cf.* previous chapter, Sections 2.1.1 and 4).

The view that there is a linear continuation from neutral representational contents to the contents of representational states is the target of Wittgenstein's last argument in *PPF*, x (§§ 106–7). Wittgenstein had critically drawn attention to

---

28 *Cf.* Schulte (1993), pp. 140f.; Frege (1879), § 2; and Chapter 1, Section 4.2.

29 Distinguishing between an element specifying the accuracy conditions of a particular representational state and an element determining the kind of its relatedness to what is represented is spelled out most explicitly in Searle's account of intentionality, *cf.* Searle (1969) and (1983) as discussed in the previous chapter, Section 3.2.

the idea of an isolable content-element already at the beginning of this section with the remark that "Moore's paradox can be put like this: the utterance 'I believe that this is the case' is used in a similar way as the assertion 'This is the case'; and yet the *supposition* that I believe that this is the case is not used like the supposition that this is the case." (*PPF* § 87) The reason why the two-component model cannot account for the difference between asserting *that I believe that p is the case* and supposing *that I believe that p is the case* is that it misunderstands the function of suppositions, or neutral thoughts, in the first place:

> Already in the *supposition*, the line is different from what you think.[30]

Schulte proposes that the 'line' Wittgenstein mentions in this otherwise rather obscure remark refers to the supposedly linear advance from supposition to assertion (*cf.* Schulte (1993), pp. 154ff.; and (1995), pp. 206ff.). This interpretation is supported by the course the argument in this section has taken until now and by an unpublished note taken down the same day (MS 137, 3.2.1948).[31] Wittgenstein here sheds doubt on the view that assertions were decomposable into a truth value-neutral representation and a truth value determinant, a mental act, or attitude, of the speaker's. The criticism is twofold. On the one hand, it is directed against the claim that there is a *linear* advance from supposition to assertion. If it makes sense to speak of an advance at all, it will be certainly misleading to think that the assertion *that I believe that p is the case* is logico-semantically continuous with the corresponding supposition *that I believe that p is the case* for the reason that it contains the supposition and therefore inherits the latter's logical properties. Whereas the assertions *that I believe that p is the case* and *that p is the case* are mutually interchangeable in ordinary circumstances, the homonymic suppositions are not. Consequently, the scopes of logical and semantic operations that can be performed in each case differ from each other, one of the effects being that Moore's Paradox arises for assertions, but not for suppositions *that p is the case and I don't believe that p is the case.*

Wittgenstein further criticises the ideas that were labelled earlier the Priority Claim and the Uniformity Claim, respectively. Priority is claimed by representation-

---

30 § 106, my translation. Original: "Die Linie liegt schon in der *Annahme* anders, als du denkst."
31 Original: "Die Linie liegt schon in der Annahme anders, als Du denkst. | Ich möchte sagen: In den Worten 'Angenommen ich glaube das' setzt Du schon die ganze Grammatik des Wortes 'Glauben' voraus. Du nimmst nicht etwas an, was Dir, sozusagen, eindeutig durch ein Bild gegeben ist, so das du dann eine Andere als die gewöhnliche Behauptung an diese Annahme anstücken kannst. Du wüsstest gar nicht, was Du hier annimmst, wenn Dir nicht schon die Verwendung von 'glauben' geläufig wäre."

alism in that 'neutral' content is supposed to be more basic than representational contents presented in a particular psychological mode or expressed in a speech act.[32] Uniformity of content across different kinds of sentences was supposed to be given in that the representation *that p is the case* constitutes the content of asserting *that p is the case* without being altered through the act of asserting. This view is problematic because when using

> [T]he words "Suppose I believe..." you are *already presupposing* the whole grammar of the word "to believe", the ordinary use, which you have mastered.—You are not supposing some state of affairs which, so to speak, is unambiguously presented to you in a picture, so that you can tack on to this supposition some assertion other than the ordinary one.—You would not know at all what you are supposing here (that is, what, for example, could be inferred from such a supposition) if you were not already familiar with the use of 'to believe'.[33]

Wittgenstein here raises doubts concerning the way in which the content-element of representational states is conceived to be constituted, more precisely, concerning the representationalist conception of states of affairs expressed by sentences like 'I believe that *p* is the case'. This conception prioritises the case of representing facts over assenting to representations of facts and entails the resultant claim that mental representations are independent of and logically prior to their linguistic manifestations. However, as Wittgenstein points out, the state of affairs represented by the representation articulated in the sentence-radical *that I believe that p is the case* is not fully intelligible without taking into account the assertive use of the expression 'I believe'. For what does one represent when the sentence 'I believe that *p*' is the content of a supposition? On the representationalist account, one thereby entertains the thought *that I believe that p* without assigning a truth-value to it. Entertaining the thought *that I believe that p is the case* bears truth conditions, but no truth value and is, in virtue of its being hypothetical, supposed to be the simpler case than the corresponding assertion. But consider the case in which Peter assumes 'I believe that *p*'. The state Peter supposedly represents in the content of his assumption is the state of affairs in which Peter's assertions 'I believe that *p*' and '*p*' are interchangeable, in which Peter's assertion '*p*, but I don't believe it' raises Moore's Paradox. In short: the state of affairs in which the

---

32 The priority at issue is a logical, not a temporal or ontogenetic priority.

33 *PPF* § 106, my translation, my emphasis. Original: "In den Worten 'Angenommen, ich glaube...' setzt Du schon die ganze Grammatik des Wortes 'glauben' voraus, den gewöhnlichen Gebrauch, den du beherrschst.—Du nimmst nicht einen Stand der Dinge an, der dir, sozusagen, eindeutig durch ein Bild vor Augen steht, so daß du dann eine andere als die gewöhnliche Behauptung an die Annahme anstückeln kannst.—Du wüßtest gar nicht, was du hier annimmst (d.h., was z.B. aus so einer Annahme folgt), wenn dir nicht schon die Verwendung von "glauben" geläufig wäre."

expression 'I believe', used by Peter in an assertive context, is transparent. The way in which the expression 'I believe' is used in an assertoric context does by no means present a more specialised, and hence derivative, use but on the contrary is an indispensable constituent of the supposedly harmless representational content of Peter's 'neutral thought'. This is to say that the representationalist claim that one could use the expression 'I believe' in hypothetical contexts without thereby bringing about the complications of the assertoric use, and that this hypothetical use were accordingly the simpler, more basic and prior use, is circular.

Remarkably, Wittgenstein emphasises that the prerequisite for sensibly 'entertaining thoughts' about one's own beliefs consists in having mastered not only the "whole grammar" of the verb 'to believe', but also its "ordinary use" (*loc. cit.*). I suggest that a consideration of the ways in which the expression 'I believe' is used will yield the conclusion that its use is more multi-faceted than suggested. Still more speaks in favour of conjecturing that, in fact, it is the hypothetical use which exceeds the assertive one with respect to the capacities its mastery requires. In assertoric contexts, the phrase 'I believe' can for the most part straightforwardly be declared redundant, adding as much to what is said to be believed as a change in one's tone of voice (or the colour of one's thought) would do. But that they are so interchangeable is not grounded in describing, *en passant*, the same psychological state of the speaker. If, as Moran's transparency model, for instance, suggests, assertions *that p* and assertions *that I believe that p* were equivalent due to containing a description of an external state of affairs (*that p*) and simultaneously a description of an internal state of affairs (*that I believe that p*), every assertion that *p* would equally be an assertion about the speaker's mind.

> So is each judgment a judgment about the one who is judging? No, it is not, inasmuch as I don't want the main consequences to be drawn to be ones about myself, I want them rather to be about the subject matter of the judgment. If I say 'It's raining', I don't in general want to be answered 'So that's how it seems to you.' 'We're talking about the weather,' I might say, 'not about me.' (*RPP* I § 750)

If the two assertions, *that p* and *that I believe that p*, were similar in virtue of having the same double referent, their consequences would be arbitrary insofar as one could optionally continue conversation with a remark about the speaker's state of mind or a line of thought with a thought about one's own beliefs, or with a statement or thought about the subject matter at stake. Instead of providing a stable and unambiguous meaning to an assertion *that p is the case*, this explanation has the consequence that, in the default case, the meaning of the assertion is undetermined. This result reflects the earlier conclusion that, if the assertion 'I believe that *p*' was simultaneously an expression and a description of one's state of mind, the default case would be the dissociative case (see previous section). Here, one would need an extra determinant in order to decide which of the two possible ways was the right continuation, talking about the matter at stake or about the speaker's state of mind, such as an additional meaning intention on part of the thinker's or speaker's.[34]

> What [then] does it mean to say that 'I believe p' says roughly the same as 'p'? We react in roughly the same way when anyone says the first and when he says the second; if I said the first and someone didn't understand the words 'I believe', I should repeat the sentence in the second form and so on. As I'd also explain the words 'I wish you'd go away' by means of the words 'Go away'. (*RPP* I § 477)

The specific similarity of assertions *that p is the case* and assertions *that I believe that p* consists in a similarity in practice, that is, how they are used, and how they are responded to. The phrase 'I believe' can be introduced, e.g. to someone who is not familiar with it, as a replacement for an assertive tone of voice, an indicator of the force with which the following sentence is stated. Accordingly, Wittgenstein mentions the similarity in use in close connection with the way in which this use is explained, by substituting the unfamiliar one with the more familiar one. In the same respect, the first-person present indicative of the words 'to say' and 'to believe' are related (§ 107). The phrase 'I say' is normally redundant in an assertion, too, since it simply verbalises what the speaker does in the moment of asserting, namely saying something. This similarity in use of 'I say' and 'I believe' makes them mutually interchangeable elements of assertions that moreover are transparent, withdrawing from the remainder of the sentence, which is, *stricto sensu*, responsible for the meaning of the whole sentence in most cases. The assertions 'I say it is raining', 'I believe it is raining' and 'It is raining' are roughly equivalent in meaning when used in normal circumstances, they count as, that is: They are meant and understood as, assertions concerning the rain. Insofar as the use of the first-person present indicative of the verb 'to believe' in assertions is replaceable by appropriate non-verbal indicators, gestures, facial expressions, tones of voice, it clearly differs from the use in hypothetical contexts. In hypothetical contexts, the expression 'I believe' indeed has the character of a report, in the sense that it participates in depicting a state of affairs from a detached, observer's point of

---

34 And a further intention determining the meaning of the meaning intention and so forth. This is to say that approaches to the meaning of sentences drawing on meaning determinants in form of meaning intentions (such as Searle's for instance) have the equally undesirable and inevitable side effect of leading into an infinite regress. This is one of the points of the remarks on meaning and rule following in *Philosophical Investigations*, to which I will briefly come back in the next sections.

view—for instance, to inform another person of it.[35] The subject matter of the suppositions 'Suppose I say it is raining', 'Suppose I believe it is raining' and 'Suppose it is raining' diverges in that the first deals with an utterance, the second with a state of mind, and only the third with a state of the weather.

The ordinary use of 'I believe' to introduce a sentence moreover involves cases in which 'I believe' roughly coincides with 'I'm not sure, but. . .', 'I conjecture. . .' or 'That's my guess' or similar expressions, which introduce a sentence of which the speaker is not fully convinced that it is true. The expression 'I believe' here serves to clarify that the statement is precisely not meant as an unmitigated assertion, but bears a lesser degree of certainty. Consequently, it cannot be omitted from the assertion *that I believe that p is the case*. But does this turn the words 'I believe' into a description of my state of mind, as the alternative to the transparent use looks like? I do not think so. For, on the one hand, although its omission in an *assertion*, i.e. an utterance spoken in an assertive tone of voice, is not possible, it can be replaced by phrases like 'It may be the case' (*RPP* I § 821) or 'possibly', or by a hesitant or doubtful tone of voice (*PPF* § 110). This indicates that the purpose of the phrase 'I believe' here, too, consists in characterising the sentence so introduced, which is concerned with the world external to the speaker's mind. If you ask me 'Is this bus going to the railway station?' I will be concerned with the route the bus takes, and if I don't know for certain that it does I will answer 'I believe it does' in order to express that it is highly probable that it does, but also to indicate that you should perhaps double check.

It is certainly true that questions, such as 'Do you know or do you merely believe it?', which demand the speaker to specify the kind of his or her attitude towards what he or she expresses with the sentence that follows, are more appropriate here than in the assertive case. Still, this does not mean that the question aims at gaining knowledge about the speaker's state of mind. This might be the case in examinations, or interrogations in court, but it can equally well aim at getting a clue how much weight one ought to attach to the statement in making up one's own mind. If the speaker responds 'I believe it, I don't know for sure', one might ask the bus driver or other passengers. If the response is 'I don't know for certain, but I'm pretty sure' one might be more willing to take the risk of entering and finding out during the bus ride whether it stops at the railway station.

What seems important to me is that the phrase 'I believe' when used in cases of uncertainty or doubt can, similarly to the assertive case, be substituted by impersonal expressions, such as 'Well. . .', or a hesitant tone of voice. Wittgenstein warns to "regard a hesitant assertion as an assertion of hesitancy" (*PPF* § 110).

---

35 *Cf.* for this understanding of 'report' Finkelstein (2008), p. 97.

Strictly speaking, as Moran advocates it, the clear-cut distinction between a strictly transparent use of the expression 'I believe' and its use in reports does not account for the nuances of uncertainty, hesitancy or doubt that lie on the continuum between expressions of thorough personal conviction on the one hand, and of the conclusion from detached self-inquiry on the other hand. Yet, they all belong to the variety of applications of 'I believe' in ordinary language. This consideration shows that it is actually misleading to characterise the transparent use of 'I believe' as that which can be replaced by an *assertive* tone of voice. Rather, transparency is given whenever the first-person present indicative is used in assertions, whether it expresses conviction or doubt, or a degree of certainty lying in between. Grasping the transparent use of the expression 'I believe' in assertions in this light appears comparable with acquiring the capacity of substituting non-verbal expressions of one's current bodily or mental condition, e.g. replacing outcries of pain with the expression 'It hurts'. In everyday contexts, the expression 'I believe' is handled more loosely than the dichotomy transparency/opacity would suggest. And here, too, its assertion appears to be at least as continuous in meaning with exclamations, non-verbal mutterings and bodily expressions, as it is supposed to be with the thought 'Suppose I believe...'.

So far, one might have got the impression that emphasising the outstanding function of the first-person present indicative of psychological concepts and acknowledging the generated asymmetry of avowals as I have done very much resembles Moran's transparency model of belief and avowals. This worry may be the more so since Moran also refers to those passages of Wittgenstein's later writings I have discussed. But this would be a misunderstanding since Wittgenstein never regards the asymmetry between the grammatical first and third person as an *epistemological* issue. On the contrary, he is careful to remark that treating it in epistemological terms is misleading because it is mistaken to speak of knowledge when characterising one's attitude towards one's experiences, including one's own beliefs, desires and intentions.[36] This mistake comes into play as soon as one conceives of experiences as independently existing facts, which could be the object of factual knowledge, and avowals of one's experiences as articulations of knowledge. The most important difference is the point in which Moran's misunderstanding of Wittgenstein is most apparent. It is Moran's claim that the sentence 'I believe that *p* is the case' is always and primarily a description of one's own state of mind because one thereby refers to a fact that exists prior to and independent of being represented in thought or speech, the fact *that oneself believes that p is the case*. The transparent use of 'I believe' is appropriate whenever this self-description

---

36 *Cf. PI* §§ 246f. Glock (1996), pp. 50–4; Hacker (1990a).

articulates a special kind of self-knowledge on part of the speaker, and turns the utterance from a report into an avowal of one's state of mind, without losing the descriptive sense. On Moran's account, this transparency belongs to the logical properties of the expression 'I believe' in assertions derived from the ontological properties of belief and of being a subject of belief.

As I explained in this chapter, Wittgenstein on the contrary straightforwardly rejects the view that an assertion of the type 'I believe that p is the case' describes the speaker's state of mind *at any rate*. Instead of conceiving of this asymmetry as an epistemic one and accordingly trying to *explain* it by means of concentrating on the mental structure that conditions the distinctive subjective relation to oneself, Wittgenstein aims at *understanding* the grammar of avowals by means of asking how they are used. In contrast to the representationalist's metaphysical interests of explaining the constitution of experience, Wittgenstein's approach is, first and foremost, a grammatical one that focusses on the way in which experience is expressed in language.

The expression 'I believe' serves to characterise the subsequent sentence and thus can be substituted by non-verbal indicators without a loss in meaning. Wittgenstein further suggests that cases in which the expression 'I believe' is used in order to describe the speaker's state of mind in an assertive context present borderline cases, whose possibility he certainly takes into consideration. These involve pathological cases of personal dissociation, for instance cases in which one's official and one's personal opinions diverge, all involving behaviour indicating that "two people were speaking from [the speaker's] mouth" (*PPF* § 105). An utterance of 'I believe' in this detached manner sounds strange, not because the utterance would lack something that was usually added to the descriptive sense, but because they seem to add an additional shade of meaning, the descriptive one, that otherwise would not be in place and ordinarily does not even belong to the use of this expression. They are at the extreme of sensibly using the expression 'I believe'. Statements in which the speaker talks about his or her beliefs in an observational manner are unusual, and it might therefore be inappropriate to respond to them with one's familiar repertoire, namely to go on talking about what the speaker asserts to believe. In the most extreme cases, there is more reason for questioning whether the utterance is meaningful at all and doubting whether the speaker is capable of using the word 'to believe' or other psychological predicates, than for taking his or her words at face value and looking for a further reason why he or she apparently fails to know his or her own beliefs.[37]

---

37 I cannot pursue this line of thought at this place. The point I indicated is made and further elaborated by John Campbell (2001), "Rationality, Meaning, and the Analysis of Delusion", *Philosophy, Psychiatry and Psychology* 8/2-3, pp. 89–100.

Since the hypothetical use of psychological predicates generally requires the capability of abstracting from one's actual situation in addition to the mastery of the ordinary use in assertions, the former turns out to be more complex, and thus logically derivative from the latter. The line advancing on the two-component model from supposition to assertion, that is from representational content to representational state is drawn in the wrong direction. Given the radical difference in meaning between the use of the first-person present indicative in assertions and supposition (after all, a hesitant assertion is not an assertion of hesitancy), it is moreover highly questionable to uphold the Uniformity Claim, that it was possible to extract a uniform, stable content-element from various representational states, and that the so distilled sentence-radical would capture the purified meaning (the objective thought, if you wish, the content-type, or the representational kind) of all its further instances. If the language-game of making assertions was indeed based on the language-game played with hypothetical, abstract contents abiding to the model $-p / \vdash p$, it would be unintelligible how the change in the logical and semantic properties of the phrase 'I believe' is brought about. For the interchangeability of the assertions 'p' and 'I believe that p' is not given for the respective suppositions. Whereas in the assertive case the phrase 'I believe' is, as it were, 'transparent', effecting that both assertions count as assertions that p, it is 'opaque' in the hypothetical case. For example, supposing *that I believe that it is raining* is quite different from supposing *that it is raining*. Because the phrase 'I believe' is part of the content of the supposition and thus belongs to the state of affairs that is assumed, it cannot be omitted or substituted unless one would explicate the substitution. In the language Wittgenstein described earlier (*PPF* § 98), in which the assertive use of 'I believe' was substituted by a change in the speaker's tone of voice, one would have to circumscribe the alteration in the supposition e.g. as 'Suppose I were inclined to say that p'. Here, it would indeed be possible to substitute the sentence with 'Suppose my brain is in a state that will under the appropriate circumstances cause me to say 'p'.[38]

Wittgenstein proceeds from the *ordinary* usage of the word 'to believe' and he does not seek to come up with a theory that brackets all instances of the expression 'I believe' together under one semantic aspect. In everyday contexts, the expression 'I believe' is used more disparately than the two-component model suggests. Notably, we do not normally suffer from the same difficulty to understand what utterances like 'I believe he will come' or 'I believe it is raining' ex-

---

38 *Cf.* Shoemaker (1975) who claims that mental terms might turn out to be fully reducible to definite non-mental descriptions (see Chapter 1, Section 3.5.1), the previous section, and *RPP* I § 501.

press as someone who tries to analyse their meaning along the lines of the model '*supposition+assent* → *assertion*'. As the presented considerations have brought to light, the two-component model is far too inflexible to account for the variety in meaning of the expression 'I believe', especially not for the asymmetry of the first- and third-person present indicative, let alone that it cannot cope with the appearance of Moore's Paradox in assertions without simultaneously being present in suppositions of the type $(p \wedge \neg B(I, p))$. As soon as one tries to unify all instances of the verb 'to believe' by subjecting it to the grammar of verbs such as 'to eat' one is likely to conceive of both the meaning of psychological concepts and the sense of assertions as simultaneously representing states of affairs and conveying information about the objective world to one another. But this is clearly not the case—in a situation in which one answers the question 'Is it raining?' with 'I believe so', it is inappropriate to reply "Don't be silly, I asked you about the weather, not about your state of mind" (*Briefe* 257; *cf. RPP* I § 750).

This matter of fact makes it seem questionable to speak sensibly of 'logico-semantic continuity' to characterise the connection of the different inflective forms of psychological predicates. Moreover, it questions the assumptions that the grammar of psychological predicates could be modelled on the grammar of other verbs although there are overlaps of their respective grammatical properties. Wittgenstein further sees the relation between the concept of belief and the 'phenomenon' of belief exactly from the opposite direction: It is not the case that the semantic and logical properties of the assertion 'I believe that p is the case' are constituted in that the sentence refers to the language-independent state of affairs *that I believe that p is the case*, but that the logical features of the assertion in question (transparency, substitutability, exclusion of certain logical operations) are constitutive of the supposedly language-independent state of affairs *that I believe that p is the case* (*cf. PPF* § 106).[39]

2.4.3 The Parting of the Lines

The preceding survey of how assertions and the expression 'I believe' behave in their natural habitat, i.e. in everyday situations, has delivered the following results. The verb 'to believe' undoubtedly has a first-person present indicative form and in this respect does not differ from non-mental verbs, e.g. 'to eat' or 'to swim'. Yet a variety of moves which it is grammatically sound to make with the first-person present indicative of other verbs normally cannot be sensibly executed with the

---

39 This point is made against Frege by Dummett (1992), ch. 10 (assertion) and consecutively by Pfisterer (2008). I will come back to it in Chapter 3.

verbs 'to believe', 'to hope', 'to intend' etc., although such moves can be made with their other inflective forms. On the other hand, other moves are possible here—assertions like 'He is going to come' and 'I believe he is going to come' most often have a similar or the same meaning. Changing the context from assertion to supposition, or the grammatical person from first- to third-person, or the tense from present to past rules out some things one can do with the words 'I believe' in present tense assertions and enables others that weren't possible otherwise. For the most part, expressions such as 'I believe', 'I wish', 'I hope' can be substituted with non-verbal expressive means. Yet, it is under certain circumstances less or not at all confusing to assert a statement such as 'I know I believe...', or 'I seem to believe', or 'I believe I hope you will come'. Here, the sense of 'I believe' diverges from its ordinary use, whose function was said to be a reinforcement of the tone of voice in which the utterance in question is made. The lines are parting, as it were; the logic of assertion and the grammar of the verb 'to believe' run side by side for some part, but not for all, and so do the language games played with assertions and suppositions (*cf. PPF* § 107). The expression 'I believe' can express many things, doubt as well as conviction. And so for assertions: The assertion 'He will certainly come' can be an expression of hope as well as of belief, anxiety as well as expectation, comfort as well as threat; it can be a description of a situation which one predicts to be the case as well as wishful thinking. Looking at a variety of situations of everyday conversation and taking one's own findings seriously could, I suggest, cure the striving for finding one single property in which all assertions and all instances of the verb 'to believe' coincide. It is the point of Wittgenstein's considerations of Moore's Paradox that one cannot investigate the meaning of a sentence by isolating it from the context in which it appears:

> Making reports is a language game with these words. It would produce confusion if we were to say: the words of the report—the uttered sentence—have a definite sense, and the reporting—the 'assertion'—adds another one to it. As if the sentence, spoken by a gramophone, belonged to pure logic; as if here it had the purely logical sense; as if here we had before us the object which logicians get hold of and consider—while the sentence as asserted, as reported, is what is *in commerce*. As one may say: the botanist considers a rose *as a plant*, not as an ornament for a dress or a room or as a delicate courtesy. The sentence, I want to say, has no sense outside the language game. This hangs together with its not being a kind of *name*. In which case one could say "I believe...'—*that's* how it is.' [...] (*RPP* I § 488, my translation)

Advocates of the two-component model make two mistakes at once: They first press the logic of assertions into the rigid system of the Fregean conception 'supposition *plus* judgement' and take their purpose to consist in telling the truth: Nothing else is necessary and sufficient to satisfy the intentions the speaker has in making an assertion. As if every statement, every report in an assertoric or indicative context could be amended by '—and this is the truth', turning the phrase into an indicator of the kind of sentence one is concerned with, similarly in function and meaninglessness to a full stop (*cf. PI* § 22). Facing the confusion that arises from this strict view when it comes to the meaning of assertions using the expression 'I believe', they secondly come up with the idea that the verb 'to believe' is used in order to refer to a psychological phenomenon. This is in turn considered an objective fact in analogy to objects and processes like tables, trees, eating or swimming. In this way, the conception of assertion condensed in Frege's symbolism is connected with the idea that sentences receive their meaning analogously to names, which directly and unambiguously designate the states of affairs they represent.

It depends, one might say, on one's interest: If one wants a neat and tidy conception of the function and meaning of language, which is easy to work with and generously abstracts from the ambiguities and muddles of everyday talk, one will be strongly inclined to proceed like the botanist in Wittgenstein's remark. The botanist engages in constructing an ideal rose in order to capture those features constituting any particular rose's being a rose (e.g. a certain sequence of genes), whilst disregarding the contexts roses are normally embedded in—be it as symbols in communication, be it as objects of aesthetic appreciation, be it to block one's neighbour's view—and the varieties of rose species that sometimes have little in common. The 'botanist' approach constructs an ideal sentence radical of the type *that p is the case* or *that S believes that p is the case* or an ideal representational content type, which timelessly captures the meaning of all their particular occurrences. And as it is the case with the ideal rose, the meaning so distilled is supposed to be unchangeably, uniformly and continuously present wherever these sentences are used, regardless the grammatical mode, tense and person, and the context in which they appear. Consequently, the assertion 'I believe that *p* is the case' cannot be connected otherwise with other instances of the verb 'to believe' than by taking it as manifesting the previously generated ideal sentence and thus ascribing the function to represent the state of affairs *that I believe that p is the case* to it.

Having thus isolated the sense of a sentence in terms of an ideal, context-independent meaning determinant, there are several questions to answer. These are, in particular, what this sense is supposed to be, and how the connection between the sense of a sentence and the sentence itself is supposed to be established. These questions equally arise for the connection between psychological expressions and their ostensible referents, psychological phenomena, and in the following section I will discuss them in this context more extensively. For the moment, I want to scrutinise the claim that understanding an utterance or thought requires grasping the sense thereby expressed, and nothing else. The two following quotations from

Wittgenstein are concerned with the question whether knowing the sense of a sentence is a necessary and/or sufficient condition in order to understand it.

> If you consider the language game with the assertion 'He is going to come', you won't hit on the idea of analysing the assertion into a Fregean supposition (a content, as it were) and the asserting of this content. Anyway it is again that notion of a process in the mind which suggests the idea of such a composition and analysis. (MS 132, 6.10.1946, quoted from/transl. by Schulte (1993), p. 146.)
> Might one speak of the sense of the words 'that he will come'? For these words are precisely the Fregean 'assumption'. Well, couldn't I explain to someone what this verbal expression means? Yes, I can, by explaining to him, or shewing him, how it is employed. (*RPP* I § 500)

In the first quotation, Wittgenstein invites his readers to imagine a situation in which the assertion 'He is going to come' is made, for instance, as an answer to another person's question 'Is Peter coming tonight?'. In this situation, the speaker might just as well have said 'I believe he is going to come', and this would not have changed the other person's reply, his or her reactions, the consequences drawn from the utterance and so forth. There is no need to worry about this similarity, and thus no inclination to further analyse these utterances, unless one has already encountered puzzling cases, such as Moore's Paradox. As Schulte points out and as I have argued, one can satisfactorily clarify what the similarity of these sentences is about once one has refrained from trying to establish a uniform analysis which explains all their instances in all conceivable situations, and instead looks into their function in different contexts. If one wants to *understand* the meaning of the sentences 'He is going to come' and 'I believe he will come' and does not bother whether one's result can be presented in as simple as possible a model conforming to logical laws, one will be able to cope with variations, asymmetries and divergences in the meaning of these sentences that depend on the kind of sentence, the speaker's intentions, the situational context, and the hearer's reactions (Schulte (1993), pp. 146ff.). Understanding the language games played with these (and any other) sentences means being capable of appropriately expressing oneself and reacting to other people's utterances, it does not additionally require being acquainted with the 'assumption' that he will come *in abstracto*.

The second quotation brings out the fact that, apart from not being necessary, it is not even sufficient to be familiar with the sense of a sentence in order to understand it. A person who does not know a word of English will not understand the sentence 'He will come' any better if one explains to him or her that these words have the meaning *that he will come*. Rather, in order to explain the meaning of this sentence, one will show the person how this sentence is used on various occasions. It is no objection to say that one could translate the sentence into the person's language, for what would one do other than saying 'The sentence 'He will come' plays the same role in English as this sentence in your language'? And how was one to teach the sentence to someone who hasn't yet acquired a native language, a child that is? The child would have to be already acquainted with thoughts, before it could learn to clothe them into words and sentences of different kinds. But what is the Fregean thought 'that he will come', which supposedly captures the meaning of this expression?[40] We don't encounter meanings differently from being in commerce, being used on particular occasions, standing in various contexts. Whether a sentence makes sense depends on whether it does what the speaker wants to do with it, and the range of things to be done with words depends on whether it can be responded to and whether there are conclusions which can be drawn from it—both of which are highly context-sensitive issues. In short, the sense of a sentence depends on how a communication or a train of thought can continue. Asserting a sentence such as "He's coming. I personally don't believe it, but don't let that disconcert you" (*RPP* I 495) is absurd exactly for this reason—it is utterly unclear what conclusions should be drawn from it, how one should respond, what the speaker wants to say. And it is in this respect, in which Moore-paradoxical sentences are similar to formal-logical contradictions, as Wittgenstein writes in his letter to Moore, and why both types of sentences should be, and usually are, ruled out from common sense.

Wittgenstein's last point in *PPF*, x is that if one goes as far as suspecting a context-independent sense in the background wherever one finds a meaningful sentence, it will seem most appealing to conceive of psychological expressions in the same way, as context-independently standing for corresponding psychological phenomena. That is to say, the two main ideas of representationalist views, the two-component model of mental states (content *plus* mode) and the idea that psychological expressions designate language-independent psychological phenomena, are interlocked such that holding one of them already motivates holding the other one, too. If one starts with the idea of a common, uniform content-element, one will sooner or later be tempted to regard particular kinds of contents as representing corresponding kinds of states of affairs. Whenever someone entertains a mental state or makes a speech act with the content 'X believes that *p*', this person is supposed to represent the psychological fact *that X believes that p*. Conversely, when one takes beliefs and other so-called propositional attitudes as definitely identifiable psychological phenomena, one will soon come across the insight that content, what beliefs, intentions and so forth are directed at or

---

40 Peter Goldie asked me once, "What is the thought 'My life is a failure'?" His example brings out even more pointedly the absurdity of the idea of an eternal and constant content, which is deeply rooted in the Fregean conception of the third realm of thought.

about, presents a suitable criterion to individuate particular propositional attitudes, makes the contents of mental states fit into well-established propositional logic, and warrants that by the expression 'X believes that p' one always refers to the same kind of phenomenon.[41]

As I argued, Moore's Paradox shows the limitations of the representationalist enterprise, even from within its own theory. And as Wittgenstein points out as early as in his immediate reaction to Moore's original presentation of the paradox, "logic isn't as simple as logicians think it is" (*Briefe* 257), as it would have to be were the two-component model to succeed. His subsequent considerations of Moore's Paradox in the context of his later philosophy of psychology uncover and disentangle several misconceptions that, among others, underlie contemporary representationalist views of the mental, particularly the striving for a theory that conforms to the laws of traditional logic, the striving to seek for uniform contents in different kinds of thoughts and utterances and the tendency to understand psychological expressions as 'names' designating corresponding phenomena.

2.4.4 Preliminary Conclusion

Following Wittgenstein, I argued that Moore's Paradox escapes all possible explanatory attempts that are made on either the two-component model of assertion or the assumption that psychological expressions designate certain kinds of language-independent facts, namely identifiable psychological phenomena. The claim that it was possible to extract a uniform content from different kinds of speech acts and mental states cannot accommodate the absurdity of asserting 'It is raining, but I don't believe it is raining'. The claim that psychological concepts denote corresponding psychological phenomena is inadequate once it comes to the asymmetries of psychological words in their different inflective forms. My argument was particularly directed against the claim that assertions involving a first-person present tense inflection of a psychological predicate always entail descriptions of one's own current state of mind. On the contrary, I argued that they never do. Consequently, in a wide range of situations in which psychological concepts are applied, the claim that meaningful sentences represent corresponding language-independent states of affairs, which lies at the core of representationalism, is

---

41 *Cf.* Schulte (1993), pp. 146ff. That the content of mental states defines their *differentia specifica* (their 'nature'), i.e. the criterion for classifying and individuating them, is central to Burge's account, for instance. It is however, perfectly unclear what the properties 'he-will-come' or 'it-is-raining', what 'aluminium-thoughts' or 'apple-wishes' should be, just as the nature of Fregean thoughts remains mysterious.

wrong. For the same class of cases the claim that generating representations of states of affairs is prior to judging them true or false, which I have termed the Priority Claim, is equally wrong.

The arrangement of the remarks in *PPF*, x suggests that Wittgenstein intends his argument from Moore's Paradox to answer their opening questions:

> How did people ever come to use such an expression as 'I believe…'? Did they at some time notice a phenomenon (of believing)? Did they observe themselves and others, and so discover believing? (*PPF* §§ 86–7, translation Hacker/Schulte)

These questions are primarily concerned with the meaning of the expression 'I believe', not with what believing 'is'. The main implication of Wittgenstein's argument from Moore's Paradox is that the expression 'I believe' is not used to ascribe a belief to oneself. The meaning of this expression does not consist in referring to a language-independent fact about the speaker's mind, not even in situations in which the expression 'I believe' is used to report on one's mental states. Accordingly, the meaning of the expression 'I believe' is not established in an act of naming a phenomenon one has noticed, or observed in oneself or others.

The main theses of representationalism were that the meaning of psychological expressions consists in designating corresponding psychological phenomena, and that these psychological phenomena are facts independent of whether they are represented. The first thesis has been sufficiently undermined with the argument from Moore's Paradox. But what follows from this for the second thesis? In the next section, I argue that in the way psychological phenomena are conceived on representationalism, it follows from the refutation of the first thesis that there are no such things as discrete psychological phenomena. This statement is neither meant to deny the possibility of meaningfully using psychological words, nor to reduce psychological phenomena to physical ones (which by contrast 'really' exist). Rather, it denies that psychological phenomena are what the representationalist conceives them to be: language-independent facts that simultaneously determine the meaning of psychological concepts and the accuracy conditions of their application.

2.5 Against Referentialism II: There is no such *Thing* as a 'Phenomenon of Belief'

The idea that mental states are identifiable phenomena that exist prior to and independently of being represented in thought or language is central to the representationalist conception of the mind. It is thought that unless mental states—

beliefs, desires, emotions, perceptions, sensations and so forth—are definite facts either mental or psychological in kind, they could not themselves present suitable objects of mental representation. In accord with the general representationalist claims, the accuracy conditions of any mental or linguistic representation of such psychological facts is determined by this fact, the truth of any judgement that a particular psychological fact obtains depends on whether it is true that this fact obtains and so forth. Representing psychological facts is accordingly treated as nothing but depicting corresponding psychological facts and as such as supposed to refer to the facts they are about.[42] The application of psychological predicates on representationalism is tantamount to ascribing a particular psychological state to a subject, whether in the first, second or third grammatical person. Since language is regarded as one way of representing states of affairs, sentences containing psychological expressions are supposed to designate corresponding psychological states of affairs. In line with that, judgements that a particular psychological fact obtains—*viz.* that someone bears a particular mental state—are true if and only if that person bears the respective mental state. Psychological facts are however supposed to exist independently of whether they are subject to anybody's judgement or thought.[43] The sentence 'Peter believes that is raining' is true if and only if the psychological fact *that Peter believes that it is raining* obtains; but Peter could believe that it is raining without this state being itself explicitly represented by himself or another person. The representationalist picture thus prioritises the existence of psychological phenomena over the existence of a language articulating them; and the meaning of this language is supposed to consist in describing corresponding psychological phenomena. Sentences concerned with the mental and mental states are thought to have the function of designation, i.e. a sentence is regarded as a sign standing for a particular state of affairs. These claims apply to type and token mental states equally: the idea of a particular class of mental states, say beliefs, is prior to and provides the meaning of the respective general psychological concept, that of believing. The existence of a particular mental state, say Peter's belief that it is raining at time t, is prior to and provides the content of the representation that Peter believes at time t that it is raining.

---

42 Of course, 'depicting' psychological facts need not involve producing a kind of visual image.
43 To which extent particular representationalist views endorse this statement depends on whether they hold a version of Shoemaker's self-intimating thesis. If mental states are constitutively self-intimating, their bearer will automatically entertain a representation of him- or herself holding the respective mental state. It is a further issue whether this kind of meta-representation is conceived as self-awareness, self-knowledge or self-consciousness. At any rate, it follows from the self-intimating thesis that representing an object involves a double cognitive achievement, representing the object in question and representing oneself as holding this representation.

Earlier in this chapter I rejected the idea that the relation between psychological expressions and psychological phenomena was one that abides the name-object model. The argument was that this model does not account for the meaning of psychological expressions in that it does not accommodate the variety of ways in which psychological expressions are used, and in that it errs in understanding this meaning as basically descriptive. I will now argue that it is not only wrong to conceive of the meaning of psychological expressions in language in terms of designation, but also that the conception of psychological phenomena as language-independent states of affairs is itself mistaken. I adopt several argumentative lines Wittgenstein has developed in *Philosophical Investigations* §§ 243–315, the remarks which are commonly known as his 'private language argument', and related issues from his remarks on rule-following.[44]

It might not be obvious that the arguments falling under the rubric of the 'private language argument' are directly applicable to the representationalist view—after all, not every representationalist straightforwardly agrees with the claim that the mind is a kind of private room furnished with mental states, as kitchens are furnished with chairs and tables. Not every representationalist is or wants to be a Cartesian, but Cartesianism in this sense is most often supposed to be the target of the aforementioned passages in Wittgenstein's *Philosophical Investigations*. Despite its drastic appearance, the comparison of the mind with an inner space, populated with thing-like objects involves two ideas which are genuinely representationalist. First, the idea that mental states constitute a particular domain of objective, truth-conferring facts. Second, the idea that if there is a substantial asymmetry between the first-person and the third-person present tense form of psychological predicates, the grammatical asymmetry will derive from an underlying epistemic asymmetry, i.e. the fact that one is in a distinguished, privileged position to be familiar with the contents of one's own mind.[45] The first idea is at the core of any representationalist view. How one decides whether to deny or affirm that the first-person present indicative of mental predicates displays a substantial epistemological asymmetry

---

44 I will not engage in the discussion whether there is such a thing as a private language argument, and if so, how many. I will follow a suggestion of Schulte's and simply refer to these remarks as *PI* §§ 243–315. *Cf.* Schulte (2011), n. 15.

45 The attribute 'substantial' is meant to reflect that the asymmetry in question derives from the ontology of mental states. A contrasting view is hold, for example, by Crispin Wright, who argues that this asymmetry is a consequence of what he calls the default case: Under normal circumstances, we credit others as well as ourselves with the best possible knowledge of our own states of mind. For this reason, we also concede the entitlement to one another to have the last word on whether judgements about them are true or false. *Cf.* Wright (1998b) and Wright (1989), "Wittgenstein's Later Philosophy of Mind: Sensation, Privacy, and Intention", *The Journal of Philosophy 86/11*, pp. 622–634.

depends on whether one agrees or disagrees with the thesis that it is a constitutive feature of individual mental states that their bearer is aware of them.[46]

However, I argued that any representationalist view confronted with Moore's Paradox will psychologise it in order to explain it, that is, it will be claimed that the subject of a Moore-paradoxical belief or assertion will know or be aware of its contents, whereas this kind of knowledge or awareness is not present in the case of another person's representational states. In other words, every representational state is not only concerned with its content, but also expresses the subject's awareness of having this representational state. So the epistemological issue on representationalism is not whether or not a person is in a special position (a more authoritative one) to know his or her own mind. Rather, it is the question as to whether the fact that he or she is better informed about his or her own state of mind is or is not a matter of an epistemic privilege (for instance, the possibility of introspection) or a matter of a distinctive kind of first-personal knowledge which obtains in addition to or is convertible into third-personal knowledge. Whether or not one distinguishes different kinds of knowing one's own mental states has an impact on the semantics of the first-person present indicative of psychological predicates. Judgements like 'I believe that p', 'I'm in pain' and so on are considered manifestations of factual knowledge of one's own state of mind at any rate, and, depending on how one decides on the matter of self-knowledge, possibly also manifestations of the distinctive, subjective kind of self-knowledge. Accordingly, first-person expressions of mental states are supposed to have a descriptive meaning at any rate, which is possibly accompanied by an additional subjective meaning.

It emerged from the last section that whether one denies or affirms that verbal articulations of one's own state of mind bear a double meaning on top of

---

46 Other than for example Parfit concludes from Lichtenberg's famous aphorism ("*It thinks*, we should say, just as one says, *it lightnings*", *Waste Books* K 76, in: Georg Christoph Lichtenberg (2012), *Philosophical Writings, Selected from the Waste Books*, transl. Steven Tester, Albany: State of New York University Press, retrieved from *Project Muse* http://muse.jhu.edu/books/9781438441986, last access March 25th, 2014) representationalism cannot allow for particular mental states without a bearer. *Cf.* Derek Parfit (1987), *Reasons and Persons*, Oxford: UP, chs. 11 and 12. The criteria of individuation of mental states comprise at least mode, content, time and ownership: My current belief that it is going to rain tomorrow does not differ from Peter's current belief that it is going to rain tomorrow, apart from the fact that the first one is mine, and the second one Peter's. As far as one can speak of 'the' belief that it is going to rain tomorrow without indication of a bearer, on does not thereby denote a disowned token belief, but a type of beliefs, which can be instantiated at different times by different people. In fact, one is talking about an abridged thought-content, *that S has the belief that it is going to rain tomorrow*. *Cf.* Frege (1819); Schulte (2011); and the previous chapter, sections 2.1 and 4.

expressing an epistemological asymmetry makes but a negligible difference in the consequences on the semantic level, as long as the claim that psychological expressions always describe corresponding psychological facts is maintained. Things are analogous in the present issue: Whether or not one holds that knowledge of one's own mental states is knowledge of a distinctive kind is irrelevant, or so I will argue, for the thesis that mental states are identifiable, independent objects, as long as one maintains that this attitude is an epistemic one. It is this *mentalist* picture of the mind Wittgenstein addresses in *Philosophical Investigations* §§ 243–315. Once again, Wittgenstein is concerned with a grammatical question, the question of how the meaning of psychological expressions is constituted, and in this context how experience is expressed in language.

The two arguments I present here, the argument from Moore's Paradox and the argument against the conceivability of a private language, are directed against what Wittgenstein takes to be a widespread but mistaken view, or better a bundle of views, of the function and meaning of psychological expressions and the 'nature' of experience and the mind. Notwithstanding his manner of writing, which suggests that he has one or several concrete views in mind at which his arguments are directed, he does not engage with particular theories of mind and language, but with certain claims he takes to be fundamental to what one might call an ideal-typical mentalist view. Among others, these permeate the idealised representationalist view, which I have explained in the last chapter. Wittgenstein certainly also objects to Augustine's, or Descartes', or Frege's respective models of the mind and language, or the view the 'author of the *Tractatus*' had once proposed. He is still more concerned with rejecting a cluster of views endorsing (some of) their central ideas. If one wants to draw attention to a particular thesis that probably is at the roots of all misunderstandings, it will be the idea that one can draw metaphysical conclusions, conclusions regarding the ontology of this or that realm of reality, from the grammar of the language, which we use to negotiate the respective issues. In this light, stating that one is not a full-fledged Cartesian, or that one does not hold a *Tractatus*-like picture of language, does not suffice to escape Wittgenstein's arguments, and it is too weak grounds to refrain from engaging with it. Particularly the argument against the conceivability of a private language is much more forceful than commonly assumed insofar as it can be turned against both the Reference and the Priority Claim with respect to both type and token mental states. This will be argued in this chapter.[47]

---

47 *Cf.* Peter M. S. Hacker (1990b), "The Private Language Arguments", in his *Wittgenstein: Meaning and Mind. Part I: Essays*, Oxford: Blackwell, pp. 1–16, and "Privacy", *ibid.*, pp.17–35.

In what follows, I will scrutinise the two versions of the claim that mental states are known in a distinctive way by their owner, which I introduced in the last chapter using the theories of Shoemaker and Moran. Both claim self-knowledge to be a constitutive feature of having mental states, but diverge in their accounts of the kind of knowledge we are concerned with. Shoemaker understands the asymmetry of first-personal knowledge as a matter of privileged access by introspection, whereas Moran takes subjective knowledge to be a special kind of knowledge. I will point to two problems that remain insurmountable on both accounts, the problem of identifying one's own mental states and establishing the meaning of psychological concepts, and the problem of re-identifying and recognising one's own mental states. At this stage, my considerations will already have provided the basis for rejecting the claim that mental states are criterially identifiable phenomena altogether and that there is something to know of in the case of one's own mental states. Finally, I will clarify once more that this conclusion does not render the language concerned with psychological expressions metaphorical (as Shoemaker's earlier proposal seems to suggest) or its functioning as a means of communication a matter of good luck, trust and social contingencies (as Kripke (1982) suggests in reaction to the relativist picture of meaning he reads into Wittgenstein).

2.5.1 Mental Privacy

In *PI* §§ 243–315, Wittgenstein once more addresses the conception that the meaning of psychological expressions is constituted in terms of reference, which has been central to my inquiry. This conception construes the meaning of psychological expressions upon an (already mistaken) idea about the meaning of language in general, which Wittgenstein discusses at the beginning of *Philosophical Investigations* (§§ 1–89) and which has become commonly known as the 'Augustinian picture of language' (*PI* § 1). Applied to psychological expressions, the model reads like this: psychological expressions are names referring to objects of a particular kind, psychological phenomena (mental states or processes). The reference between name and object is established by a kind of 'baptism': A mental state becomes in some way or another manifest to consciousness, is captured by attending to it, and associated with a name, say, 'belief that it is raining' or 'pain' or 'visual image of a yellow lorry'. The reference relation so established between psychological expression, object and our knowledge of it is supposed to explain what use we make of them. That the meaning of words is established in accord with this picture is very plausible for the realm of physical, commonly accessible objects and facts and agrees with the common experience that many expressions are taught by means of ostensive definition, that is, drawing attention to an object and saying, for instance, 'This is a chair'.[48]

In *PI* §§ 243ff., Wittgenstein explains his notion of a private language as a language that is invented by a single person in order to write down or articulate his or her own experiences and captures the genuinely subjective way in which he or she is aware of them. Thus, a 'private language' does not work like a cipher, it does not conceal facts which are in principle knowable by others, but serves to articulate the subjective aspect of one's experiences. Since this aspect cannot be conveyed to another person (after all, nobody has *my* pain), a private language cannot be used and understood by others. The privacy of experiences is explained as an epistemological notion,[49] in the sense that there is a special way of knowing one's own experiences that is both exclusively available to their bearer and authoritative: "[O]nly I can know whether I am really in pain, another person can only surmise it."[50]

   The epistemological question is placed in the foreground by representational-ism. Once psychological phenomena are regarded as facts that exist independently of anybody's judgements about them, statements of the type 'X is in S' present ver-

---

48 The assumption that objects and states of affairs in one's proximal physical environment were discernible by themselves is, of course, central to externalism and naïve realism. This presupposes that "[t]he world divides into facts" (*TLP* 1.2) unless one grants conceptual capacities being at work even in the most primitive cases of representation. See the sections on representational content in Chapter 1 and John Campbell (2000), "Wittgenstein on Attention", *Philosophical Topics 28/2*, pp. 35–48, here pp. 35f. As Campbell rightly points out, one of the main interests of Wittgenstein's later writings is to reject this view as a convenient, but misconceived picture already in this seemingly simple case. Similarly, Stroud regards the 'private language argument' (especially *PI* § 258) as continuous with the preceding remarks on rule-following, and suggests to interpret it as an instance of Wittgenstein's general argumentation against the view that meaning is constituted by reference. *Cf.* Barry Stroud (1983), "Wittgenstein's 'Treatment' of the Quest for 'a language which describes my inner experiences and which only I myself can understand'", in Stroud (2000), *Meaning, Understanding, and Practice*, Oxford: UP, pp. 67–79. Analogously, the aforementioned §§ 398–411 investigate the referentialist view with respect to the word 'I'. I will confine my argument to the class of expressions I am interested in here, the psychological ones, although I am in unanimous agreement with both.
49 The use of the words 'privacy' and 'private' in connection with knowledge, possibly the most familiar combination, is one among a variety of other uses that can be found in Wittgenstein's later writings. For examples of nouns to which Wittgenstein attributes the word private, and for a very illuminating and structuring overview over Wittgenstein's relevant use of 'privacy' see Schulte (2011).
50 *PI* § 246. Note that Wittgenstein's interlocutor here does not claim that first-personal knowledge of one's own experiences is infallible, nor that it is constitutive for having experiences.

ifiable descriptions of states of affairs in any of their grammatical forms, including their first-person present indicative, 'I am in S'. Their first-person asymmetry is conceived as resulting from an epistemological distinctiveness of the way in which mental states are known first-personally—the way in which 'only I can know' my own experiences—either in terms of privileged access or in terms of a distinctive kind of self-knowledge. On either alternative, considering first-person asymmetry in epistemological terms has the consequence that the meaning of psychological expressions has to be established in private. For even if verbs like 'to believe', 'to wish', 'to see' and so on were used to describe my mental states as well as yours, Peter's or other people's, the yardstick of whether they describe their objects accurately would remain the person's own judgements, precisely because he or she is the only one who can really know, not only surmise, whether he or she has a particular mental state. Their 'real' reference thus can only be known by oneself. Therefore, the relation between psychological phenomena and psychological expressions has to be established in private, even if one might find it convenient to choose a repertoire of signs that are already in use. The entire process of individuating mental states, attaching signs to them and using these signs again whenever the state reoccurs is controlled by the subject alone, precisely because no other person has access to the referent.

In *PI* § 258, Wittgenstein describes how the meaning of psychological expressions is established according to this picture. A person intends to record the recurrence of a particular mental state and, for this purpose, associates it with a sign, 'S'. Whenever the state occurs, the person notes 'S' in his or her diary. Wittgenstein writes:

> I first want to observe that a definition of the sign cannot be formulated.—But surely, I can give one to myself as a kind of ostensive definition!—How? Can I point to the sensation?—Not in the ordinary sense. But I speak, or write the sign down, and at the same time I concentrate my attention on the sensation—and so, as it were, point inwardly.—But what is this ceremony for? For that is all it seems to be! A definition serves to lay down the meaning of a sign, doesn't it?—Well, that is done precisely by concentrating my attention; for in this way I commit to memory the connection between the sign and the sensation.—But "I commit it to memory" can only mean: this process brings it about that I remember the connection *correctly* in the future. But in the present case, I have no criterion of correctness. One would like to say: whatever is going to seem correct to me is correct. And that only means that here we can't talk of correctness.[51]

---

51 Notably, the term 'sensation' can be substituted, for the present purposes, with 'mental state' without changing the applicability and force of Wittgenstein's argument. Further, using ostensive definition for the purpose of establishing the reference relation between mental states and psychological expressions would be one among several kinds of definition that would be possible

In the passages which follow the above passage in *Philosophical Investigations*, Wittgenstein makes efforts to attack the conception formerly introduced from various directions. The two argumentative lines most applicable to the present case are already outlined in this remark. On the one hand, it is not possible to formulate a definition of a term in private. And even if one seemingly succeeded in doing so, on the other hand, the definition would be useless, because one would lack the means to check whether one henceforth uses the term in accordance with one's earlier definition. I will take up these arguments in turn to refute the representationalist claims concerning the relation of thought and language which is characterised by reference of the latter to the former, and priority of the former over the latter.

2.5.1.1 Constitution: Private Ostensive Definition

Let us assume with the representationalist that psychological phenomena are possible objects of discovery, individuable facts with definite boundaries constituting the meaning of corresponding psychological concepts. What is necessary to establish a system of signs denoting these facts under the given circumstances? Wittgenstein describes the process as follows. First of all, one has to fix the referent, a particular mental state S. This step requires awareness of the state in question, and, more importantly, focusing on it with one's attention. It is not enough to have the mental state one intends to name among the states one is conscious of, one also has to individuate it for being able to 'point' to it.[52] Since one can only surmise another person's mental states and since attaching a symbol to a referent as elusive as Schroedinger's cat will not be likely to deliver a uniform concept, one will choose a mental state of one's own. Then, one will define a symbol, 'S', which one intends to refer to this (kind of) mental state in the future, by concentrating on the mental state and maybe thinking, with determination, 'I hereby name thee S'. One has to 'catch' the object one wants to name, as it were, bring it before one's mental eye and call it by a name. The original mental state has the character of a sample, which provides both the referent and the criterion of correctness for one's further using the word 'S'.

Establishing a psychological concept so conceived proceeds by private ostensive definition, a process that is supposed to work analogously to explaining an observational concept or an individual name by demonstration. For example, if,

---

here. Consequently, proposing an alternative way of defining mental concepts, say by analytic definition, general concepts (Evans) or familiarity with a sample (Burge), would not present an option to escape from Wittgenstein's argumentation. I will come back to this point in Chapter 3.
52 *Cf.* Campbell (2000), p. 38.

at a crowded party, I point into the crowd saying 'This is my friend Peter', you will follow my pointing, single out the individual and henceforth know the person my frequent mention of Peter refers to. And if I don't know what the word 'sepia' refers to, you might search for a sepia-coloured object, point to it and say 'This is called 'sepia'', and I may henceforth be able to use the word. In the case of demonstrable objects, the picture is that "attention to objects and their properties is what provides us with our knowledge of the references of terms, and this knowledge of reference is what explains the use that we make of the terms" (Campbell (2000), p. 39). The meaning of psychological concepts is supposed to be established and used in the same way.

I indicated earlier that one might take publicly available concepts for one's own mental states instead of inventing a new symbolism. One would do so, for example, when one is taught the word 'belief' in learning one's first language. But this would not make the process of connecting word and referent less private, for neither the connection (the concentration of one's attention) nor the referent (the mental state) is available to the teacher or any other person. All one would do in this case is establishing a (private) connection between a public term and a private state or experience.[53] Similarly, it is of course possible to create new signs for objects or properties and also experiences one has never come across earlier. On his island, Robinson Crusoe might come across a bird or might experience a sensation, which he has never had before, and call it by a name. Robinson Crusoe, however, is not inexperienced in individuating birds or sensations. He is a full-fledged language-user who happens to be stranded in solitude. Robinson Crusoe is capable of creating new symbols *within* compartments of language he acquired at an earlier time, he has learned how to single out and recognise birds and sensations, and a variety of ways in which one can talk about both of them. In this respect, his way of inventing symbols is a far cry from the creation of a private language. The 'private linguist' faces the task to create the semantics and the syntactical rules of his or her language on his or her own.

So what is wrong with the picture presented in *PI* § 258, according to which the meaning of psychological concepts is constituted by demonstratively establishing a sample? The first difficulty results from the idea that the meaning of psychological words is established by associating them with one's own mental states by means of ostensive definition. To make this work, one has to be capable of attending to one's own mental states whilst giving them a definition. This requires a coherent

---

53 *Cf.* Schulte (2011), pp. 4f., who refers to a relevant passage in Ludwig Wittgenstein, *Philosophical Occasions 1912–1951* (*PO*), ed. by James C. Klagge, Alfred Nordmann, Indianapolis: Hackett 1993, p. 220.

understanding of what 'concentrating one's attention' is. But a point Wittgenstein makes earlier in *Philosophical Investigations* (§§ 28–9) is that the use of the word 'attention' is disparate already within the public domain of physical objects and properties.

> And what does 'pointing at the shape', 'pointing at the colour' consist in? Point at a piece of paper.—And now at its shape—now at its colour—now at its number (that sounds odd!).—Well, how did you do it?—You'll say you 'meant' something different each time you pointed. And if I ask how that is done, you'll say you concentrated your attention on the colour, the shape, and so on. But now I ask: how is *that* done? [...] But do you always do the *same* thing when you direct your attention to the colour? [...] One attends to the colour sometimes by blocking the contour from view with one's hand, or by not focusing on the contour of that thing, or by staring at the object and trying to remember where one saw that colour before. One attends to the shape, sometimes by tracing it, sometimes by screwing up one's eyes so as not to see the colour clearly, and so forth. I want to say: this and similar things are what one does *while* one 'directs one's attention to this or that'. (*PI* § 33)
>
> There are, indeed, what may be called 'characteristic experiences' of pointing, say, to the shape. For example, following the contour with one's finger or with one's eyes as one points.— *This*, however, does not happen in all cases in which I 'mean the shape', and no more does any other characteristic process occur in all these cases.—But even if something of the sort did recur in all cases, it would still depend on the circumstances—that is, on what happened before and after the pointing—whether we would say 'He pointed at the shape and not at the colour'. [...] in certain cases, especially when one points 'at the shape' or 'at the number' there are characteristic experiences and ways of pointing—characteristic, because they recur often (not always) when shape and number are 'meant'. But do you also know of an experience characteristic of pointing at a piece in a game, as a *piece in the game*? (*PI* § 35)
>
> So, one could say: an ostensive definition explains the use—the meaning—of a word if the role the word is supposed to play in language is already clear. So if I know that someone means to explain a colour-word to me, the ostensive explanation 'That is called sepia' will enable me to understand the word. (*PI* § 30, all quotations translated by Hacker/Schulte.)

With respect to attention, the upshot of these passages is that although attending to an object seems to be a simple thing to do, it is neither easily manageable, nor is attending a unique process itself. However, both would be required if one set out to establish a language for one's own mental states—one would already have to know how to direct one's attention to one's own mental states, and one would need to do so in a coherent way to secure that the relation between mental state and concept provided the grounds for using this relation in the future as a sample to refer to mental states of the same kind. If 'attending to one's beliefs' meant a different thing on different occasions it would be a matter of hope or sheer luck to always end up with thereby having singled out an object of the same kind as the original sample.[54]

---

54 *Cf.* Wright (1989), pp. 622f.

Attention not being a good guide to one's own mental states, the boundaries of the target itself, the mental state, are as nebulous as the road leading towards them. On the one hand, one cannot distinguish one mental state from one hundred mental states of the same kind without a criterion to do so.[55] On the picture of mental states drawn on representationalism, mental states have definite boundaries that determine the boundaries of the concepts referring to them. One might reply by offering several criteria of individuation for mental states, such as mode, content, time, and the person having them. Given that person and time are the same in the moment of defining a psychological concept by private ostensive definition, content and mode have to serve as the respective criteria. If one takes content to be the criterion to distinguish two mental states of the same kind, one will thereby not attend to the mental state, but to their contents. Thereby, however, one would precisely *not* bring the mental state itself into the position where it could be associated with a word, in one's focus of attention. This consideration brings out once again that one attends to one's own mental states by attending to their contents, not by attending to the states themselves.[56]

And if one attends to representational contents in order to individuate mental states, one will soon encounter the very same problem. For what separates one representational content from another one? Is it the proposition, which renders the content in language? But what is a proposition? A sentence of a natural language. So maybe the thought or content-type expressed by a proposition? But what is a thought, in contrast to a hundred thoughts? An entity in the third realm? How do I count all thoughts or content-types instantiated in the contents of my current beliefs? As a complex of elementary representational contents, contained by one single belief, expressed by a conjunction of elementary sentences, as what the early Wittgenstein suggests (and the later rejects)? Or as a multitude of single beliefs? And what then, once more, individuates a single belief? The problem of individuation will be inevitable at a sooner or later stage of theorising along these lines. But if it is not even possible to individuate representations without the help of language, one cannot compare them with objects either.

On the other hand, one and the same content can, according to the representationalist picture, figure as the content of various mental states of different

---

55 Schulte (2011), p. 5, *PO*, p. 243.
56 See Section 3.2.2 of this chapter. For belief, the case is made in *PPF*, x, for perceptual experience in *PI* §§ 275–7; for mental states in general in Campbell (2000), pp. 39–42. As a side-effect, the consideration also uncovers a disanalogy between attending to one's own mental states and attending to physical objects, such that it becomes more questionable than ever to construe a model of discovering and designating psychological phenomena as the rock-bottom of the meaning of psychological concepts.

kinds. So one might propose to individuate mental states by their psychological mode, rather than their content (only). But the private linguist lacks the capacities for distinguishing a *belief* that it is raining from a *wish* that it is raining. For this purpose, he or she would have to have a criterion by which a particular state could be categorised one way or another—say, a distinctive 'feeling' of belief or wish. However, it was the point of the ostensive definition to provide a sample as a criterion to recognise one's mental states in the future. So it might be thought that one could proceed by first defining a word for one kind of mental state and continuing by comparing other mental states with the so created sample, working oneself from the category word set in this way towards other ones. This does not however solve the following difficulty:

> What reason have we for calling 'S' the sign for a *sensation*? For 'sensation' is a word of our common language, which is not a language intelligible only to me. So the use of the word stands in need of a justification which everybody understands.—And it would not help either to say that it need not be a *sensation*; that when he writes 'S' he has *Something*—and that is all that can be said. But 'has' and 'something' also belong to our common language.—So in the end, when one is doing philosophy, one gets to the point where one would like just to emit an inarticulate sound.—But such a sound is an expression only in a particular language-game, which now has to be described. (*PI* § 261)

As Wittgenstein remarks here and in the earlier passages of *Philosophical Investigations* quoted above (§§ 30–5), defining a word by ostensive definition requires understanding what kind of thing the object of one's pointing is. If Peter was to explain the word 'sepia' to me by pointing with his hand to a pack of pasta and I didn't know that he meant the colour, I could mistakenly believe that the word 'sepia' referred to a particular shape or a recipe or the packaging.[57] It does not become clear from the pointing alone that 'sepia' is a colour-word. I would need to know the context of the pointing. In this case, it is relatively easy—I might have not been able to imagine the colour 'sepia' in an earlier conversation and Peter might have promised to show me a sepia-coloured object on some occasion. I might simply ask Peter what he meant. Still, understanding his reply 'Why, I meant the colour', requires me to have an understanding of colours beforehand, which consists among others in being capable of using it appropriately (*cf. PI* § 30).

The same goes for mental states. In order to define the meaning of a psychological word by concentrating one's attention to a mental state, one must already

---

[57] It is in fact more complex: How do I know that Peter was pointing at anything? Why do I follow his hand and do not look into the other direction? What enables me to understand that he is giving me an explanation?

be capable of individuating mental states, one has to have a grasp of what kind of thing one thereby was attending to. This requirement has already emerged from the argument from Moore's Paradox for beliefs. Representing that I believe that *p* presupposes having mastered the common use of the verb 'to believe', otherwise one would not have an idea of the object one means to represent at all. This claim is generalisable: Referring to one's own mental states requires some prior grasp of what one is looking for, and this means, first and foremost, a grasp of how the term 'mental states' is commonly used. But since *ex hypothesi* the ostensive definition is performed in private, familiarity with the public use of psychological concepts would not help, because, as I have pointed out earlier, connecting public terms, even the most general category 'mental states' with one's own mental states would be an act of one's own, which is not comprehensible for anybody else. Therefore, one could only *hope* that what one has individuated is what others call a mental state, and, as Wittgenstein remarks in *PI* § 261, one could not even be sure that one has thereby individuated *anything* at all. One could not distinguish whether or not one had, by means of pointing inwards, hit one's target, whether or not one had arrived at the right one, whether or not one had individuated nothing at all, and whether or not one had even aimed at anything at all.

As a possible line of defence, a proponent of representationalism could grant all this whilst stating that, in fact, this argument sustains what he or she has claimed from the beginning, that mental states are truth-conferring facts independent of and prior to psychological expressions, and that the capacity of having mental states includes the capacity of individuating them. And this is just what Shoemaker's self-intimation thesis and Moran's transparency claim are about. Once would say that within the domain of one's own psychological facts (or at least, within a subclass of this domain), judgements to the truth of particular facts are infallible, although these facts are contingent facts, and obtain independently of the judgements, and although the judgements in question deliver genuine factual knowledge of the states in question. As in the ordinary case of contingent observational facts, there is a contrast here between what is judged to be the case with one's mental states and what is the case. But differently from the ordinary case, one need not have a criterion to distinguish between what seems right to oneself in judging *that one is in S* and the fact *that one is in S*. One need not verify one's judgements under any conditions—the fact that one judges, or can judge that one has a particular mental state entails that one's judgement is true. If one adds the claim that knowing one's mental states is constitutive for having them to the presupposition that having mental states is prior to having words to designate them, "there will be both a genuine distinction between the judging and the state of affairs judged and no possibility of that kind of ascertainable contrast" (Wright (1989), p. 624). If there is no possibility of going amiss in recognising one's own mental states, the discussion how one can make sure that one does not fail to individuate them seems obsolete.

One could even go so far as to state that in the privacy of one's own mind one knows one's way about perfectly well, whereas confusion only enters once one acquires the suggested public ways of coming to know one's own mental states. In Moran's example of the psychoanalytical setting, the analysand was said to hold two contradicting beliefs about herself, which she arrived at by two different methods. Upon consideration of the subject-matter whether her brother betrayed her in the past on her own, she arrives at the belief that he didn't and, according to the transparency model, also at the belief that she believes that he didn't. Considering her own behaviour and feelings, events in the past and so on in the way the psychoanalyst had done and suggested to her, she arrives at the conclusion that she believes that her brother betrayed her.

As Moran interprets his example, the reason why the analysand holds contradicting beliefs about her own mental states is that she arrives at the judgements 'I believe that my brother betrayed me' and 'I believe that my brother did not betray me' in two ways. How can the analysand determine which of her judgements is true, i.e. which belief she really holds? Considering the grounds she had for judging either way has brought about the trouble and thus can be ruled out as a possible way of deciding the question. The analysand must decide only by comparing the two judgements, that she believes that her brother betrayed her, and that she does not believe that her brother betrayed her, which judgement originates from her actual belief and which one from the belief she holds in virtue of considering herself from her analyst's point of view. To make this possible, Moran appeals to there being a distinct 'phenomenology' of the truly first-personal judgement (Moran (1997), p. 156). Whatever this term is supposed to mean here, he apparently takes it to provide a criterion that lies beyond the judgement itself (say, a feeling of conviction) and thus seems to relativise his own claim that judgements of one's own beliefs are not in need of verification by further criteria.

One might now say that the relevant criteria, say, a feeling of truth or conviction, come with having mental states, but this would just raise the question how one identifies the criteria themselves and so threaten to lead into infinite regress. And appealing to objectively observable criteria whose presence could for instance be ascertained by imaging techniques again raises the question how the connection between the publicly available criterion and the privately accessed mental state and its intrinsic subjective criterion could be established (*cf. PI* § 270).

This is why Wittgenstein is right in concluding that the meaning of psychological concepts cannot be established by means of ostensive definition or an analogous definitory act,[58] given the representationalist assumption that this process serves to identify facts that provide the referents of corresponding expressions and thereby both justify and explain the way we make use of these expression in language. It is very natural to assume that attention plays a role in defining the meaning of words, and Wittgenstein does not deny that it does. But it does so only in contexts in which the person who is supposed to establish or to learn a word has a prior grasp of what he or she is to do with the word, which is not and cannot be given in the present case. And even if one succeeded in establishing a stable relation between a psychological state and a psychological expression, which enabled one to use the word reliably in the presence of the state, this relation would not have the intended effect, being able to meaningfully use the expression on future occasions, not even if the meaning consisted in designating its supposed referent.

2.5.1.2 Recognition and Identification

The point of the "ceremony" Wittgenstein describes in *PI* § 258 was to connect a word with a mental state in order to establish the reference relation that is supposed to constitute the meaning of the sign, and to turn the uttering of sounds into a meaningful expression.[59] If one succeeds in establishing the meaning of a sign in private, by ostensive definition or otherwise, the referent will henceforth take a double role; it will serve as a warrant for the meaning of the sign and provide the criterion of correctness for its use, functioning as a kind of sample or yardstick by which one could check actual uses of the sign. The idea is simple: In cases of uncertainty about the use of the expression, or in order to understand what another person means with it, one could look up the original reference relation as in a dictionary, as it were, and check whether the use at issue is in accord with one's original intentions.

---

58 An analytical definition, for instance, would employ expressions from either public or the person's private language, and equally would have to be connected with the *definiendum*. So the respective arguments I have just cited would apply again.

59 This almost literally circumscribes Searle's understanding of meaning: The speaker's intentions cause a sequence of sounds to be a meaningful sentence expressing what the speaker intends the sentence to express. *Cf.* Searle (1983), ch. 6; above, Chapter 1, Section 3.2, and below, Chapter 3, Section 2.1. What Searle seems not aware of is that his description renders acts of constituting the meaning of particular utterances by meaning intentions declarations in his sense. According to his own account, this is to say that the possibility of making meaningful utterances already presupposes linguistic conventions of the sort 'the utterance of a sound counts as a speech act of this sort in this language'. To me, this seems indeed a rather plausible statement about meaning. Regrettably, Searle maintains that, the need for a common vocabulary notwithstanding, having meaning intentions is prior to being able to utter meaningful sentences.

The only fault in this idea is that the sample has to be retrieved from memory: One has to remember what one did in associating expression and sample, and one has to remember *correctly*. But since, *ex hypothesi*, the entire process was performed in private, one has no criterion at one's disposal to decide whether one remembers the connection between expression and mental state correctly. The potential failure of memory does not only concern the sign one had chosen earlier (this would be as if a German native speaker forgets the English expression for 'Es regnet'), but extends as well to the other elements of the name-giving ceremony, individuating the referent and attending to it.

First of all, one could lose track of the referent itself:

> 'Imagine a person who could not remember *what* the word 'pain' meant—so that he constantly called different things by that name—but nevertheless used it in accordance with the usual symptoms and presuppositions of pain'—in short, he uses it as we all do. Here, I would like to say: a wheel that can be turned though nothing else moves is no part of the mechanism. (*PI* § 271)

The kind of error in remembering the original reference relation Wittgenstein describes here is that one could diverge from the originally intended use of the symbol by applying it to various states without noticing the difference between the objects one designates at every instance—indeed without anybody noticing. What has gone wrong here is that one does not reidentify a mental state as the mental state, which one originally used in establishing the reference relation, because one has forgotten what the referent was. And because, as regards one's own mental states, there is no criterion for whether one 'means' the *same* referent at every instance one uses a particular psychological concept, the referent plays the role of an 'idle wheel', it has nothing to do with constituting the meaning of the word.

Furthermore, 'concentrating one's attention' does not designate a uniform phenomenon, not even in the non-mental domain of facts, such that it is doubtful whether a reliable reference relation could be established at first place. An analogous point concerns 'retrieving the sample from memory'—both *attending* to an object and *remembering* the connection between word and object (themselves 'psychological phenomena') have to be carried out in private. But under these conditions, it is not only indeterminable whether one remembered the meaning of a word correctly in the sense that one remembers the right object, but also whether one does the right thing in remembering. To adapt Wittgenstein's remark, it might be the case that one does, without noticing, various things whilst 'concentrating one's attention' and 'remembering the referent'. So one may conclude that the processes that supposedly are sufficiently made clear with these notions equally do not participate in constituting the meaning of a psychological expression.[60]

---

60 *Cf.* Wright (1989), pp. 626–629.

A distinction between what *seems* to be right and what is *in fact* right cannot be drawn for either recognising the referent of a word or for the process of recognising. In absence of a public measure of correctness, it is impossible to state the similarity or identity of different processes, events, and experiences; whether a later event is a reoccurrence of an earlier one or something else. Establishing a reference relation between a psychological concept and a mental state in a private definitory act does not provide a stable meaning of the word across different uses even if one succeeded in connecting word and state on a single occasion because the relation is not sustainable by the person alone. But one will not even come so far in one's attempt to create a meaningful language for one's own mental states because one cannot even make the first step: connecting a word and a mental state.

2.5.2 Summary

The picture of mental states as discrete, judgement-independent phenomena suggests that the relation between psychological concepts and mental states is one of reference. Constituting meaningful expressions for mental states therefore requires bringing about the respective reference relations, which involves at least individuating a referent and connecting it with a concept in a definitory act. I have argued that it is impossible to carry out this procedure under the assumption that the epistemology of one's own mind is not the same as the epistemology of other people's minds. So one comes across the idea that psychological concepts have a double sense: a public one applicable to others, and a private one, capturing the distinctiveness of first-personally knowing one's own mental states. This assumption inevitably has the consequence that the subjective meaning of psychological concepts has to be constituted in the way Wittgenstein describes in § 258 as the 'invention' of a private language.

The idea of a private language, however, is nonsensical for several reasons. The first mistake is to construct the act of defining psychological expressions in private in analogy with explaining words by pointing at objects in the common world. Attending to an object is not even here a uniform phenomenon, let alone within the 'private' realm of one's mind. Further, without having already a prior understanding of what mental states are, one cannot individuate the referents, neither numerically (one belief or a hundred?), nor qualitatively (the belief or the wish that it is raining?).

The second mistake is to believe that one could recognise the reoccurrence of the mental state one has used as a sample to constitute the meaning of a particular expression. Recognising a mental state requires being able to distinguish between situations in which the state in question is actually present, and in which it only seems to be present. But a single person cannot possibly establish a criterion by which he or she could make the distinction, on pain of becoming entrapped in a never-ending regress of further criteria, each determining the correctness conditions of the previous one's application.

The definitory process was supposed to create a 'sample' as a standard regulating the future use of the sign. Defining a word is explaining its meaning and specifying a rule for its correct application. Yet, without a context clarifying the role the sign one wants to introduce is supposed to play in language, and without criteria distinguishing the difference between those applications which are in accord with the meaning of the sign and those which only seem to be, the semantics of a language cannot be established (not to mention its syntax). Both conditions are not fulfilled in case of initiating a language by privately connecting one's own mental states with sounds whilst intending to henceforth refer to the state with the sound.

> That's why 'following a rule' is a practice. And to think one is following a rule is not to follow a rule. And that's why it is not possible to follow a rule 'privately'; otherwise, thinking one was following a rule would be the same as following a rule. (*PI* § 202)

This is to say that drawing solely on definitions without taking notice of their contextual conditions does not suffice for constituting the semantic rules of a language and for explaining the meaning and the use of words. This conclusion is possibly most comprehensible when one is concerned with the notion of a 'private language', less so when considering the everyday practices of explaining this or that by pointing at things and properties in one's field of vision, for instance, or of checking dictionaries or instruction manuals in order to check the meaning of a word, the operation of a machine and so on. Yet, one easily forgets in these situations that the descriptions, demonstrations and explanations one is concerned with are intelligible only against a practical grasp of describing, demonstrating and explaining. Searle defines 'declarations' as those speech acts, which bring about what they represent. More precisely "all declarations bring about institutional facts, facts which exist only within systems of constitutive rules, and which are, therefore, facts by human agreement" (Searle (1983), p. 172). They require a background of social institutions in order to succeed (*ibid.*, pp. 171f.). That defining the meaning of a sequence of sounds—in a definition, or in a meaning intention—belongs to the declarative class and can therefore not be performed in private remains unmentioned.

Finally, if it is indeterminate what kind of thing a mental state is, it does not play a role in constituting the meaning of a psychological expression. It is therefore irrelevant to both, understanding and having the capacity to correctly apply psychological expressions, whether psychological phenomena *exist* as language-independent facts, or whether they do not (*cf. PI* § 261, quoted above).

Suppose that everyone had a box with something in it which we call a 'beetle'. No one can ever look into anyone else's box, and everyone says he knows what a beetle is only by looking at *his* beetle.—Here it would be quite possible for everyone to have something different in his box. One might even imagine such a thing constantly changing.—But what if these people's word 'beetle' had a use nonetheless?—If so, it would not be as the name of the thing. The thing in the box doesn't belong to the language-game at all; not even as a *Something*: for the box might even be empty.—No, one can 'divide through' by the thing in the box; it cancels out, whatever it is.

That is to say, if we construe the grammar of the expression of sensation on the model of 'object and name', the object drops out of the consideration as irrelevant. (*PI* § 293)

These two remarks nicely sum up the conclusion for what I argued in this chapter: The assumption that psychological words stand for corresponding mental states is neither necessary nor sufficient for understanding the meaning of psychological expressions. Remarkably, the more anxiously one attempts to keep hold of the referent in order to grant that psychological words are meaningful and not, for instance, abbreviations of behavioural descriptions or more precise descriptions of neurophysiological ongoings (the definition of psychological concepts is given in the realm of utmost certainty, the realm of one's own mental states, whereupon one has authoritative and infallible knowledge) the more elusive the referent becomes. Its boundaries are continuously blurred, until its existence becomes indeterminable and it eventually inaudibly escapes. It is illusory to believe that one could, for the sake of providing an imperturbable grounding for the meaning of psychological concepts, bypass the ambiguities and variations of their everyday use and ignore their complex entanglement in social interactions.

This conclusion substantiates the conclusion from Moore's Paradox: The idea that there were a uniform meaning common to all grammatical forms of the word 'to believe', namely describing or denoting a definite phenomenon of believing and allocating it to a bearer, does not account for the use of the word, particularly, it does not accommodate the irregularities and situational variations in using them. Moore's Paradox remains unintelligible on this very assumption, independently of what the origin of the asymmetry of the term 'I believe' is supposed to consist in, as long as this is conceived as an epistemological one, as a property of the way in which one refers to one's own mental states.

2.6 Conclusion

In this chapter, I developed two arguments against the representationalist theory of mind taking up two arguments of Wittgenstein's, the argument from Moore's Paradox and the argument against the conceivability of a private language. In particular, I argued that Moore's Paradox provides the basis for rejecting the claims I specified in the last chapter as the central presuppositions of representationalist views—the Reference Claim, the Uniformity Claim, and the Priority Claim—together with their conception of the mind as being constituted from discrete mental states which were structurally analysable into two components, a psychological mode and a representational content, as well as their interlocking conception of language as one way of representing reality. I will now summarise my argument and its conclusions.

2.6.1 Summary

At the outset of this chapter (Section 1), I reconsidered Moore's Paradox and stated one's again that the representationalist view cannot properly solve it. Moore's Paradox consists in that a sentence of the form 'p is the case, but I don't believe p is the case' is absurd when asserted in the first-person present indicative, although it can be true, although it is not absurd in kinds of sentences other than assertions, and although it ceases to be absurd when the first-person present tense of 'to believe' is changed into a different grammatical tense or person. That is, in representationalist terms: if the state of affairs expressed in the assertion is referred to from another temporal or personal perspective (Moore (1993), pp. 208ff.).

If one's views concerning both assertion and the grammar of the verb 'to believe' are already settled, as they are by the representationalist framework, Moore's Paradox must be regarded as the problem that Moore-paradoxical assertions are absurd although they can present true descriptions of reality. As I have argued, this approach necessarily renders asserting a Moore-paradoxical sentence equivalent to asserting a formal-logical contradiction. Yet, Moore-paradoxical sentences are absurd when asserted, but not contradictory. Hence, the representationalist explanation of Moore's Paradox is false.[61]

I introduced Wittgenstein's considerations of Moore's Paradox with a brief contextualisation of how he encountered the paradox and which position it takes within his later philosophy (Section 2). Remarkably, Wittgenstein attaches much weight to Moore's Paradox; it frequently appears in his later manuscripts. Following Wittgenstein's suggestion, the first move in approaching Moore's Paradox consists in concentrating on the grammar of assertions of the kind 'p is the case, but I don't believe that p is the case' instead, i.e. precisely on what is unnegotiable

---

61 Section 3.1 presents a concise version of this argument.

on representationalism, the 'logic' of assertion and the meaning of the expression 'I believe'.

Setting aside the representationalist framework for a while and choosing this radically different approach has far-reaching implications for the understanding of both issues (Sections 3 and 4). Investigating Moore's Paradox in this way reveals that modelling the structure and function of assertions upon the two-component model and conceiving of the meaning of the expression 'I believe' as designating a corresponding state of mind has unbearable consequences. First of all, given these interlocking conceptions Moore's Paradox cannot be resolved: Either, Moore-paradoxical assertions are transformed into assertions of formal-logical contradictions, or the absurdity does not arise at first place. There is no way of accommodating the specific absurdity of Moore-paradoxical assertions given the rigid model of assertion and the fixation on specifying a common referent constituting the meaning of psychological expressions.

What is more, surveying the ways in which the expression 'I believe' is used in assertions brings to light that the variety of acceptable usages is far more diverse than the representationalist conception of meaning as reference allows. This suggests that even if the claim that the meaning of psychological expressions is constituted in this way was true, it would not explain, that is, it would not help to understand the meaning of psychological expressions on particular occasions.

Thirdly, I argued that trying to solve Moore's Paradox whilst maintaining the Fregean model of assertion and the referentialist conception of the meaning of psychological expressions, as the representationalist views I have discussed do, yields conclusions that contradict these very claims themselves. Most importantly, I tried to show that there is no way to reconcile the asymmetry of the first-person present indicative of the verb 'to believe' with its supposed function to attribute a discrete state of mind to its user. Every attempt of doing so resulted in either violating the Uniformity Claim, and thus being incompatible with the two-component model, or the Reference Claim. This is to say that Wittgenstein's considerations of Moore's Paradox, which I have been drawing on throughout my argument, eventually show that representationalism is self-defeating.

In the last section of this chapter I developed an additional argument against the assumption that mental states were those discrete phenomena explaining and constituting the meaning of psychological expressions and providing the correctness conditions of their use. Based on Wittgenstein's remarks on rule-following and his (so-called) private language argument I argued first that representationalist views have to endorse the conception of a private language of psychological expressions, which is outlined and successively rejected in *Philosophical Investigations* §§ 243– 314. Thereby, I sought to demonstrate secondly that drawing on a reference relation obtaining between psychological expressions and mental states is neither necessary nor sufficient to explain either what constitutes the meaning of psychological expressions and how they are used in language. It turned out that, contrary to the representationalist theory, it is perfectly irrelevant to questions concerning the meaning of language of psychological expressions whether there are such things as psychological phenomena.

2.6.2 Belief, Assertion, and Truth

I have pointed out in the last chapter (Section 3.8) that there is nothing on representationalist accounts that rules out the possibility of sensibly asserting or believing the sentence 'I falsely believe'. More precisely, the assertoric moment of belief, i.e. their being truth-directed, cannot be provided for. The referentialist position concerning the meaning of psychological predicates, which is central to representationalism, cannot account for the asymmetry of the expression 'I believe', that is, their transparency *when used in assertions*. It is, however, exactly this characteristic in virtue of which the assertions 'p is the case' and 'I believe that p is the case' are similar and in virtue of which 'I believe' is generally substitutable by other verbal or non-verbal expressions. Contrary to the representationalist view, the opaque use of the verb 'to believe' (e.g. in suppositions, in other tenses than the present tense, or for other grammatical persons) comprises the transparent use of its first-person singular present indicative, which for its part never exerts a referential function. The opaque use of 'I believe' in suppositions or other hypothetical contexts has turned out more complex than the transparent one, and more importantly, secondary to the latter (Section 4.2 of this chapter). That is, the 'line' (*PPF* § 106) runs in the reverse direction than representationalist views assume, from assertion to supposition on the one hand, from the assertive to the descriptive use of 'I believe' on the other hand. That the line from the descriptive to the transparent use of 'I believe', that is the line from reference to use breaks down means that representationalist accounts of mind and language yield a false order of priority. The line runs from assertion to supposition, from language to thought.

    This is to say that the concept of belief representationalist views employ is not derived from the properties of its alleged referent, the phenomenon of believing, but that it presents an extrapolation from the verb 'to believe' as it is used in everyday language. The similarity of the assertions 'p is the case' and 'I believe that p is the case' is exploited to the effect that the truth-directedness of assertion is inscribed in its alleged mental precursor, belief. Notably, not every aspect of the meaning of 'I believe' is thus accommodated. Its meaning, so constructed, is restricted to the point in which the concepts of assertion and belief touch (*PPF* § 108), to cases in which the expression 'I believe' is used emphatically, in order to express one's conviction of the following proposition's being true (as it is the case, for instance, in court). All other uses of 'I believe'—the hesitant one, the uncertain one, the guessing one—are omitted by this procedure. Dummett is right to question the Fregean treatment of "assertion as the expression of an interior act of judgment" and to consider Frege's notion of judgement to actually consist in "the interiorization of the external act of assertion" (Dummett (1992), p. 362). Modelling judgement and belief on assertion and, in a second step, disparaging this move as a move for 'pedagogic' purposes only (Searle) delivers an abridged understanding of the concept of believing and runs into the problems surrounding Moore's Paradox.

It follows that the 'logic of assertion' proposed on representationalism and, more fundamentally, on Frege's view, i.e. the conception of assertion as a statement that receives its meaning as well as its truth-directedness from the belief (or judgement) it simultaneously articulates, is radically mistaken. Not every assertive statement is simultaneously a statement about the speaker's mind, be it explicit or implicit, as not every assertion containing the expression 'I believe' is (*cf. RPP I* § 750). But not every assertion is a statement *about* the truth of what is thereby asserted, as the analysis of assertion into judgement *plus* proposition suggests. For what more is said with the sentence '*p* is true' than is said with '*p*'? That assertions are assessable with respect to their truth and falsity is not brought about by tacking a judgement onto a (neutral) proposition. It is not an additional, but an essential feature of ordinary sentence-statements in everyday talk.[62] Here, too, the strict line drawn between assertions and propositions results in over-emphasising the alleged complexity of the former and the alleged simplicity of the latter, which tempts into prioritising the ostensibly simple over the ostensibly complex case and thus into a simplistic conception of language. It is, as Wittgenstein writes, one of the points of Moore's Paradox that "logic isn't as simple as logicians think it is" (*Briefe 257*), and my aim in this chapter was to show why.

Ironically, though, the solution to Moore's Paradox is simpler than it is thought to be. Because the assertions '*p*' and 'I believe that *p*' are similar Moore-paradoxical assertions are similar to assertions of overt contradictions. They are thus akin to assertions like "I am [hereby] lying" (*RFM I* App. III § 12) or "I can't speak a word of English" (*RPP* I 503). Their absurdity consists in their being spanners in the

---

62 *Cf. PI* § 22 and Ludwig Wittgenstein, *Remarks on the Foundations of Mathematics* (*RFM*), ed. by Georg Henrik von Wright, Rush Rhees, G. E. M. Anscombe, transl. G. E. M. Anscombe, 3rd, revised edition, Oxford: Blackwell 1978, Part I, Appendix III; Pfisterer (2008); and Chapter 1, Section 3.8.

works of language—they neither continue nor give a clue as to how to continue a conversation, they question which language game has been played hitherto, whether or not a language game has been played at all. With asserting a Moore-paradoxical sentence one mocks the most important rule governing the use of assertion, i.e. their being intended to be true statements, one does not simply violate it (cf. Z § 691). Yet, assertions can exert several communicative functions, their truth-directedness being one of them. For this reason, it might become intelligible or even appropriate to use a Moore-paradoxical or contradictory assertion under certain circumstances. In such cases, the speaker should not be understood as intending to make a true statement—and doing so would be inadequate. Rather, the situation demands for other standards than truth to evaluate his or her statement, and to seek for other ways of understanding than taking the speaker by his or her words. Whether or not a Moore-paradoxical assertion is absurd, whether or not it is thus admissable, depends on the context in which it is made, on the speaker's intentions equally as on what language game is currently played and the hearer's or addressee's reactions and interpretations.

Nothing comparable is available in the mental realm, that is in the case of Moore-paradoxical belief or judgement. Although asserting 'I falsely believe that p' is absurd in the same sense asserting 'p is the case, but I am lying' is one cannot even absurdly judge or believe a Moore-paradoxical sentence. This possibility is ruled out conceptually, not commonsensically; Bernard Williams' slogan 'beliefs aim at truth' ought to be read as a grammatical statement concerning the function of the word 'belief' and the corresponding verb 'to believe', not as a metaphysical one concerning the functional properties of 'belief'. The same holds for the notion 'judgement': Being an extrapolation from assertion, the functions of judgement are exhausted by judging something true. Other than in the case of assertion that is, there are no further communicative or other purposes a judgement could fulfil. In contrast to the truth-directedness of assertion, whose origin is normative in character, the truth-directedness of judgement is thus teleological, or constitutive in character (cf. Pfisterer (2008), p. 13) in that nothing that is not truth-directed can qualify as a judgement. Because the transparency of the expression 'I believe' renders sentences like 'I falsely believe…' or 'p is the case, but I don't believe it' falsities they are dysfunctional as instruments for judgement. It is therefore not a normative requirement (as Moran thinks), but a conceptual impossibility to judge a Moore-paradoxical sentence. It is a normative requirement, though, that there *be* Moore-paradoxical judgements and beliefs if the continuity of different kinds of sentences (from supposition to judgement to assertion) and inflections (from 'Peter believes' to 'I believe') is to be preserved at all cost. On a closer look, the expressions 'Moore-paradoxical belief' and 'Moore-paradoxical judgement' turn out to be oxymorons. This result should eventually disrupt the line drawn, on Frege's view, from supposition to assertion and, on representationalist views, from thought to language.

2.6.3 Not a Something, but not a Nothing, either

My conclusion so far is a negative one; it is a rejection of the representationalist view with respect to its ontological claims (mental states are discrete phenomena, depending on a bearer, but independent of being the object of linguistic and non-linguistic representation), its epistemological claims (mental states are something to know about even in one's own case), its metaphysical claims regarding the structure specifically of belief and assertion (complying with the two-component model) and its resultant claims about the meaning and function of psychological expressions (designating such phenomena). This may be criticised for being un-satisfactory. One might expect either a sceptical conclusion with regard to both the possibility of being right or wrong in using grammatical and semantic rules (as Kripke famously concludes from his interpretation of *Philosophical Investigations* § 201) and the existence of the mind beyond behavioural expressions, the 'inner realm' beyond the material, the 'outer' world. Or one might demand a counter-theory to representationalism, an alternative conception of the mind and its interrelations with the material world and language, which might prevent what one might suppose to be inevitable—the denial of the reality of the mind, or the reduction of mental states to entities of a different ontological kind, physiological occurrences or behavioural sequences, for instance.

> 'But you will surely admit that there is a difference between pain-behaviour with pain and pain-behaviour without pain.'—Admit it? What greater difference could there be?—'And yet you again and again reach the conclusion that the sensation itself is a Nothing.'—Not at all. It is not a Something, but not a Nothing either! We've only rejected the grammar which tends to force itself on us here.
> The paradox disappears only if we make a radical break with the idea that language always functions in one way, always serves the same purpose: to convey thoughts—which may be about houses, pains, good and evil, or whatever. (*PI* § 304, transl. Hacker/Schulte)

The aim of my inquiry was not to develop a theory of the mind. I intended to inves-tigate some of the ways in which we use a certain domain of language, the domain of psychological expressions, particularly in assertions. Thereby, I intended to criticise specifically two metaphysical conclusions drawn from this usage, the claim that language conforms to the two-component model, and that its meaning is constituted by reference to, and consists in depicting, or representing indepen-dently existing states of affairs. The argument from Moore's Paradox has rendered them inadequate with respect to their respective *explananda*. Adopting several remarks from Wittgenstein's argumentation against the coherent conceivability of a private language, my last argument sought to demonstrate that it is neither sufficient nor necessary to assume the existence of such independent states of affairs, in order to clarify the grammatical questions surrounding assertion and the word 'to believe'.

Rejecting representationalism on these grounds by no means yields a sceptical position with respect to either the 'reality' of the mind or to the possibility of investigating the grammar of language. Rather, breaking with its core ideas allows for better understanding the diversity of both the role assertions have to play in language and the meaning of 'I believe' and other psychological expressions. The expectable result will not consist in a simple and necessarily simplistic theoretical model of how language ought to work, wasn't it for the inexactness of everyday talk and the laziness of commonsense, but in an outline of the 'grammar' of the linguistic phenomena we are trying to understand. This requires us dropping the rigid models of the logic and semantics of language, with which I was concerned throughout my inquiry. It requires to investigate the use of the respective concepts and kinds of sentences we are trying to understand, including the situational and linguistic contexts in which they are applied, the intentions which are involved in using them, the typical responses of others (*cf.* Schulte (1993), pp. 155ff.).

In the following chapter I will follow these lines in giving an outline how the meaning of the word 'to believe' is constituted and the interlocking question how the 'logic' of avowals could be formulated, if not by means of traditional logic. I will reply to several possible objections from a representationalist viewpoint, and offer an alternative conception of expressions of belief.

3 'I Believe' in Practice

The conception of language inherent in representationalism proceeds from the claims that sentences from a natural language articulate mental content and structurally comply with the two-component model, just as mental states do. Both claims are inherited from the general representationalist framework manifesting the view that language is an extension of thought. This account is supposed to account for three *explananda*: (1) that linguistic expressions have a definite meaning at first place, which is uniform across various contexts; (2) that particular applications of linguistic expressions can be assessed in terms of veridicality or truth; (3) that there is something that amounts to being able to apply and understand linguistic expressions. This conception, which I have called a *referentialist* position, grasps the meaning and grammar of linguistic expressions, psychological or otherwise, in terms of reference; that is, as determined by the respective objects, concepts or states of affairs they are supposed to designate, and by the internal structure of the content they articulate. As I have elaborated in the first chapter, the capacity to use any linguistic expression, to understand it in conversation as well as to apply it oneself in order to represent an object, presupposes familiarity with the respective referential object, be it in terms of conceptual knowledge of its defining criteria or be it in terms of perceptual acquaintance with a sample. A consequence of this conception is that the semantic and grammatical properties of linguistic expressions reflect the constitution of the objects they refer to. Consequently, questions concerning the meaning and/or the grammar of particular linguistic expressions are supposed to be answerable by investigating the metaphysics of the phenomena they describe. Applying this strategy to Moore's Paradox, the representationalist approaches to solving it have led into an investigation of the state of affairs supposedly described by Moore-paradoxical assertions, and thus eventually into investigations concerning the metaphysics of belief.

In the previous chapters, I argued that this strategy necessarily yields both a wrong solution to Moore's Paradox and an inadequate conception of the meaning of the expression 'I believe'. I have arrived at the conclusion that turning to the metaphysics of belief is of no use when it comes to understanding either the meaning of the expression 'I believe' or the logic of assertions of belief. I instead proposed to focus on the role they play in language, the ways in which they are used in practice. In this chapter, I first reply to some possible objections against this proposal from a representationalist point of view and reject three further accounts of meaning, scepticism, 'stipulativism', and 'expertivism', all of which seem to develop a practice-based account of meaning. Both the representationalist objections as well as the three latter accounts rely on a misconception of the interrelation of meaning, use and practice. Moreover, all of them involve the misconceptions that there is a gap between the meaning of a linguistic expression and its particular applications, and analogously between the significance of expressions of one's state of mind and 'the facts' about one's state of mind. Having discerned this gap, I clarify the thesis that the meaning of the verb 'to believe' lies in the way it is used and outline a suggestion how to better understand its use in assertions of one's own beliefs, avowals. In the next chapter, I will close with some remarks on the lesson to draw from Moore's Paradox.

3.1 Objections

From the thesis that the meaning and grammar of psychological concepts consist in how they are used, it follows that knowing the meaning of a psychological concept amounts to mastering its use. This is to say, being able to competently apply a psychological concept is both necessary and sufficient for understanding it. Consequently, neither knowing the definition of a psychological concept in terms of possessing a corresponding formal or general concept (as the Generality Constraint requires), nor acquaintance with the object it refers to, nor the two together matter for the possession of a psychological concept. Moreover, as I argued in the last chapter, the meaning of a word is not constituted by reference to either a sample (as Burge thinks) or a formal concept (as Evans claims). I will now discuss four objections against my proposal. My replies to them will help to clarify the view I am advocating.

3.1.1 The Objection from Circularity

The first objection charges the claim 'The meaning of a word is its use in the natural language it belongs to' with circularity in two respects. Its proponent conceives of the claim as defining the meaning of a psychological concept from a natural language (a 'material concept') with a description of its use in the language, or as a conjunction of its concrete uses. That is, the meaning of a psychological concept is allegedly defined by a list of its past uses, or suitable examples of its use. The resulting 'definition-in-use' (Fodor) of a psychological concept thus contains the respective concept not only as the *definiendum*, but also in the *definiens*. Hence, it is circular.[1]

---

1 *Cf.* Jerry A. Fodor (2008), *LOT 2: The Language of Thought Revisited*, Oxford: UP, ch. 2.

The objection continues, the ability to apply a psychological concept requires possessing the grammatical rules governing its application. Giving a grammatical rule for the application of a psychological concept in terms of use contains the respective concept, for instance, in the following way 'Use the word 'to believe' as a regular verb in English'. Thus, mastery of the grammar of a psychological concept equally requires knowing the semantics of the psychological concept in question (for instance, 'to believe'). Hence, mastering the syntactical rules of psychological concepts requires a definition of the concept in question, and this cannot be provided by a definition-in-use (since this is circular).

Therefore, the objection concludes, understanding the meaning of psychological concepts in terms of their use in a natural language fails as an account of meaning and as an account of concept-possession. In other words: It fails to constitute the meaning and grammar of psychological concepts. This shows (says the objection) that the use of a material psychological concept in fact presupposes a definition of the corresponding 'formal concept', which comprises the relevant semantic and grammatical rules. Possessing a particular psychological concept accordingly requires *prior* knowledge of what the concept refers to, either by knowing the definition of the corresponding formal concept, or in virtue of being acquainted with the referent of the respective concept. This is provided for on representationalism, but not on the 'meaning-is-use' account.

This objection interprets the thesis that the meaning of psychological concepts is constituted in use as defining the meaning of psychological concepts with a conjunction of their past applications. This 'definition-in-use' of a word would thus consist in a collection, a list of sentences, in which the word is applied. Accordingly, knowing the meaning of a particular psychological concept would amount to knowing that it is used in the ways specified by the list. Yet, each example from the list contains the word in question, that is, understanding any one of them requires acquaintance with its meaning. Therefore, no definition-in-use, even if it consisted in a complete list of all instances of the word in question, could ever ground the meaning of a material psychological concept.

Likewise, the objection conceives of the competence of applying a psychological expression in a natural language as knowing its meaning and its grammatical rules, that is, knowing that the expression in question is used in the way specified by the respective semantic and grammatical rules. This knowledge is supposed to distinguish a rule-informed use of a material concept from a use that is merely in conformity with the respective syntactical rule. In rule-informed concept-application, it is said, the user of the concept intends to follow the (semantic and syntactical) rules governing its application. That is, following the respective rules must figure in the content of the speaker's intention to apply the concept competently, and thus he or she must know that the concept in question is governed by the respective rules. Yet, a syntactical rule on the 'meaning-is-use' account mentions the psychological concept in question. This is to repeat that the rule-informed use of a psychological concept requires knowing its semantics, and this cannot be provided on pain of circularity.

The objection concludes that the competent use of the verb 'to believe', for instance, presupposes that one knows what believing is, that one is acquainted with the phenomenon of believing, or that one could give an analytical definition of the formal concept corresponding to the English word 'belief'. The objection takes it for granted that the acquisition of particular material concepts or other expressions from a natural language amounts to a kind of translation of the formal concepts one already has at one's disposal into the vocabulary of a natural language, or from a kind of 'baptism' of an object with which one is already acquainted. Learning to competently use the verb 'to believe', would accordingly require possessing a corresponding idea of what a belief is (the formal concept), or being acquainted with the state of believing. In learning, one would establish a translational relation between one's idea of belief and the material verb 'to believe' or 'attach' the name 'to believe' to a state of believing once it occurs.

However, the objection misconceives of the thesis that 'The meaning of a word is its use in the natural language it belongs to', to the effect that it misses the point. The objection misunderstands the claim as aiming at equating the meaning of particular psychological concepts with the totality of its previous or possible applications in the respective natural language, and at equating knowing how to use a such a concept with knowing these applications. According to the objection, this conception imagines the meaning of a psychological concept to be constituted in a way similar to the manner in which a dictionary explains the meaning of a word by giving a descriptive definition of its meaning and a list of examples. Conceiving of the meaning of a psychological concept in terms of its use would supposedly amount to a dictionary entry that contains only a list of examples whilst omitting the definition of the word.

I take it to be obvious that this would not provide a satisfactory account of meaning—in this respect, the objection is quite right. Yet, this could not possibly be my position. For, as I argued in the last chapter, knowing the definition of a material psychological concept is neither necessary nor sufficient for understanding its meaning, *regardless of the form the definition takes*—be it a list of examples, be it a 'translation' of a formal concept, be it an analytical or ostensive definition of its object. It is impossible to discern the boundaries of the respective *definiens*—be it a 'formal concept' or a sample of the referential object—without having an idea what kind of thing the *definiens* is supposed to be, to what other concepts it semantically relates, and how it can syntactically be combined with other concepts. Replying that this is exactly the information provided by the definition and presupposed by the use of the corresponding material concept is not of any use. For even if one knew all this and further knew what a definition is, one would know it in private, that is, for oneself, perfectly detached from a public language shared by others. In this case, however, it would be impossible to establish a connection of semantic correspondence between one's private definition of a particular formal concept, or one's sample established from one's private acquaintance with an object and a particular word from a natural language. For other than in the case of translating a German word into English, one *relatum*, the formal concept and its definition, could be accessed by one person only. Therefore, there would neither be a criterion of correctness whether one had chosen the right formal concept or the right sample, respectively, as the content of a particular material concept, nor a warrant that everyone was using the respective material concept for the same (kind of) formal concept or referential object; one could not even state whether one was referring to the same formal concept at every instance of applying a particular material concept.

It goes without saying that a comparison between the definition of a formal concept and a material concept, or a comparison of *my* definition of a formal concept with *your* definition or *Peter's* definition of the formal concept in question would not yield the desired results. For the definition of a material concept, a word from a common language, would have to be given in a public language, in which case the problem is reinforced: one would have no means at hand to match one's private definition, be it ostensive or analytic, with the public definition. The same applies to comparing one another's definitions of particular formal concepts. The only means one would have at hand to do so is sharing a language, and one could not establish the required correspondence between one's own formal concept and a material concept at first place. So it is irrelevant to the meaning of a particular material concept whether one possesses a definition of formal concepts, be it a general or particular one, and whether everybody possessed the same formal concepts (*cf. PI* §§ 261, 264f., 270–2, and 293 as quoted above). *A fortiori*, understanding the semantic as well as the syntactical rules of a particular material concept is a capacity independent of whether there is something like the possession of a 'formal concept' in terms of knowing its definition prior to acquiring the capacity of using the material concept; not to mention that, in the light of what has been said hitherto, it seems hardly possible to give a coherent notion of, say, the 'formal concept' in the first place.

3.1.2 The Objection from Productivity

The second objection claims that understanding the meaning of psychological concepts in terms of their use in a natural language cannot explain the *productivity* of a natural language, that is, its speakers' capacity of composing an in principle infinite number of different meaningful sentences from a finite number of concepts, and their capacity of understanding words even when applied in previously unfamiliar sentences.[2] Yet, defining the meaning of a material concept with its use considers the concept in a number of given sentences. However comprehensive the 'definition-in-use' of a material concept is, it can only cover a finite number of applications. Thus, there will always be an application, which is not contained by the 'definition-in-use', and consequently must be considered meaningless. Moreover, the enlisted examples are context-bound and hence cannot account for understanding or using a word in an unknown context, in connection with other concepts than the familiar ones. This however contradicts the idea of productivity. In other words, if the meaning of a particular word was defined by either the totality or a description of its 'old' uses, the resulting definition would not provide the meaning of the word in 'new' sentences.

On the contrary, the objector continues, to account for productivity, meaning and grammar of a concept must be determined in isolation, i. e. detached from its actual uses, and the resulting definition must grant the meaning of the concept for all its possible uses independently of its actual use, it must, as it were reach beyond its past and present applications. A definition by the sum of 'old' uses is insufficient for two reasons; it does not account for new occurrences of a word and it does not allow for contextual variations in use. The objection concludes that productivity presupposes *compositionality*, the idea that the meaning of every complex linguistic expression (i.e. sentences or phrases) in a natural language is determined by nothing but its structure and the meanings of its constituents (i.e. words).[3] That is, the productivity of a natural language requires that the mean-

---

2 The possibility of infinite sentences intuitively seems implausible. However, the keyword is 'recursive reiteration': From six concepts only one can combine an infinite number of sentences. They differ in their internal structure in that the concepts are bracketed together in different combinations, for instance: (Katie swims) and (Peter sings) and (Katie sings and Peter swims) and (Katie swims and Peter sings) and (Katie sings or Peter swims) and (Katie swims or Peter sings) etc. Notably, this procedure presupposes an atomistic theory of meaning, a prior syntactical differentiation of sentences, and a prior determination of the syntactical function of individual concepts. *Cf.* Zoltán Gendler Szabò (2008), "Compositionality", *The Stanford Encyclopedia of Philosophy*, Edward N. Zalta (ed.), http://plato.stanford.edu/archives/win2008/entries/compositionality/, last access September 19th, 2012.

3 *Cf.* Fodor (2008), ch. 1; Gendler Szabò (2008).

ing of a material concept derives from a corresponding formal concept, and that the grammatical rules of a natural language equally derive from formal rules, which are possessed prior to learning one's first natural language. Definitions-in-use are thus neither necessary nor sufficient for constituting a meaningful language.

Let me first point out that I am primarily concerned here with the meaning of *psychological* concepts. For this case, the objection reads: In order to understand why we can meaningfully apply and understand a word like 'to believe' in infinitely many sentences, we must assume that we know its meaning in virtue of knowing its definition and its grammar, that is, that we already know its reference (the phenomenon of believing) and its grammatical rules.

On this conception, the formal concepts or objects corresponding to material psychological concepts and their grammar, which together grant compositionality and, *a fortiori*, productivity, are present in a person's mind prior to his or her possession of material psychological concepts. Furthermore, the mental states designated by these formal concepts, which could serve as samples to constitute their reference, also exist in the person's mind prior to his or her having acquired the corresponding words. Finally, the connection between formal concepts and their respective referents equally is established in the person's mind before the person learns to use psychological terms in a natural language.

From this view follows that, in case of psychological concepts, both the level of representation (the respective formal concepts and syntactical rules) and the level of reference (mental states) as well as their connection (the definition of the former by the latter) are *private* in the sense of *Philosophical Investigations* § 258. Therefore, as I argued in the previous chapter, *neither* of them plays a role in constituting the semantics and syntax of material psychological concepts, that is, psychological words belonging to a natural, shared language. As explained before, the reasons are twofold. First, no such conception can bridge the gap obtaining between private samples, or formal concepts and grammar, and material concepts and grammar, respectively. Second, it is impossible to determine whether the connection between a psychological expression from a natural language and the allegedly corresponding mental state is established correctly, that is, whether the person uses the right word for a particular mental state.

In short, what happens among the formal concepts, prior grammatical rules and mental states within a person's mind is entirely irrelevant for both the constitution and function of the semantic and syntactical rules of words like believing, expecting, hope, love, pain and so forth. It is irrelevant, that is, whether formal concepts and mental states are related in the right way, in the wrong way, or not in any way at all. It is equally irrelevant whether the person applies the formal concepts at his or her disposal according to the right syntactical rules, or to any rules at all. And it is irrelevant whether formal concepts of mental states refer to something, or nothing at all. As I argued in the last chapter, the so assumed 'mental' language containing ostensible abstract rules for grammar and meaning of psychological concepts cannot be connected with a natural language of psychological expressions. Accordingly, the idea that the use of psychological expressions would derive from a connection of their 'mental' semantics and syntax with the corresponding elements in a natural language, makes no sense. Yet, if formal concepts and abstract syntax do not constitute the use of psychological words in a natural language, they cannot provide the idea of productivity with respect to psychological words and its inherent idea of semantic continuity, either. Therefore, the objection is void.[4]

The two objections I have discussed, are based on a misconception of the proposal to understand the meaning of psychological words in terms of their use. For this proposal does not entail the claim that a descriptive definition of a concept, i.e. a list of all its past instances, or an empirical law induced from them, is either necessary or sufficient for explaining the meaning of a particular concept. The proposal neither reduces the meaning of a word to a collection of (past) samples, nor does it equate semantic rules to a kind of stimulus-response mechanism. On the contrary, being able to use a word includes being able to use it on occasions, which one had not yet encountered, or in combinations with different words.

It is erroneous to think that the capacity to use a word meaningfully requires possessing a definition of an allegedly corresponding formal concept, as it is erroneous to think that it is only in virtue of designating a referent, or in virtue of there being a general rule prescribing the use of a word on every occasion that a word could be used on different occasions whilst maintaining a uniform meaning. This latter claim was rejected in the last chapter, where I have argued that, given the assumption that concepts had a constant or uniform meaning, Moore's Paradox

---

4 Although I cannot spell out an argument against compositionality and the related idea of logical atomism more generally in this place, I think that this conception of the meaning of sentences is highly questionable in itself. For it seems that compositionality, being a formal or functional principle, alone cannot account for sentences that have no meaning although each of their constituents has a definite meaning and although they display a syntactically correct structure. Earlier, I have drawn attention to such a sentence, namely 'Milk me sugar!' (*PI* § 498) This sentence is composed of words with a definite meaning and is in accord with the grammatical rules of English. Yet, it is nonsensical. Another example, of course, is the sentence 'It is raining, but I don't believe it is.' That is, the principles suggested by accounts based on compositionality are to coarse-grained to accommodate such cases. Their generating infinite possible applications exceeds the scope of meaningfulness. Therefore, they are insufficient to give a complete account of meaning.

cannot be accounted for. Second, a common referent is neither necessary nor sufficient as a criterion of correctness of and for granting semantic continuity between particular applications of a material concept. On the contrary, the idea that a general rule, as it is supposed to be provided by a formal concept and/or its definition, was either necessary or sufficient or both to make the application of a material concept in particular cases possible, inevitably leads into an infinite regress of rules determining the meaning of each preceding rule. As Wittgenstein argues in *Philosophical Investigations* §§ 139–242, this regress results in the paradox that rules, which for instance come in the form of definitions, are both necessary and irrelevant for determining their applications:

> This was our paradox: no course of action could be determined by a rule, because every course of action can be brought into accord with the rule. The answer was: if every course of action can be brought into accord with the rule, then it can also be brought into conflict with the rule. And so there would be neither accord nor conflict here. [...] (*PI* § 201)

This is to say that even if the meaning of a material concept was determined exclusively by a general rule defining the corresponding formal concept, as the objection contends, it would be impossible to decide whether the respective material concept was applicable because one would lack a criterion to distinguish between a correct and an incorrect use. For this, one would need an additional rule deciding about the applicability of the first rule, a third rule to determine whether the second rule applies and so forth.[5] In short, the competence of applying material concepts correctly, whether in a novel, in an entirely unfamiliar situation, or in a situation that resembles a situation one has experienced in the past, cannot sufficiently be grounded in either definitory knowledge of formal concepts or non-conceptual acquaintance with the objects they allegedly refer to. It is therefore neither necessary nor sufficient to draw on formal concepts in order to explain the meaning of mate-

---

5 This is basically the conclusion which unfortunately lead Kripke into adopting scepticism about the possibility of rule-following behaviour, most prominently in Kripke (1982). Kripke is wrong for the very same reason as the advocate of the objection, he thinks that a general rule is necessary to make following a rule possible, but, other than the proponent of the objection, has understood (and read) Wittgenstein so far as to see that this is inconceivable. Hence, he concludes, that rule-following is inconceivable, that a rule is a Nothing, as it were. The reply here is, as above, that it is not a Nothing, but not a Something, either (*cf. PI* § 293). Kripke's scepticism is a position which follows from the insight that one's desire for an unambiguous definition of a rule, covering all possible applications, must necessarily remain dissatisfied. The point Wittgenstein makes is that it is a misunderstanding to frame the question what following a rule is as a choice between taking abstract rules to determine their particular applications, and the denial that there was something like rule-following behaviour. I will come back to scepticism regarding the meaning of psychological expressions in Section 2 of this chapter.

rial concepts, as it is neither necessary nor sufficient to possess formal concepts for being a competent user of a natural language. In other words, definitions of whatever kind, whether ostensive, or analytic, or descriptive, neither constitute the meaning of words, nor regulate their use, nor is their acquisition necessary or sufficient for learning a language at first place.[6] What definitions can do is help someone who is already a competent user of a native language in learning a second or third language, just as an instruction manual can help someone, who knows how to use it, to operate a machine, or exercise a certain practice. But in order to make use of a definition, one must already be able to use it. And this is something the appeal to reference cannot account for.

3.1.3 The Objection from Workability

One might argue that setting aside ontological issues concerning the mind and setting aside the question as to how the meaning of psychological concepts is constituted, representationalism presents a workable theory which explains how the mind functions. After all, representationalism is not dedicated to yielding a theory of the semantics of psychological expressions. That it nevertheless does so is only a side-effect.

There are two replies to this objection. First, the representationalist conception of the mind claims that the mind divides into individual mental states that comply with the two-component model of thought. But, as I argued in the last chapter, the two-component model is necessarily unable to account for explaining the phenomenon of Moore-paradoxical belief, the phenomenon allegedly underlying Moore-paradoxical assertions.[7] Borderline cases probe a theory for its adequacy. Moore's Paradox presents such a case for representationalism. If representationalism is a theory of the mind, as the objection claims, it ought to be expected that it covers borderline cases. Since it cannot cope with the case arising from Moore's Paradox, it is false.

Second, representationalism indeed presupposes a particular conception of the meaning of psychological expressions, the view that their meaning consists in

---

6 For a more thoroughgoing analysis of and a detailed argument against Fodor's version of representationalism, *cf.* Daniel D. Hutto (2008), *Folk Psychological Narratives. The Sociocultural Basis of Understanding Reasons*, Cambridge (MA): MIT Press.

7 I have pointed out in my conclusion of the last chapter that the notion of a Moore-paradoxical belief is incoherent. However, once the claim that linguistic expressions derive their characteristics from corresponding phenomena is in place Moore-paradoxical beliefs become the primary *explananda*.

describing, or referring to discrete mental states. Representationalism claims to be a theory about the phenomena they refer to, and employs psychological expressions in order to describe the function of the mind. It is certainly unproblematic to use psychological expressions in hypothetical, or scientific contexts in general (for instance, in the supposition 'Suppose I believe it is raining'). Notwithstanding, it is erroneous to assume that one would thereby deliver a description or an explanation of the internal structure and function of an independently existing object of scientific investigation, called 'the mind' in commonsense language, precisely because this theory is framed third-personally. As it is irrelevant to the use and meaning of a particular psychological expression whether or not it has referent, it is, by analogy, irrelevant to the working of the representationalist theory whether it is theory of *something* (the mind) or rather *nothing* (a chimera). So it seems appropriate to raise a question concerning the use of the representationalist enterprise—even if it did, as stated, function as a theory (which it doesn't, see above), its self-declared aim, discovering the function of the mind, could not be fulfilled because both existence and constitution of the object it claims to be about is indeterminate, and cannot be determined. In short, it is not clear what representationalism is about, and it cannot ever be made clear. What one can investigate, of course, is the function of the brain; but doing so will not yield insights concerning the function of the mind. One can engage in empirical psychology, but then one must not forget that, in contrast to terminology of physics or chemistry, the concepts employed by psychology are concepts from commonsense, they are not technical terms. And of these commonsense terms, there is is only a very limited aspect that is accessible by the third-personal method representationalist theories regard the most promising one, which is the use of psychological expressions for the purpose of explaining and predicting one another's behaviour. But this is secondary to more common uses, such as expressing one's state of mind, justifying one's actions, or exchanging one's views on some matter or other. One can, of course, investigate the meaning of psychological concepts. But for this purpose one must not give in to the inclination, as Burge (1986) does, that their meaning is constituted by reference to something, which is yet awaiting discovery and to which the use commonsense makes of these very concepts is but an approximation for lack of better knowledge (*cf. PI* § 130).

3.1.4 The Objection from Externalism

The objections I discussed so far reject both my negative conclusion that the representationalist theory of mind is infeasible and my positive claim that the meaning of psychological expressions, and thus the boundaries of psychological phenomena, are constituted by their use in a linguistic practice. My reply was that, given the arguments of the preceding chapter, it is impossible to reconstruct the meaning of psychological expressions by drawing solely on the mental resources of individuals. Even if their was reason to assume (which I argued there is not) that someone might succeed in establishing the semantics, grammar and conditions of usage of psychological expressions on his or her own any attempt to translate such a private language into public talk would not succeed—especially since the objector's point was to guarantee that, in using psychological expressions, everybody was referring to the same (kind of) phenomena.

The objection from externalism equally employs the theoretical framework of representationalism familiar from Chapter 1 and rejects the claim that the meaning of psychological expressions is constituted by and consists in their way of being used in a language in its most radical and encompassing form. But it approaches the issue from another and in some way more differentiated viewpoint. As explained in Chapter 1, externalism is distinctive with regard to its view on the constitution of representational *content*. Rather than solely drawing on the individual's mental or cognitive resources (e.g. formal concepts) in explaining the origin of representation it takes the referents of representational content, and thus the reference of linguistic expressions, to constitutively depend on the representational subject's relations to its physical and social environment. That is, it locates the factors determining representational content and thus the decisive criterion for individuating mental states, i.e. their 'representational kind', *outside* the individual's mind rather than *inside*. Thus, it can allow language and social conventions to play a certain role in the constitution of representational states. In particular, the position in principle recognises that the identity of certain kinds of mental states depends on linguistic conventions concerning the semantics of the concepts involved individuating their content, given that certain conditions are in place. However, in contrast to the negative conclusion of my last chapter it obtains a referentialist position with respect to psychological concepts. It maintains the claim that representational states are distinctive psychological states or phenomena that are ontologically language-independent 'facts' and as such provide the reference for psychological expressions. If language plays a role for the individuation of representational states it must be contingently, or indirectly so and must not interfere with the essential inalterability of particular (token) mental states. Therefore, the objection might be framed, the meaning of the corresponding psychological concepts is constitutively independent of there being respective communicative practices: Their primary meaning is to refer to the corresponding psychological states, any further communicative function psychological concepts may exercise is piggybacking on their original referential, or descriptive function. Without qualification, that is, the claim that the meaning of psychological concepts is constituted by their use is, from a representationalist viewpoint, false.

The relevant point for my investigation is that on the externalist (or anti-individualist or naïve realist) version of representationalism, too, psychological concepts belong to those concepts the referents of which are per se determinate. Their referents, mental states, constitute a distinctive class of psychological phenomena the structure of which complies with the two-component model. Particular mental states belong to a certain psychological kind, or mode, and are individuated by their veridicality conditions (their representational kind, or content), their bearer, and time of occurrence. In virtue of their influence on certain non-psychological concepts linguistic practices may influence the individuation of mental states only attributively (by influencing their contents), not substantially—a belief is a belief is a belief, regardless of how the word 'belief' is used in a particular community, discourse or conversation. Consequently, the meaning of the words 'belief' and 'to believe' (*pars pro toto*) figuring in the contents of representational states equally invariably consists in referring to the corresponding psychological state, the state of believing something, or more briefly the corresponding belief. Compared with the previously discussed view, the externalist or anti-individualist position simply replaces formal concepts with determinate observable phenomena as the alleged referents of psychological concepts.

Yet, this is precisely not the case, as my arguments in the previous chapter sought to establish. There are no such things as mental states—mental states are not 'Somethings' (despite there equally not being 'Nothings'). For, on the one hand, no external standard can determine the meaning of particular applications of psychological concepts, be it facts about the individual's mental system, be it facts in the external world, as follows from the arguments from rule-following and the inconceivability of a private (sensation-)language. On the other hand, by the argument from Moore's Paradox, no account that deems the meaning of psychological concepts to be constituted by *reference* to independent psychological, mental, or representational states can accommodate the irregularities of their first-person singular present indicative. No representationalist account can dispense with overloading the meaning of the expression 'I believe' with a referential function (as its original one), apart from all other functions it might accomplish in commonsense talk, on pain of rendering it meaningless. And it cannot declare psychological concepts to concepts the extensions of which are (partly) constituted by linguistic practice on pain of giving up the Priority Claim, the claim to the ontological priority of thought over language. And it cannot make an exception for the reference of the first-person singular present indicative and declare this form exclusively to be constituted by linguistic conventions on pain of violating the claim to the uniformity of content, the principle according to which the objects represented by mental content are perspective-independent, of postulating a further, distinctive category of 'first-person psychological states' and/or a distinctive first-person kind of reference to psychological states, thus sliding into the quagmires of self-knowledge and private languages.

So the question is not as to what influence linguistic practices have on determining the 'nature' (Burge), or content of representational states (for here, representational states are already postulated as the referents of psychological expressions), but as to whether or not referentialism with regard to psychological concepts presents a coherent account of the meaning of psychological concepts. Not the individuation, but the individuability of mental states was at stake. Yet, fixing the boundaries of the ostensible referents of psychological expressions, whether third-personally (by observation) or first-personally (by private definition), necessarily fails. The third-personal use of psychological expressions *includes* the irregularities of the first-personal one, and the first-personal one cannot be established in absence of an already established practice of using psychological concepts, especially in the first-person singular present indicative. Inasmuch as the representationlist theory of mind maintains referentialism with regard to psychological expressions it is false, and should it discard referentialism there would not be that much of representationalism left.

3.1.5 Scepticism or Stipulation?

In the light of the preceding considerations, the answer to Wittgenstein's questions from *PPF*, x is primarily negative: However the meaning of the verb 'to believe' was brought about, it was certainly not by discovering and designating a discrete phenomenon of believing, neither in myself or in others, and it was equally not by attaching a sign to a general concept giving this sign a definite meaning. The meaning of a psychological expression does not, so much is clear, consist in something external, or beyond, or over and above the use of the respective expression in a natural language. The representationalist approach to the meaning of psychological concepts confronts a paradox that runs analogously to the paradox of rule-following presented in *PI* § 201: No referential object can determine the meaning of a concept, because every application of the concept can be brought to match or mismatch the referential object specified. It results that the strategy representationalist accounts employ, i.e. shifting the investigative focus from a grammatical to a metaphysical level, in order to account for its three *explananda*—the meaning of psychological expressions and its uniformity across various contexts, the possibility to assess the veridicality of their instances, and the competence of using and understanding them—does not succeed. For the presumed metaphysical level of psychological phenomena is both inaccessible and, independently of that, irrelevant with regard to the *explananda*.

If, in other words, there is no such thing as a phenomenon of believing, nor anything else that could ground the meaning of psychological expressions and the correctness of their applications, is it possible at all to use psychological expressions meaningfully and non-arbitrarily? Is there a non-vacuous sense in which any such application can be assessed in terms of veridicality?

Given the preceding considerations, there is a strong inclination to deny these questions and to turn towards scepticism about meaning, at least with respect to the meaning of psychological expressions, which one might, but need not, complement with a reductive account of mental states on the metaphysical level. A sceptical position about the meaning of psychological concepts, framed on Kripke's scepticism about meaning in general, reads as follows: There is no fact that could possibly determine the meaning of psychological concepts, external to the linguistic practice in which they are used. Therefore, there is nothing that distinguishes meaningful from meaningless applications, nothing that could possibly decide whether a particular application is veridical or not, and nothing that explains that a psychological concept is used to mean one thing rather than another on a particular occasion; for example, a belief rather than a wish or even a non-mental object, the moon, say. More precisely, there is neither a fact that determines whether a particular application of a psychological concept is meaningful, i.e. used to refer to a psychological fact, nor a fact that determines whether it is veridical, i.e. whether it matches a corresponding state of mind. Hence, the sceptic might conclude, there is no meaning to psychological expressions, and no correctness or incorrectness to their particular applications.

This problem arises in particular for the first-person present indicative because in this case there are no publicly accessible criteria by which the subjectively given presence of a mental state could be confirmed. As a consequence of the distinction between having and representing a mental state, the individuation of a mental state by means of a first-personal ascription cannot be tracked by anyone except the subject. By contrast, the epistemological grounds for ascribing mental states to others can in principle be shared insofar as one can check with others whether they would arrive at the same judgement given the same evidence. Yet, ascribing a mental state to someone else also remains beyond verifiability because the only kind of 'authentic' epistemological access to the state itself (other than by observation, guess or inference) is the subjective one, and this has proven unreliable. So the sceptic concludes that it is impossible to state whether a particular application of a psychological concept is meaningful, i.e. refers to a corresponding psychological state, whether it is correct, i.e. in accord with the general use of that concept and, *a fortiori*, whether any such application is veridical.[8]

---

8 *Cf.* Kripke's summary of his interpretation of the 'private language argument', which he presents as a 'sceptical solution' to similar questions about meaning in general in Kripke (1982), pp. 107–13.

Kripke's answer to this sceptical 'challenge' would be that one ought to reconsider what statements concerning the meaning of particular applications of a psychological concept and definitions explicating the general meaning of psychological concepts are supposed to do. He suggests that a particular application of a concept is correct if it does not deviate from the way the concept is in general applied. Stating that a person uses a particular concept correctly depends on whether he or she does so reliably on various occasions. That a concept has a stable meaning comes down, in Kripke's opinion, to the 'brute fact' whether the individuals of a particular community agree in its applications. The significance of stating whether someone's way of applying a particular concept is in accord with the common use consists in that this fact decides about the person's inclusion or exclusion in the respective community (at least with respect to the use they make of language). Questions of truth or veridicality do not occur on the picture Kripke draws, apart from the laconic statement that "if everyone agrees on a certain [instance of a concept, us.], then no one will feel justified in calling [this instance, us.] wrong" (1982, p. 112). In a nutshell, Kripke takes the sceptic to show that there are no facts deciding questions of meaning and truth with regard to the use of the expressions from a natural language. Yet, it is not entirely pointless to state whether someone applies an expression correctly or incorrectly at a particular instance because this decides about this person's membership in the community speaking the language in question. And, fortunately, it can be done—an observer (say, an ethnologist investigating the culture of a particular community, or a member or committee within this community who is endowed with observing the other member's speech behaviour) will be able to state whether or not a particular application of a word is meaningful and whether or not the word is used correctly, which simply amounts to whether or not it accords to the community use. Though there is no *fact* that could decide the questions concerning meaning and correctness of particular applications, there is an *authority* who can make judgements to this effect with the help of a non-metaphysical standard of meaning and correctness (the community's behaviour).[9]

Scepticism is motivated by the ostensible insight that it is impossible to determine whether a particular application of a psychological concept is meaningful, correct or veridical because there is no epistemologically satisfactory way of accessing the referential object of the application in question. Yet, scepticism about the meaning of psychological concepts is not a necessary consequence of concluding that meaning and truth of psychological concepts are not determined by reference

---

9 This is a very brief summary of the view Kripke imputes to Wittgenstein. For a more comprehensive one, see Finkelstein (2008), pp. 33–5.

to independently existing phenomena. And the view that their meaning and correct application are exhausted by a majority's using them in more or less the same way, is not a necessary, and not necessarily a good interpretation of the thesis that both are constituted in a linguistic practice. Against Kripke's answer to the challenge of meaning-scepticism, Wright thus suggests to rethink what decides whether a particular ascription of a psychological states is meaningful on the one hand, and veridical on the other hand.

Wright's answer to scepticism about meaning is that whether a concept is used with a particular meaning depends on what the person using it means with it. What the person means with a concept is conceived roughly as a kind of meaning intention. In this respect (though not in others), Wright's account of how it comes that particular uses of psychological expressions have a particular meaning, namely in virtue of the person's meaning intentions, runs analogously to Searle's conception of meaning. Consequently, in order to clarify questions of meaning one must look at the conditions determining the truth of judgements about a person's intentions.

Wright agrees with Kripke on rejecting the claim that the veridicality of ascriptions of psychological states depends on whether they succeed in referring to corresponding, but independently existing mental phenomena. By contrast, Wright's position locates the origin of veridicality concerning statements about a person's psychology in some kind of 'stipulative' or 'constitutive' judgement.[10] Accordingly, the facts about a person's mind determining whether ascribing a psychological state to him or her is true, e.g. an intention to apply a word with a particular meaning, are (partly) constituted by the judgements made about the person's state of mind. The yardstick for the truth or falsity of a judgement 'S is in state M' is provided by the person's own first-personal judgements on the matter. This is due to the person's entitlement to decide on and thereby (partly) constitute his or her state of mind. This entitlement, which constitutes, on Wright's view, the authority of first-personal ascriptions of mental states, eventually is grounded in the practice governing the application of psychological concepts. That is, according to Wright, at the bottom of assessing the truth of particular ascriptions of mental states lies a kind of stipulation, a judgement, which simultaneously constitutes the fact it judges to be true.[11]

One might feel uncomfortable about Wright's appeal to first-personal authority in explaining both meaning and veridicality conditions of psychological expres-

---

10 Finkelstein hence refers to Wright's position as 'stipulativism' or 'constitutivism'. I will use these terms for Wright's position in the following. *Cf.* Finkelstein (2008), ch. 2, especially pp. 39ff.
11 *Cf.* Wright (1986); Wright (1998b); Finkelstein (2008), ch. 2; Searle (1983), ch. 6; and my discussion of Searle's account in Chapter 1, Section 3.2.

sions because it (to some extent) removes the first-personal use of psychological expressions from the truth-evaluable range of applying them. For it seems that on Wright's account, whatever a person judges to be true of his or her mental constitution, will henceforth be true. The absence of a public corrective for judgements concerning a person's state of mind equally affects the meaningfulness of psychological expressions in that whatever the person's meaning intentions are— i.e. whatever he or she means in using psychological expressions—is equally up to the subject. Conditioning a person's meaning this or that with his or her words thus makes meaning a volatile, and eventually arbitrary notion. The most obvious seeming remedy will be to relocate the origin of the meaning of psychological expressions, and thus their conditions of application, in some common practice of creating 'meanings' or referents by determining the boundaries of (psychological) concepts.[12] On this suggestion, the reference, and so the meaning, correctness and veridicality of applying psychological expressions are objective, but not ontologically independent of a linguistic practice. Whether or not a particular application of a word is meaningful or meaningless, correct or incorrect, veridical or non-veridical, is a matter of whether or not it is in accord with the previously established standard. In absence of there being a metaphysical fact deciding whether or not this is the case, the authority of judging particular instances of words to be in accord or disaccord with the standard resides in those who know the standard best, a group of experts, say—botanists for applying the word 'rose', physicians for 'arthritis', logicians for 'negation', or the psychologist for 'believing'. On this 'expertivist' account, just as on Wright's view, correctness and veridicality of particular applications of psychological concepts are grounded in judgements. The two positions diverge with respect to the authority entitled to make valid judgements concerning issues of meaning, correctness, and truth—everyone in one's own case (Wright) or an individual or a group of experts (Burge)—and with respect to generating the judgements in question, i.e. by stipulation (Wright) or comparison with expert knowledge (Burge).[13]

---

12 This is an adaptation of Burge's 'social anti-individualism' (*cf.* Burge (1979, 2003)). Burge would deny its applicability to psychological expressions in the given form, since, on his account, they do not belong to those concepts whose extensions are socially constituted—he considers psychological states language-independent phenomena. He could, however, agree with the weaker version of this view that though the reference of psychological concepts is not constituted by linguistic practice, the allocation of psychological concepts to psychological phenomena is, and in this sense also the meaning, correctness and veridicality of their application.

13 *Cf.* Burge (1979); Burge (1986); and Chapter 1, Section 2.1.5. A side-effect of relying on experts when it comes to making judgements concerning the meaning and correctness of particular applications is denying the subject's having the last word on what he or she means with his or her

The three accounts, Kripke's scepticism, Wright's constitutivism and Burgean ex-pertivism, seek to escape the dilemma representationalist accounts face with regard to questions of truth and meaning concerning the use of psychological expressions. The dilemma for representationalist and, more generally, referentialist accounts is that, on the one hand, there must be a stable reference to an independently existing phenomenon in order to grant that psychological expressions are meaningful and in order to assess their particular instances in terms of veridicality. On the other hand, neither a discrete phenomenon nor a formal definition can serve to establish the reference in question. Both Kripke and Wright take this as the lesson from their reading Wittgenstein's arguments on rule-following and the conceivability of a private language. Kripke continues by straightforwardly denying that questions of meaning and correct application are what they seem to be, namely questions of meaning and correct application, rather than questions of inclusion or exclu-sion into a speakers' community. The sceptical conclusion delivered in this way is interpreted as being the upshot of Wittgenstein's considerations, which Kripke (wrongly) sees terminating with the paradox Wittgenstein formulates in *PI* § 201 (quoted above).[14]

Wright takes Wittgenstein's argument to lead towards a point where scepticism seems unavoidable and, in a streak of 'quietism' (Wright), to break off without answering the questions as to what a meaningful use of a word amounts to and whether it is possible to specify conditions under which the use of psychological concepts can be judged veridical. He counters Kripke by deliberately parting with his interpretation of Wittgenstein (the 'community view') and adopting a kind of constitutivism with regard to meaning and veridicality. As Finkelstein rightly points out (2008, chs. 2 and 4), Wright thereby lets a main assumption of what I

---

words. In cases of 'incompletely understanding' an expression, i.e. lacking full (expert) knowledge of its referent, the person making a statement might not be aware of what he or she actually says or thinks by employing them. *Cf.* Burge (1979), especially pp. 104ff.; Burge (2006), pp. 174ff.; Burge (2003), pp. 683f.; and the critique in Donald Davidson (1987) "On Knowing one's own Mind", in his (2001), *Subjective, Intersubjective, Objective*, Oxford: UP, pp. 15–38, here pp. 26ff. and 37f.

14 Kripke's interpretation of Wittgenstein's remarks on rule-following and private language was shown categorically wrong at an early stage of discussion. It yet seems a widespread phenomenon in philosophical literature to refer to Kripke, or 'Kripke's Wittgenstein' when reporting on or trying to make sense of the passages on rule-following in *Philosophical Investigations*. For two arguments against Kripke's interpretation and an encompassing explanation why it is problematic both as an interpretation of *Philosophical Investigations* and as an independent position, see Warren Goldfarb (1985), "Kripke on Wittgenstein on Rules", *The Journal of Philosophy* 82/9, pp. 471–88; and, from each different directions, Gordon Baker, Peter Hacker (1984), *Scepticism, Rules and Language*, Oxford: Blackwell; BarryStroud (1990), "Wittgenstein on Meaning, Understanding, and Community", in Stroud (2000), pp. 80–94; and Davidson (1992), pp. 111–3 and 117–21.

have treated as the representationalist account of language go without question, that both meaning and truth of a statement about a person's psychology have to be determined by something *external* to the statement—in his case, an individual judgement. Remarkably, Wright's proposal has significant overlaps with both Kripke's and Searle's respective accounts of meaning (Searle as a proponent of the view Wright seeks to reject as 'platonist'). Similarly to Kripke, Wright conditions questions of the meaning of (psychological) expressions and the correctness of their particular instances on additional, retrospective agreement, although Kripke takes this agreement an empirical matter of 'brute facts', whereas Wright's account is normative in aspiration. And similarly to Searle, Wright conditions the meaning of utterances on the speaker's intentions, although he takes their existence a matter of judgement, rather than as a matter of fact.

The expertivist view agrees with Kripke (against Wright and Searle) that the person's meaning intentions are not decisive for settling this question.[15] Yet, it denies that a person's meaning something is in principle indistinguishable from a person's meaning nothing at all, and it denies that questions of meaning and correctness straightforwardly reduce to coincidence with a community use. Similarly to Searle, it takes the meaning of a person's utterances an objectively and unambiguously discoverable matter of fact, and similarly to Wright, it takes the determination of the meaning and correctness or incorrectness of particular applications a matter of authoritative (expert) knowledge and/or judgement.

Scepticism, constitutivism and expertivism have in common that they understand the paradox framed in *PI* § 201 as a real paradox, and as a paradox that is supposed to show the impossibility of determining the meaning of linguistic expressions and the conditions of their applicability theoretically, i.e. by reference to a rule specified by a definition or a sample. The conclusions they draw from this with regard to questions of meaning are, however, questionable. Scepticism generally is an unsatisfactory position; and once it begins denying truisms, it tends towards dubiosity. The truism in question is that psychological expressions are meaningfully used and understood, that there are practices of correcting one another and that it is possible in many cases to state whether their use on particular occasions is justified. The constitutivist position Wright advocates and the expertivist position adopted from Burge acknowledge the rule-following paradox as well as the validity of the truisms just listed and recommend a non-metaphysical, non-sceptical remedy to accommodate both of them.

---

15 *Cf.* Burge's criticism of Grice's account in Burge (1979), pp. 140f.; and his (2003) reply to Davidson (1987).

Yet, both proposals do not only agree on the paradox, their respective solutions also fall prey to the same problems that concern any referentialist account of meaning in that they, too, seek to establish the meaning and the correctness conditions of psychological expressions by something independent of and external to their particular instances. But a judgement as to the meaningfulness and correctness of instantiations of psychological concepts itself is open to doubts of the very same kind as those concerning judgements that a particular psychological fact obtains. There is no reason why making judgements concerning a person's state of mind ought to be in need for a further judgement that declares them meaningful and/or veridical, while these judgements are in this respect beyond doubt. In other words, grounding meaning and correctness in judgements about meaning-intentions and accordance with whatsoever equally lapses into hypostatising an external constituent of meaning or invites a vicious regress—after all, the meaning of the allegedly meaning-setting judgements has to be established by a further judgement as to the presence of a meaning intention for the first one, and so on, independently who is conventionally or otherwise endowed with the authority over making such judgements.[16]

Scepticism, stipulativism and expertivism are not good replies to the questions of meaning which representationalist accounts are unable to answer. All seek to avoid the regress problem raised on the assumption that there must be (a) 'Something' in addition to the various instantiations of a concept that makes them meaningful and open to assessment in terms of correctness. For this purpose, they refer to a kind of practice of deciding questions concerning meaning and correctness that (might) arise on particular occasions. They conceive of judgements stating whether a particular application of a linguistic expression is meaningful and/or veridical as a kind of declaration in Searle's sense, statements that simultaneously create the fact they assert to be true. For this reason, the infinite regress affecting the determination of their meaning is accompanied by an infinite regress of practices that endow the respective class of judgements with the capacity of creating facts about meaning and veridicality.[17] Kripke accounts for this practice as a practice of stating

---

16 *cf.* Finkelstein (2008), pp. 43f.; Davidson (1992), p. 116; and Davidson (1987).

17 *Cf.* Searle (1983), pp. 171f. Notably, Searle explicitly denies that linguistic meaning in general is grounded in declarations, being well aware of the vicious circle that would enter by defining one linguistic convention with another, see Searle (2010), pp. 111–5. Yet, his conception of meaning intentions formally coincides with his conception of declarations in that meaning intentions, too, create the fact they cite, namely a person's representing a particular state of affairs with a sequence of sounds. For meaning intentions to succeed, an external rule is required that establishes the correspondence of linguistic expressions and represented content. That is, individual statements

deviations from the standard use of a term, which is determined by coincidence on how a term is applied by the individual members of a speakers' community, that serves the purpose of judging a person's belonging to the community in question. Wright, in contrast, introduces a practice of making constitutive judgements concerning meaningfulness and correctness of the use of linguistic expressions backed by a practice regulating the authority over making such judgements, which supposedly delivers steadfast statements of veridicality and meaning. Similarly, the expertivist view posits a common practice of constituting meaning and conditions of correct application (let this be scientific or discursive), complemented by a practice of recognising the authority of experts over supervising the previously established standards of meaning and correctness and making judgements as to this effect.

Generously speaking, we are thus concerned with three interpretations of the thesis that the meaning of a linguistic expression lies in its use. And in contrast to the objections outlined above, they do not interpret the notion 'use' solely in a theoretical sense, as definition-in-use, but make efforts to account for the linguistic and extra-linguistic practices regulating this use. However, the meaning-constituting practices as conceived here receive the same status the presence of an empirical phenomenon or the possession of a formal concept have on a representationalist view, namely the status of determinants of the meaning of linguistic expressions from beyond their use. In this sense, the meaning of linguistic expressions again is reified and detached from their actual usage to the effect that there is an unbridgeable gap opening between meaning and use. The three accounts join forces with accounts that attempt to determine the semantic and grammatical rules of a natural language by means of drawing on 'theoretical' entities in that they take the paradox concerning meaning seriously. That is, they equally assume that there is a gap between the level of language in use, and an alleged level on which this use is regulated. However, the suggestion to bridge the gap by drawing on practices instead of definitions does not and cannot succeed as long as practices equally decompose into components of use and components of meaning. Especially on Wright's account it becomes visible that this is the case—the determinants of meaning (a special class of judgements) are of the same kind as the things whose meaning has to be determined, namely particular kinds of sentences. Conceiving of meaning-constituting practices as external or additional to the use of language on particular occasions turns out to be of as much explanatory force as understanding the use of an expression as a conjunction of all past uses criticised above. If an

---

equally require a linguistic practice that determines their meaning as well as their being meaningful statements *independently* of the statements themselves.

attempt to grasp meaning in terms of use or practice ought to succeed, it must not consider particular uses *detached* from general practices or rules, but as entangled and embedded in them.

3.1.6 Summary

In this section, I rejected four objections to the thesis that the meaning of an expression is constituted by its use in the language it belongs to, the objection from circularity, the objection from productivity, the objection from workability, and the objection from externalism. Based on my elaborations in the last chapter, I argued that no theory will succeed in either, explaining what the mind is and explaining the constitution of meaning and conditions of applicability of psychological concepts. I further explained that this argument extends to a specific conception of the notion 'use', namely as a 'definition-in-use' (Fodor), roughly a definition of a word based on a list or a comprehensive statement of its past uses. I presented three further accounts that react to the incapability of deducing the meaning of a word as well as its conditions of applicability and the competence to use it from reference by replacing reference to a (theoretically) definable level of meanings with practices of agreement on particular instances of linguistic expressions as determinants of their meaning. However, this understanding of the interrelation of the notions 'meaning', 'use' and 'practice' also proves inadequate in that it comes down to equally assuming that the meaning and grammar of linguistic expressions must be something external to their use on particular occasions. That is, the gap between meaning and language that is obviously present on a reference-based account of meaning is here reinstantiated, albeit more covertly. It does not open between definition and use, but between meaning or meaning-constituting practice and use to the effect that the paradoxicalities concerning meaning-constitution that affect the representationalist as well as other definition-based views reappear.

3.2 Meaning in Practice

In the last section, I presented two misreadings of the thesis that meaning is constituted in use, and not by reference, the critical one advanced from a representationalist viewpoint, and the approving one resulting in a sceptical, a stipulativist, and what I have called an expertivist position, respectively. The common denominator of representationalism, scepticism, stipulativism and expertivism has turned out to be the assumption that questions of meaning and correctness of linguistic expressions are located and have to be settled on a different level from their actual uses. For this reason, all of them face the difficulty of bridging the alleged gap between meaning and use, without any of them being able to satisfactorily overcome the paradoxicalities arising from that.

Consequently, I suggest that we give up the attempt to find an external determinant of the meaning of linguistic expressions, in particular of psychological ones, and to take Wittgenstein's remark that "the meaning of a word is its use in the language" more literally, especially in this domain (*PI* § 43). Following some remarks of Wittgenstein's and an argument Finkelstein develops from them, I clarify what the alleged gap between meaning and use consists in. I continue with a brief outline of how the interrelation of the notions practice, meaning and use can be made intelligible without falling prey to the misinterpretations presented in the foregoing section. Finally, I will bundle the observations on the commonsense use of the expression 'I believe' from the last chapter into a suggestion what one does with assertively stating it when 'avowing one's state of mind'. It will turn out that this requires reconsidering the meaning of psychological expressions just as well as the logic of assertion.

3.2.1 The 'Gap of Meaning'

Throughout the last sections, I argued that conceptions of meaning in terms of reference, meaning intentions and stipulative judgements are prone to lapse into a vicious infinite regress of meaning determinants that manifests the rule-following regress Wittgenstein describes in *PI* §§ 139–242. For this reason, they are confronted with a paradox about meaning analogous to the rule-following paradox framed in *PI* § 201: Nothing that persists over and above the particular uses of an expression can determine its applications, because everything can be brought into accordance with the respective determinant. The point Wittgenstein originally makes here is that the rule-following paradox rests on a false assumption, the assumption that there is a gap between a rule and its application that had to be bridged by interpreting the rule. The analogous misunderstanding as regards the meaning of psychological expressions consists in assuming that there is a *gap* between a level of intentionality and content on the one hand, and a level of expression (sounds or other physical realisers) of representational states on the other hand. The gap concerns both components of representational states, mode and content: How does it come that a sentence expresses representational content? and how does an utterance express a particular mental state, e.g. a belief rather than a desire? These questions motivate Searle's conception of speech acts—articulations of content in a natural language—as involving a double level of intentionality. The capacity of sentences to articulate content, which is the topic of this section, is supposed to be brought about by the meaning intention, whereas their capacity of expressing a particular intentional state of the speaker's is captured in the sincerity condition of the respective statement. I will discuss this in the following section.

The assumption of a gap between the level of intentionality and the level of expressions is, *pars pro toto*, pinpointed in the way Searle frames the "problem of meaning":

> [T]he problem of meaning in its most general form is the problem of how we get from the physics to the semantics; that is to say, how do we get [...] from the sounds that come out of my mouth to the illocutionary act? (Searle (1983), p. 27)

Searle's difficulty is almost literally raised by Wittgenstein's interlocutor:

> 'There is a gap between an order and its execution. It has to be closed by the process of understanding.'
> 'Only in the process of understanding does the order mean that we are to do THIS. The *order*—why, that is nothing but sounds, ink-marks.—' (*PI* § 431, transl. Hacker/Schulte)

The assumption Wittgenstein's interlocutor states here tempts into the view that there must be a determinant of meaning, something that endows entities from a physical world with subjective modes and representational contents, a referential object, say, which is pointed to by the speaker's meaning intention. The mistake Searle makes, and in which he is joined by the other representationalist views discussed in the last chapter as well as by Kripke and Wright, consists in assuming that meaningful utterances and written sentences are "something more" (Searle (1983), p. 163) than mere utterances of sounds or ink marks on paper. It is an expression of astonishment that we understand each other, that instructions are carried out, orders obeyed, techniques exercised, rules followed—in the light of the possibility of misunderstanding one another, of lying, pretending, disobedience, failure and defection in general—and that this is the normal case. It seems as if there was some magic power, some mystery about meaning, contrasting the simultaneous desire to get a metaphysically firm hold on it, framed as an explanatory necessity.

There are cases of doubt, to be sure: Sometimes it is actually unclear what another person means, sometimes one mishears what he or she says, or cannot read his or her handwriting. Expressions can become obsolete when they are no longer used or change their meaning over time or across different cultural contexts. Especially when translating a text from a foreign language, one needs to interpret the expression, look out for other clues as to which aspect of its meaning, or which translation is the right one, check with dictionaries, or ask someone for his or her opinion. Sometimes one intentionally deviates from the standard usage of a word, for instance when writing poetry. On other occasions, misunderstandings are unavoidable, sometimes one overlooks the relevant facet of someone else's utterance, sometimes one misinterprets it, sometimes one thinks one knows better what he or she means and does not rely on his or her actual words. Notwithstanding, speaking of doubt makes sense only against the background of a normally well-functioning practice:

> It may easily look as if every doubt merely *revealed* a gap in the foundations [of the meaning of a word, us.]; so that secure understanding is possible only if we first doubt everything that *can* be doubted, and then remove all these doubts.
> The signpost [as an example of a statement, us.] is in order—if, under normal circumstances, it fulfils its purpose. (*PI* § 87)

Cases of intentional or unintentional defection, failure or doubt can only arise once a practice in which these cases are entangled, be it the practice of following signposts, be it the practice of mutual understanding by means of a natural language, has already been established. Moreover, only people who participate in this language can be said to fail in following its rules, to misunderstand them, or to doubt the applicability of expressions in a particular case. It is possible that one has doubts when following a rule, when for example an order is given in a misleading way, or that one does not succeed in carrying out an instruction. However, the possibility that a rule and its application, or the way in which an utterance is meant and the way in which it is understood in a particular case come apart does not show that a gap would in principle open between them, which had to be overcome in every particular case. If there is doubt how an instruction is or ought to be understood, or whether it has been carried it out correctly, this is a matter of a particular application. In such a case, one might try to interpret the instruction, or to compare one's current situation with a similar situation which one has experienced in the past, or of which one has been told by other people. Or (and this is most often the best way) one asks another person how an utterance has been or might have been meant. But if an interpretation was always necessary, if the gap between meaning and understanding was the default case, there would be no understanding at all, not of the original expression, and not of its interpretation, either. And in this case, one could not even meaningfully raise doubts concerning the correct application of a rule, or concerning the possibility of rule-following behaviour: On the one hand, it is meaningless to speak of deviance from rules where there are none. On the other hand, doubting itself is a 'move' in an already established game, the game of understanding, of taking one another by one's words, of communicating in a shared language. Without there being meaningful utterances at first place there would not be anything to doubt, and without there being a practice of doubting nothing could even be meant and understood as a doubt.[18]

3.2.2 Practical Entanglement

I suggest we take Wittgenstein's claim seriously that "[f]or a *large* class of cases— though not for *all*—in which we employ the word 'meaning' this word can be explained thus: the meaning of a word is its use [*Gebrauch*] in the language" (*PI* § 43).[19] The meaning of an expression is not something standing 'behind' the expression, whose task it were to grant its meaning and regulate its application. This thesis needs further qualification, particularly in the light of the two misconceptions reviewed above. Wittgenstein employs the German word *Gebrauch*, which is generally translated into 'use', though it is also translatable into 'custom' or 'practice'. It comprises both a facet of actual application and a normative or conventional facet, pointing out that the ways in which a word is in fact used and the rules specifying how it should be used are mutually constitutive matters. In this sense, the notion 'use' reappears in *Philosophical Investigations* § 199, which Wittgenstein closes with clarifying his conception of what it is to follow a rule:

> It is not possible that there should have been only one occasion on which only one person followed a rule. It is not possible that there should have been only one occasion on which a report was made, an order given or understood, and so on.—To follow a rule, to make a report, to play a game of chess, are *customs* (usages [*Gebräuche*], institutions).
> To understand a sentence means to understand a language. To understand a language means to have mastered a technique. (*PI* § 199, transl. Hacker/Schulte)

---

18 *Cf. OC* §§ 624–6: "A doubt without an end is not even a doubt" (§ 625).

19 Hacker draws attention to the context in which this remark stands. Wittgenstein's claim in *PI* § 43 is to be understood as a counter-thesis to the claim that the meaning of words is constituted by reference that Wittgenstein criticises in the passages preceding this remark. For Wittgenstein, the use of a word encompasses the linguistic and extra-linguistic practices in which it is embedded. Conversely, these practices are sustained and comprised in their being used on particular occasions. *Cf.* Hacker and Baker (2009a), "Meaning and Use", in Hacker and Baker (2009b), *Wittgenstein: Understanding and Meaning. Part I: Essays,* [2]Oxford: Blackwell, pp. 129–58. Wittgenstein's explicating the meaning of a word by its use in *Philosophical Investigations* takes up the analogous explication at the beginning of the *Blue Book*. Here, it appears with less qualification ("But if we had to name anything which is the life of a sign, we should have to say that it was its *use*." (p. 4, original emphasis)), but similarly to the quoted passage from *Philosophical Investigations*, it counters the claims that, first, there is a definite and general answer to the question as to what the meaning of a word is; that, second, the answer is 'reference'; that, third, words and sentences are lifeless signs, was it not for their having a meaning so conceived.

Formulating in a slogan "the meaning of a word is its use" abridges Wittgenstein's remark by the important phrase "*in the language*" (*PI* § 43, my italics). The meaning of a word or a sentence is, as I said earlier, not confined to the sum of its particular applications, which could sensibly be considered in isolation. This would reduce the meaning of a word to the regularity of its occurrence, and questions of meaning to questions of speech behaviour (another suspicion often raised against (Kripke's) Wittgenstein). That the meaning of a particular expression is indeterminable in general does not imply that it would be indeterminable and/or indeterminate in particular applications. This conclusion would overlook that in most cases the meaning of a particular word can be specified, for example that 'obsolete' means 'out of use'. Explaining a word in this way, however, replaces one linguistic expression with another, it does not exhibit any 'deeper' fact. What is said is that the word 'obsolete' is used in the same way as the expression 'out of use'.[20] Thus, explanations of this sort are helpful only if one has already learned a language and is familiar with the practice of using one or the other. What a word or sentence means at a particular occasion depends on the place it has in a language as well as on the intentions with which it is used and the reactions of a listener or reader. It is clear that the meaning of words and sentences is, considered in isolation, indeterminable, for example:

> It is quite possible that a sentence, e.g. 'It is raining', is at one time uttered as an assertion, at another time as a supposition (even if it is not prefixed by 'Suppose')—what renders it one, what the other? On the one hand I want to answer: the game in which it is used. On the other hand: the intention with which it is uttered. How do these two tally with each other? [...] 'I intended the sentence as a supposition'—how do I explain that?—I intended the game. I can only explain this movement as the opening of a chess match by explaining the game of chess.[21]

This is to say that the meaning of a word or sentence at a particular instance, its use, depends on the context in which it is embedded in two respects. On the one hand, the meaning of an utterance depends on the *situational* context, in which it is used, e.g. on whom one is speaking to, on the context in which the conversation takes place. On the other hand, a particular application of a word is not independent of the *over-situational* practices in which it is entangled in that one can only intend a particular use of an expression if one intends it as an expression within a certain domain of language.

---

20 *Cf. PI* § 201, Stroud (1990), pp. 87ff.
21 Ludwig Wittgenstein, MS 136, 10.1.48, transl. in Schulte (1993), pp. 153f.; *cf. PI* § 205. See my discussion of Searle's account of meaning in Chapter 1, Section 3.2. As explained there, Searle does not acknowledge that intending a word or a phrase to mean something presupposes the relevant practice, the 'game' in Wittgenstein's note.

The situational context includes the activities in which one is presently engaged as well as the reactions and responses of another person. The meaning of the word 'bank' is not unambiguous when it is used within a conversation about the financial crisis, although it can just as well be used for a riverbank or as the name of a particular Underground station on a different occasion. There are cases, in which questions of meaning arise, for sure. But in answering them, one does not reveal what *really* stands behind the sounds or marks on paper one is concerned with. Rather, one will explain how one has intended to use the word, and how it is used within the practice it belongs to—what game is currently played, so to speak. All such explanations will succeed only if the person has some understanding of the practice. Unless a person is familiar with monetary practices, he or she will neither understand, nor be enabled to use the word 'bank' when explained as replaceable by 'financial institution'. To someone unfamiliar with the respective practice, explaining the meaning of a word will involve explaining the practice, and eventually, when all possible explanations have been exhausted, end with stating "This is simply what I [or we, us.] do." (*PI* § 217) If one is familiar with the context in which an utterance is made, if, that is, there is agreement on the setting in which the utterance takes place, if both speaker and hearer participate in the same or similar cultural practices (or 'forms of life') one will face little difficulties to understand one another even if some words and expressions are used in an unfamiliar, unprecise or even wrong way. The productivity of language, its flexibility to integrate new or borderline uses of particular expressions does not, as Fodor thinks, originate from every word's having a particular referent that is invoked in every single application, but from every word's being embedded in a sentence, a sequence of sentences, a conversation, a linguistic practice and eventually in extra-linguistic practices—that is, precisely from its *limitations* in being sensibly applied. Hence, to "understand a sentence means to understand a language. To understand a language means to have mastered a technique" (*PI* § 201, transl. Hacker/Schulte)—and nothing else is necessary and sufficient for using and understanding one another in language.

The particular use of a word or sentence is rooted in the *practices* in whose context it occurs. These include domains of language that belong to certain linguistic and extralinguistic conventions, institutions and customs, the language of the builders Wittgenstein presents in the opening passages of *Philosophical Investigations* is one such example (*cf.* particularly §§ 2, 8), others are the language of mathematics, the language of cricket, or the language of hip-hop. In that Wittgenstein conceives of language in terms of practice, or "technique" (*PI* § 199), and of words and expressions in terms of "instruments", or "tools" (*PI* §§ 11–4) he emphasises that speaking a language belongs to a "form of life" (*PI* § 23); that it is grounded in activity, in shared ways of living and shared perspectives on the world. Regularity, the repeated use of an expression or the reoccurrence of certain patterns of behaviour under similar circumstances, is as central to practices as coinciding ways of behaviour and perception are:

> Following a rule is analogous to obeying an order. One is trained to do so, and one reacts to an order in a particular way. But what if one person reacts to the order and training *thus*, and another *otherwise*? Who is right, then?
>
> Suppose you came as an explorer to an unknown country with a language quite unknown to you. In what circumstances would you say that the people there gave orders, understood them, obeyed them, rebelled against them, and so on?
>
> The common human ways of acting are the framework of reference by means of which we interpret an unknown language.[22]

In the end, agreement in one's way of engaging in activity constitutes the basis not only for understanding one another in one's own language, but equally for understanding one another across the boundaries of a particular language. The grounding of meaning in temporally extended practices, and the meaningful use of a word on a particular occasion are interdependent. It is nonsensical to think that the meaning of a word were constituted in private, on one's own. It equally makes no sense to consider an expression meaningful, if it is uttered on a single occasion only, and never again (which would be a consequence if the meaning of a word was something different from its use). That is, an utterance has no meaning if it does not belong to a language, i.e. unless it is embedded in eventually extralinguistic practices. And it will not be understandable unless one agrees in one's practices, unless one shares basic ways of acting.

Conversely, a practice, which is not exercised, is 'dead' in a literal sense—it does no longer play a role anybody's life. In the same sense, words, or whole languages, which are no longer used, are dead. What remains from the ancient languages of the Middle East, for instance, are marks, burnt into clay, or scratched into stone, bereft from the meaning they used to have. These signs are dead because the forms of life in which they were integrated have ceased to exist; and not because their referents would have been eradicated. Hieroglyphs are still interpretable as signs, but only insofar as we can translate them into a sign-system, which is *now* in commerce, which we now use in our practices. We need to give them an interpretation, or a

---

22 *PI* § 206,the first and second paragraph translated by Hacker/Schulte, the third by me. Following a suggestion of Goldfarb's, I translated '*gemeinsame menschliche Handlungsweise*' as 'common human ways of acting' instead of 'common behaviour of mankind' (Anscombe) and 'shared human behaviour' (Hacker/Schulte). *Cf.* Warren Goldfarb (2010), "Rule-Following Revisited", in Jonathan Ellis, David Guevara (eds.), *Wittgenstein and the Philosophy of Mind*, Oxford: UP, pp. 73–90.

series of interpretations, which connects them with our 'form of life', our customs and institutions. And the 'framework of reference', that is, the basis for comparing our form of life with other forms of life—past or present—is *agreement* in basic ways of engaging with the world, the "common human ways of acting". Yet, 'agreement' in one's practices is not a result from thematic negotiations or reflection on what ought to be done, a matter of joint decision whether a particular action was used in accord with a particular rule, or coincidence in ways of behaviour. Wittgenstein clarifies this notion in his closing remarks on rule-following:

> 'So you are saying that human agreement decides what is true and what is false?'—What is true or false is what human beings *say*; and it is in their *language* that human beings agree. This is agreement not in opinions, but rather in form of life.
> It is not only agreement in definitions, but also (odd as it may sound) agreement in judgements that is required for communication by means of language. This seems to abolish logic, but does not do so.—It is one thing to describe methods of measurement, and another to obtain and state results of measurement. But what we call 'measuring' is in part determined by a certain constancy in results of measurement. (*PI* §§ 241–2, transl. Hacker/Schulte.)

Drawing attention to the notion 'agreement' as an indispensable element of meaning thus ought not to be understood as coinciding behaviour, as Kripke does, or as a collective judgement on the meaningfulness and/or correctness of particular uses. It is not a matter of "opinions" (*PI* § 241) or decisions whether a sentence is true or false, whether a rule has been followed or not in a particular case. But it is not solely a matter of "definitions" (§ 242), of having a common level of reference external to the particular uses of a word, either. Rather, the framework of language (definitions) and the things we do with language within this framework (particular judgements) are inseparable from one another; just as the practice (the 'methods') of measuring is in part dependent on there being a certain constancy in its results. Agreement on both is manifested as well as constituted in the use of language, it is not something preceding, or grounding, or (functionally or causally) determining language.[23] We do not step beyond language, neither in investigating meaning in philosophy, nor in using meaningful sentences in everyday life.

In brief, saying that the meaning of a word just is its use is not tantamount to saying that the meaning of a word consists in the sum of its past uses enlisted in a descriptive definition, say, as the objection from compositionality suggests. Neither does the 'use' of a word consist in an instructive rule, such as 'use the word *W* to designate object *O* in context *C*', as the objection from circularity suggests— although both a definition and an instructive rule in this sense can be given for

---

23 *Cf.* Goldfarb (2010).

many words. In this case however, both definition (a synonym or a semantic rule) and instructive rule are extrapolations from the 'use' of a word. They can *describe*, but not *prescribe* its meaning. In order to understand such a rule, one must already be familiar with these kinds of rule. That is, one must know which place in language the word they define has, and one must know the role it takes in language. In short: One must have understood its use.

I made this point in the last chapter in the context of giving a definition by pointing to an object: Understanding someone's ostensive definition 'This is called sepia', requires understanding that 'sepia' is a colour-word, and understanding what colour-words are, that is, how they are used. If one mistakenly thinks that 'sepia' is used for a certain shape of pasta, one will be surprised at finding the word 'sepia' in connection with photographs. Although ostension can play and in many cases actually plays a major role in teaching and learning a language, the ostensive definition of 'sepia' itself does not provide for its use unless the use of what is thereby defined is already understood.[24]

Once one conceives of meaning as situated in the practices of using language, rather than as being something over and above them, the question, 'What *grants* that there is a uniform meaning across all instances of a word?' becomes obsolete. Understanding the meaning of a word or sentence, an utterance or a text, an assertion or an order, thus, is understanding their use, and understanding their use is exercised in using them.

3.2.3 The Use of 'I Believe'

In this section I focus first on the meaning of first-personal statements using psychological predicates, so-called 'avowals' of one's state of mind. I want to come back to two points I mentioned earlier, the supposed conflict between the expressivity and truth-functionality of such statements, and the function of avowals as descriptions. I will then investigate what we understand by the word 'believing' and make a proposal what the expression 'I believe' means in everyday language drawing on the examples given in the previous chapters.

3.2.3.1 Avowals: Expressive Statements
On representationalism, the relations between the meaning and the use of a word, and mental states and their behavioural and linguistic expression, are conceived

---

24 *Cf.* Barry Stroud (2003), "Ostension and the Social Character of Thought", *Philosophy and Phenomenological Research* 67/3, pp. 667–74.

analogously as relations between two independent *relata*. I rejected this conception for the case of meaning in the last section arguing that the problem in fact does not arise because there is no gap. I turn now to rejecting the conception on the same grounds for the case of mental states.

Searle observes that different kinds of utterances are used to express different kinds of mental states. Orders, for example, usually express the desire that they be obeyed; assertions express the speaker's beliefs. Thus, we can infer from someone's statements to his or her state of mind. Subsequently, Searle follows a similar train of thought as Wittgenstein's interlocutor in *Philosophical Investigations* §§ 431–436. The consideration might be put as follows. There is a gap between the desire and the utterance or written instruction, by means of which an order is given. This gap needs to be closed. Now, the question is, how is the gap closed? How does the order express the desire? This question is similar to the question discussed in the last section, what bridges the gap between the representational content of a word or sentence and its manifestation in a language? It differs in that it asks for how the utterance manages to express the speaker's mental state, its sincerity condition, rather than how it is supplied with content.

The common view underlying the different answers conceives of utterances as well as gestures, movements or facial expressions as 'artificial devices' by means of which one communicates to another person that one currently has a certain mental state. Finkelstein characterises this view as follows:

> Our movements and their effects are, in themselves, without determinate *psychological* content. In order to understand how bodily movements may be expressive of a particular mental condition, we need to see what gives them psychological significance. If they are to be understood as psychologically significant, movements [...] must somehow be *invested* with content (e.g., via interpretation [or meaning intention, us.]). (2008, p. 90, original italics.)

The reply to this view is analogous to the previous reply: So presented, the conception presupposes that mental states are discrete psychological entities, or states, or processes that are distinct from bodily behaviour and linguistic or non-linguistic utterances, which accompany the bodily movements and utterances that express the states in question. Yet, in everyday life, situations are omnipresent in which orders are given, understood and executed without any gaps appearing either between the desire expressed in the order and the utterance of the order, or the order and its being understood and carried out. The desire that a certain action be performed is simply expressed in the interplay of the sentence, instructive gestures or facial expressions, by means of which an order is given, just as this behaviour simply means that this and that should be carried out. It is understood in that the order is obeyed. Only if one disregards the contextual frame of giving orders or instructions, of having a philosophical argument or a conversation about the weather, will one be inclined to believe that the desires, beliefs, hopes and fears expressed in these situations are something detached from what obviously happens in the situations themselves.[25]

Following the two-component model, one can say that utterances of meaningful sentences at any rate reflect the speaker's mind by means of their illocutionary force, regardless of whether their content refers to a mental state of the speaker's or to an independent state of affairs. This is different in avowals. Conceived as assertions in which the speaker uses the first-person present indicative of a psychological predicate, avowals apparently express a mental state of the speaker's, a belief that what he or she says is true, and additionally represent the mental state cited in their content. Accordingly, avowals seem to display a double gap between utterance and the speaker's mind, the gap between their illocutionary force and the belief expressed, and the gap between their content and the state cited. Avowals of belief are even more special in that they represent a belief of the speaker's and express the speaker's belief that he or she actually has the belief specified in the content. An avowal of a belief *that p is the case* thus seems to emphasise the truth of a state of affairs twice, by representing it as the content of the belief avowed and simultaneously expressing that one believes that one's belief *that p is the case* is true. However, what else is said, in this manner, than with the simple statement '*p*'?

    Much of the confusion originates, as it seems to me, from commonly using the word 'avowal' for statements employing the first-person singular present indicative of psychological predicates. This current use as a technical term goes back to

---

25 This suggestion has been framed by Axel Seemann as the insight that bodily and experiential ('mental') properties are equally constitutive for the meaning of what Strawson (1959) has called '*P-predicates*' ('*P*' for '*psychological*'), i.e. predicates whose applicability involves an ascription of consciousness to the respective subject. Taking up Strawson's notion, Seemann argues that it is indispensable to take both components into account, a person's bodily changes and his or her experiential states, when it comes to understanding one another's states of mind. I perfectly agree with Seemann and I am in principle sympathetic to the idea of grasping the relationship of the experiential and bodily components of states of mind, like sadness, joy, expectation etc., as constitutive, mutual interdependence. Yet, I am reluctant to particularly draw on Strawson's formulation because he considers the competence of P-predicates as underlying a constraint analogous to Evans' Generality Constraint (the latter is based on the former). I agree with Burge (2010) that, as becomes clear already from the title of his book, Strawson advocates a metaphysically and cognitively overly demanding account of mental concepts, which involves both a body-mind dualism and a meaning-language dualism. *Cf.* Axel Seemann (2008), "Person Perception", *Philosophical Explorations* 3, pp. 245–62; Seemann (2010), "The Other Person in Joint Attention. A Relational Approach", *Journal of Consciousness Studies* 22, pp. 161–82, and Chapter 1, Section 2.1.4.

Gilbert Ryle.[26] Ryle uses the word 'avowals' synonymously with "unstudied utterances" (pp. 181ff.), first-person statements articulating one's occurrent emotions, sensations and feelings, as well as so-called propositional attitudes, such as beliefs, desires or intentions. He characterises them as immediate expressions of one's state of mind that employ "explicit interest phrases" (p. 183), such as "I want", "I hope", "I intend", "I guess", but also "I dislike", "I am depressed", "I feel hungry" or "I feel a tickle" (all examples are Ryle's, *cf.* pp. 101f., 183). Avowals contrast with other sentences applying psychological concepts in that they are *immediate*, i.e. not based on self-observation, and typically accompanied by characteristic behaviour, gestures, tones of voice, or facial expressions.

I find Ryle's coinage of the term 'avowal', though convenient and meanwhile well-established in philosophical discussion, somewhat unfortunate because its original use overlaps to a large extent with the respective usage of the words 'confession', and 'declaring oneself', and is akin to the use of 'vow' and 'vowing'. Similarly to the notions 'judgement' and 'assertion', it roots in the language appropriated in jurisdiction and liturgy and so invokes the associated actions— confessing one's mind (to a priest) or (a)vowing that one will speak nothing but the truth; asserting that this is the truth (against another person's statement) and settling a question by judging that *this* is the case. Using the term 'avowals' coextensively with the term 'unstudied utterances' credits their particular everyday applications with a special communicative weight which they, ordinarily, have not. It suggests that such statements served to uncover what is otherwise hidden, i.e. some fact about the speaker's mind, to articulate what is otherwise the speaker's privileged self-knowledge, and thereby to draw attention to the speaker's mind, away from the conversational subject at issue. Yet, as my examples in the last chapter illustrate, this is usually not the case. Quite to the contrary, taking statements containing psychological predicates in the first-person singular present indicative primarily as *descriptive* statements, statements of facts *about* the speaker's mind and shifting the conversational topic accordingly is most often inappropriate.[27] The expression 'unstudied utterance' brings better out

---

26 Gilbert Ryle (1949), *The Concept of Mind*, London: Hutchinson, here pp. 101f. and 181–185.

27 Think of the example from Wittgenstein's *Letter to Moore*: "If I ask someone 'Is there a fire in the next room?' and he answers 'I believe there is' I *can't say*: 'Don't be irrelevant. I asked you about the fire, not about your state of mind!'" (*Briefe 257*) It is inappropriate for the first speaker to rebuke the second for shifting the topic from the fire to the second speaker's mind and thus taking a transparent use of the expression 'I believe' for an opaque one. Reversely, it would be awkward to take Macbeth's ponderings about daggers primarily at face value, as utterances about objects in his visual field, rather than as expressions of his at this stage of the drama already severe mental distortion. This is to say again that unstudied utterances and ordinary statements are much more

what I think is one or even the most important characteristics of such statements, namely their being spontaneously uttered, without drawing on evidence or further considerations.

The motivation for the idea to credit the content of unstudied utterances with a descriptive function was to grant its representational function, which was found indispensable for such a statement's being assessable in terms of veridicality and thus first and foremost being a statement (and not only the utterance of sounds), and that the first-person present indicative of psychological predicates has the same meaning as their other inflections. It was assumed that this could not be the case if they in contrast had only the function of expressing the state of mind they cite. It was deemed inconceivable, that is, that expressions could in themselves consist in ordinary assertive statements and so stand on a semantic continuum with ascriptions of mental states to others.

The need for ascribing a descriptive function to avowals in addition to their expressive function, which is for the most part agreed upon, arises on a particular understanding of the notion 'expression', which is often connected with a remark of Wittgenstein's in the *Blue Book*. There he writes:

> To say, 'I have pain' is no more a statement *about* a particular person than moaning is. (*BB*, p. 67, original emphasis)

Wittgenstein here emphasises the continuity (not: the identity) of expressive statements with more 'natural' expressions of one's state of mind primarily in order to distinguish them from descriptions and reports, as the following remarks from *Remarks on the Philosophy of Psychology* show:

> A cry is not the description of a state of mind, even though a state of mind can be inferred from it. (*RPP* II § 723)
> If a cry is not a description, then neither is the verbal expression that replaces it. The utterances of fear, hope, wish, are not descriptions. [...] (*RPP* II § 728)

Wittgenstein is often misread as holding a position which one may call 'expressivism'. On this position, statements using the first-person present indicative of psychological predicates, that is, avowals or 'unstudied utterances' of one's state of mind, are regarded as *nothing but* meaningless sounds, 'natural expressions' of one's state of mind, such as yawns, moans, groans, certain gestures and move-

---

similar regarding to their function as expressions of their speaker's mind than the strict distinction between assertion and expression and the insistence on the representational or referring function of psychological predicates tolerate—and this is just to reformulate what Moore's Paradox reveals.

ments. Given this assumption, avowals would indeed lack truth-aptness, and would be detached from other-person ascriptions of psychological states. That this is not Wittgenstein's position becomes clear from his remarks on Moore's Paradox in *Philosophical Investigations*, which I discussed above:

> Imagine a language in which 'I believe it is so' is expressed only by means of the tone of the assertion 'It is so'. In this language they say, not 'He believes' but 'He is inclined to say…' and there exists also the hypothetical 'Suppose I was inclined to say etc.', but not the expression 'I am inclined to say'.
> Moore's paradox would not exist in this language; instead of it, however, there would be a verb lacking one inflexion. (*PPF* § 98)

Expressivism—Moran's 'Presentational View'—conceives of the meaning of avowals as expressive *in opposition to* the alleged descriptive sense of statements using psychological predicates in any other grammatical form. It thereby makes a similar mistake as views conceiving of avowals primarily as descriptive in meaning (see Chapter 2, Section 3.2.3). For both views assume that psychological concepts generally designate corresponding psychological phenomena, but do something else or something additional in the first-person present indicative, and consequently stumble inevitably over Moore's Paradox. Yet, psychological predicates do not designate corresponding psychological phenomena even in grammatical forms *other* than the first-person present indicative. So it is not only erroneous to insist on avowals having both, an expressive and a descriptive meaning, it moreover leads up the garden-path in that its prejudgements on the constitution of their meaning in general obstruct considerations of their meaning in particular cases.

It is worth reconsidering Wittgenstein's remark from the *Blue Book* quoted above. Reading it as saying 'To say, 'I have pain' is just another way of moaning', as a proponent of expressivism and his or her opponents unanimously do, is a misinterpretation. What Wittgenstein denies is not that avowals are truth-functional statements, but that they are statements that inform their hearer *about* a particular person and his or her current state of mind. In Wittgenstein's view, unstudied utterances are not descriptions of an independently existing psychological fact about oneself that could otherwise not be communicated to another one, but belong to the various ways of expressing one's state of mind. Wittgenstein takes avowals to be partly substitutions, partly extensions of 'natural' expressive behaviour. For instance, sensation-words such as 'pain' "are connected with the primitive, the natural, expressions of the sensation and used in their place. A child has hurt himself and he cries; and then adults talk to him and teach him new exclamations and, later, sentences. They teach the child new pain-behaviour."[28] With respect to

---

28 *RPP* I §§ 458–9; *PI* § 244; *cf.* Glock (1996), pp. 50f.; Schulte (1993), chs. 8 and 9.

their expressive function, they are *similar* to expressive behaviour, exclamations, gestures and facial expressions.

Yet, unstudied utterances are not *identical* with cries, moans, frowning and so forth. And their meaning does not consist in designating such expressions, although they are, in certain circumstances replaceable by them. One's current and overall state of mind is manifest in a variety of movements, gestures, facial expressions, courses of actions, exclamations and verbal utterances, and in this sense entangled in a situation. Unstudied utterances belong to these manifestations of one's state of mind, and in this sense are on a par with non-linguistic utterances. Sometimes, they are replaceable with shorter exclamations, or non-verbal utterances, or a tone of voice. And unstudied utterances are full-fledged sentence statements, and as such on a par with other sentence statements. As Finkelstein argues, the point of rejecting that avowals were about *something* was not to say that they expressed *nothing*, but that they express no *thing* (Finkelstein (2008), ch. 6.2, drawing on *PI* § 304). The choice between articulating either 'something' or 'nothing' at all is a wrong choice because it involves a pre-decision on the function of language and communication, namely "to convey [and exchange] thoughts—which may be about houses, pains, good and evil, or anything else you please" (*PI* § 304); and on their alleged 'satisfaction'—to say the truth, and nothing but the truth.[29] This however presupposes a certain ontology of what is expressed by psychological concepts, an ontology that hypostatises states of mind in analogy to individual objects in the physical world. And this conception of mental states has been shown to be irrelevant for the meaning of psychological concepts.

Aiming at reconciling the expressiveness of avowals with their truth-functionality and their potential to enter inferential processes, Finkelstein suggests to understand avowals as statements that are expressions *and* assertions at the same time. This formulation seems to me misleading for, on the one hand, it comes too close to Moran's overloading avowals with both a descriptive and an additional expressive function. Yet, endowing avowals with this double function has turned out no good guide to their meaning, but a good guide into *aporia*, as I have argued in the last chapter (Section 3.24 and 3.2.5). On the other hand, Finkelstein's proposal seems to be captured by the very dichotomy between expression and truth-functionality it seeks to mitigate. But it seems to me that the price for counting avowals as *as-*

---

29 Evans, for example, regards communication as exchange of information. *Cf.* Evans (1982), p. 310: "For it is a fundamental, though insufficiently recognized, point that communication is *essentially* a mode of transmission of knowledge"; and Ch. 9. This opinion permeates all previously discussed views, and persists through all views that take for granted that thinking and (meaningful) language are always *about* something.

sertions stricto sensu is too high in that it interprets their truth-functionality as truth-evaluability and thus reinvites the question as to what constitutes their truth and truth conditions. Thus, Finkelstein risks to dilute his otherwise so illuminating account of the meaning of avowals as being constituted by the place and function they have in what he calls the 'weave of life'[30] There is yet an emphatic use of 'unstudied utterances', by which someone earnestly and sternly speaks his or her mind, and I think it is appropriate to call such statements 'avowals', or *assertive expressions* of one's mind—for they are made in an assertive manner. But this is not to say that they were 'expressive assertions', i.e. both expressions and reports of one's state of mind. As I have mentioned above, this use of the first-person singular present indicative of psychological expressions is best to substitute by other expressive means.

As an alternative to Finkelstein's proposal, I suggest to interpret the truth-functionality of unstudied utterances not in terms of truth-evaluability, but in terms of their being sentence-statements and *as such* essentially truth-functional. This is not to say that unstudied utterances were a kind of Fregean assumptions (or their representationalist equivalent, i.e. neutral contents), which bear truth-conditions but have not been assigned a truth-value by their subject. This would assimilate avowals to statements made from Moran's theoretical point of view to one's own mind, i.e. a perspective from which one can only surmise, or hypothesise, or make inferences about one's state of mind without being in any epistemologically better position than other people are, and would thus lapse into the representationalist-*cum*-referentialist view of the meaning of unstudied utterances that I have throughout opposed.

Rather, unstudied utterances *constitute* the measure for truth and falsity as regards statements concerning the speaker's state of mind and thus belong to the "game of truth-functions" (*RFM* I App. 3 § 2) without being truth-evaluable themselves. By means of unstudied utterances, the speaker sets the standard by which *further* statements concerning his or her state of mind are evaluable in terms of truth and falsity. They are not incontestable;[31] but contesting them will not result in proving them false. Rather, it will result in reinterpreting one's situation,

---

30 The phrase originally is Wittgenstein's (or Anscombe's, respectively), *cf.* PPF § 2: "'Grief' describes a pattern which recurs, with different variations, in the weave of our life."

31 As Ryle observes, statements using the first-person present indicative of psychological predicates that lack any behavioural accompaniment can hardly be taken seriously as *avowals*. It is hard to take a person's statement 'I am suffering from severe depression' seriously if the person otherwise gives the impression of brimming over with life, say, amidst a light-hearted conversation on the dance-floor at a party. The point Ryle makes is that, first, the authority of such statements is not independent of their truthfulness, that, second, their truthfulness or credibility depends on

choosing different words, maybe changing one's mind: Changes, that is, which affect the evaluative framework for the speaker's further conduct as well as for others' interactions with him or her.[32]

I suggest that we gain a better understanding of the meaning of unstudied utterances offside discussing their truth-functionality, by focusing on the multiple functions they have 'in commerce'. Although there is no 'one' characteristic that was common to all instances of unstudied utterances and could provide their *differentia specifica*, I find it harmless to characterise them as statements that usually serve to make one's own behaviour intelligible to another person, or to make sense of one's own conduct and experiences for oneself, in the larger narrative of one's life. Although they do not convey information about oneself in employing the first-person present indicative of a psychological predicate—they do not articulate representational content about oneself—they reveal aspects of one's state of mind, for example, in that they allow another one to make inferences from them. One might say that by avowing one's state of mind, one gives another person a clue at hand how to understand one's doings, as if one said "See the action in this light."[33] With making an avowal, one highlights one aspect of how one experiences the situation on different levels of abstraction and to a variable degree.[34] This, however, is not an exclusive feature of unstudied utterances—any utterance can be interpreted as an expression of the speaker's state of mind. And what 'making oneself intelligible to others' means again depends on the particular case. Moreover, avowals need not primarily mean to express the state they cite. Asserting 'I believe it's raining' can equally be an expression of belief (and not necessarily only of the belief *that it is raining*) as an expression of remorse or release, as it can be a report on the weather.

This is to say that by expressing one's state of mind with an avowal one enables another person to respond in a more refined, and possibly more appropriate way than he or she might be able to do by attending to one's behaviour only. They rather help him or her to gain orientation within, or an overview over the situation and responding appropriately—just as a signpost helps to find one's way about, to recognise where one is, where one has come from, and how one can continue. That is, they help the other to understand how one experiences one's current situation, how the world looks from one's own standpoint, what

---

the context in which they uttered, that is on there being a possible interpretation of their author's situation in which they can coherently be integrated.

32 *Cf.* Severin Schroeder (2006), pp. 169f.

33 Anscombe (2000), p. 21.

34 This proposal is spelled out in Matthew Soteriou (2007), "Content and the Stream of Consciousness", *Philosophical Perspectives* 21, pp. 543–68.

one is going to do. Eventually, expressing one's state of mind with words needs not always serve communication, just as bodily or facial expressions of one's state of mind need not be communicative in purpose. The similarity of avowals with more primitive expressions among others results from that they are often issued spontaneously, like yawns or sudden movements. What one does with an avowal, how it is understood and acted upon, which aspect of one's experience one highlights and on which level of abstraction depends on the context.

On this understanding, it becomes obsolete to insist on counting 'unstudied utterances'—expressive statements of one's state of mind using the first-person present indicative of a psychological predicate, or 'avowals'—as *assertions*, even the more as assertions according to the restrictive conception of assertion deriving from Frege's view. Grasping avowals as assertions in this sense, articulations of judgements to the truth of a proposition, additionally blocks the view from what is actually done by expressing one's state of mind by means of words and sentences. Here, the gap discussed in the last section reappears: Considering a statement in isolation neither renders its meaning, nor its purpose, nor the conditions making it successful. Consequently, there is nothing that would distinguish a statement from the mere utterance of sounds—was it not for a specific content providing its meaning, in terms of conditions of veridicality or satisfaction, and its illocutionary force, specifying its purpose and conditions of success (Searle's 'direction of fit'). However, this genuinely Cartesian way of separating statements into a subjective (an 'intellectual act') and an objective component (a 'content') has been revealed incoherent and to not even fulfil the function its adherents ascribe to it, to unambiguously determine the meaning of every single statement.[35] Even according to Searle's taxonomy of speech acts, which knows five and only five different classes, indicative statements can be subsumed, when considered in isolation, under (at least) three classes, assertions, expressions and declarations. One might well doubt whether this list is, in fact, exhaustive, given the multitude of things one can do, and actually does, with language[36]—and accordingly whether the 'satisfaction' of different sentences is comprehensively grasped as conditioned eventually on their veridicality only. On the contrary: Just as the meaning (and grammar) of language and its practice must be accounted for together—and, in the end, be anchored in common human ways of acting—the meaning of any particular statement cannot

---

35 *Cf.* Chapter 2, particularly Sections 3.2 and 4, and the preceding sections of this chapter.
36 A small selection, listed in *PI* § 23, might contain giving and obeying orders, reporting or speculating about an event, forming and testing a hypothesis, making up and reading a story, asking, thanking, cursing, greeting, playing...

be separated from the use it is made of; and, eventually, not in isolation from its context.

Once one has noticed that avowals are statements like any other sentence statement is, and once one has recognised that statements are with what we play the game of truth-functions, it is, of course, tempting to highlight this supposed common denominator of all statements and continue one's investigation by isolating avowals from their environment in practice and trying to pinpoint what exactly makes them truth-functional statements and what exactly constitutes their truth-conditions. Truly articulating one's mind amounts to nothing more than speaking openly, honestly and sincerely, whether one uses psychological predicates or not. And besides truth, other criteria matter, even more, when it comes to understanding one another—truthfulness, sincerity, authenticity, to name a few. Classifying avowals as Fregean or Searlean assertions tempts into wrongly analysing them according to the two-component model, suggesting that their main function consists in describing one's state of mind and conveying this information to another person. Thereby, the various other facets that are to the meaning of expressions of one's state of mind beyond their truth-functionality and the richness of their communicative functions equally escape from sight as their entanglement into practices and situations of communication.

In summary, 'avowals' are ordinary statements, meaningful sentences by means of which one expresses one's state of mind. They involve the first-person present indicative of a psychological predicate or a substitute, a person-neutral phrase or related accompanying behaviour that is roughly equivalent in meaning. Their meaning consists in revealing one's state of mind in terms of highlighting certain aspects of one's current experiences and thereby making one's own situation intelligible, for others as well as for oneself. Which aspects of one's current experiences one articulates, to which extent one does so, and how one's avowal is understood, depends first and foremost on one's situational context, broadly understood as involving one's own feelings and experiences, one's thoughts and other doings, one's interactions with others and one's possible hearers, and the events occurring in one's surroundings.

3.2.3.2 The Meaning of 'I Believe'

What then *is* the meaning of the expression 'I believe'?—When confronted with this question, one "feel[s] that [one] can't point to anything in reply to [it] and yet ought to point to something." (*BB*, p. 1) So one is tempted into pointing at something beyond the level of words, to something more substantial represented by the sign in language, in order to avoid the conclusion that there is nothing designated by the word 'believe'. Yet, the straightforward answer, following from referentialism about meaning and unanimously offered by representationalist views, 'Well, to refer to a discrete psychological phenomenon, the state of believing', has been shown to produce a 'mental cramp' (Wittgenstein) instead of presenting a satisfactory reply. And the choice between 'something' or 'nothing' as potential candidates for the meaning of the verb 'to believe' has turned out a false one. For it arises only upon one's preliminary decision to answer the question by looking away from language as it is used, as if one could leave the level of signs behind and concentrate on what there really matters, the level of reference. What happens on the other side of the alleged gap between meaning and use, i.e. beyond the practice of language, however, has proven irrelevant for what we do within.

Staying, in contrast, *within* the practice of language, the meaning of the verb 'to believe' can be approached by answering two questions, namely: How is the word 'to believe' used in everyday language?, and What aspect of our experiences do we highlight when saying 'I believe...'? In the last section I suggested that the first-person singular present indicative of psychological predicates is used to highlight some aspect or other of one's own current experiences, or state of mind, and thereby makes one's doings intelligible to others. Further, I proposed that such unstudied utterances are both truth-functional and expressive statements, and yet are not truth-evaluable statements *about* one's state of mind. They present the linguistic extension of exclamations and non-linguistic expressions of one's state of mind, gestures, facial expressions, groans and moans and so forth. This might seem implausible in the case of believing, because believing apparently lacks characteristic behavioural expressions as compared with being afraid, feeling pain, or to some extent even expecting something. Looking at the actual practice, the expression 'I believe' is used assertively just as the first-person present indicative of other psychological expressions. For a wide range of cases, the expression 'I believe' can be substituted by equivalent expressions, such as 'I'd say', or a tone of voice, for instance, an assertive one, or a doubting one. In the last chapter, I mentioned the use of 'I believe' in reply to the question, 'Is this the bus to the station?'—'I believe it is', once uttered with confidence, once in a hesitant tone of voice. If one is confident that the bus is going to the station, or if one knows it is, the utterance 'I believe it is' can be replaced with the simple assertion 'Yes, it is'. If one does not know for certain, one can say instead 'I think so; but I'm not sure'. What is meant with the expression 'I believe' in the respective situations becomes—usually sufficiently—clear from the context, i.e. additional features of the situation, in this case, the speaker's tone of voice. Similarly, the utterance 'I believe the financial crisis will not be overcome until next year' may be replaced with 'I'd say the financial crisis will not be overcome until next year', with 'As I estimate the situation, ...', or 'The financial crisis will certainly not be overcome until next year'. In these and other similar cases, the expression 'I believe' characterises the speaker's statement, as a tone of voice would do, or an adverbial phrase. Still, the expression 'I believe' does not designate an assertive tone of voice. Thus, I think it is innocuous to say that asserting a sentence like 'I believe it is raining', asserting 'It is raining', or opening one's umbrella are, in certain contexts, typical expressions of one's belief that is is raining.

In the remaining remark of *Philosophy of Psychology – A Fragment*, Section x, which I have left unconsidered until now, Wittgenstein presents his view of the grammar of 'to believe', that is, what kind of expressions it belongs to as well as what it expresses:

> This is how I'm thinking of it: Believing is a state of mind. It persists; and that independently of the process of expressing it in a sentence, for example.[37] So it's a kind of disposition of the believing person. This is revealed to me in the case of someone else by his behaviour; and by his words. And so just as well by the utterance 'I believe...' as by the simple assertion—Now what about my own case: how do I myself recognize my own disposition?—Here I would have to be able to do what others do—to attend to myself, listen to myself talking, making inferences from what I say!
> My attitude to my own words is wholly different from that of others. (*PPF* §§ 102–3, transl. Hacker/Schulte.)

Wittgenstein characterises believing as a "state of mind"[38] that has a temporal extension, and further as a "kind of disposition", which persists over time independently of being expressed in a certain way. It is expressed in behaviour as well as in utterances, which simultaneously reveal it to other people. Ascribing the state of believing to another person is based on attending the other person's behaviour, listening to what he or she says, and making inferences from what he or she says. The attitude to one's own statements introduced with 'I believe...', however, is radically different.

---

37 The second sentence of this remark is especially hard to translate and any translation is likely to provoke misunderstandings. The German reads: "Er dauert an; und unabhängig vom Ablauf seines Ausdrucks in einem Satz, z.B." Anscombe translates: "It has duration; and that independently of the duration of its expression in a sentence, for example." In contrast to Hacker/Schulte, she emphasises the temporal extension of the state of believing. I suggest to read it like this: "It persists in time; and does so independently of the course its expression takes, for example in a sentence." This is not as concise as the original, but I think it will make clearer what Wittgenstein does and does not say.

38 According to Schulte (1996), this is a *grammatical* statement, i.e. a characterisation of the *word* 'believing', not an ontological claim. He draws attention to *PI* §§ 572–3, in which Wittgenstein calls 'expectation' "grammatically, a state", and compares it with "being of an opinion, hoping for something, knowing something, being able to do something" (§ 572).

This remark distinguishes Wittgenstein's position from three conceptions of 'believing'. First, it excludes behaviourism, although Wittgenstein uses the notion 'disposition' (though not in a functionalist sense)—believing is more than behaving in certain ways, and more than having a mental state with certain functional properties. Second, it excludes the position Finkelstein has called 'stipulativism' and ascribed to Wright—whether someone is in a state of believing is independent of his or her own or anybody else's judgement. Third, though less obviously, Wittgenstein here rejects the conception, which I have been criticising so far, according to which believing is a discrete mental phenomenon. In contrast to this view, Wittgenstein says here that the state of believing persists independently of *how* it is expressed, he does not say that it persists independently of *whether* or not it is expressed in words or behaviour. Moreover, recall that this view entails the claim that someone's believing is an objective fact even from the person's own perspective. The difference between the grammatical first and third person was conceived as an epistemological difference, a difference in the way in which one comes to know of one's own or other people's beliefs, respectively. In contrast, the difference between first and third person here is not conceived as a difference in *knowledge*,[39] but in grammar. It does not concern one's attitude to one's own *beliefs*, as opposed to other people's beliefs, but concerns the attitude to one's own *expressions* of belief. One's attitude towards one's own expressions of belief contrasts with one's attitude towards other people's avowals in the same way as one's attitude towards one's own facial expression contrasts with one's attitude towards another person's facial expression (Finkelstein (2008), pp. 100–2).

Two points in Wittgenstein's remark seem to me particularly important. First, that he characterises believing as a *state* of mind as opposed to a momentary or timeless occurrence. Second, that he grasps believing as a 'kind of disposition'. The first characterisation emphasises the temporal extension of believing and is related to the thesis that mental states are situated in a person's life—in his or her doings, experiences, feelings, concerns; the events occurring in his or her environment, his or her interaction with others and so forth. This is also to propose that mental states are dynamic states, in the sense that their significance and expressivity can vary over time and across different contexts. The second characterisation of belief as 'disposition' departs from its conception as a state directed towards a specific object of which it aims to yield a true picture. Taking a related passage of *Philo-*

---

39 In the last chapter, I have drawn attention to various occasions at which Wittgenstein states that sentences like 'I know I believe…' are, for the most part, nonsensical. The passage from the *Blue Book* (pp. 65–68) quoted earlier supports this interpretation.

sophical Investigations into consideration (§§ 572–83), it suggests to distinguish believing and grammatically similar states (like expecting, hoping or knowing) from thinking, in that in a state of believing, one does not permanently focus on or attend to a particular object.

Drawing attention to the temporal dimension of mental states, Finkelstein proposes to understand context-dependency as applying to the individuation of psychological states just as to the individuation of content. He claims that one should "never [...] ask after someone's mental condition in isolation, but only in the context of the events of his life" (Finkelstein (2008), pp. 110f.). For what makes one's state of believing, considered at a single moment, a state of *believing*, rather than another state of mind? Conversely, what makes an expression of belief an expression of *belief*, rather than another state of mind? There are no specific criteria, no unambiguous signs, not even more than merely 'typical' or characteristic experiences and actions involved in believing, by which one could determine whether a person holds a belief at a particular moment. This is to say that the situational context, that is, the person's feelings, his or her own statements, his or her expressive behaviour, what is happening in the person's surroundings, does not only make an expression of a mental state intelligible, but also crucially contributes to the possibility of interpreting one's own or another person's doings in terms of particular mental states, say, the belief that it might start raining at any moment, rather than the desire for an apple. For this reason, one needs to take the situational context into account, which 'surrounds' the moment one is interested in, in order to understand one's own or another person's state of mind at this moment as a state of believing. Calling 'believing' a (temporally extended) state of mind as Wittgenstein does, first and foremost draws attention to the need for considering a person's state of mind in the context of his or her doings, feelings, interactions with others, and the events involved in the situation, i.e. as one aspect of a holistic system. My assertion 'I believe it will be raining later' makes sense as an expression of *belief* rather than of hope or fear, only in the light of my preceding and subsequent doings and experiences. *Vice versa*, my acting and experiencing in a particular situation might be made sense of by interpreting them as expressions of a certain state of mind even if I do not have any explicit thoughts on that matter. So, for instance, my cleaning up my living room, preparing tea for two, looking at the clock, becoming impatient at a certain time make sense as expressions of my *expectation* that Peter will come to tea at a certain time (*cf. BB* p. 21). My thoughts, however, might have been addressing the absurdity of Moore-paradoxical sentences, remembering the nice French restaurant Peter took me in London, or whatever you like.

This example illustrates what was said in the last section, namely that the assertive use of psychological predicates first and foremost serves to make one's own or someone else's doings, experiences and statements intelligible by interpreting them in a certain light, as expressions of the person's state of mind. Individuating psychological states proceeds just in this way, by focusing on segments of a person's life and present them as coherent phenomena in the light of the person's relevant states of mind. Our interpretations in terms of psychological expressions might vary depending on how wide or narrow we choose the focus, that is, what temporal extension we consider, which aspects of the situation we highlight (*cf.* Soteriou (2007)). In a broader context, the doings interpreted above as my expecting Peter to come to tea can equally be interpreted as expressing my amicable feelings for Peter, as expression of my general hospitality, my faible for both company and tea, or an instance of the custom of drinking tea. The particular phenotypes of segments titled 'belief that it is raining', or 'expectation that Peter comes to tea' will both vary in detail and sufficiently overlap to call them by the same name—but what we count as variation or commonality and whether we thus interpret the segment one way or another, again, is a matter of context, the interpreter's one as well as the interpreted person's one.

As Finkelstein notes, this is *not* to disregard the significance of particular moments in experiencing. It is not to deny that one can experience an overwhelming emotion in a single moment, that one can form and drop a belief in a single instance, or that one can justifiably state that someone has a particular belief at a certain point of time. And this is not to deny that one can report or describe one's state of mind, and that one does so by means of using psychological predicates in the first-person singular; but if one does so, one considers one's state of mind in its temporal extension, in its dynamics and its various manifestations. One does not choose the first-person present indicative, but other grammatical forms of psychological predicates, and the resulting statements are not only truth-functional, but also truth-evaluable. Yet, the individuation of mental states by means of unstudied utterances, self-reports as well as by means of making a statement about another person makes sense only in consideration of the context in which they occur, as the truth of any statement using psychological predicates does. Just as there is no fact about a certain sequence of behaviour that would make it the instance of following a rule and no fact about a particular statement that would determine its meaning, there is no fact about a mental state that would individuate it as a particular one, rather than another one or none at all. The idea that mental states were individuable 'psychological phenomena', recognisable by their mode and/or content, conceals just this adaptation from Kripke's 'sceptical paradox' in order to prevent its otherwise inevitable sceptical consequence that mental states are 'Nothings', as it were. But again, the choice between denying the existence of the mind and hypostatising mental states is a false choice resulting from a mistaken view about language, *viz.* the assumption that the question as whether someone is or is not in a particular state of mind must be unambiguously determinable independently of whether and how this question is decided. If one considers one time slice of a person's psychological life *in isolation*, what happens there will lack any significance. Neither an avowal, nor an ascription of a state of mind to another person will make sense if one focuses on one single moment only. Consequently, it makes no sense to assess their veridicality by means of concentrating on a particular moment as it is irrelevant whether, in this moment, there is or is not any-thing that would decide on that question.

In that Wittgenstein grasps believing as a "kind of disposition" (*PPF* § 102), he draws attention to a further point, which tends to go amiss on a conception of belief in accordance with the two-component model, as a discrete psychological attitude directed towards a concrete, specifiable object. For regardless of how one spells out the psychological mode of what the word 'belief' supposedly refers to, be it an intentional state (Searle), a functional state (Shoemaker) or a normative state (Moran), one characterises 'believing' as being *about* something. The state of affairs specified as the content of one's belief appears as the *endpoint* of one's mental activity. It is treated as the object one's mind is directed to, as if it figured in the focus of one's attention. This conception is fostered by grasping belief as aiming at, being satisfied by, or committing the believer to the truth of the state of affairs constituting the content of the belief in question and conditioning the veridicality of believing on a correspondence between its content and the object so represented. This view of believing results in the view that the function of believing is limited to recognising what is true about the world, which requires abstracting from one's current situation. Believing here appears as a vehicle which aims at leaving one's own experiences, one's own point of view behind whilst approaching an impersonal, an 'objective' stance towards what is the case in the world.

But this does not adequately account for either, the temporal dimension and the situational entanglement of believing as a *state of mind* expressed by one's doings as well as by one's assertions that things are this way or that way. Believing is involved in engaging with one's environment, rather than aimed beyond one's own position. The significance of a belief, the role it plays in a person's life, varies from situation to situation; as the ways in which a belief can meaningfully be expressed.

In principle, it is not entirely wrong to understand, as Moran does, beliefs as constituents, rather than inhabitants of one's mind to the effect that finding out what one's beliefs are is performed by focusing on what they are about. However, it is wrong to conceive of belief as context-independently individuable phenomenon, on Moran's view, as commitment from rationality to the truth of a proposition.

For Moran's conception of belief results in the claims that firstly, the veridicality of judgements about whether someone has a particular belief is unambiguously assessable in a given moment, and that secondly, the transparency of questions concerning one's state of mind towards questions concerning the world derives from an equally transparent relation between beliefs and self-knowledge of belief.[40] Yet, most of what constitutes one's own perspective on the world cannot sensibly be rendered the outcome of one's own deliberative judgements. There are too many propositions one would assent to if only one ever had the opportunity of doing so. Allocating each of them to single corresponding beliefs that were tacitly built into one's mental constitution, and requiring the existence of any of these beliefs as a warrant for the truth and sensibility of one's avowals neglects that every use of the expression 'I believe' as well as every assertion can express (infinitely) many states of mind, not only the respective content-identical belief.

In contrast to Moran, I propose to make use of Wittgenstein's characterisation of believing as a 'kind of disposition', which seems to enable the development of a more adequate understanding of the connection of 'belief' with the basis of one's experiences and doings. Using the notion 'disposition' means to conceive of believing as part of one's situational and over-situational background from which one proceeds in one's doings. The linguistic expression of belief so understood serves to give orientation about one another's situation, one's perspective on it and one's interpretation thereof. Belonging to one's background, 'beliefs' are not individuated entities. In this sense, what a person believes is manifest in his or her doings and utterances without necessarily becoming thematic to that person as beliefs about particular states of affairs. Ascribing a belief to other people articulates what they take for granted in their engagements with the environment. It is a kind of interpretation of their behaviour, which can be more or less appropriate. Articulating one's belief expresses a part of one's situational background, for instance, in form of a statement concerning one's situation, or explicating what one, in general, takes the world to be. However, 'what one takes the world to be' does not amount to the totality of propositions one believes to be true. Articulating one's state of mind either by using the phrase 'I believe' or by a simple assertion does not describe one's position, for there is no one-to-one relation between expression and disposition. It is misleading to speak about 'beliefs' as 'constituents' or 'parts' of one's background, for this can be understood

---

40 Considering transparency an idiosyncratic, if not exclusive feature of one's attitudes towards one's own beliefs and intentions furthermore seems to neglect other 'transparent' uses of psychological predicates, e.g. the question 'do you believe that Macbeth actually sees a dagger?' expresses at least as much interest in settling a matter concerning Macbeth as in acquiring information about the other person's mental constitution.

as suggesting that one's 'beliefs' were, after all, discrete elements which *together* with other such elements form an interlocking structure. And this would amount to relapsing into the conception of the mind as a pre-structured system, which I have proposed to abandon.

Searle here spots a dilemma between recognising that what he calls the 'Background' is not by itself structured into intentional states, but presents a continuous stream on the one hand, and possessing a very limited conceptual repertoire for investigating this background, on the other hand. So writes Searle, "we tend to lapse into an Intentionalistic vocabulary" when articulating it (1983, p. 156). However, as I hope to have sufficiently made clear, there is in principle no difficulty There is a dilemma only on the mistaken assumption that psychological expressions represent corresponding psychological phenomena—and that discourse or theorising about the mind could only be successful if it revealed true insights into the 'real' structure of the mind. Once one drops the assumption that individuating psychological states on a level of discourse must reflect the *actual* individuation of psychological phenomena one can see that there is an innocuous way of speaking of individual beliefs, hopes, expectations and desires as being part of the background of one's experiences and doings—alongside with skills, dispositions, and practices. Still, one has to bear in mind that a single belief is individuated in that it is expressed in an avowal or in an ascription of belief to another person, and that its individuation depends on its being embedded in the stream of life.[41] We can sustain the claim that the use of psychological concepts underlies conditions of truth and veridicality—though not in terms of correspondence, but of truthfulness—and that a person's state of believing persists independently of anybody's judgement, independently of "the course its expression takes in a sentence", as Wittgenstein writes (*PPF* § 102). Yet, it is only in virtue of someone's articulating one aspect of a person's state of mind as a state of believing *that p is the case* that this state becomes individuable *as* this person's belief *that p is the case*. Once it is made thematic, a belief can be reconsidered, reformulated, assessed with respect to its truth or falsity and so on. But these are moves in the language we use to express ourselves, to make sense of one another's states of mind, to make our doings intelligible to one another, and eventually, to make it possible to respond to one another appropriately. Disregarding the extent to which psychological expressions are entangled in our efforts to achieve mutual understanding in linguistic and non-linguistic practice will eventually leave their significance opaque.

---

41 *Cf.* Soteriou (2007), pp. 561ff.; and Finkelstein (2008), ch. 4.

3.2.4 Conclusion

In conclusion, unstudied utterances, or avowals are ordinary statements, by means of which one expresses one's state of mind, that is, one's perspective on one's current situation. As statements, avowals are truth-functional in that they set the yardstick against which the truth of further statements concerning the speaker's state of mind. Their truth-functionality yet is not their only function, and certainly not their most significant one. Whether an avowal is truthful or hypocritical, sincere or insincere, appropriate or inappropriate matters, and not whether or not what is said presents an accurate description of the speaker's state of mind (since in absence of language-independently existing psychological phenomena this cannot be made a satisfiable requirement). Avowals do not describe, but reveal one's state of mind—not necessarily and not exclusively by explicitly citing a particular state of mind—in that they highlight certain aspects of one's current experiences and thereby make one's own situation intelligible, for others as well as for oneself. Which aspects of one's current situation one articulates, to which extent one does so, and how one's avowal is understood, depends first and foremost on one's situational context, broadly understood as involving one's own feelings and experiences, one's thoughts and other doings, one's interactions with others and one's possible hearers, and on the events occurring in one's surroundings.

Conceiving of the meaning of 'I believe' as *either* expressive *or* observational is one-dimensional and does not account for the actual diversity of its use. Conceiving of the meaning of 'I believe' primarily as a description of a corresponding mental state further detaches it from non-linguistic expressions of belief, and additionally removes it from everyday usages. Yet, the very same avowal of belief has different meanings in different situations. The meaning of an expression of belief, be it verbally or non-verbally, depends on the speaker's feelings, experiences, doings, interactions with others, and events happening in his or her surroundings, as well as on the responses it elicits. I have further argued that an expression of belief is unintelligible, if one considers it in isolation, i.e. as an articulation of a momentary mental state. Analogously, it is unintelligible to conceive of beliefs as phenomena whose presence could be determined by looking at a single moment in a person's life. Further, conceiving of belief as a uniform phenomenon, be it in terms of commitments to truth, or in terms of discrete mental states, does not account for the temporal dimension of believing. It conceives of 'belief' as a static, or a timeless phenomenon, and neither understanding does justice to the situational entanglement of believing. The variability in impact on one's doings and significance of a certain belief at different moments of one's life, are thus equally neglected, to the effect that 'believing' becomes an even more volatile and abstract notion, and that 'beliefs' eventually escape from the reach of our language.

4 Epilogue: The Legacy of Moore's Paradox

4.1 The Lessons of Moore's Paradox

What lessons might be drawn from Moore's Paradox? The most significant ones are those formulated in Wittgenstein's letter to Moore and in the remarks on Moore's Paradox published in *Philosophical Investigations*. In the letter, Wittgenstein notes that Moore's Paradox has unsettling consequences for traditional views in and about logic and, at the same time, warns against 'psychologising' the origin of the paradox. In Section x of *Philosophy of Psychology – A Fragment*, he develops an argument from Moore's Paradox against both, the logic of assertion evolving from Frege's philosophy and the 'mentalist' conception of belief as a discrete phenomenon, which I have presented as a plausible adaptation of Frege's logic in the philosophy of mind, exemplified by the representationalist theory of mind.

In contemporary philosophy, the significance of Moore's Paradox is systematically underestimated. Against Wittgenstein's advice, Moore's Paradox is typically treated as a paradox concerning a particular constellation of psychological facts, and as such is supposed to reveal ontological insights concerning the structure and function of the mind. This approach to Moore's Paradox has been shown to misconceive the origin of the paradox in the first place, and consequently to arrive at a wrong explanation of the absurdity of Moore-paradoxical assertions, reducing them to assertions of formal-logical contradictions. Remarkably, though rarely noticed, this result contradicts the guiding assumptions of this approach itself, that is, that Moore-paradoxical assertions are absurd, but neither contradictory nor meaningless, and that this conflict first and foremost generates Moore's Paradox, which is considered to be the contrast between the inassertability and the possible truth of Moore-paradoxical sentences.

Concentrating on the contrast between the absurdity of Moore-paradoxical assertions and their possible truth tempts one into transforming a grammatical question into an ontological inquiry. Instead of using Moore's Paradox as an opportunity to investigate some peculiarities of the verb 'to believe' and its first-person present indicative in relation to the function of assertion, the absurdity of Moore-paradoxical assertions is read into the situation they supposedly represent. Hence, the investigative focus is turned away from ostensibly superficial questions that are bound up with the manifestations of language in everyday use, such as the logic of assertion and the use of the verb 'to believe'. That the logic of assertion and the function of the verb 'to believe' are already pre-established matters inevitably obstructs the approach to Moore's Paradox that Wittgenstein suggests.

Unsurprisingly so—for understanding Moore's Paradox as a paradox concerning the logic of assertion and the concept of believing undermines precisely those views which are taken for granted, i.e. the view of assertion as judgement *plus* proposition—or proposition *plus* judgement—and the conception of the meaning of the verb 'to believe' as describing a corresponding, discrete mental phenomenon. Its impact thus affects the foundations of propositional logic as well as those aspects of philosophy of mind which consider the mind to be a phenomenon suitable for theoretical investigation.

Before I offer a solution to Moore's Paradox, I will summarise the consequences to be drawn from the paradox understood as a phenomenon revealing insights about particular regions of language.

4.1.1 The Logic of Assertion

In response to Moore's presentation of the paradox, Wittgenstein writes that Moore's discovery reveals "something about the logic of assertion" (*Briefe* 257). In the light of the preceding argument, Wittgenstein's remark can and ought to be read in two ways: First and most obviously, the absurdity of sentences like 'It is raining, but I don't believe it is' tells us something about the logic of *assertion*, about what Wittgenstein would call the 'language games' played with assertions, how they are used, what one can do with them, for what purpose and so on. In particular, it shows that there are, in commonsense, limitations on what can be asserted intelligibly that do not coincide with the limitations logic deduces from its pre-established body of laws which regulate the function and structure of language. In this way, the absurdity of Moore-paradoxical sentences shows something about the *logic* of assertion, that is, about the conception of assertion formulated by Frege and sustained by his successors. Eventually, thus, the impact of Moore's Paradox extends to all philosophical engagements with language sustaining Frege's central ideas, Searle's analysis of speech acts and Burge's externalist model of thought being among the most obvious of such implementations.

Frege's conception of assertion relies on the ideas of content and uniformity. Assertions are considered articulations of judgements about the truth of a proposition. The meaning of linguistic expressions is supposed to be constituted by the sense they convey, their function is conceived as the truth or falsity of the sense they articulate. The meaning of language is extracted from language as it is 'in commerce' (Wittgenstein), but considered to persist within a realm of timeless and perspectiveless validity (Frege's 'third realm', the realm of thought). Hence, the meaning of language is uniform, as is its grammar. Meaningful expressions are so in one way, that is they are meaningful in virtue of the sense which they articulate. Concepts designate concepts, names objects, sentences thoughts, independently of their grammatical and situational context. Linguistic expressions inherit their semantic and grammatical properties from the content they express and so inevitably reflect the properties of the object they describe.

Moore-paradoxical assertions have no place within such a rigid logic of assertion. The instruments logic has at its disposal are too coarse to acknowledge their characteristic absurdity, and the assumption of uniformity prevents logicians from examining it other than in terms of veridicality and uniformity of content. Yet, Moore-paradoxical sentences are neither fish nor fowl—they are neither meaningless, nor sensible; neither contradictory, nor assertable. Their absurdity is a non-arbitrary, grammatical matter, although it arises for a single grammatical form only—the first-person present indicative of the verb 'to believe'. The ambivalence of Moore-paradoxical sentences makes it impossible to account for their absurdity within a theoretical system that is fundamentally based on binary principles— which both the Fregean conception of language and the representationalist theory of mind essentially are. The logic of assertion is a system that requires 'either-or' choices. Accordingly, the solutions to Moore's Paradox offered by proponents of a traditional logic must either declare Moore-paradoxical sentences contradictory, or deny their absurdity altogether. Either way, though, brings Moore's Paradox to a dissolution, not to a solution, since Moore's Paradox has turned out to be a 'neither-nor' phenomenon. Insofar as they oscillate between sense and nonsense, Moore-paradoxical sentences remain wayward to logic and continuously resist logical analysis.

Moore's Paradox shows that not everything that *has* a sense in logic *makes* sense in language. Not all logically possible moves are possible moves in everyday language—the conjunction of two independent, each perfectly meaningful propositions, can issue in an absurdity that successfully evades the logically accessible domain of language. And *vice versa*—the range of possible uses of the expression 'I believe' in commonsense extends to moves (substitution) and relations (similarity) unprovided for by logic. The referentialist black-and-white picture of meaning emerging from searching for the meaning of linguistic expressions in general and for meaning-preservation across various of their particular instantiations has proven inadequate to capture the grey areas and flexibility of ordinary language. This is manifest particularly in the inability of referentialism to account for the oscillation of the first-person present indicative of psychological predicates over the wide range of its expressive functions. Focussing on assertion in commonsense use instead uncovers gaps, not only between logic and language, but in logic itself. The first legacy to take from Moore's Paradox thus is that "logic isn't as simple as logicians think it is" (*Briefe* 257). Logic, when exercised as an exact science, does not deliver an adequate understanding of language, of its structure, function and meaning as well as of the role it plays in human life. The pursuit of universality and simplicity, reflected in the focus on veridicality and uniformity of content, results at best in oversimplifying the subtleties and variability of language in practice, at worst in ignoring extensive regions of its meaning and use.

4.1.2 The Conception of Belief

The conception of belief challenged by Moore's Paradox is paradigmatically exemplified by the representationalist theory of mind, although its significance extends to further models of the mind common in philosophy as well as in the empirical sciences. They share the view that concepts and other kinds of expressions from natural languages designate corresponding referents external to the language itself—be it entities, phenomena or formal concepts; be it facts, thoughts, or ideas. The meaning of the word 'belief' and the corresponding verb 'to believe' are accordingly supposed to refer to a discrete, language-independent psychological phenomenon, the phenomenon of believing, and to do so independently of the grammatical and pragmatic context of its occurrence as well as of the perspective from which it is used.

Yet, the absurdity of Moore-paradoxical sentences shows that this is clearly not the case. Contrary to the assumption built into the mentalist view, the expression 'I believe' does not describe a person's state of mind, individuated by a content that is articulated by the following sentence. In ordinary statements, the expression 'I believe' is similar in meaning to expressions like 'I'd say', 'I'm not sure' or impersonal ones like 'Possibly', and thus replaceable by any of them. Accepting the ordinary use of the expression 'I believe' on the view discussed, however, would admit a lacuna in the inflection of the verb 'to believe', interrupting the uniformity of content that is supposedly generated by its inflective forms in virtue of their supposed common reference to an objective state of affairs. Remarkably, the move intended to remove this grammatical irregularity by reducing it to an ontological and/or epistemological one goes to the other extreme. For on the assumption of a distinctive subjective access to one's own mental beliefs, the alleged referent of the expression 'I believe' is removed from a publicly accessible sphere and relocated to the privacy of one's own mind. In other words, the approach to the meaning of the word 'to believe' chosen by mentalist accounts does not, by any means, render beliefs to be objective facts, but, on the contrary, a subjective and ultimately omissible phenomenon. That this conception is indefensible, again, is shown by the way in which the expression 'I believe' is replaceable by other expressions, even impersonal ones; and the extent to which its meaning depends to a large extent on other expressive means accompanying its use in a concrete situation. Adhering to the alleged necessity of an external warrant for both meaning and grammar of everyday expressions for the purpose of anxiously avoiding only the slightest possibility of doubt regarding meaningfulness and correctness of language in use, first and foremost provokes doubt on the possibility of meaning and veridicality not only in a single case, but general doubt of the most radical sort, the sceptical one. For it irreversibly pulls meaning and language apart, lapsing into a series of metaphysical dualisms, that of subject and object, of mind and world, experience and expression of experience, to name but a few. It thus unavoidably yields the conclusion that nothing would serve to reunite these extremes; and in particular, that *no thing* would serve as good as *some thing* as a stable determinant for the meaning of the word 'to believe'. That Moore's Paradox arises on this view shows that what happens in the mental realm, reified in the way described, is entirely irrelevant for the grammatical and semantic conditions of its use.

More importantly though, transforming the absurdity of Moore-paradoxical sentences from a grammatical into a metaphysical problem resulting from the hypostatisation of both meaning and mind, not only generates Moore's Paradox, but also predetermines the approach to solving it by drawing on 'psychological facts' that allegedly are implicitly conveyed by asserting or believing a proposition. This suggestion is not only an inadequate way of handling a phenomenon that concerns commonsense communication, but, when subsequently thought through, issues in a result that contradicts its own assumptions, given that this approach set out to avoid the contradictoriness of Moore-paradoxical sentences on pain of losing the referential function of 'I believe'. Hence, turning one's investigative focus away from the manifestations of linguistic expressions in everyday life towards the ostensible metaphysics of their referents turns out to be not only irrelevant, but moreover obstructionary when it comes to gaining insights in such important areas of language as the language used to articulate and communicate one's own state of mind to one another. Likewise, attempts to isolate uniform criteria for the presence or absence of particular states of mind leaves the investigator to choose between returning empty-handed or stipulating a theoretical chimera whilst deferring the possibility of gaining access to it into an indeterminate future.

The legacy to be drawn from the fact that Moore's Paradox remains, and will remain, unsolvable under these conditions is that if one really wants to understand the meaning of the expressions used in everyday language one has to gain an overview of their grammar *in practice*. Proceeding in this way will only succeed if one dispenses with the tendency to isolate superficially uniform phenomena and instead considers them in all the variety and heterogenity of their use. Likewise, if one is interested in gaining a substantial understanding of the mental one has to look at its manifestations and be prepared to accept that a metaphysically steadfast explanation of the mind is in principle unavailable.

4.1.3 The Legacy of Moore's Paradox

I have pointed out at various places where the Fregean logic of assertion and the mentalist conception of belief support and complement each other. If one considers the meaning of language to be constituted by reference one will not make an exception of, but rather insist on this claim in the case of psychological expressions. The Fregean picture of language in particular fosters a representationalist view of the mind in two respects. When used in the subordinate clause of indirect speech, the function of a proposition changes from reference to attribution. It further serves to qualify the main predicate of the sentence. From there it is only a small step, if any, to conceiving of propositions articulating the content of mental predicates as individuating the mental state thus designated. Conceiving of the structure of utterances in terms of the two-component model additionally provides reasons to adopt an analogous conception of the structure of mental states. Apparently, this is supposed to enable the establishing of the commensurability of different types and tokens of sentences or mental states in virtue of a common element, a sentence-radical, whose function is to articulate their uniform content and thus refer to a common state of affairs.

Confronted with a Moore-paradoxical sentence, such as 'It is raining, but I don't believe it is raining', these claims require considering the two conjuncts as incommensurable because the crucial phrase 'I believe' effects a change in the status of the subsequent proposition. However, conceiving of the two instances of the proposition 'It is raining' in the given Moore-paradoxical sentence as separated by the expression 'I don't believe', precludes taking seriously the idea that the double appearance of the sentence 'It is raining' makes Moore-paradoxical sentences similar to contradictions, since the first appearance must be considered to be a statement about the outer world, the second one a description of the speaker's inner realm. In everyday talk, one cannot mitigate the impression that one is contradicting oneself that arises from sincerely stating a Moore-paradoxical sentence merely with 'don't be silly, I'm talking about myself, not the weather'. That this most promising and obvious approach to the absurdity of Moore-paradoxical sentences is straightforwardly ruled out, again, results from the dualist metaphysics manifest in the alleged gaps between meaning and language, and mental content and world.

In conclusion, Moore's Paradox challenges the way in which traditional logic conceives of the function of language, its meaning and grammar, and its claim and promise to render a substantial as well as universal foundation of language in abstraction from its manifestation in concrete situations. The case runs parallel for the representationalist theory of mind, which similarly frames a rigid model of the function of the mind, its structure and significance, whilst claiming and promising to deliver substantial insights into the ontology of the mental and, *a fortiori*, into the meaning of psychological concepts. Confronted with the notoriously vague and complex use of natural languages in everyday situations, logicians tend to seek and find uniform explanations for linguistic phenomena. Likewise, the representationalist way of dealing with the uncountable and multifarious expressions of experience presents an attempt to extract from them a uniform class of phenomena, content-bearing states, and to further investigate them *in abstracto*. Remarkably, both propositional logic and the representationalist theory of mind develop coherent, well-functioning models of their respective targets, of language and the mind. Notwithstanding, once the resulting systems are scrutinised for their applicability to language and communication on the one hand, and to the mind and the meaning of psychological expressions on the other hand, they do not only prove *incapable* of answering questions about meaning and mind arising from commonsense in *theory*, they equally turn out to be *irrelevant* for understanding language as well as the manifestations of the mental in the *practice* of everyday life. The representationalist's and the logician's striving for utmost generality and ideal simplicity is rendered idle:

> The more closely we examine actual language, the greater becomes the conflict between it and our requirement. (For the crystalline purity of logic was, of course, not something I had *discovered*: it was a requirement.) The conflict becomes intolerable; the requirement is now in danger of becoming vacuous.—We have got on slippery ice where there is no friction, and so, in a certain sense, the conditions are ideal; but also, just because of that, we are unable to walk. We want to walk: so we need *friction*. Back to the rough ground! (*PI* § 107, transl. Hacker/Schulte)

4.2 'It is Raining, but I don't Believe it is'

In most everyday situations, sentences like 'It is raining, but I don't believe it is' are absurd in the sense elaborated in Chapter 2. There are no appropriate responses, no ways of sensibly continuing a conversation from this point. Hence, their assertion is, for the most part, meaningless although one can imagine special, borderline cases, in which a sentences of this kind presents a meaningful expression of one's present situation—think of a friend's telephone call, saying in a stern voice 'My mother died this morning, but I don't believe it'. Their absurdity in more ordinary contexts consists in their being similar to contradictions, which equally are 'ruled out' from commonsense precisely because—*ex falso omnia*—every response to a Moore-paradoxical assertion is, as every response to the assertion of a contradiction, appropriate and inappropriate, right and wrong at the same time. They do not contribute to making a situation intelligible and so cannot help in our understanding of one another. Moore-paradoxical assertions and assertions of formal-logical contradictions are not only similar with regard to their structure, but also to their function in language as "wall[s] indicating that we can't go on here" (*Z* § 687). That Moore-paradoxical assertions are ruled out by commonsense is due to their being similarly dysfunctional as contradictions are. That Moore-paradoxical assertions are in commerce nonetheless results from their restricted functionality under special circumstances. Acknowledging that the sense of sentences, the significance of gestures, and the meaning of faces depend on multiple factors provided by the situational circumstances and over-situational practices they are embedded in, releases the pressure of delving into deceptive metaphysical depths in order to find out what really lies at the bottom of the stream of everyday understanding and enables recognising that beyond the surface, nothing is hidden. And only by focussing on this surface, the relief-like structure immanent in the grammar of our expressions will become visible.

Accepting the absurdity of the sentence 'It is raining, but I don't believe it is' instead of running up against it, and recognising the similarities and dissimilarities among the uses of various concepts and kinds of sentences in commonsense holds the solution to Moore's Paradox. Moore's Paradox arises only if the absurdity of Moore-paradoxical sentences, i.e. their usual meaninglessness and dysfunctionality, is contrasted with the functions they *ought to have* given the presuppositions of traditional logic and the representationalist conception of the mind—they ought to be meaningful, given the independent reference of their conjuncts; they ought to be assertable, given the non-absurdity of the corresponding suppositions; and they ought to have the same logical and grammatical properties as statements of the very same facts issued from another perspective or at a different time, given that meaning is timeless and perspective-independent. These requirements on the meaning of language have eventually proven to belong to a vain endeavour to find an explication of what is easily intelligible in commonsense on a level far removed. In the course of trying to press the flexibility of language to integrate and cope with borderline cases in practice into the rigid norms dictating the limits of language in theory, the intellect acquires bumps rather than understanding. We are free, in philosophising, to choose between ignoring them or taking them seriously as occasions to scrutinise what we ordinarily take for granted. As the paradoxes arising in the context of understanding concerning what it means to follow a rule, and how the meaning of expressions of experience is constituted, Moore's Paradox, too,

> [D]isappears only if we make a radical break with the idea that language always functions in one way, always serves the same purpose: to convey thoughts—which may be about houses, pains, good and evil, or anything else you please. (*PI* § 304)

Abbreviations of the Works
of Ludwig Wittgenstein

BB   *Blue Book*, in: *The Blue and Brown Books*, Oxford: Blackwell 1958, pp. 1–74.
BrB   *Brown Book*, ibid., pp. 75–185.
Briefe 257 "Letter to G. E. Moore", October 1944, in *Cambridge Letters. Correspondence with Russell, Keynes, Moore, Ramsay and Sraffa*, ed. by Brian McGuinness, Georg Henrik von Wright, Oxford: Blackwell 1995, pp. 315–7.
LWPP   Ludwig Wittgenstein, *Last Writings on the Philosophy of Psychology. Preliminary Studies for Part II of Philosophical Investigations. Letzte Schriften über die Philosophie der Psychologie. Vorstudien zum zweiten Teil der Philosophischen Untersuchungen*, 2 Volumes, ed. by Georg Henrik von Wright, Heikki Nyman, Oxford: Blackwell 1982.
MS   Manuscripts from Wittgenstein's *Nachlass*, Bergen Electronic Edition, Oxford: UP c1998-. The manuscripts are referred to by the numbers from Georg Henrik von Wright's catalogue.
OC   *On Certainty*, ed. by G. E. M. Anscombe, Georg Henrik von Wright, New York: Harper & Collins 1969.
PI   *Philosophical Investigations. Philosophische Untersuchungen*, ed. by G. E. M. Anscombe, Georg Henrik von Wright, transl. G. E. M. Anscombe, ^{2}Oxford: Blackwell 1958.
PI   *Philosophische Untersuchungen. Philosophical Investigations*, transl. Peter M. S. Hacker, Joachim Schulte, 4th, substantially revised edition, Oxford: Blackwell 2009.
PU   *Philosophische Untersuchungen. Kritisch-genetische Edition*, ed. by Joachim Schulte, Frankfurt: Suhrkamp 2001.
PPF   "Philosophie der Psychologie – Ein Fragment. Philosophy of Psychology – A Fragment", in *Philosophische Untersuchungen. Philosophical Investigations*, transl. Peter M. S. Hacker, Joachim Schulte, 4th, substantially revised edition, Oxford: Blackwell 2009, pp. 182–243.
PO   *Philosophical Occasions 1912–1951*, ed. by James C. Klagge, Alfred Nordmann, Indianapolis: Hackett 1993.
RFM   *Remarks on the Foundations of Mathematics*, ed. by Georg Henrik von Wright, Rush Rhees, G. E. M. Anscombe, transl. G. E. M. Anscombe, 3rd, revised edition, Oxford: Blackwell 1978.
RPP   *Remarks on the Philosophy of Psychology. Bemerkungen über die Philosophie der Psychologie* Vol. 1, ed. by G. E. M. Anscombe, Georg Henrik von Wright, Oxford: Blackwell 1980.
RPP II   *Remarks on the Philosophy of Psychology. Bemerkungen über die Philosophie der Psychologie* Vol. 2, ed. by G. E. M. Anscombe and Georg Henrik von Wright, Chicago: Chicago University Press 1980.
TLP   *Tractatus logico-philosophicus. Logisch-philosophische Abhandlung*, ed. by Joachim Schulte, Frankfurt: Suhrkamp 2003.
Z   *Zettel*, ed. by G. E. M. Anscombe, Georg Henrik von Wright, Oxford: Blackwell 1967.

Bibliography

(2014, March). "radical, adj. and n.". In J. Simpson and E. Weiner (Eds.), *OED Online*. Oxford: Oxford University Press.

Anscombe, G. E. M. (2000). *Intention*. Cambridge (MA): Harvard UP.

Baldwin, T. (Ed.) (1993). *G. E. Moore: Selected Writings*. London: Routledge.

Baldwin, T. (2010). "George Edward Moore". In E. N. Zalta (Ed.), *The Stanford Encyclopedia of Philosophy* (Summer 2010 ed.).

Bar-On, D. (2004). *Speaking my Mind. Expression and Self-Knowledge*. Oxford: Oxford University Press.

Bar-On, D. (2009). "First-Person Authority: Dualism, Constitutivism, and Neo-Expressivism". *Erkenntnis 71*, 53–71.

Biesenbach, H. (2011). *Anspielungen und Zitate im Werk Ludwig Wittgensteins*. Number 22 in Publication from the Wittgenstein Archives at the University of Bergen. Bergen: The Wittgenstein Archives at the University of Bergen.

Bilgrami, A. (1998). "Self-Knowledge and Resentment". See Wright (1998a), pp. 207–42.

Biro, J. and P. Kotatko (Eds.) (1995). *Frege, Sense and Reference: One hundred Years Later*, Volume 65 of *Philosophical Studies Series*. Dordrecht: Kluwer Academic Publishers.

Black, M. (1948, May). "Introductory Note". *The Philosophical Review 57*(3), 207–8.

Burge, T. (1979). "Individualism and the Mental". See Burge (2007), pp. 100–50.

Burge, T. (1986). "Individualism and Psychology". See Burge (2007), pp. 221–53.

Burge, T. (1996). "Our Entitlement to Self-Knowledge". *Proceedings of the Aristotelian Society 96*, 91–116.

Burge, T. (2003, November). "Social Anti-Individualism, Objective Reference". *Philosophy and Phenomenological Research 67*(3), 682–90.

Burge, T. (2006). "Postscript to Individualism and the Mental". See Burge (2007), pp. 151–81.

Burge, T. (2007). *Foundations of Mind*. Oxford: Oxford University Press.

Burge, T. (2010). *Origins of Objectivity*. Oxford: Oxford University Press.

Campbell, J. (1999, Spring & Fall). "Immunity to Error through Misidentification and the Meaning of a Referring Term". *Philosophical Topics 26*(1 & 2), 89–104.

Campbell, J. (2000, Fall). "Wittgenstein on Attention". *Philosophical Topics 28*(2), 35–48.

Campbell, J. (2001, June-September). "Rationality, Meaning, and the Analysis of Delusion". *Philosophy, Psychiatry and Psychology 8*(2-3), 89–100.

Carroll, L. (1872). *Through the Looking-Glass, and what Alice Found there*. London: Macmillan.

Cassam, Q. (Ed.) (1994). *Self-Knowledge*. Oxford University Press.

Chalmers, D. (2004). "The Representational Character of Experience". In B. Leiter (Ed.), *The Future for Philosophy*. Oxford University Press.

Coope, C., P. Geach, T. Potts, and R. White (1972). *A Wittgenstein Workbook*. Berkeley and L. A.: University of California Press.

Crane, T. (2003). "The Intentional Structure of Consciousness". In A. Jokic and Q. Smith (Eds.), *Consciousness: New Philosophical Perspectives*, pp. 33–56. Oxford: Oxford University Press.

Davidson, D. (1987). "On Knowing one's own Mind". See Davidson (2001), pp. 15–38.

Davidson, D. (1992). "The Second Person". See Davidson (2001), pp. 107–21.

Davidson, D. (2001). *Subjective, Intersubjective, Objective*. Oxford: Oxford University Press.

Descartes, R. (2008 [1641]). *Meditations on First Philosophy*. Oxford World's Classics. Oxford: Oxford University Press.

Dummett, M. A. E. (1981). *The Interpretation of Frege's Philosophy*. Cambridge (MA): Harvard University Press.

Dummett, M. A. E. (1992). *Frege: Philosohy of Language* (2 ed.). London: Duckworth.

Edgley, R. (1969). *Reasons in Theory and Practice*. London: Hutchinson.

Evans, G. (1982). *The Varieties of Reference*. Oxford: Clarendon Press.

Finkelstein, D. H. (2008). *Expression and the Inner*. Cambridge (MA): Harvard University Press.

Fodor, J. A. (2008). *LOT 2: The Language of Thought Revisited*. Oxford: Clarendon Press.

Frege, G. (1879). *Begriffsschrift, eine der arithmetischen nachgebildete Formelsprache des reinen Denkens*. Halle: Louis Nebert.

Frege, G. (1891). "Funktion und Begriff", Vortrag, gehalten vor der Jenaischen Gesellschaft für Medizin und Naturwissenschaft am 9.1.1891. See Frege (1962), pp. 16–37.

Frege, G. (1892a). "Über Begriff und Gegenstand". *Vierteljahrsschrift für wissenschaftliche Philosophie 16*, 192–205.

Frege, G. (1892b). "Über Sinn und Bedeutung". *Zeitschrift für Philosophie und philosophische Kritik 100*, 25–50.

Frege, G. (1918/19). "Der Gedanke". *Beiträge zur Philosophie des Deutschen Idealismus 2*, 58–77.

Frege, G. (1948, May). "Sense and Reference". *The Philosophical Review 57*(3), 209–30.

Frege, G. (1956, July). "The Thought: A Logical Inquiry". *Mind 65*(259), 289–311.

Frege, G. (1962). *Funktion, Begriff, Bedeutung: Fünf logische Studien*. Göttingen: Vandenhoek & Ruprecht.

Frege, G. (1980a). "Begriffsschrift". See Frege (1980e), pp. 1–20.

Frege, G. (1980b). "Function and Concept". See Frege (1980e), pp. 21–41.

Frege, G. (1980c). "On Concept and Object". See Frege (1980e), pp. 42–55.

Frege, G. (1980d). "On Sense and Meaning". See Frege (1980e), pp. 56–78.

Frege, G. (1980e). *Translations from the Philosophical Writings of Gottlob Frege*. Oxford: Blackwell.

Gendler Szabò, Z. (2008). "Compositionality". In E. N. Zalta (Ed.), *The Stanford Encyclopedia of Philosophy* (Winter 2008 ed.).

Glock, H.-J. (1996). *A Wittgenstein Dictionary*. Blackwell Philosopher Dictionaries. Oxford: Blackwell.

Goldfarb, W. (1985, September). "Kripke on Wittgenstein on Rules". *The Journal of Philosophy 82*(9), 471–88.

Goldfarb, W. (2010). "Rule-Following Revisited". In J. Ellis and D. Guevara (Eds.), *Wittgenstein and the Philosophy of Mind*, pp. 73–90. Oxford: Oxford University Press.

Green, M. and J. N. Williams (2007a). "Introduction". See Green and Williams (2007b), pp. 3–36.

Green, M. and J. N. Williams (Eds.) (2007b). *Moore's Paradox. New Essays on Belief, Rationality, and the First Person*. Oxford: Clarendon Press.

Hacker, P. M. S. (1990a). "Privacy". See Hacker (1990c), pp. 17–35.

Hacker, P. M. S. (1990b). "The Private Language Arguments". See Hacker (1990c), pp. 1–16.

Hacker, P. M. S. (1990c). *Wittgenstein: Meaning and Mind. Part I: Essays*, Volume 3 of *An Analytic Commentary on the Philosophical Investigations*. Oxford: Blackwell.

Hacker, P. M. S. (1990d). *Wittgenstein: Meaning and Mind. Part II: Exegesis §§243-427*, Volume 3 of *An Analytic Commentary on the Philosophical Investigations*. Oxford: Blackwell.

Hacker, P. M. S. and G. P. Baker (1984a). *Frege. Logical Excavations*. Oxford: Blackwell.

Hacker, P. M. S. and G. P. Baker (1984b). *Scepticism, Rules and Language*. Blackwell.

Hacker, P. M. S. and G. P. Baker (2009a). "Meaning and Use". See Hacker and Baker (2009b), pp. 129–58.

Hacker, P. M. S. and G. P. Baker (2009b). *Wittgenstein: Understanding and Meaning. Part I: Essays* (2 ed.), Volume 1 of *An Analytic Commentary on the Philosophical Investigations*. Oxford: Blackwell.

Hacker, P. M. S. and G. P. Baker (2009c). *Wittgenstein: Understanding and Meaning. Part II: Exegesis §§1-184* (2 ed.), Volume 1 of *An Analytic Commentary on the Philosophical Investigations*. Oxford: Blackwell.

Heal, J. (1994). "Moore's Paradox: A Wittgensteinian Approach". *Mind 103*(409), 5–24.

Hieronymi, P. (2009). "Two Kinds of Agency". See O'Brien and Soteriou (2009), pp. 138–62.

Hutto, D. (2008). *Folk Psychological Narratives. The Sociocultural Basis of Understanding Reasons*. MIT Press.

Huxley, A. (1994). *Brave New World*. Harper & Collins.

Jackson, F. (1982, April). "Epiphenomenal Qualia". *The Philosophical Quarterly 32*(127), 127–36.

Jäger, C. and W. Löffler (Eds.) (2011). *Epistemology: Contexts, Values, Disagreement. Proceedings of the 34th International Wittgenstein Symposium*, Volume 34, Heusenstamm. Austrian Ludwig Wittgenstein Society: Ontos.

James, W. (1890). *The Principles of Psychology (Two Volumes)*. New York: Dover.

Jokic, A. and Q. Smith (Eds.) (2003). *Consciousness: New Philosophical Perspectives*. Oxford: Oxford University Press.

Köhler, W. (1933). *Psychologische Probleme*. Berlin: Julius Springer.

Konzelmann Ziv, A., K. Lehrer, and H. B. Schmid (Eds.) (2011). *Self-Evaluation. Affective and Social Grounds of Intentionality*, Volume 116 of *Philosophical Studies*. Dordrecht: Springer.

Kriegel, U. (2004, July). "Moore's Paradox and the Structure of Conscious Belief". *Erkenntnis 61*(1), 99–121.

Kripke, S. (1982). *Wittgenstein on Rules and Private Language*. Cambridge, MA: Harvard University Press.

Kuusela, O. and M. McGinn (Eds.) (2011). *The Oxford Handbook of Wittgenstein*. Oxford: Oxford University Press.

Lau, J. and M. Deutsch (2014). "Externalism about Mental Content". In E. N. Zalta (Ed.), *Stanford Encyclopedia of Philosophy* (Spring 2014 ed.).

Lichtenberg, G. C. (2012). *Philosophical Writings, Selected from the Waste Books*. Albany: State University of New York Press.

Lycan, W. G. (2008). "Representational Theories of Consciousness". In E. N. Zalta (Ed.), *The Stanford Encyclopedia of Philosophy* (Fall 2008 ed.).

Lycan, W. G. and J. J. Prinz (Eds.) (2008). *Mind and Cognition. An Anthology* (3rd ed.). Blackwell Philosophy Anthologies. Oxford: Blackwell.

Moore, G. E. (1993). "Moore's Paradox". See Baldwin (1993), pp. 207–12.

Moran, R. (1997). "Self-Knowledge: Discovery, Resolution and Undoing". *European Journal of Philosophy 5*(2), 141–61.

Moran, R. (2001). *Authority and Estrangement. An Essay in Self-Knowledge*. Princeton: Princeton University Press.

Moran, R. (2003). "Responses to O'Brien and Shoemaker". *European Journal of Philosophy 11*(3), 402–19.

Moran, R. (2004). "Anscombe on Practical Knowledge". *Philosophy 55 (Supplementary Volume)*, 43–68.

Nagel, T. (1974, October). "What is it like to be a Bat?". *The Philosophical Review 83*(4), 435–50.

O'Brien, L. (2003). "Moran on Agency and Self-Knowledge". *European Journal of Philosophy 11*(3), 375–390.

O'Brien, L. and M. Soteriou (Eds.) (2009). *Mental Actions*. Oxford University Press.

Pacherie, E. (2007, January). "The Sense of Control and the Sense of Agency". *Psyche 13*(1), 1–30.

Parfit, D. (1987). *Reasons and Persons* (2 ed.). Oxford University Press.

Peacocke, C. (1996). "Our Entitlement to Self-Knowledge". *Proceedings of the Aristotelian Society 96*, 117–58.

Peacocke, C. (2003). "Action: Awareness, Ownership, and Knowledge". See Roessler and Eilan (2003), pp. 84–111.

Peacocke, C. (2009). "Mental Actions and Self-Awareness (II): Epistemology". See O'Brien and Soteriou (2009), pp. 192–215.

Pfisterer, C. C. (2008). "Moore's Paradox, Behaupten, Urteilen". *Conceptus 91*, 41–62.

Pfisterer, C. C. (2009). "Gedanken beleuchten. Frege und Davidson zum Problem der Prädikation". *Deutsche Zeitschrift für Philosophie 57*(4), 583–95.

Pfisterer, C. C. (2011, March). "Ist Glauben ein psychisches Phänomen?". (MSS) Draft paper presented at Vienna.

Putnam, H. (1975a). The meaning of 'meaning'. See Putnam (1975b), pp. 215–71.

Putnam, H. (1975b). *Mind, Language, and Reality*, Volume 2 of *Philosophical Papers*. Cambridge: Cambridge University Press.

Ratcliffe, M. (2008). *Feelings of Being. Phenomenology, Psychiatry and the Sense of Reality*. Oxford: Oxford University Press.

Recanati, F. (1995). "The Communication of First-Person Thoughts". See Biro and Kotatko (1995), pp. 95–102.

Rey, G. (1989). "Towards a Computational Account of *Akrasia* and Self-Deception". See Rorty and McLaughlin (1989), pp. 264–96.

Roessler, J. and N. Eilan (Eds.) (2003). *Agency and Self-Awareness: Issues in Philosophy and Psychology*. Oxford: Clarendon Press.

Rorty, A. O. and B. McLaughlin (Eds.) (1989). *Perspectives on Self-Deception*. Berkeley: University of California Press.

Ryle, G. (1949). *The Concept of Mind*. Hutchinson.

Sartre, J.-P. (1970). *Das Sein und das Nichts. Versuch einer phänomenologischen Ontologie*. Hamburg: Rowohlt.

Savigny, E. v. and O. R. Scholz (Eds.) (1996). *Wittgenstein über die Seele*. Frankfurt: Suhrkamp.

Schmid, U. (2011). "Where Individuals Meet Society. The Collective Dimensions of Self-Evaluation and Self-Knowledge". See Konzelmann Ziv et al. (2011), pp. 253–73.

Schmid, U. (2013). "From Sharing a Background to Sharing One's Presence: Two Conditions of Joint Attention". See Schmitz et al. (2013), pp. 147–62.

Schmitz, M., B. Kobow, and H. B. Schmid (Eds.) (2013). *The Background of Social Reality. Selected Contributions from the Inaugural Meeting of ENSO*, Volume 1 of *Studies in the Philosophy of Sociality*. Dordrecht: Springer.

Schroeder, S. (2006). "Moore's Paradox and First-Person Authority". *Grazer Philosophische Studien 71*, 161–74.

Schulte, J. (1993). *Experience and Expression. Wittgenstein's Philosophy of Psychology*. Oxford: Clarendon Press.

Schulte, J. (1996). "Es regnet, aber ich glaube es nicht". See Savigny and Scholz (1996), pp. 194–212.

Schulte, J. (2011). "Privacy". See Kuusela and McGinn (2011), pp. 429–50.

Searle, J. R. (1969). *Speech Acts. An Essay in the Philosophy of Language*. Cambridge: Cambridge Unicersity Press.

Searle, J. R. (1983). *Intentionality: An Essay in the Philosophy of Mind*. Cambridge: Cambridge University Press.

Searle, J. R. (1995). *The Construction of Social Reality*. New York: The Free Press.

Searle, J. R. (2010). *Making the Social World. The Structure of Human Civilization*. Oxford: Oxford University Press.

Seemann, A. (2008, September). "Person Perception". *Philosophical Explorations 11*(3), 245–62.

Seemann, A. (2010). "The Other Person in Joint Attention. A Relational Approach". *Journal of Consciousness Studies 22*, 161–82.

Shakespeare, W. (1994). *Macbeth*. Penguin Popular Classics. London: Penguin Books.

Shoemaker, S. (1968). "Self-Reference and Self-Awareness". *The Journal of Philosophy 65*(19), 555–67.

Shoemaker, S. (1975, May). "Functionalism and Qualia". *Philosophical Studies: An International Journal for Philosophy in the Analytic Tradition 27/5 27*(5), 291–315.

Shoemaker, S. (1988). "On Knowing one's own Mind". See Shoemaker (1996), pp. 25–49.

Shoemaker, S. (1995). "Moore's Paradox and Self-Knowledge". See Shoemaker (1996), pp. 74–93.

Shoemaker, S. (1996). *The First-Person Perspective and other Essays*. Cambridge: Cambridge University Press.

Shoemaker, S. (2003). "Moran on Self-Knowledge". *European Journal of Philosophy 11*(3), 391–401.

Shoemaker, S. (2009). "Self-Intimation and Second-Order Belief". *Erkenntnis 71*, 35–51.

Siegel, S. (2010). *The Contents of Visual Experience*. Oxford: Oxford University Press.

Siegel, S. (2011). "The Contents of Perception". In E. N. Zalta (Ed.), *The Stanford Encyclopedia of Philosophy* (Winter 2011 ed.).

Soteriou, M. (2007). "Content and the Stream of Consciousness". *Philosophical Perspectives 21*, 543–68.

Strawson, P. F. (1959). *Individuals. An Essay in Descriptive Metaphysics*. University Paperbacks. London: Methuen.

Stroud, B. (1983). "Wittgenstein's 'Treatment' of the Quest for 'a language which describes my inner experiences and which only I myself can understand'". See Stroud (2000), pp. 67–79.

Stroud, B. (1990). "Wittgenstein on Meaning, Understanding, and Community". See Stroud (2000), pp. 80–94.

Stroud, B. (2000). *Meaning, Understanding, and Practice*. Oxford: Oxford University Press.

Stroud, B. (2003, November). "Ostension and the Social Character of Thought". *Philosophy and Phenomenological Research 67*(3), 667–74.

Williams, B. (1970). "Deciding to Believe". See Williams (1973), pp. 136–51.

Williams, B. (1973). *Problems of the Self*. Cambridge: Cambridge University Press.

Williams, J. N. (1979). "Moore's Paradox—One or Two?". *Analysis 39*(3), 141–2.

Wirz, B. (2014, June). *Was Licht bedeutet und Dunkel verstehen lässt. Philosophie zwischen Affirmativität und Negativität*. Ph. D. thesis, University of Basel, Basel.

Wright, C. (1986). "On Making up One's Mind: Wittgenstein on Intention". In P. Weingartner and G. Schürz (Eds.), *Logic, Philosophy of Science and Epistemology. Proceedings of the*

11th International Wittgenstein Symposium, Schriftreihe der Wittgenstein Gesellschaft, Kirchberg/Vienna, pp. 391–404. Hölder-Pichler-Tempsky.

Wright, C. (1989, November). "Wittgenstein's Later Philosophy of Mind: Sensation, Privacy, and Intention". *The Journal of Philosophy 86*(11), 622–34.

Wright, C. (1998a). *Knowing Our Own Minds*. Oxford: Clarendon Press.

Wright, C. (1998b). "Self-Knowledge: The Wittgensteinian Legacy". See Wright (1998a), pp. 13–45.

Wright, C. (2007, December). "Rule-Following without Reason: Wittgenstein's Quietism and the Constitutive Question". *Ratio 20*(4), 481–502.

Zalta, E. N. (2014). "Gottlob Frege". In E. N. Zalta (Ed.), *The Stanford Encyclopedia of Philosophy* (Spring 2014 ed.).

Index